STD

P9-AFS-490

THE NEW FIELD BOOK OF
Reptiles and Amphibians

THE NEW FIELD BOOK OF
Reptiles

DORIS M. COCHRAN
Former Curator of the Division of Reptiles and Amphibians, The Smithsonian Institution

COLEMAN J. GOIN
Professor of Biological Sciences, University of Florida, and Research Associate, Carnegie Museum

New field book of reptiles

and Amphibians

More than 200 photographs and diagrams

G. P. Putnam's Sons, New York

Copyright © 1970 by the Estate
of Doris M. Cochran and by Coleman J. Goin.

Library of Congress Catalog
Card Number: 69–18168

PRINTED IN THE UNITED STATES OF AMERICA

TO OLIVE,
who deserves a better dedication

Picture Credits

THE authors and publisher wish to express appreciation to the following individuals and institutions for their gracious permission to reproduce photographs:

Mrs. Carden (Constance) Warner: Plate 1, a, c, d, e; Plate 2, a–f; Plate 3, a, c–e; Plate 4, a, c–f; Plate 5, a, b, e, f; Plate 6, a–f; Plate 7; a–d, f; Plate 8, a–c, e, f; Plate 9, a, c–f; Plate 10, a, b, d–f; Plate 11, a, d–f; Plate 12, a, d–f; Plate 13, a–d, f; Plate 14, a–f; Plate 15, a, d, f; Plate 16, b, d–f; and Figures 9, 41, 44, 61, 71, 74, and 76.

Dr. R. S. Simmons: Plate 1, b, f; Plate 3, b; Plate 4, b; Plate 5, c, d; Plate 11, b; Plate 12, b, c; Plate 15, e; and Figures 1, 3, 10, 11, 12, 14, 24, 33–39, 53, 54, 63, 67–69, 73, 84.

James A. Honey: Plate 8, d; Plate 9, b; Plate 10, c; Plate 11, c; Plate 15, c; and Figure 4.

Dr. Howard K. Gloyd: Figures 75, 77, 78, 80, 82, 86, 90.

Nathan W. Cohen: Plate 13, e; Plate 15, b; Plate 16, a.

Dr. Charles J. Stine: Plate 16, c and Figure 96.

Dr. Archie Carr: Figures 49–52.

Robert J. Ellison: Figure 25.

University of Florida—Leonard Giovannoli: Figures 16, 17, 30, 42, 43, 46, 47, 60, 64, 65, 70, 83, 85, 89, 91, 93.

Carnegie Museum—Dr. M. Graham Netting: Figures 21, 22, 27, 29, 81.

Carnegie Museum—Dr. C. J. McCoy: Figures 8, 15.

The American Museum of Natural History: Figures 2, 13, 18–20, 23, 26, 28, 31, 32, 45, 56, 59, 62, 72, 79, 94, 95, 97–100.

The San Diego Zoo: Figures 5–7, 48, 55, 57, 58, 87, 88, 92.

The United States National Museum: Figure 40.

Preface

THIS book is intended as an introduction to the salamanders, frogs and toads, turtles, crocodilians, lizards, and snakes now known to occur in the United States, including Alaska and Hawaii. It is hoped that by using the summary of diagnostic features in the species accounts, the illustrations, and the information concerning geographic distribution of the various species, the beginner will be able to identify the majority of the amphibians and reptiles he encounters. Where more detailed information regarding the variation and life history of the species is desired, the reader is referred to the volumes listed in the selected references.

In the making of this book we have, of course, become indebted to many people. We have called upon friends for help in illustrating this book and our friends have been generous. The following have made some of their personal photographs available to us: Dr. Archie Carr, Dr. Nathan W. Cohen, Robert J. Ellison, Dr. Howard K. Gloyd, James A. Honey, Dr. R. S. Simmons, Dr. Charles J. Stine, Robert Tuck, and finally Mrs. Carden Warner, who supplied the majority of the photographs. Dr. M. Graham Netting made Carnegie Museum photographs taken by him and Dr. C. J. McCoy available; Dr. Charles Shaw made certain San Diego Zoo pictures accessible to us. And Dr. H. K. Wallace gave us permission to use Department of Zoology, University of Florida, pictures taken by Leonard Giovannoli. We have also availed ourselves of the photo resources of the American Museum of Natural History, New York. To all these we owe our thanks. For the line drawings and other assistance we are indebted to Mrs. Charles Newman and Mr. Paul Laessle. Dr. James Peters of the United States National Museum has given us the benefit of his advice and help on a number of occasions. We are indeed grateful to them. Finally, our biggest debt of all is to Olive B. Goin. Not only has she reviewed the entire manuscript and given us the benefit of her editorial talents but she has also helped appreciably with the drudgery of typing and retyping, checking figures, preparing legends, and the many other details that go into the preparation of a volume of this kind.

DORIS M. COCHRAN
COLEMAN J. GOIN

Contents

Photographs and Diagrams

The color plates appear as a unit after page 170.

SIRENS AND SALAMANDERS

xi

FROGS AND TOADS

CROCODILIANS

TURTLES

SNAKES

Introduction

It has been said that to know the name of an animal is to know the animal itself. While this may not be quite true, certainly the first stage in becoming familiar with any kind of animal is to learn its name and what it looks like. This book was written with the hope that it will help you learn something about the amphibians and reptiles in the United States.

The amphibians are backboned animals that lack any covering of the skin—fur, feathers, or scales. They have no paired fins, as fish do, and always have at least one pair of legs, though these are sometimes so small that they may escape notice unless looked for. Amphibians lay their shell-less eggs in water or in moist places on land. Representatives of three of the four living orders of amphibians, the sirens, the salamanders, and the familiar frogs and toads, are found in the United States.

The reptiles are also backboned animals. They are covered with scales, rather than with feathers or hair as birds and mammals are. They have no gills, as fish do, and no fins. They may or may not have legs. They lay shelled eggs on land or else keep the eggs in the body of the mother until they hatch. The reptiles of the United States are grouped into the turtles, the crocodiles and alligators, and the familiar lizards and snakes.

The study of amphibians and reptiles is formally known as *herpetology*. The reason for grouping the study of the class *Amphibia* and the class *Reptilia* into a single science is simply historical. Compared to the fish or birds they both are relatively small classes, and they both are collected and preserved with essentially the same techniques; as a result, the early herpetologists became thoroughly acquainted with members of both groups. Today, most herpetologists tend to specialize and study just turtles or just salamanders or just snakes. With more detailed studies of small groups and with an ever-increasing number of students of herpetology, our knowledge of amphibians and reptiles has increased tremendously in recent decades. Of one thing we can be sure, though—not a single species of amphibian or reptile in the United States is so well known that there is not more to learn about it. Good, careful observations of the everyday habits of even our most common forms may lead to significant studies on behavior and ecology.

There is no general rule of thumb that can be used to insure always finding amphibians and reptiles when you look for them, but if you keep certain facts in mind, it may help. All the salamanders have more or less smooth, soft skins that must be kept moist if they are to survive. Obviously, then, they should be searched for in moist places. Under rocks, along stream courses, and under logs around the edges of ponds are good places to look for the more aquatic salamanders, while more terrestrial ones can often be found under logs lying on the forest floor or under rocks buried in the soil and leaf mold on a hillside.

The males of most of our native frogs and toads call the females to the mating site. Since many of them congregate in large choruses during the breeding season, it is quite often possible to collect a number of individuals at one time from these breeding congresses.

Since the reptiles, with their impervious scales, are not confined to moist places, it is more difficult to say just where they can be found. Of course, aquatic forms of snakes and turtles should be searched for around the edges of streams and lakes. Many small snakes and lizards live under logs, rocks and other debris on the forest floor, just as do the salamanders, and many of the former can be found while searching for the latter. In very wet country *and* in desert country, snakes are inclined to crawl onto the surfaces of paved roads at night, and at times, large numbers can be found by driving slowly along such roads and locating the snakes by means of the automobile headlights.

In using this handbook, you will naturally turn to the pictures first. Pick out the one that most closely resembles your specimen and then refer to the description of the species. If you decide your specimen does not belong there, check any similar species that may be listed. If you are still at a loss, read the account of the genus to be sure you are in the right group. Where only one species occurs in a genus, the genus is not defined. Pay attention to ranges. The distributions given simply reflect our knowledge at this time, and it is possible for an animal to be found outside the known range. But in general, if a form is said to be restricted to the Mississippi Valley, you would not expect to find it in a ravine in Oregon or in the desert of the Southwest.

Many people find it extremely pleasant to have a hobby of collecting and studying snakes, and it is indeed a hobby to be encouraged, but a word of caution is in order. It is nothing less than foolhardy to handle live poisonous snakes unless one's vocation requires it. This does not mean, though, that no snake should be handled. The easy way to resolve the dilemma is to learn first of all to recognize every poisonous snake in your vicinity; then you know that any other snake you see is harmless. Since the kinds of harmless snakes in any area in our country far outnumber the kinds of poisonous ones, the task of learning to recognize the poisonous ones is usually not too difficult.

The hobby of studying amphibians and reptiles is a fascinating one. For most of us, the many hours of pleasure we get from it repay manifold the initial effort we have to expend in becoming acquainted with them.

Sirens and Salamanders

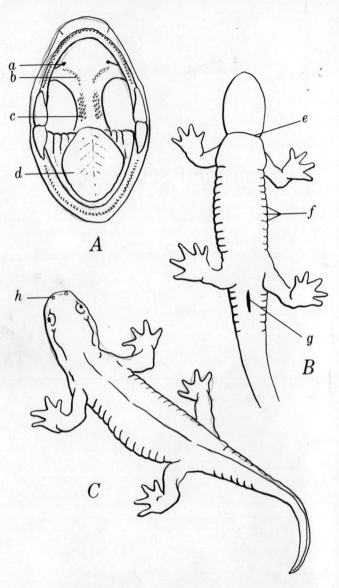

ANATOMICAL PARTS OF THE SALAMANDER

A. Open mouth of salamander showing (a) internal nares, (b) vomerine teeth, (c) parasphenoid teeth, and (d) tongue.

B. Ventral view of salamander showing (e) gular fold, (f) costal grooves, and (g) vent.

SALAMANDER GLOSSARY

Adpressed limbs: The front legs are pressed back along the side of the body, and the hind legs are pressed forward.

Cloaca: A common chamber into which the digestive, excretory, and reproductive tracts empty. It opens to the outside through the vent.

Costal grooves: A series of vertical grooves along the sides of the body between the front and hind legs of most salamanders.

Gular fold: A fleshy fold across the throat.

Intercostal fold: The fold of flesh between two costal grooves on the side of most salamanders.

Internal nares: The openings of the nasal passages in the roof of the mouth.

Nares: Nostrils. The outer openings are called the external nares.

Nasolabial groove: A groove running from the nostril to the edge of the upper lip on each side in some salamanders.

Neoteny: Retention of larval characteristics in the adult as a result of environmental factors.

Palatine teeth: Teeth on the roof of the mouth.

Parasphenoid teeth: Teeth on the roof of the mouth of some salamanders, usually well behind the internal nares and arranged in longitudinal series.

Parotoid glands: Large mucous glands on the head.

Premaxillary teeth: Teeth in the front part of the upper jaw.

Vomerine teeth: Teeth on the roof of the mouth between or just behind the internal nares, usually arranged in rounded patches or in transverse series.

Vent: The posterior opening of the digestive, excretory and reproductive systems.

Sirens and Salamanders

THESE animals are amphibians. They have moist skins unprotected by scales, and since they lose body water easily through the skin, they must stay in moist surroundings to prevent desiccation. Unlike frogs and toads, they have elongated bodies, relatively long tails, and relatively short legs. Sirens have only one pair of legs, the front ones; salamanders have two pairs, though they may be so small as to be easily overlooked. In general build, many salamanders resemble small lizards, from which they can be told by the absence of scales and of claws on the toes.

In identifying salamanders, remember that dorsal refers to the back, lateral to the side, and ventral to the underside. Most salamanders show a series of grooves, the costal grooves, down the sides of the body. The number of these grooves may be important in identification. Make your count beginning with the one over the front leg (it may not be well developed) and ending with the one just in front of the hind leg (two grooves may fuse here—count both). Remember, though, that there may be some individual variation; the number given in the text is the one found in most specimens.

Between the costal grooves are the intercostal folds. The length of the legs in proportion to the length of the body is expressed by giving the number of intercostal folds between the adpressed limbs. Push the front leg back along the side of the body and the hind leg forward, and count the folds between the tips of the toes.

Occasionally, it may be necessary to open a salamander's mouth to check some detail. In Dusky Salamanders, Shovel-nosed Salamanders, and Hubricht's Salamander, the lower jaw is fixed in position by heavy muscles, and the upper jaw must be raised to open the mouth. Some salamanders have a tongue attached in front, free at the sides and behind; in others the tongue is mushroom-shaped, attached by a central stalk and free all around the edge.

All of our salamanders lay eggs. In Hellbenders, fertilization is external; in the others it is internal. After a more or less elaborate courtship, the male deposits a little jellylike mass, the spermatophore, which is capped with a packet of sperm. The female picks this up with the lips of her vent. The eggs may be deposited in water or on land. Those laid in water hatch into aquatic larvae. These larvae look more like adult salamanders than a tadpole looks like a frog—they have the same general body shape, and the legs are already developed. They have three external gills on each side, with an opening, the gill slit, in front of each, and a tail fin which may extend forward along the back. Some salamanders and all sirens retain the gills as adults and live out their lives in the water as permanent larvae. Others absorb the gills as adults but remain thoroughly aquatic. Still others absorb the gills and move out on land, to return to the water only to breed. Sometimes salamanders that normally are terrestrial may fail to metamorphose because of some environmental condition, such as lack of iodine in the water. They become sexually mature and are able to reproduce but retain larval characteristic and remain in the water. This condition is called neoteny, and the animals are said to be neotenic. When the eggs are laid on land, the salamanders usually lose the gills before hatching and have no aquatic stage.

SIRENS, FAMILY SIRENIDAE

The sirens belong to the only living family representing the order Trachystomata and are quite different structurally from all other living amphibians. They are permanent larvae in the truest sense, being aquatic throughout life and having external gills. They are elongated, eellike animals, completely lacking hind limbs and with small front limbs which are useless in locomotion. The jaws are covered with horn. The eyes are minute. Two genera of this family are known, both North American.

Sirens, Genus *Siren*

These large sirens have hands with four fingers and three pairs of gill slits. Adults lack light stripes on the sides of the body, but stripes may be present in the young. One member of this genus has the distinction of being one of the two largest amphibians in the New World. It and *Amphiuma* are exceeded only by the Asiatic Giant Salamanders of the family Cryptobranchidae. There are two species.

Greater Siren, *Siren lacertina*

This siren may attain a length of over 36 inches, though few exceed 30 inches. To the casual observer, it looks like an eel, but a close examination reveals the presence of front limbs, each with four digits. The external gills appear as plumy growths on the sides of the neck just in front of the arms. The tip of the tail is rounded. The skin is smooth, not rough as in the true eel, and is gray or olive-colored, frequently with many round black spots on the head, back, and sides and a series of yellow dashes along the sides. Young ones have a light lateral stripe that disappears as they mature. There are usually 38 to 39 costal grooves. These animals are found in many different kinds of shallow-water habitats on the coastal plain from the vicinity of Washington, D.C., to southern Alabama and south through peninsular Florida.

Lesser Siren, *Siren intermedia*

These sirens are similar to the Greater Siren but never grow as large. The race of the Lesser Siren present in the region where the two species overlap has a maximum length of 15 inches and 31 to 34 costal grooves. Like the Greater Siren, it is strictly aquatic. There are three races.

Eastern Lesser Siren, *Siren i. intermedia* (Plate 1a)

This siren does not grow longer than 15 inches. Its black or brown back and the darker and more uniformly colored belly will help separate it from the Greater Siren. It has 31 to 34 costal grooves, and the tip of the tail is pointed. This race is found along the coastal plain from South Carolina to central Florida and west to southeastern Mississippi.

Western Lesser Siren, *Siren i. nettingi*

Like the Eastern Lesser Siren, this subspecies is small, reaching a maximum length of only $16\frac{7}{8}$ inches. It is gray or olive above, with small scattered black spots, while the belly is dark with many light spots; and there are no distinctly paler areas around the jaws, gills, limbs, or vent. There are 33 to 37 costal grooves. This race is found from southern Mississippi to eastern Texas and north in the Mississippi Valley to Illinois and Indiana.

Rio Grande Siren, *Siren i. texana*

The Rio Grande Siren approaches the Greater Siren in size, reaching a maximum of $24\frac{1}{2}$ inches in length. There are usually 37 to 38 costal grooves. The back is olive to gray, with many small black dots on the head and back. The belly is light-gray, and pale areas occur at the jaws, gills, limbs, and vent. This race is found along the Rio Grande valley in southeastern Texas.

Dwarf Siren, *Pseudobranchus striatus*

Found only in Florida and the southern parts of Georgia and South Carolina, the eellike Dwarf Sirens live secretive lives among clumps of water plants or in mud in ponds or bogs. None exceeds $8\frac{1}{2}$ inches in length. Like their large relatives, the true Sirens, they lack hind legs, but their front limbs have only three fingers, and they have only a single gill slit on each side. There are light stripes present along the sides. Little is known about their breeding habits. There are five races of the single species.

Narrow-striped Dwarf Siren, *Pseudobranchus s. axanthus* (Figure 1)

The absence of bright-yellow or orange stripes on the back characterizes this form. It is a dark, rather muddy gray, with vague lighter gray stripes on the sides. It has about 35 costal grooves between the front limb and the vent. It reaches a maximum size of $8\frac{1}{4}$ inches. When it is in danger, it gives a yelping sound, opening its mouth when the yelp is emitted. This habit of yelping and its fancied similarity to the sound made by a dog, may be a reason for the popular name of "mud

Fig. 1. Narrow-striped Dwarf Siren, *Pseudobranchus s. axanthus*

Fig. 2. Marbled Salamander, *Ambystoma opacum*

puppy" or "water dog" given to these and other salamanders in Georgia, where they are objects of superstitious fear to many humans. It is found from extreme southern Georgia south through Florida to the region of Lake Okeechobee.

Everglades Dwarf Siren, *Pseudobranchus s. belli*

This race has between 29 and 33 costal grooves, fewer than those of the other subspecies known. Its maximum size is 6 inches. Its stripes are much brighter than those of the Narrow-striped Dwarf Siren, and its belly is light-gray with buff spots. This form is apparently confined to the southern half of Florida where it was first collected in quantity among masses of dead water hyacinths which had been destroyed by spraying.

Gulf Hammock Dwarf Siren, *Pseudobranchus s. lustricolus*

This race has about 34 costal grooves, and its light dorsolateral stripes are bright-orange or yellow, followed by a yellowish or silvery white lateral stripe. Its belly is black with light mottling. Somewhat larger than the others, its maximum recorded size is $8\frac{1}{2}$ inches. It is likewise known to give a yelping call when seized. It lives in stagnant bogs, nearly buried in muck. In an aquarium simulating its natural habitat, one remained in a vertical position in the muck at all times, except when it darted to the surface to gulp air, retreating at once to its muddy bed. It is confined to Gulf Hammock on the west side of the Florida peninsula.

Broad-striped Dwarf Siren, *Pseudobranchus s. striatus*

The dark dorsal stripe is not divided by three narrow light ones, but has at the most a single indistinct pale middorsal stripe. Its sides have a broad yellow stripe, and its belly is dark, marbled with yellow. Its maximum size is 6 inches. It stays in living clumps of water hyacinths. This race is found from southern South Carolina to southeastern Georgia.

Slender Dwarf Siren, *Pseudobranchus s. spheniscus*

The narrower head and more pointed snout set this form apart from any of the others yet known. It has two bright-tan or yellow stripes on each side of the body. It has about 34 costal grooves and is 6 inches long when fully grown. It lives in shallow ponds, especially in those containing cypress and black gum trees, and may be collected by dredging up and examining the debris from the pond bottom. It is found in south central and southwestern Georgia and the northern panhandle of Florida from Baker to Gulf and Leon counties.

GIANT SALAMANDERS AND HELLBENDERS, FAMILY CRYPTOBRANCHIDAE

These are squat, ungainly water animals that never completely metamorphose. The adults lack eyelids and retain the larval teeth.

Although they never leave the water, they do undergo a partial metamorphosis, for the adults lose the gills, though one gill slit may remain open. This family contains the largest known living amphibians: *Andrias japonicus*, the Japanese Giant Salamander, reaches a length of 5 feet, and a slightly smaller form is known from the Asiatic mainland. The only North American genus, *Cryptobranchus*, while only about half as long, is nevertheless among the largest salamanders in the United States.

Hellbender, *Cryptobranchus alleganiensis*

This peculiar creature is known to modern fishermen as a stealer o bait, and some people still regard it as harmful, though it is entirely innocuous. Its skin looks too loose for it. The wrinkled folds on the sides of the heavy, flattened body serve as aids to respiration and are often kept in motion while the animal is resting on the bottom of the pond, where oxygen is not abundant. Its gray, black, or dull-brown color, often irregularly spotted, renders even its big body practically invisible among the rocks and debris of the bed of a stream or river. Hellbenders mate in late summer. The male digs a nest beneath a flat stone in the stream bed and allows any female heavy with eggs to enter. She deposits her eggs in two long beadlike strings, producing as many as 450 eggs at a laying. Several females have been known to lay their eggs in the same nest. The male discharges the whitish, cloudy seminal fluid over them to bring about external fertilization. He stays at the opening of the nest to guard the developing eggs during their incubation time of ten to twelve weeks. Larvae are a little over an inch at hatching and are light with darker spots. They begin to lose the gills when they are approximately 5 inches long and eighteen months old. There are two races.

Hellbender, *Cryptobranchus a. alleganiensis* (Plate 1b)

The throat is sparsely spotted with black, and the body and tail are usually black-spotted. A single pair of gill slits can usually still be seen ventrally in the adults. Judging by the growth rate of captive specimens, this Hellbender attains a size of about 20 inches in five years. The maximum reported length is 29½ inches. One individual lived for twenty-nine years in captivity. This race ranges from southern New York to extreme northern Georgia and Alabama and west through central Missouri.

Ozark Hellbender, *Cryptobranchus a. bishopi*

The gill slits have a tendency to close in adults of the Ozark Hellbender. The largest recorded specimen was about 22½ inches long. The throat is usually spotted with black, and the dark color on the body and tail is mostly in large blotches. This race is found in the Black River system of southeastern Missouri and northeastern Arkansas.

AMBYSTOMIDS, FAMILY AMBYSTOMATIDAE

These are mostly sturdily built, broad-headed salamanders, small to medium in size. Costal grooves are present, though they may be rather hard to see in some. There is no nasolabial groove running from the nostril to the lip. Neoteny is rather common in this family. Neotenic adults are large (6 to 14 inches) and stout-bodied, with well-developed gills and distinct costal grooves. The body is pigmented, the eyes normal. The family is found only in North America. Of the four genera, one is confined to Mexico, two are found only on the west coast of the United States and Canada, and one is widespread, occurring from Alaska to Mexico and from the Atlantic to the Pacific.

Mole Salamanders, Genus *Ambystoma*

Except in the western parts of northern California, Oregon, and Washington, any salamander belonging to this family will also belong to this genus. In this region the family includes the Pacific Giant Salamander, which is large and heavily built, with a marbled pattern, and the Olympic Salamander, which is small and slender, with big pop eyes. As their popular name suggests, Mole Salamanders spend most of their time underground. At the breeding season, some congregate in large numbers in their natal pond, and for a few days the water is churned white by their activities. Just as suddenly as they came, they leave when the eggs are fertilized and laid, and for almost another year it is a clever collector who manages to discover the adults in their hiding places. On rainy nights, however, they may venture out to feed on earthworms and other small invertebrates. As captives, they usually make good pets, as some may learn to accept bits of raw meat from one's fingers. The ease with which they may be kept makes them very desirable laboratory animals, and countless experiments have been performed with them. Several kinds are neotenic. Neotenic adults have a broad dorsal fin that extends nearly to the head. This is especially common where iodine, necessary to successful metamorphosis, is in short supply. Some adults grow to 13 inches in length. Twelve species are found in the United States. The Long-toed Salamander and the Northwestern Salamander are confined to the northwest; nine other species are found only in the eastern half of the country; and the wide-ranging Tiger Salamander covers most of the range of the genus.

Spotted Salamander, *Ambystoma maculatum* (Plate 1c)

The rows of golden or orange spots down each side of the back on a shiny black background make this salamander one of the most striking in appearance. The sides are dark-gray, the belly slate-gray and unspotted. It has been recorded as an albino, in which the yellow spots persisted on a creamy white ground. The record size of an adult is 9 inches. In March or April in the northern states the full-grown ones return to their breeding ponds, swimming around in a courtship "dance" and rubbing one another with their noses. Eggs numbering from a dozen to 250 or more are deposited by the female in a large mass, clear or whitish at first, then often acquiring a greenish tone from the symbiotic algae that live in the egg mass. The incubation period is between 31 and 54 days, depending on the water temperature. The larvae are about $\frac{1}{2}$ inch long at hatching and greenish yellow with dark spots on the back. Gills are present, also small, budlike structures representing the forelegs, but hind legs do not develop until some time later. After a larval period of 61 to 110 days, they have increased to $3\frac{1}{2}$ inches and are ready to transform. A year later the young salamander is about 4 inches long and is ready to breed by the following spring. This widespread species is found in woodland ponds during the breeding season, and occasionally in humid places at other times. It ranges from Canada to southern Georgia and west to eastern Kansas, Oklahoma, and Texas.

Marbled Salamander, *Ambystoma opacum* (Figure 2)

White or silvery crossbars distinguish this salamander from the Spotted and Tiger Salamanders, which usually have yellow or golden spots. There are four to seven of these bands, which narrow on the back and widen on the upper parts of the sides, sometimes uniting to alternate with large black spots set off from the ground color. There are usually 11 costal grooves. The Marbled Salamander is less aquatic than the Spotted Salamander, often preferring dry hilly regions, although it may be found in damp sand or gravel near streams. It breeds in autumn, the female depositing 50 to 200 eggs on land in a shallow hole under debris, where she remains until rain floods the nest, after which the larvae hatch. The incubation period is variable, depending on moisture and temperature; if the autumn rain is scant, the eggs may not hatch until the following spring. The larvae are $\frac{3}{4}$ inch long at hatching, and by June, the usual transformation season, they are from $2\frac{1}{2}$ to nearly 3 inches long. When they are fifteen to seventeen months old or by the fall of the year following their transformation, they are old enough to breed. The maximum size of the adult is 5 inches. This is another widespread form, occurring from Massachusetts to central Florida and west to eastern Oklahoma and Texas.

Mole Salamander, *Ambystoma talpoideum*

Its large head and feet seem out of proportion to the rather small body of this salamander, whose maximum size is only 4 inches. There are 10 costal grooves. The pattern consists of a wide brown dorsal stripe, lightening on the tail, with many small dull bluish-white flecks above in lichenlike patches. The belly is gray, with more and larger light blotches. Because it burrows, it is seldom found except at breeding time—January and February in the Gulf states. Eggs are laid in temporary shallow ponds near gum trees or in pine woods. The larvae grow to nearly adult size before losing their gills, and metamorphosis is usually complete by May. Occasionally this salamander is neotenic.

It is found along the coastal plain from central South Carolina to central Florida, west to eastern Texas and north in the Mississippi Valley to southern Illinois. There is apparently a disjunct population in western North Carolina and eastern Tennessee and another in southeastern Oklahoma.

Small-mouthed Salamander, *Ambystoma texanum*

The ground color is a deep-brown to black, blotched with grayish or yellowish lichenlike patches above and on the sides. There are usually 14 costal grooves. The head and mouth are relatively small when compared to other members of the genus. Its blackish unspectacular pattern conceals it well among the damp debris along streams and ponds where it likes to burrow in the soft soil. It often lives in abandoned crayfish burrows, seldom going into the water except to breed. Eggs are laid singly or in clusters attached to stems of water plants in February and March. When hatched, the larva is ½ inch long or a little less, its back olive-green with squarish spots. It transforms in May or June when about 2¾ inches in length, its maximum when full-grown being 9¼ inches. This species ranges from Ohio to southern Iowa and south to the Gulf Coast from Mississippi to eastern Texas.

Ringed Salamander, *Ambystoma annulatum*

The handsome pattern of narrow, yellowish, usually regular rings on a dark-brown to black background makes this a rather easily recognized species, but it is so secretive except when breeding that it is seldom noticed. The belly is dark with small scattered light spots. There are 15 costal grooves. Adults may reach 8 inches in length. When heavy autumn rains come, Ringed Salamanders congregate in large numbers in small pools, where each female lays up to 150 eggs in clusters, some fastened to vegetation but most of them scattered on the bottom. Spring breeding has been observed, and at that time eggs are laid under logs on land, the hatching (in the laboratory) of these eggs beginning ten days later. More study on different phases of its life history is needed. This species is found from central Missouri through northwestern Arkansas to northeastern Oklahoma.

Flatwoods Salamander, *Ambystoma cingulatum*

This is a small species, adults not exceeding 4½ inches. The ground color is black, frosted with many light-gray flecks or reticulated above, and with narrow vertical lines on the sides between the costal grooves, of which there are thirteen or fourteen. There are two races.

Frosted Flatwoods Salamander, *Ambystoma c. cingulatum*

The belly is black with scattered gray spots. The grayish irregular dorsal pattern on a black ground suggests frost to some or lichens to others; at any rate, it is well concealed in the slash pine and wire grass flatwoods of its rather restricted range along the coastal plain from extreme southern North Carolina to northeastern Florida.

Reticulated Flatwoods Salamander, *Ambystoma c. bishopi*

This salamander has a dark belly with minute pale flecks, giving a salt-and-pepper effect. It is found from southwest Georgia and north-west Florida to extreme southeastern Mississippi.

Northwestern Salamander, *Ambystoma gracile*

Members of this species are the only ones in the genus to have large kidney-shaped parotoid glands behind the eyes. They are large, stout-bodied salamanders with 11 costal grooves. There are two races.

Brown Salamander, *Ambystoma g. gracile*

The popular name comes from its uniform seal-brown color, although the glandular regions of the parotoids, sides of head, upper part of tail and belly are lighter. The upper tail ridge is strongly glandular and thicker than the lower edge. In the Olympic Mountains there may be small yellow spots on the back. Adults reach 7¾ inches. The Brown Salamander frequents humid areas, hiding under logs and other debris or sometimes staying in ponds near sea level or as high as 8,000 feet. Eggs are deposited between January and July, depending on altitude and other factors, and hatch in two to four weeks. This race is found along the Pacific Coast from northern California to Vancouver Island and the adjacent mainland of British Columbia.

British Columbia Salamander, *Ambystoma g. decorticatum*

The parotoid glands are less pronounced in this race, and the tail is not noticeably thickened above. It is chocolate-brown above, with numerous small, dull, irregular white spots. The belly is light-brown. Adults may reach 8½ inches. This race extends from British Columbia into southern Alaska.

Jefferson Salamander, *Ambystoma jeffersonianum*

These are moderately slender for Mole Salamanders, with long toes. Adults are lead-colored to brown above, with small pale-blue flecks on the lower sides (sometimes lacking in old adults). They may reach a length of 7¾ inches. Young ones may have small pale-blue dots on the sides of the head, body and tail, also on the throat, which are absent in large, old adults. They breed in March or early April. A single female lays over 200 eggs in the breeding pond, placed in small clusters on submerged plant stems or twigs. In thirty or forty-five days the larvae hatch, then being just over ½ inch in length. After a period varying between eight and eighteen weeks, they transform when they have reached a length of nearly 2 to 3 inches. The next year the young grow to 4½ inches and are old enough to breed by the following spring. This species ranges from Vermont to northern Virginia and Kentucky and west to Illinois.

Blue-spotted Salamander, *Ambystoma laterale* (Plate 1d)

Unlike the preceding species, adults of the Blue-spotted Salamander retain the blue and white spots on a bluish-black ground throughout their lives. It is very easy to confuse the two kinds, as their ranges overlap in New York and New England, and hybrids are frequently found. The toes are proportionately shorter in the full-grown Blue-spotted, however, and it is smaller, less slender, and darker. Adults reach 6¼ inches. This hardy little creature extends farther north than any other eastern Mole Salamander, being found to fifty-three degrees north latitude in Labrador and Ontario. It ranges south to northern New Jersey and west to Minnesota.

Mabee's Salamander, *Ambystoma mabeei*

This small, stoutly built salamander grows to a length of 4 inches. Its head is relatively small and its toes quite long compared to others of the genus. It has 13 costal grooves. Its sober coloration of deep-brown to black with flecks of dull-tan or gray conceal it under bark or fallen logs where it hides, its habitat seeming to be similar to that of the Flatwoods Salamander. It is found on the coastal plain of North and South Carolina.

Long-toed Salamander, *Ambystoma macrodactylum*

This salamander has a broad tan or greenish-yellow middorsal stripe with irregular edges, which is sometimes broken into irregular blotches or mottling. The sides are brown to black, usually sprinkled with tiny white flecks, and the belly is dark-brown or sooty. There are usually 12 costal grooves. Adults may reach 5 inches. Five races have been described.

Western Long-toed Salamander, *Ambystoma m. macrodactylum*

The dorsal stripe is yellowish or greenish and becomes vague on the head. The dorsal ground color is gray. This race is found from western Oregon north to Vancouver Island.

Eastern Long-toed Salamander, *Ambystoma m. columbianum*

The dorsal stripe is bright-yellow to tan and wider than the distance between the nostrils. On the head the stripe is broken into spots. This race is found from western Montana and eastern Idaho north into Canada.

Santa Cruz Long-toed Salamander, *Ambystoma m. croceum*

The dorsal stripe is orange-yellow on a dark, usually black, ground color and is narrower than the distance between the nostrils. This race is known only from Santa Cruz County, California.

Northern Long-toed Salamander, *Ambystoma m. krausei*

The yellow, unbroken dorsal stripe continues onto the snout. It is narrow, widest just behind the eyes, and there is a patch of the same color on each eyelid. This is the most widely distributed race, ranging from central and western Idaho through eastern and central Oregon and Washington, north nearly to Alaska.

Southern Long-toed Salamander, *Ambystoma m. sigillatum*

The dorsal stripe is narrower than the distance between the nostrils, bright-yellow, and often broken into spots. There are small yellow spots on the head. This race is found from southern Oregon southward through northern and northwestern California.

Tiger Salamander, *Ambystoma tigrinum* (Plate 1e)

These are large, stoutly built salamanders with blunt heads, small eyes, and tubercles on the undersides of the feet. There are no conspicuous parotoid glands. The color and pattern are very variable in this widely distributed species. Usually there are large and conspicuous light spots or bars on a dark background, but sometimes the dark color is reduced to a network or series of spots on a lighter background. Many are neotenic, especially in the Western United States, where the neotenous larvae become very large, often nearly 13 inches. These larvae have external gills and a well developed tail fin. Those that do transform and come out on land usually stay in burrows during daylight hours and are thus difficult to find. Breeding occurs in the spring, when great numbers of adults appear at the ponds to lay their eggs. Some of the subspecies deposit their eggs in a large mass, as do the Spotted Salamanders, but others fasten the eggs singly or in small clusters to stems of water plants. There are eight races.

Eastern Tiger Salamander, *Ambystoma t. tigrinum*

The back, sides and belly are marked with olive-yellow or brownish-yellow spots on a dark-brown or black ground color. There are 12 costal grooves. This is a very large race—adults may reach 13 inches. It is found from Long Island south to northern Florida and west to extreme southeastern South Dakota and eastern Texas.

Gray Tiger Salamander, *Ambystoma t. diaboli*

In this race the back is grayish or brown with small, round black spots, and the belly is dull-yellow. There are usually 12 costal grooves. The maximum size is $12\frac{1}{4}$ inches. This race is found from central Nebraska and extreme southeastern Wyoming south through most of New Mexico and Texas into Mexico.

Barred Tiger Salamander, *Ambystoma t. mavortium*

In this race the pattern consists of vertical yellow bars often reaching from the middorsal to the midventral line and sometimes confluent on the lower part of the side. The back is dark-brown or black, the belly often with irregular dark blotches. Adults may reach 8⅜ inches. It is found from southwestern Minnesota and northwestern South Dakota, north into Canada.

Blotched Tiger Salamander, *Ambystoma t. melanostictum*

In this race the light dorsal spots are dull yellow, tending to fuse into large, irregular blotches on a dark-brown or black ground color. The top of the head and the snout are usually light. There are 13 costal grooves. Adults may reach 8⅝ inches. This race ranges from northern Nebraska, northwestward into Canada and west to central and northern Idaho and the eastern half of Washington.

Utah Tiger Salamander, *Ambystoma t. utahensis*

The back is grayish or brown with small, round black spots, and the belly is gray and unspotted. Adults may reach 9 inches. This race is found from southern Wyoming, south through the western half of Colorado and most of Utah into northwestern New Mexico and northern Arizona.

Arizona Tiger Salamander, *Ambystoma t. nebulosum*

This race is like the Utah Tiger Salamander, but the belly is light, mottled with dark spots. Maximum size is slightly over 9 inches. This race is found in central Arizona and west central New Mexico.

Sonora Tiger Salamander, *Ambystoma t. stebbinsi*

In this race there are twenty-five to forty-five golden-brown or yellowish spots between the limb insertions, with larger ones on the sides and tail. The belly is brown, sometimes with a few small golden spots. Maximum size is 12⅞ inches. This form is known only from the Huachucua Mountains of southern Arizona.

California Tiger Salamander, *Ambystoma t. californiense*

There are a few large orange or yellow dorsolateral spots (seldom any spots in the middorsal area) and large yellow spots on the sides. The belly is gray with a few small dull-yellow spots along the center. Adults may reach 8³⁄₁₆ inches. This race is found in central western California.

Pacific Giant Salamander, *Dicamptodon ensatus* (Plate 1f)

The genus *Dicamptodon* differs from the related *Ambystoma* in having indistinct costal grooves. There are no tubercles under the foot, and the fourth toe of the hind foot has three segments. From *Rhyacotriton*, the other member of the family found in the United States, it differs in its much larger size, smaller eyes, and in having a brownish back with black marblings. The only known member of its genus, *D. ensatus*, attains an adult length of 12 inches, and its stout body and heavy limbs give an impression of even greater size. It is one of the few salamanders to make sounds when disturbed; the voice has been described as a scream, a bark, or a rattle. It is nocturnal, but sometimes appears during the day. Adults eat land snails, slugs, beetles, moths, and flies, and may even devour other amphibians and small rodents. The larvae take aquatic insects, water snails, and small crayfish. Apparently the eggs are laid in early spring underground near the outlet of a spring. The larvae wriggle down to a mountain brook and seem to metamorphose during their second summer, when they are 6 to 8 inches long. Neotenic adults have the dorsal fin confined to the tail. This species lives in damp forests along the coast in Santa Clara County, California, north to southwestern British Columbia, and in northern Idaho and western Montana in a discontinuous distribution.

Olympic Salamander, *Rhyacotriton olympicus* (Figure 3)

Barely exceeding 4 inches in total length, these big-eyed little salamanders are brown or olive above, yellow or orange beneath. There are 13 to 15 costal grooves, including 1 each in axilla and groin. The sex of an adult can be told by the shape of the vent; in the male the vent forms squarish posterior lobes with light tips, which are visible even when looking at the animal from above. Apparently the eggs are laid in June, in running water, attached singly to the lower surfaces of stones. The eggs are relatively large, and not many are laid, the average per clutch being five. There are two races.

Northern Olympic Salamander, *Rhyacotriton o. olympicus*

The back is chocolate-brown, the belly is yellowish-orange, sometimes with brown mottlings on the throat and a few dark spots on the belly and tail. There are usually some fine white spots along the sides. These little salamanders are found in or beside spring seepages in western Washington and northwestern Oregon, west of the Cascades.

Southern Olympic Salamander, *Rhyacotriton o. variegatus*

The greenish-yellow body is heavily blotched with black to brown irregular patches, while the lower surfaces are rather thickly covered with small black flecks, which are not concentrated on the throat, as are the dark spots of the northern race. Although very young larvae are nearly white below, their bellies become spotted as they grow, thus differing from the larvae of their northerly relative. This race is found in northern California and southwestern Oregon. Intergrades are recognized from the central coast of Oregon diagonally northeastward into Lewis County, Washington.

Fig. 3. Olympic Salamander, *Rhyacotriton olympicus*

Fig. 4. California Newt, *Taricha torosa*

AMPHIUMAS, FAMILY AMPHIUMIDAE

This family is found only in the Southeastern United States and contains only a single genus. Amphiumas are big, dark, semilarval, aquatic animals, with long cylindrical bodies and minute, easily overlooked front and hind legs.

Amphiumas, Genus *Amphiuma*

Adults of this aquatic genus develop lungs, as do the *Cryptobranchidae*. Although the gills are lost, a pair of gill slits remains throughout life. Vibrations in the water which might denote the presence of danger or of food are detected by means of lateral line organs similar to those found in fishes. Amphiumas are also sensitive to ultraviolet light, which can harm their skin. They defend themselves by biting, and the sharp little teeth in their strong jaw can cause a painful wound. The three forms now recognized are easily told apart. As their common names indicate, they differ in the number of toes.

Two-toed Amphiuma, *Amphiuma means* (Plate 2a)

There are only two toes on each foot. The belly is dark-gray, with no sharp color change from the dorsal and lateral dark tones. This salamander is a favorite in laboratories and has been known to live for twenty-seven years in captivity. Having only tiny arms and legs, its elongated body somewhat suggests that of an eel, but of course, it lacks the eel's fins. It can move around slowly on swampy land, however, and lays its eggs above water level in shallow depressions beside fallen trees or in similar protected places, the female remaining to guard her eggs. These are laid in long beadlike strings lying in a mass. The incubation period is believed to be five months. The young larvae are 2 inches long when hatched, with short white gills that are contrasted with the dark brown of the body. They transform when they are less than 3 inches long. The maximum size of the adult is about 35 inches. They stay in definite lairs or retreats, to which they return after foraging for invertebrates, fish, frogs, small snakes, and even the smaller individuals of their own kind. They prefer to live in marshes or in muddy lakes and streams. They are found along the coastal plain from southern Virginia to southern Mississippi and south through peninsular Florida.

Three-toed Amphiuma, *Amphiuma tridactylum*

This species has the legs slightly better developed, though still tiny, with three toes on each foot. The belly is light-gray, sharply set off from the dark color of the back and sides. Calcareous streams seem to be preferred by this form, although they are sometimes taken in drainage ditches and swamps. A maximum of 40 inches has been recorded. A large female was found in the drying bed of a cypress swamp coiled around a mass of about 150 eggs under a large log.

The young apparently hatch in the late fall. Food of adults consists of crayfish, clams, earthworms, insects, spiders, small fish, and snails, with an occasional salamander or frog.

This species is found from southeastern Missouri to the Gulf of Mexico and from northern Georgia west to southeastern Oklahoma and eastern Texas.

One-toed Amphiuma, *Amphiuma pholeter*

This is small for an Amphiuma, the largest specimen not reaching 11 inches. The limbs are very minute and have only one digit apiece. There is little difference in color between the back and belly but the general tone is lighter than that of the Two-toed Amphiuma. This species is presently known only from Levy, Jefferson, Liberty and Calhoun counties, Florida.

NEWTS, FAMILY SALAMANDRIDAE

Members of this family usually metamorphose completely and spend at least part of their time on land. Most of them are found in the Old World. There are only two genera in this country, one in the East, one in the West. Adults of the Western Newts are typically terrestrial, though they must return to the water to breed. Adults of the eastern form are usually found in water, though there is often a terrestrial stage between the aquatic larva and aquatic adult. There is no naso-labial groove between nostril and lip and there are no costal grooves. Newts are small to moderate in size with brightly colored bellies, yellow, orange, or red, and with rough skins in the terrestrial stages.

Eastern Newts, Genus *Notophthalmus*

This genus is found from southern Canada through all the eastern United States and into Mexico. Usually these newts are terrestrial for at least a year after transformation from the larval stage, and during their presence on land they are mostly brick-red or coral, meriting their popular name of Red Eft. In a year or so they return to the water permanently. While terrestrial, the skin becomes roughened and thick, and the tail is rounded, but upon resuming aquatic habits, the skin is much smoother, and the tail is laterally compressed (rudderlike) to act as a swimming device. Sometimes the Red Eft stage is bypassed, and the larva metamorphoses directly into the aquatic adult. Newts seem always to search for food, whether in their native ponds or in an aquarium, eating worms, insects, small snails, baby frogs, and frogs' eggs in the wild state or bits of hamburger or canned pet food in captivity. Their skin secretes a noxious substance when they are injured, so that relatively few of the larger animals prey upon them. There are three species.

Newt, *Notophthalmus viridescens*

These newts look as if they had been sprinkled with black pepper. There may also be an irregular dorsolateral row of bright-red spots.

These spots may be elongated to form a broken, black-bordered red line on the trunk and posterior part of the head. The other two species of Eastern Newts differ in pattern. In Striped Newts the red line is not heavily bordered with black, is usually unbroken on the head and trunk, and continues onto the tail. Black-spotted Newts have larger round black spots on the back. There are four races of this species.

Red-spotted Newt, *Notophthalmus v. viridescens* (Plate 2b)

The Red-spotted Newt has dorsolateral rows of black-bordered red spots. The aquatic adults are olive to brown above, yellow on the belly. These newts stand the cold very well and may often be seen swimming under a film of ice in their native ponds. The annual sexual changes in the male begin during the winter. A broad fin develops on the tail; the vent becomes protuberant; and black horny growths appear on the inner thigh surfaces and on the tips of the toes. Actual mating takes place in the spring. Internal fertilization is effected by means of spermatophores. A female lays between 200 and 375 eggs, each one fastened to an aquatic plant away from swift currents. Depending on the depth and temperature of the water, the eggs hatch in three to five weeks. The larvae do not complete their metamorphosis until the following autumn. The maximum length of this newt is 5 inches. It ranges from the Maritime Provinces of Canada south to southern Georgia and Alabama, west to eastern Michigan and northeastern Mississippi.

Broken-striped Newt, *Notophthalmus v. dorsalis*

This newt is much smaller than the preceding, becoming no longer than $3\frac{3}{8}$ inches. The black-bordered, broken red stripe along the sides of the head and body distinguishes it from the Red-spotted Newt, and the usual breaking up of this stripe on the trunk and its absence on the tail separate it from the Striped Newt. The eft has the red stripe indistinctly dark-bordered and a general body color of reddish brown. This race is found along the coastal plain of North and South Carolina.

Central Newt, *Notophthalmus v. louisianensis*

This form is 4 inches long at its maximum. Although considered a close relative of the Red-spotted Newt, the Central Newt has no red spots as a rule. However, from Michigan southward to the Gulf of Mexico, intergradation with the Red-spotted Newt occurs, and individuals with small red spots may be seen, but these spots are only partly encircled by black rings. The belly is yellow, with only a few scattered black spots. At breeding time the tail fins of the male are particularly high, and a row of dark spots on the upper and lower fins extends to the tip of the tail. Apparently the Red Eft stage does not always take place in this form, the newts remaining among the water plants to transform and retaining traces of external gills in the adult stage. This newt ranges from Minnesota to the Gulf Coast of Texas and extends eastward through southern Alabama and Georgia and northern Florida to southern South Carolina, so that here its range is east of that of the Red-spotted Newt.

Peninsula Newt, *Notophthalmus v. piaropicola*

The Peninsula Newt has a heavily spotted orange or yellow belly and black dorsal color, distinguishing it from its near relatives. Like the Central Newt, it lacks red spots. When fully grown, it measures 4⅛ inches in length. Its subspecific name means "dweller among water hyacinths" (*Piaropus*), although the efts hide under debris on the banks of ponds. This newt is found in peninsula Florida.

Striped Newt, *Notophthalmus perstriatus*

An unbroken bright red stripe along the sides of the head and body characterizes this newt. The stripe continues onto the tail, where it is usually broken. The red-orange eft also has stripes similar to those of the adult, whose maximum size is only 3⅛ inches. Adults frequent shallow ponds in the piney woods, and efts often stay in rather dry surroundings. Neotenic individuals as large as the aquatic adults are sometimes found. In these, the larval gills are retained throughout life, but the reproductive organs become functional just as in the normal adult. The Striped Newt is found in northern and central Florida and southern Georgia.

Black-spotted Newt, *Notophthalmus meridionalis*

This newt is quite easily recognized because of the large black spots over the upper and lower surfaces of its body and the lack of red in its coloration. It is one of the largest of its genus in the United States, growing to 4⅛ inches in length, thus equaling the Peninsula Newt. Although there are not many swamps or lagoons within its range, it is fairly abundant wherever such standing water does occur. It has rougher skin when adult than do most of the other newts of this genus. It is known to breed in March and April, and the female attaches her eggs singly to pieces of debris in the water. It is found in southeastern Texas and adjacent Mexico.

Pacific Newts, Genus *Taricha*

The genus *Taricha* is found in states west of the Rocky Mountains, in Canada and in southern Alaska. Newts of this genus grow considerably larger than those of the eastern *Notophthalmus* and are uniformly dark above, without any of the bright dots or lines that characterize the eastern forms. They do not have a terrestrial eft stage, although adults roam at will on the river banks, especially in wet weather. The Red-bellied Newt is known to migrate back each year to the pond in which it was hatched.

Red-bellied Newt, *Taricha rivularis*

The eyes are large and uniformly dark. The body is black or dark-brown above, this color extending well onto the lower limb surfaces and crossing the vent as a broad, dark band. The belly and upper sides of the digits are red. The sides of the upper jaw and most or all of the lower eyelids are light. The snout is shorter, usually with a light area between the nostrils. This newt lives in the coastal redwood belt north of San Francisco Bay, in mountain streams of rapidly moving water. As soon as the spring floods have passed, spawning begins during March and April. The spermatophores are fastened firmly to the rocky stream bed, where the female finds them and picks them up with her cloaca, fertilization being internal. Clusters of eggs are subsequently attached to the lower surfaces of submerged rocks or to vegetation. Many females may lay their eggs on the same stone as seventy egg masses have been found on the underside of a single stone in an area of approximately 100 square inches. This newt ranges from Sonoma to Humboldt counties in California.

Rough-skinned Newt, *Taricha granulosa*

The eyes are small in this species, and there are silvery patches on the iris. The body is light- to dark-brown above, contrasting sharply with the yellow to orange, occasionally reddish, belly. There is sometimes an indistinct reddish color on the tops of the digits. The sides of the upper jaw are usually dark; if they are light, the light color does not extend up onto the lower eyelids. The skin is rough except in the breeding male. Adults may reach $8\frac{1}{4}$ inches. There are two races.

Northern Rough-skinned Newt, *Taricha g. granulosa*

This handsome newt has very little dark blotching on the belly. During most of the year, most individuals prefer cold permanent streams, but some stay under pieces of bark or other debris on the bank, and in autumn they may often be seen crawling around on cloudy or rainy days, searching for food. In cold or very dry weather they live underground or in fallen logs, and consequently are much harder to observe. In spring they gather at their favored breeding sites, although sometimes spawning begins in late December. The small eggs are laid singly or in small clusters, usually attached to aquatic vegetation. When the larva is about $1\frac{1}{2}$ to 3 inches long, it is ready to begin metamorphosis, usually completing this process in August. When they are about four years old and about 4 inches in length they are sexually mature. They range from Santa Cruz County, California, north to southern Alaska.

Crater Lake Newt, *Taricha g. mazamae*

Numerous dark blotches on the belly and the usual presence of a black stripe across the vent distinguish this race from its near relatives. Stomach analyses show that it is a predator, taking many kinds of small insects and other invertebrates, as well as amphibian eggs, algae and occasionally dead arthropods, this last indicating a scavenging habit. This form is known from a rather small area on the slope of Mount Mazama in Crater Lake National Park, Oregon, but may occur in other parts of the Cascades at high elevations.

California Newt, *Taricha torosa* (Figure 4)

The eye is somewhat larger than in the Rough-skinned Newt but also has silvery patches on the iris. The back is light-brown to reddish, lightening gradually to the light color of the belly. The light color on the upper jaw extends onto the lower eyelids. There are two races.

Coast Range Newt, *Taricha t. torosa*

This salamander is yellowish-brown to dark-brown above, light-yellow to orange below. The upper eyelids and snout are not usually light-colored. The tail fins of the breeding male are well developed. It lives in the coastal ranges in the relatively still water of streams and pools that are not necessarily permanent. During the summer drought when its ponds dry up, it comes out on land and stays in damp spots under logs, stones, and in rodent burrows, but must return to the water after the spring rains in order to breed. It is often active by day, especially in cloudy weather. It is found from Mendocino County southward to San Diego in California.

Sierra Newt, *Taricha t. sierrae*

This newt is reddish-brown to chocolate-brown above, usually burnt-orange below. The tail fins of the breeding male are less well developed. When disturbed, it arches the tail over the flattened body to reveal the bright-orange color underneath, and a poisonous milky substance for its defense may be secreted from its tail glands. It frequents the foothills and western slope of the Sierra Nevada up to an altitude of 7,000 feet.

MUDPUPPIES AND THEIR ALLIES, FAMILY PROTEIDAE

This is another small family of strictly aquatic salamanders, with only two genera, one in Europe and one in the United States. They never metamorphose, but as adults they retain three pairs of bushy red gills and two pairs of open gill slits and fail to develop eyelids. Both front and hind limbs are present, and there are four toes on each foot. Sirens have only front legs; Amphiumas have less than four toes; and Hellbenders lose the gills as adults and have a wrinkled fold of skin along the side. Other aquatic or neotenic salamanders have five toes.

Mudpuppies and Waterdogs, Genus *Necturus*

The popular but misguided belief that these aquatic salamanders bark like a dog gives rise to their common name. Their voice at best is only a small squeak, inaudible to human ears more than a short distance away. They have plumy, dark-red gills on each side of the neck that are retained as respiratory organs throughout their lives. The hind feet have four toes, instead of five, as in most other salamanders. Their colors are rather dull, to harmonize with the river bottom on which they live, but the particular arrangement of spots is a diagnostic feature used in telling the different forms apart. Adult maximum size is useful in identifying them, since the smallest is not known to exceed 7¼ inches, while the largest is over 19 inches in length. Except in one case, the species occupy different ranges so the locality at which they are taken should be considered.

Mudpuppy, *Necturus maculosus* (Plate 2c)

Mudpuppies are large and rather flat-bodied, with relatively few large, rounded, rather diffuse black spots on a ground color of yellowish or reddish-brown to dark-brown, dark-gray or almost black. The belly is usually pale and may be marked with dark spots. There is a dark stripe through the eye. Mudpuppies tend to be larger and darker in the northern part of their range, smaller and more lightly colored in the South, and the extremes are sometimes considered separate races. The size of the Mudpuppy's gills indicates the temperature and oxygen content of its surroundings, for where the water is warm and stagnant, the gills are large and are kept in motion, while they are small and contracted in clear, cool water.

Mating takes place in autumn, and sometimes a pair will stay in the same spot at the bottom of the pond afterward. The male deposits spermatophores consisting of a jellylike base, on top of which the sperm lie in a whitish mass. The female retains these until the following spring, when she attaches her eggs singly on the lower surface of a submerged stone or log and remains with them during their incubation and sometimes longer. The eggs when first laid are light-yellow, and each is about ¼ inch in diameter. They hatch in thirty-eight to sixty-three days, the quicker time in water of milder temperature. The larvae are nearly 1 inch long when hatched, with well-developed front limbs and fingers. The hind limbs are short and directed backward, with little indication of toes at this time. The color of the larva is very different from that of the adult, as it has a broad, dark middorsal stripe from the snout extending onto the tail, bordered on each side by a narrower yellow stripe from the gills onto the basal third of the tail. These stripes may be retained by the adult, especially in the southern part of the range. The side of the body is dark, becoming lighter below and fading into the yellow tone of the belly. When the young are about 8 inches long and five years of age, they become sexually mature. The maximum adult size is about 19 inches. This species is found from western New Hampshire to eastern North

Dakota and from Canada south to extreme northern Georgia and northwestern Texas. Populations, probably introduced, have been reported from Maine and Rhode Island. South of New York it is not found in the Atlantic drainage, and in the southeastern states it occurs north of the range of the Waterdog.

Waterdog, *Necturus beyeri*

Waterdogs are smaller and more profusely spotted than Mudpuppies and the spots are more distinct. The ground color is brown. The spots may be scattered irregularly or more or less arranged in rows. The maximum size is $10\frac{7}{8}$ inches. Waterdogs are apparently more active in winter than in summer and are sometimes taken by fishermen on baited hooks. There are three races.

Gulf Coast Waterdog, *Necturus b. beyeri*

Adults appear squat and heavily built, with short tails and blunt heads. The back has a light-tan network over the dark-brown dorsal tone, breaking this ground color into spots in irregular rows or at random, while the belly is also spotted in the adult. The belly spots are smaller than those on the back. This race is found in shallow streams from eastern Texas to the Pearl River drainage in southeastern Louisiana and southwestern Mississippi, where it intergrades with the Alabama Waterdog.

Alabama Waterdog, *Necturus b. alabamensis*

This form is quite similar to the Gulf Coast Waterdog, but is more slender and has fewer and usually smaller and more diffuse spots and an immaculate white belly. It occurs in streams where there is debris on the bottom under which it can hide. It is found from western Georgia and the panhandle of Florida to the Pearl River drainage in Louisiana and Mississippi.

Neuse River Waterdog, *Necturus b. lewisi*

This is one of the most heavily spotted members of the genus. It is very similar to the Gulf Coast Waterdog, but the spots on the belly are about the same size as those on the back. It seems to prefer larger rivers with deeper water, and thus it is more difficult to collect than those living in shallow streams. It has sometimes been taken on fishing lines. It is found in the Neuse and Tar river systems of North Carolina.

Dwarf Waterdog, *Necturus punctatus*

This $7\frac{1}{4}$-inch salamander is soberly colored, its back being dark-brown, purplish, or black, with a few lighter spots. Its belly is bluish-white. It stays in sandy streams among the debris on the bottom. Females taken during the winter and early spring were heavy with eggs; hence they probably nest and lay their eggs in spring. It is found on the coastal plain from Virginia to central Georgia.

LUNGLESS SALAMANDERS, FAMILY PLETHODONTIDAE

This is the largest family of salamanders and is the one to which most of our common salamanders belong. They are small to medium in size, with two pairs of limbs. Adults usually lack gills, but they do not have lungs; they take in oxygen through their moist skins and the lining of the mouth and throat. A small nasolabial groove runs from the nostril to the lip on each side. (This is not easy to see without a lens.) Many are terrestrial, and some even lay their eggs on land and do not have an aquatic larval stage. Others are terrestrial as adults but return to water to breed. Still others are aquatic; most of these lose the gills as adults, but a few retain them. Several are blind, white, cave-dwelling forms. This family is widespread in the New World, ranging from Canada to northern South America, but only two species are found in Europe.

Climbing Salamanders, Genus *Aneides*

These are smooth-skinned salamanders with well-developed eyes and well-developed limbs. There are five toes on the hind feet, and the toes are unwebbed. There is no constriction at the base of the tail. The tongue is attached in front, free at the sides and behind. The posterior part of the upper jaw is sharp-edged but lacks teeth. One species of this genus is found in the Appalachians, the other four occur in the western United States. The green color of the eastern form separates it from all other salamanders in its area; one or two of the western forms also show a greenish tone occasionally. They do not have a stripe down the back, as many of the Woodland Salamanders do.

Green Salamander, *Aneides aeneus*

The spreading toes and flattened body allow this salamander to climb over the face of a cliff and hide in damp crevices, although it is found also on the ground under logs or stones and may even climb trees at times. The green, lichenlike markings on the dark ground color make it hard to see in such surroundings. As many as nineteen eggs are laid at one time, adhering to one another by their sticky outer envelopes, the whole cluster attached to the nesting surface with several short strands of mucus. Apparently the young ones remain in the guardianship of the female for some time after they hatch. Adults may reach 5½ inches in length. This species is found in the Appalachians, from extreme southwestern Pennsylvania and southern Ohio to northern Alabama.

Black Salamander, *Aneides flavipunctatus*

These salamanders are solid black to dull-greenish above, with or without light spots, and the belly is black with scattered gray dots. There are 3 to 5 intercostal folds between the toes of the adpressed limbs. Adults reach 6 inches in length. There are two races.

Speckled Black Salamander, *Aneides f. flavipunctatus*

The back is black or suffused with pale-greenish, with or without light spots. The lips of the cloaca are white or nearly so. There are usually 12 or occasionally 13 costal grooves. The head is relatively narrower and the tail less compressed than in the Santa Cruz Black Salamander. This creature is found in forested areas in rockslides where seepage occurs, and in similar damp locations, though seldom actually in water. The tail is prehensile, and the salamander has a curious habit when disturbed of jumping forward for several inches by striking the tail forcibly against the ground while using the hind legs for the leap. Spiders and beetles seem to constitute its food. The eggs, about twenty-five in number, are attached by individual short stalks to a common base, in turn attached to a stone or other solid protecting substance, sometimes underground. This race is found in the coastal mountains of California from north of San Francisco Bay to Humboldt County.

Santa Cruz Black Salamander, *Aneides f. niger*

The back is shiny black, sometimes with minute white markings, and the lips of the cloaca are black. There are usually 13, occasionally 14 costal grooves. The head is relatively broader and the tail more compressed than in the Speckled Black Salamander. This race is found in Santa Clara, Santa Cruz, and San Mateo counties, California.

Sacramento Mountain Salamander, *Aneides hardyi*

The back is brown in this species, with or without lighter mottlings, and the belly is a light purplish-brown. There are 3 to 5 intercostal folds between the adpressed limbs. This is the smallest of the Climbing Salamanders—adults may reach $3\frac{3}{16}$ inches. This salamander frequents the tops of the Sacramento, Capitan, and White Mountains of southern New Mexico. It is found in the coniferous forests from 8,000 to 9,600 feet. The clouds, fog, and occasional rainfall provide moisture which it needs in its hiding place under logs and in fissured rock. Not much concerning its reproduction has come to light, although a cluster of three developing eggs was found inside a hollow fir log in August. It was suspended from the top of the cavity, and an adult female, which may have been guarding the eggs, was nearby.

Arboreal Salamander, *Aneides lugubris*

The toes are relatively long in this Climbing Salamander. When the limbs are pressed along the sides, the digits overlap or are separated by only one intercostal fold. The back is dark brown, usually with definite light spots. There are typically 15 costal grooves, sometimes 14 or 16. The head is broader behind the eyes and the limbs and feet heavier than in the Clouded Salamander. As its popular name suggests, this salamander is a climber of trees, having been found at least 60 feet above the ground in a deserted tree mouse's nest. As many as thirty-five have been collected in a single cavity of a coast live oak during the summer. It also stays under rocks and logs on the ground where it is damp. Mine shafts, cellars and rodent burrows are other favorite hiding places. It is nocturnal and insects and isopods form a large part of its food. Its wide, sharp teeth also enable it to bite off fungus which grows on the inside of tree cavities. Eggs are found in summer in clusters of twelve to eighteen, underground, or attached to material on the ground or in tree holes. The adult female and possibly the male also protect the eggs until they hatch three or four months later. Adults may reach $7\frac{1}{2}$ inches. This species is found in the coastal ranges of California from Humboldt County south to Lower California, on islands off the coast, and in the foothills of the central Sierra Nevada.

Clouded Salamander, *Aneides ferreus*

This is another long-legged species in which the tips of the digits overlap or are separated by no more than $1\frac{1}{2}$ intercostal folds when the limbs are adpressed. The back is marked with large, irregular grayish blotches composed of minute light flecks. There are 16 or 17 costal grooves. The limbs and feet are more slender and the head not so broad as in the Arboreal Salamander. The Clouded Salamander may stay in rotting logs in open clearings, but is an agile climber and perhaps the most arboreal of all the Climbing Salamanders. It feeds on small arthropods with similar habits of hiding. The eggs are usually deposited in late summer or fall, numbering nine to seventeen, often with a milky strand from each egg twisted around those from the other eggs, and finally attached inside a cavity in an old log. This species is found from the Columbia River in Oregon to Mendocino County, California, in the coastal ranges, and on the lower western slopes of the Cascade Mountains in Oregon.

Slender Salamanders, Genus *Batrachoseps*

Like the Ensatinas, salamanders of the genus *Batrachoseps* are found only in the Pacific states, although they do not range north of Oregon. Their elongated, more or less wormlike bodies, long tails, and short limbs with four toes on each foot make them recognizable at once. This variable group is in need of further systematic study. At present, three species are recognized.

California Slender Salamander, *Batrachoseps attenuatus* (Figure 5)

The tiny limbs are scarcely longer than the width of the body in this diminutive salamander. The belly is dark, finely speckled with light. Adults usually have a broad dorsal stripe of some shade of red, brown, or yellow. There are 18 to 21 costal grooves. Adults seldom exceed 5 inches in length.

Fig. 5. California Slender Salamander, *Batrachoseps attenuatus*

Fig. 6. Monterey Salamander, *Ensatina e. eschscholtzi*

Northern Slender Salamander, *Batrachoseps a. attenuatus*

The dorsal stripe is light and often well defined and the sides are less distinctly light-dotted than in the southern race. The leg extends over 3 to 3½ costal folds when adpressed. These creatures are terrestrial, being found in valleys and meadows in both damp and dry soil. When not in motion, they coil up as most snakes do, with the head toward the center and lying on the upper loop of the body. In moving slowly, they can crawl by using their small legs, but when in danger, they move quickly by undulating or lashing the body. Their weak limbs are not useful to burrow into hard soil, but they can slip easily into any convenient hole or crevice for moisture or food. Like most terrestrial salamanders, they eat earthworms, slugs, and small arthropods such as sowbugs, millipedes and insects. Breeding occurs in June and July. Eggs may be laid underground or among dead leaves in late fall and winter, with four to twenty-one eggs in a cluster, and the time of hatching is usually in the spring. This race is found along the Pacific coast from southwestern Oregon to Los Angeles County, along the western slopes of the Sierra Nevada, and on Santa Cruz Island, California.

Southern Slender Salamander, *Batrachoseps a. leucopus*

The dorsal stripe is often dark and the sides are distinctly light-dotted in this race. The leg extends over 4 costal folds when adpressed. This race probably prefers dryer situations, as it is found from San Diego and Imperial counties, California, south into Lower California.

Oregon Slender Salamander, *Batrachoseps wrighti*

This species has larger legs which are considerably longer than the width of the body. There are 6 to 7 costal interspaces between the tips of the digits when the limbs are adpressed. The belly pattern consists of a fine black network with blotches of white. Adults may reach 3¾ inches. Essentially a woodland species, these small salamanders may be found under pieces of bark near springs or in seepage areas. They also coil the body and hold the head much like a snake when at rest. Eggs are laid in a rosarylike string in the late spring. The females do not appear to brood them, but probably remain near until hatching, which occurs in October. This species is found in a limited region in north central Oregon.

Pacific Slender Salamander, *Batrachoseps pacificus*

Though still small, these salamanders are somewhat stouter in build than the other two Slender Salamanders. There are usually 18 to 21 (and occasionally 17 or 22) costal grooves. The dorsal stripe of the adult is often faint or lacking, and the belly is light with small black flecks. Adults may reach 7 inches in length.

Channel Islands Slender Salamander, *Batrachoseps p. pacificus*

The eyes are larger in this race and the limbs relatively longer. The leg covers $5\frac{1}{2}$ to $6\frac{1}{2}$ intercostal folds when adpressed and there are 9 to 11 intercostal folds between the tips of the toes when both limbs are adpressed. There are 17 to 20 grooves. The dorsal stripe is obscure or absent. These salamanders hide under leaf litter and rocks, where they may congregate in considerable numbers. This form is found on islands opposite Santa Barbara and Ventura counties in southern California.

Garden Slender Salamander, *Batrachoseps p. major*

In this race the eyes are smaller and the limbs relatively shorter, the leg covering 4 to $4\frac{1}{2}$ intercostal folds when adpressed. There are usually 19 costal grooves. The white speckling on the belly is often dense, and the vent is usually not margined with black. This is the only mainland representative of the *pacificus* group, occurring in alluvial soil along the coastal plain of southern California, and along certain river drainages where coast live oaks are plentiful. They estivate during the hot summer months. Eggs apparently are laid in winter, clusters numbering between fifteen and twenty.

Catalina Island Slender Salamander, *Batrachoseps p. catalinae*

This race resembles the Garden Slender Salamander, but there are usually 20 to 22 costal grooves. The belly has a black network laterally, and the white speckling in the center is weak. The vent is usually black-margined. This form is said to be fairly common during the rainy season under surface litter, and it is often found in considerable numbers in excavations for ditches and cellars. When the dry season comes, it goes into the deepest burrow it can find. It is found on Santa Catalina Island.

Dusky Salamanders, Genus *Desmognathus*

These are short-bodied, rather stoutly built salamanders with the hind legs longer and stouter than the front legs and with five digits on the hind feet. The tongue is attached in front, free at the sides and behind. The openings of the internal nares are conspicuous. These variable creatures are abundant over their range but are often puzzling even to professional herpetologists because of their changing patterns at different ages. In adults there is usually a pale diagonal bar from the eye to the angle of the jaw. In this respect they differ from the Shovel-nosed Salamander and Hubricht's Salamander, which lack this light bar. These two genera, as well as the Dusky Salamander, have the lower jaw immovable, opening the mouth by lifting the upper jaw and head. All other Lungless Salamanders have the conventional lower jaw movement to open the mouth.

Dusky Salamander, *Desmognathus fuscus*

The tail is triangular in cross section and keeled above. The toes of the adpressed limbs are separated by 2 to 4 intercostal folds. The dorsal pattern is very variable and changes with age. Young have two rows of large, light spots on the back and sometimes two rows of small, pale, rather indistinct spots on the sides. The spots are more or less obscured by the spread of dark pigment in older individuals. On the tail the large spots fuse with a median stripe to form a broad, zigzag light line. The belly may be light, more or less spotted, or marbled with dark, or dark with light spots. In large, old adults it may be almost uniformly dark. Adults of the larger, heavily built Black-bellied Salamander have a uniformly black belly and usually two rows of light dots along the side. In the Southern Dusky the tail pattern is a narrow line. The pattern is faint in the Central Dusky, and the belly is lightly but uniformly pigmented. Seal Salamanders also have the belly pale and usually uniformly pigmented. Other members of the genus have the tail rounded in cross section. Three races of the Dusky Salamander are here recognized.

Northern Dusky Salamander, *Desmognathus f. fuscus*

Several individuals of all ages may be found under wet leaves or woodland debris in seepage from springs and brooks. Very young ones around 2 inches in length often are brilliantly colored with orange or reddish paired spots along the back on a tan background. The spots are bordered laterally by a dark, wavy line. Later the spots tend to fuse into a light dorsal stripe, and with age the back darkens to a dark-brown which sometimes obscures the median stripe. The belly is usually mottled with gray or brown. Breeding takes place in spring, and eggs are deposited in small clusters from June to August under stones or logs near water, where the female stays curled around them until they hatch. Adults may reach 5¼ inches in length. This race ranges from Maine, south at least through central Georgia and west through Ohio. The ranges of this and the Spotted Dusky in the central Gulf states have not been worked out.

Black Mountain Dusky Salamander, *Desmognathus f. welteri*

Except for its larger size and darker, blotched belly, the Black Mountain Dusky is much like the Northern Dusky. Adults may reach 6½ inches. Its range is restricted to eastern Kentucky and adjacent parts of Virginia.

Spotted Dusky Salamander, *Desmognathus f. conanti*

The Spotted Dusky is attractively colored with golden or reddish-gold dorsal spots beside the midline, which are sometimes separate but often fused into serrated crossbands. This juvenile pattern is retained except in darkened old males. The bar behind the eye is yellow or orange. Adults lose their vomerine teeth, as do others of the *fuscus* group, but have enlarged and recurved premaxillary teeth. The belly is heavily mottled. It is a small race—adults may reach 4¾ inches in length. This lowland race is found from southern Indiana south through western Kentucky and probably through Mississippi.

Southern Dusky Salamander, *Desmognathus auriculatus*

The tail is keeled above, triangular in cross section. Young have a wide, pale, dark-bordered, middorsal stripe with irregular borders and several rows of whitish or reddish spots along the sides. Traces of spots can usually be seen even in large, dark adults. Variation in color and pattern is great, and the belly may be either dark or light. There is a narrow, light median line on the tail. The toes of the adpressed limbs are separated by 3½ to 5½ intercostal spaces. These salamanders can often be found in cypress ponds and stagnant pools, as well as in spring runs. They occur along the coastal plain from southern Virginia, south through central Florida and west into eastern Texas.

Central Dusky Salamander, *Desmognathus brimleyorum*

This is another of the group that have triangular, keeled tails. While this brown or grayish species usually has a row of small, light dots along each side of the back, its pattern is not conspicuous. The belly is uniformly and lightly pigmented. The female lays up to thirty-six eggs in strings in decaying wood and remains with them until they hatch. During dry weather she is said to take them into a hole where more dampness is found, bringing them back to the surface at the next rain. Adults may reach a maximum of 7 inches, though most do not exceed 5½. This race occurs in northeastern Texas, Arkansas, and southeastern Oklahoma.

Mountain Salamander, *Desmognathus ochrophaeus*
(Plate 2d)

The tail is oval or nearly round in cross section and is not keeled above. There is a broad, light, dark-bordered stripe down the back. The Pigmy Salamander, Cherokee Salamander, and Alabama Salamander, which also have rounded tails, are only about half the size of the Mountain Salamander. There are two races.

Allegheny Mountain Salamander, *Desmognathus o. ochrophaeus*

The median dorsal stripe is light-tan, gray, or reddish, with straight edges. (It is obscure in old individuals.) The belly is lightly pigmented and scarcely mottled. There is a small, light bar from the eye to the angle of the jaw. Adults may reach 4 inches. This salamander is quite terrestrial, as it is often found under logs or in moss at some distance from the nearest stream, although it is also collected with the Northern Dusky Salamander along the banks of streams. Mating takes place in late summer and autumn and probably also in the spring. The eggs, numbering up to fourteen, are attached by a stalklike process of the outer egg envelope to the undersides of stones or logs. This salamander is found in mountainous areas from New York to Tennessee.

Blue Ridge Mountain Salamander, *Desmognathus o. carolinensis*

The median light dorsal stripe has irregular edges. It may be yellow, red, brown, or gray. Old adults are bluish-black above. The belly is finely pigmented with black in the young, heavily reticulated with black in old ones. Adults may reach 4⅜ inches. This highly variable form resembles the preceding in breeding habits. As a rule, the Blue Ridge Mountain Salamander prefers a wetter environment, although it is not in any sense aquatic. It is found in the mountains from southern Virginia to Georgia. (See also Jordan's Salamander, *Plethodon jordani*.)

Seal Salamander, *Desmognathus monticola*

This is another salamander that has the tail triangular in cross section. The belly is light, at least anteriorly, and the back is tan, brown or gray, usually with darker markings. They are rather large for Dusky Salamanders—adults may reach 5¾ inches. There are two races.

Appalachian Seal Salamander, *Desmognathus m. monticola*

The back is marked with conspicuous light spots outlined in black or with heavy vermiculations, the sides are mottled and sometimes have a row of light dots, the belly is uniformly and lightly pigmented. These interesting animals do indeed suggest a seal by their fleshy necks and their big, projecting eyes, which reflect light like a cat's when seen by flashlight at night when they are at the entrance of their burrows. By day they hide in shady ravines and beside mountain brooks under logs, bark, and stones and sometimes in muddy rivulets. As many as thirty eggs have been reported for a single laying, the female remaining coiled around them. They are found in mountainous country from southwestern Pennsylvania to northern Georgia and Alabama.

Virginia Seal Salamander, *Desmognathus m. jeffersoni*

A lowland barrier separates this form geographically from the preceding, from which it is readily distinguished by its much lighter color. The back is tan to gray, with small, round, dark spots, or may lack a pattern. The belly is light but mottled or spotted with dark. This race lives in cold, swift-running, mountain streams, and apparently prefers small terrestrial millipedes and isopods as food, instead of the numerous kinds of aquatic insect larvae in its streams. It is found in the Blue Ridge Mountains of Virginia.

Pygmy Salamander, *Desmognathus wrighti*

This tiny salamander has the tail oval or nearly round in cross section and has a broad, reddish-brown or tan dorsal stripe, often with a dark herringbone pattern down the center. The sides are lightly pigmented, and the belly is flesh-colored. Adults reach only 2 inches in length. This high-altitude salamander frequents spruce and fir forests from the Great Smokies northward to southern Virginia at heights of 3,500 to 6,500 feet. It is entirely terrestrial, lurking under stones and logs by day.

Cherokee Salamander, *Desmognathus aeneus*

This is another minute salamander with a tail rounded in cross section. The belly may be mottled brown and white, and there is a broad, light dorsal stripe. There are two races.

Cherokee Salamander, *Desmognathus a. aeneus*

The dorsal stripe has nearly straight edges in this race. It is reddish brown with irregular dark flecks or with a narrow, dark line in the center, continuous with a Y-shaped mark on the head. The belly is mottled brown and white. Adults may reach 2 inches in total length. Living under dead leaves and debris near small streams and seepage areas, its small size and dead-leaf coloring conceal it admirably. Sexually mature females carrying thirteen eggs in the ovaries have been reported. It is found in extreme southwestern North Carolina and northern Georgia.

Alabama Salamander, *Desmognathus a. chermocki*

The dorsal stripe is tan or yellow and has wavy edges and sometimes a faint herringbone pattern in the center. The belly is very light and rarely mottled. Adults may reach 2¼ inches. This salamander is also found near seepage areas on hillsides and in ravines. Females curled around their eggs in hollow logs or under leaves have been found in February, March, and April. The recorded number of eggs per clutch is between five and sixteen. They are attached to one another by extensions of the egg envelopes, but apparently have no stalk for the attachment of the whole cluster to the sheltering surface. This race is found in north central Alabama.

Black-bellied Salamander, *Desmognathus quadramaculatus*

The tail is triangular in cross section. The belly is uniformly black in adults, flecked with yellow in the young, and the back is black with small, irregular greenish blotches. There are usually two rows of light dots on the side. This is the largest *Desmognathus*, reaching a length of 7⅜ inches. It likes rocky mountain streams above 2,500 feet in forested ravines and is very elusive as it darts away among the stones. Unlike most of its relatives, it sometimes comes into the open by day to bask on the wet rocks. Eggs from one laying may number between twenty-five and forty and are attached singly to the lower side of a rock, either in water or just above it, very much in the manner of the Seal Salamander. Eggs with developing embryos have been found during July and August. The larvae transform when they are between 2 and 3½ inches in length. It is found from southern West Virginia, south through the mountains to northern Georgia.

Ensatina, *Ensatina eschscholtzi*

These often brightly colored salamanders have five toes on the hind feet, and the swollen tail is set off from the body by a constriction at its base. The genus is restricted to the Western coastal states, British Columbia, and northwestern Lower California. Seven forms have been recognized, all belonging to a single species. Intergrades between the various races are common. They live in damp to nearly dry surroundings, the northern forms being abundant in redwood, fir, and oak stands, the southern ones often frequenting canyons where the humidity is acceptable to them. The sexes can be told apart by the tail length—in males the tail is as long as or longer than the body, while it is shorter in females. The male also has a longer and blunter snout, while in the female it is shorter and rounded. They feed upon small invertebrates, such as earthworms, spiders, and insects that live under dead leaves, into which the salamanders can creep for the sake of moisture. When the weather is very dry, they retreat into deep holes or rock crevices, as they cannot burrow in hard ground. After the first heavy rains in the fall, adults and young emerge to feed and to replenish the water in their body tissues. In high mountains and in the north, where freezing occurs in winter, the salamanders must retreat underground to escape the frost. They breed in February and March after an elaborate courtship ritual, and eggs are laid in spring or early summer. Not many egg clusters have been found, but the female had remained with these. The time of hatching has not been ascertained, but very young ones appear with the fall and winter rains. The salamanders live in colonies, and many tend to remain in the home area indefinitely, as the same marked individuals have sometimes been recaptured over a period of three years.

Monterey Salamander, *Ensatina e. eschscholtzi* (Figure 6)

In this race the back is reddish brown above, plain or with darker blotches. The belly is white, pale-orange, or yellowish and lacks black dots. The dark color of the sides is usually even with or above a line between the upper attachment of the limbs. The iris of the eye is dark-brown without a yellow or brassy color. The toes are whitish above. Adults reach $5\frac{5}{16}$ inches. This race is found in the coastal region of southern California.

Yellow-blotched Salamander, *Ensatina e. croceator* (Figure 7)

This race is blackish above with light, usually yellowish blotches. The blotches are smaller and more irregular than in the Large-blotched Salamander and are usually not squarish. There is a large blotch on

Fig. 7. Yellow-blotched Salamander, *Ensatina e. croceator*

Fig. 8. Cave Salamander, *Eurycea lucifuga*

the head behind each eye, but these blotches do not join to form a U-shaped mark. The eyelids are usually without markings. Adults reach 5⅞ inches. This race occurs in the interior mountains in Kern County, California.

Large-blotched Salamander, *Ensatina e. klauberi*

This is another blotched race, the blotches large, squarish, and usually orange in color. The blotches behind the eyes frequently unite to form a U-shaped mark and are more extensive than in the Yellow-blotched race. They reach farther down on the side of the head and may join light-colored markings on the eyelids. This is the largest of the races, reaching 5⅞ inches. It is found in the interior mountains of extreme south central California.

Oregon Salamander, *Ensatina e. oregonensis*

This is one of the unblotched races, plain brown to blackish above. The dark color of the sides is usually irregular and mottled and reaches below a line connecting the upper level of the attachments of the limbs. The belly is whitish or faintly spotted with orange or yellow and marked with uniformly distributed black dots. The eyelids are dark. Adults reach 5⅛ inches. This is the most widely distributed of the races, ranging from British Columbia south through western Washington and Oregon to north of the San Francisco Bay area. Its range is interrupted along the coast of southern Oregon and northern California by that of the Painted Salamander.

Painted Salamander, *Ensatina e. picta*

This race is brown above, blotched with black and yellow or orange. The ventral surfaces are yellow or orange, uniformly sprinkled with dark dots. The iris of the eye has a yellow or bronzy patch. This is the smallest of the Ensatinas, adults reaching 4⅛ inches. It is found in a narrow strip along the coast in extreme southern Oregon and northern California.

Sierra Nevada Salamander, *Ensatina e. platensis*

This is another of the spotted races of the interior mountains. It is gray to brown above, with orange spots which are smaller, more numerous, and more irregular than are those of the Large-blotched Salamander. The tips of the digits are spotted. The blotches on the head are more irregular and do not form a U-shaped band. It reaches 4⅞ inches. This race is found in the Sierra Nevadas. It intergrades with the Yellow-eyed race in the west central foothills.

Yellow-eyed Salamander, *Ensatina e. xanthoptica*

This unblotched race has a conspicuous yellow eye patch. The belly is orange and either unmarked or with a few black dots that tend to occur in clumps. Adults reach 5⅜ inches. This race occurs in the vicinity of San Francisco Bay and on the western slopes of the Sierra Nevadas, where it intergrades with the preceding race.

Brook Salamanders, Genus *Eurycea*

These are slenderly built salamanders with moderate to long, compressed tails and with five toes on the hind feet. The hind legs are not noticeably larger than the front. The tongue is supported on a central pedicel and is free all around the edge. The Brook Salamanders are found in or near small bodies of fresh water—where their chief enemies, the fishes, are not common. Most of them are yellow or yellowish, at least on the lower surface. Known only from eastern North America, the nine species fall easily into three groups which differ somewhat in habitat. The first three species given here are usually found in or near the edges of streams beneath rocks and leaves. Their tails are proportionately shorter than those of the next group. The Long-tailed and Cave Salamanders are somewhat more terrestrial, though they are often found near streams. They are also frequently found in or near caves. The last four species are neotenic. Adults remain in the water and retain their gills. They are found in springs and streams, frequently in or near caves.

Aquatic Salamander, *Eurycea aquatica*

This is a moderate-sized, stocky Brook Salamander with 13 costal grooves and a tail usually shorter than the head and body. A light dorsal band extends to the tip of the tail. The sides are dusky-black, and the belly is plain or lightly stippled. While most of the entirely aquatic Brook Salamanders are also neotenic, this one loses its gills and transforms into a normal adult. Clear streams with gravelly beds, where the salamanders conceal themselves among the aquatic plants, are the chosen dwelling places. The females produce an unusually large number of eggs at a laying, as many as ninety-six being recorded. Adults may reach 3⅜ inches. It is definitely known only from Jefferson County, Alabama, but may also be present in northwestern Georgia, northeastern Mississippi, and southwestern Tennessee.

Two-lined Salamander, *Eurycea bislineata*

These Brook Salamanders have a light middorsal stripe bordered on each side by a distinct black stripe. There are 14 to 15 costal grooves, and the digits of the adpressed limbs are separated by 3 or more intercostal folds. They are more slender and have somewhat longer tails than the Aquatic Salamanders but are more similar to that species in build than to the very long-tailed members of the next group. There are three races.

Northern Two-lined Salamander, *Eurycea b. bislineata*

In this race the dorsolateral dark stripe is irregular, containing small, light spots and not reaching to the tip of the tail. The sides are mottled. There are 15 costal grooves. Adults may reach 4½ inches. A slender, dainty creature which hides in wet places under stones and logs, this salamander may stray into woodlands during summer rains. They breed from January to April, and the clutch of about thirty eggs is attached to a stone in running water. Several females may choose the same place for their eggs. The larvae are less than ½ inch long at hatching and transform when two or three years old and about 3 inches in length. This race ranges from Canada south through all of the eastern United States to Virginia and eastern and central Tennessee and west to southern Illinois.

Southern Two-lined Salamander, *Eurycea b. cirrigera*

The scientific name of this form comes from the well-developed cirri, which project downward from the nostrils of the adult males. These cirri are projections of the nasolabial grooves which help free the nostrils of water. The males of several other plethodontid salamanders also have cirri developed to a greater or lesser extent. In this race there are 14 costal grooves, and the dark dorsolateral stripes usually continue to the tip of the tail. The sides are mottled with brown and white or with a series of white spots above the legs; the belly is yellowish. Adults may reach 4 inches. This form is found on the Atlantic coastal plain and Piedmont in swamps and near springs, from North Carolina south to northern Florida and west to the Mississippi River. The breeding and egg laying habits are similar to those of the northern race.

Blue Ridge Two-lined Salamander, *Eurycea b. wilderae*

The dark dorsolateral stripe is heavy, with a straight upper edge, and continuous on the basal half of the tail, becoming broken into a series of spots toward the end. The sides have definite, irregular black spots. There are 15 costal grooves. This is the largest race—adults may reach 4¾ inches. It prefers elevations above 2,000 feet, and individuals have been found on the highest peaks of the southern Blue Ridge chain. They wander into the forest far from water but hide in damp situations under moss and forest debris. The young transform when about 1½ inches in length.

Many-ribbed Salamander, *Eurycea multiplicata*

These little salamanders lack the well-developed dark longitudinal stripes of the Two-lined; they have 19 to 20 costal grooves, rather than 13, as the Aquatic has; and their tails are shorter than those of the Long-tailed and Cave Salamanders. There are two races.

Many-ribbed Salamander, *Eurycea m. multiplicata*

Primarily aquatic, this creature sometimes is found on land under stones and debris, both inside and outside caves. The brilliant yellow lower surface and yellowish back, plus the high number of costal grooves, distinguish it from other Brook Salamanders. Adults may reach 3½ inches in total length. It is found from north central Arkansas to southeastern Oklahoma.

Gray-bellied Salamander, *Eurycea m. griseogaster*

The back is gray or brown with a broad middorsal light stripe, edged by a poorly defined black line on either side or with the upper part of the sides darker than the back. The belly is a uniform yellowish-gray. This is a slightly smaller race, adults not exceeding 3¼ inches. Like its close relative, the Many-ribbed, the Gray-bellied Salamander has a high number of costal grooves. Its gray color is unusual in the genus, where most of the forms are yellow. This one lives in quiet pools under stones. The larvae are more uniformly colored than the adults, and some reach a length of 2¾ inches before transformation. This race occurs in southwestern Missouri, northwestern Arkansas, and northeastern Oklahoma.

Long-tailed Salamander, *Eurycea longicauda*

These slender salamanders have the tail decidedly longer than the head and body. There are 14 costal grooves, and the digits of the adpressed limbs are never separated by more than 2 intercostal folds, and they often meet or overlap. There is a definite broad dorsal light stripe. Adults may reach 7⅛ inches. Three races have been described.

Long-tailed Salamander, *Eurycea l. longicauda* (Plate 2e)

The light dorsal stripe encloses small, irregular black spots and has elongated dots on either side. The sides are marked with separate black spots, and the sides of the tail with black vertical or crescentic bars. The belly is yellow and unspotted. The vertical black bars on the tail make it rather easy to recognize. It is mostly terrestrial, found under the usual litter and also under rocks near streams and often in caves. Larvae metamorphose when about 2½ inches in length. The young one has a relatively shorter tail than the adult. This race ranges from southern New York to northwestern Georgia and west to northeastern Arkansas and southeastern Missouri.

Three-lined Salamander, *Eurycea l. guttolineata*

In this race a narrow black middorsal line is present in the tan or yellow dorsal stripe. The upper parts of the sides are black, the belly mottled with gray and dull-yellow, and the tail is yellow with vertical black bars separated by narrow interspaces. This form may travel some distance from water but usually stays in wet places below springs, along streams, and in swamps. The larvae transform when nearly 2 inches in length. The race is found from Virginia, south to the panhandle of Florida, and west to the Mississippi River.

Dark-sided Salamander, *Eurycea l. melanopleura*

The back and tail have a median tan or yellow stripe marked with many small, dark spots; the sides below are dark-brown with scattered light spots; and the belly is spotted and mottled. This form frequents the dimly lit mouths of caves but may also be found outside along streams, usually on land, but sometimes in the water. It is found in the highlands of Arkansas, Missouri, and eastern Oklahoma.

Cave Salamander, *Eurycea lucifuga* (Figure 8)

This is another slender, long-tailed form. There is no definite broad dorsal stripe. The ground color of the back and sides is yellow to reddish-orange, marked with many small black spots, which occasionally form a dorsolateral linear series. The belly is light-yellow. Adults may reach 7⅛ inches. This terrestrial salamander also frequents the entrances of caves, climbing on the walls and ledges in search of small invertebrate food but is sometimes found in damp locations outside caves. Their prehensile tails help them in their climbing activities. They occur in limestone regions from Virginia to eastern Oklahoma and from southern Indiana south to northern Alabama and Georgia.

San Marcos Salamander, *Eurycea nana*

This tiny creature is the smallest of the Brook Salamanders, as it measures only 2 inches when full grown. It is a neotenic form with gills, brown above, with a row of dorsolateral yellowish dots, and white or yellowish on the belly. The eyes are normal. It lives among water plants in a large, shallow spring at the head of the San Marcos River in central Texas. Like the other neotenic salamanders, much more information is needed on its breeding habits.

Texas Salamander, *Eurycea neotenes*

As with the other neotenic species, adults retain the gills. These salamanders are yellowish above, with a mottled pattern but without distinct dorsolateral dark stripes. The belly is whitish, and the eyes are usually normally developed. Adults may reach 4⅛ inches. The three races that have been described are differentiated solely on internal characters, so that live, intact specimens can be identified only by locality. The habits of all three are probably identical.

Bexar County Salamander, *Eurycea n. neotenes*

This race has been reported from Edwards and Uvalde counties to the vicinity of Austin, Texas. It lives among dead leaves in shallow pools and springs inside and outside caves along the Balcones Escarpment.

Fern Bank Salamander, *Eurycea n. pterophila*

Known only from Fern Bank Spring, near Wimberly, Hays County, Texas.

Cascade Cavern Salamander, *Eurycea n. latitans*

Known from Cascade Cavern, Kendall County, and Turtle Creek, Kerr County, Texas.

Valdiva Farms Salamander, *Eurycea troglodytes*

This is another neotenic form with gills. As a cave dweller, it is light-gray with white dots above and indistinct yellowish stripes along the sides of the body and upper surface of the tail. The eyes are degenerate, since they are never needed. In appearance, its long slender limbs and flattened snout suggest the Texas Blind Salamander, but the latter is white and has only 11 costal grooves, while this species has 13. It is known only from northwestern Medina County, Texas.

Oklahoma Salamander, *Eurycea tynerensis*

This neotenic form prefers cold, shallow streams with gravelly beds, among stones or around the roots of water plants. It has a dark-gray-dotted back, and the belly is pale and translucent, allowing eggs and viscera to be seen through the body wall. The limbs are small and slender, as in most permanently aquatic salamanders. It differs from all the other neotenic Brook Salamanders in having a greater number of costal grooves—19 or 20. The external gills are short and dark. Adults may reach $3\frac{1}{8}$ inches. It is found in northeastern Oklahoma, extreme southwestern Missouri, and northwestern Arkansas.

Spring Salamanders, Genus *Gyrinophilus*

These attractive, stoutly built, orange or reddish, and usually black-spotted salamanders may be confused with the genus *Pseudotriton* —the Red and Mud salamanders—which they resemble in size, proportions, and color. The Spring Salamanders usually have a light bar running from the eye to the nostril, dark-bordered below and sometimes above. Red and Mud salamanders do not have such a stripe. Both are found in the Eastern states. There are two species of Spring Salamanders, one a neotenic, cave-dwelling form. As the common name indicates, they are often found in or near springs or other clear, cool waters.

Spring Salamander, *Gyrinophilus porphyriticus*
(Figure 9)

Adults metamorphose and have well-developed eyes and eyelids. The larvae differ from the neotenic Tennessee Cave Salamanders in having larger eyes and narrower, less flattened heads. There are four races.

Northern Spring Salamander, *Gyrinophilus p. porphyriticus*

The back is tan, reddish, or light-salmon, strongly mottled with darker, sometimes with chevron-shaped marks or dark reticulations;

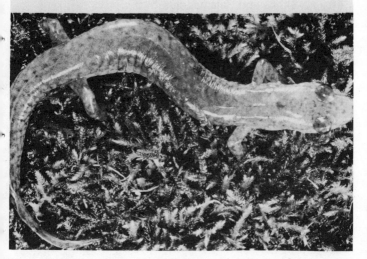

Fig. 9. Spring Salamander, *Gyrinophilus porphyriticus*

Fig. 10. Georgia Blind Salamander, *Haideotriton wallacei*

the belly is flesh-colored, with small, scattered black dots. The maximum size is 8⅝ inches. This form and its allies used to be called Purple Salamanders in reference to their color after preservation, but in life they are mottled salmon, brownish-pink, or reddish. They live by day in springs and cold mountain streams and in nearby forests under logs or wet debris, wandering around in search of food at night. Mating occurs in autumn, but egg laying may take place from spring through late autumn. The clutch varies between 44 and 132, the eggs being attached singly by an enlargement of the outer envelope to the lower side of a stone or other immersed object. Recently hatched larvae are about 1 inch in length. Probably they remain in the larval stage for three years, maturing when they are some 5½ inches in length. This race is found from southern Maine to eastern Ohio and central Virginia. South of Pennsylvania it is confined to the Appalachian region, where it apparently intergrades broadly with both the Kentucky Spring Salamander and the Carolina Spring Salamander as far south as northern Georgia, Alabama, and northeastern Mississippi.

Kentucky Spring Salamander, *Gyrinophilus p. duryi*

The reddish back and sides are marked with conspicuous dark dots, those on the back usually arranged in dorsolateral rows but occasionally scattered over the entire dorsal surface. The spots are small, few, and widely separated. The throat is unspotted, but there are a few small dark dots on the lower jaw. This smaller form (to 6½ inches) is much in need of study as to its life history and larval development. It is found in southern Ohio, eastern Kentucky, and extreme southwestern Virginia and West Virginia, intergrading to the north, east, and south with the Northern Spring Salamander.

Blue Ridge Spring Salamander, *Gyrinophilus p. danielsi*

The reddish back is marked with numerous large, dark spots which often unite to form elongated blotches. The chin has many small, dark dots, but the belly is almost unmarked. The maximum size is about 8 inches. This race is found in the mountains of western North Carolina and eastern Tennessee.

Carolina Spring Salamander, *Gyrinophilus p. dunni*

In this race the dorsal spots are small and usually separate, though they sometimes join to form indistinct chevrons. The belly is usually plain but sometimes shows a few dark dots. The edge of the lower jaw is often spotted, but the throat is never heavily marked. This race does not exceed 6¾ inches. It prefers a lower elevation and is seldom found above 3,500 feet. Its breeding habits have not yet been recorded. It is found from southern North Carolina and extreme southeastern Tennessee, south into western South Carolina and northern Georgia, intergrading with the northern race in a broad band from North Carolina to northern Alabama.

Tennessee Cave Salamander, *Gyrinophilus palleucus*

Although the last to be discovered, this species is already well known because of our interest in its cave-dwelling habits. It has small, lidless black eyes, a broad, flattened head, and rich red gills. Apparently it does not metamorphose in nature, but laboratory specimens can be induced to metamorphose by treating them with hormones. They lose the gills, develop eyelids, and become mottled in appearance. Three races have been described.

Sinking Cove Cave Salamander, *Gyrinophilus p. palleucus*

This race is a pale flesh color, without pigment. Adults reach 6⅗ inches. It is found in caves in southeastern Tennessee.

Big Mouth Cave Salamander, *Gyrinophilus p. necturoides*

This race is pigmented. The dorsal ground color varies from a reddish brown to a deep purplish brown and in larger specimens is marked with large blackish spots. Two rows of small white dots extend along the side. The belly is gray. Adults reach 7⅖ inches. This race is known only from Big Mouth Cave in southeastern Tennessee, but what appear to be intergrades between it and the preceding race have been taken in Blowing Cave in northeastern Alabama.

Berry Cave Salamander, *Gyrinophilus p. gulolineatus*

This race is also pigmented and has a distinctive dark stripe on the anterior half of the throat. It is known from Grundy and McMinn counties, Tennessee.

Georgia Blind Salamander, *Haideotriton wallacei*
(Figure 10)

The only subterranean blind salamander from east of the Mississippi was first taken from a 200-foot-deep well near Albany, Georgia. It has since been found in underground waters of caves in southern Georgia and northern Florida. It has no external eyes, though small, dark eyespots may be present in young individuals. The external gills, present throughout life, are long and deep-red in color. The rest of the body is light-pinkish, almost iridescent. The head is elongated and flattened. When moving around in a tank, its slender legs assist locomotion, but when stimulated by an unusual vibration, it swims very rapidly around the aquarium trailing its legs, propelled by undulations of its body and tail alone. Out of the water it seems completely helpless and unable to walk. The largest known specimen was 3 inches long, but most do not exceed 2 inches.

Four-toed Salamander, *Hemidactylium scutatum*

While no salamander is "easy" to identify, the Four-toed Salamander has three characteristics which, in combination, set it off from all others: The hind foot has four toes, instead of the usual five; the white belly has many small black spots; and the tail is constricted at the base. When pursued, the caudal constriction is the place at which a voluntary and practically bloodless shedding of the tail can take place, just as it does in some lizards. The tail muscles continue to twitch, attracting the pursuer, while the tailless salamander inconspicuously makes his escape, in time growing another appendage. Its dorsal color, like that of a reddish-brown leaf, its small size, and its slow mode of progression, with frequent stops, render it very difficult to see on the forest floor. Mating occurs in late summer and early autumn by means of spermatophores picked up by the female's cloaca and retained during the winter hibernation. In spring a regular migration by the females to the breeding place near water takes place. About thirty eggs are produced by a single female, who lies on her back at the time, laying each egg by itself and attaching it by its sticky coating to sphagnum moss or grass roots. Several females may lay at the same place, and often a few remain to guard the eggs until they hatch after an incubation period of thirty-eight to sixty days. At hatching the tiny larvae measure only $\frac{1}{2}$ inch in length and are attractively colored in orange, yellow, and green, with dark marks. After six weeks, they transform at a length of $\frac{3}{4}$ to 1 inch. They are mature sexually in $2\frac{1}{2}$ years. Adults do not exceed $3\frac{1}{2}$ inches in total length. It is found in sphagnum swamps and adjoining wooded areas from Maine, south to central Alabama and west to Wisconsin. Scattered colonies are reported from Georgia, Florida, Louisiana, Arkansas, and Missouri.

Web-toed Salamanders, Genus *Hydromantes*

These salamanders have five toes on the hind feet, and the toes are joined by webbing. The tongue is attached by a central stalk and is free around the edge. This is the only genus of salamanders found in both the New World and the Old World. We have three species in California, while several others occur in southern Europe. They are all quite similar, with comparatively short tails and rather subdued colors. They do not much exceed 4 inches in length.

Mount Lyell Salamander, *Hydromantes platycephalus* (Figure 11)

This species is flattened, with a short tail and short legs. There are $\frac{1}{2}$ to $1\frac{1}{2}$ intercostal folds between the toes when the limbs are adpressed. The back is mottled, matching the granite rocks among which it lives. The belly is dusky, flecked with white. Frequenting the higher elevations of the Sierra Nevadas from Sequoia National Park to Sonora Pass, usually from 5,000 to over 10,000 feet, this salamander is nearly independent of the covering of dead leaves and other vegetation sought by most others. It gets the required moisture under rocks at the edge of water coming from melting snow—seldom actually going into the water, but staying on wet rock or earth. It is nocturnal as a rule and

Fig. 11. Mount Lyell Salamander, *Hydromantes platycephalus*

Fig. 12. Limestone Salamander, *Hydromantes brunus*

feeds upon small terrestrial creatures, such as centipedes, spiders, termites, beetles, and flies. Since snow forces it to remain underground more than half the year, most of the egg development probably takes place there. From six to fourteen ova have been found in adult females. The webbed feet make it possible for the salamander to climb over rocks, as the foot becomes almost a suction cup in walking. The short, blunt tail is used almost as a walking stick, as it is curled on the ground so the tip points forward when the animal goes downhill, thus serving as a brake. When the animal goes uphill, the tail is straightened and swings from side to side as a balance.

Shasta Salamander, *Hydromantes shastae*

The body is not so flattened in this species, and the legs are longer; when the limbs are adpressed, the toes overlap by $\frac{1}{2}$ to $1\frac{1}{2}$ intercostal folds. The back is mottled and may be gray-green, tan, or reddish. The tail is usually yellowish. There are white blotches on the belly. This is typically a cave dweller but may be found under rocks in the open in wet weather. Females lay their eggs in moist caves in summer and brood them. The Shasta Salamander is found only in the region of the headwaters of the Shasta Reservoir in northern California at elevations of 1,000 to 2,500 feet.

Limestone Salamander, *Hydromantes brunus* (Figure 12)

This species has a longer tail, longer legs, and longer toes than the Mount Lyell Salamander. The tips of the toes overlap when the limbs are adpressed by $1\frac{1}{2}$ intercostal folds. Adults are uniformly brown above, pale below, with yellow on the underside of the tail. Young are pale-yellowish-green above. This form is known from the lower Merced Canyon in Mariposa County, California, at altitudes of 1,200 to 2,500 feet.

Shovel-nosed Salamander, *Leurognathus marmoratus*

There are five toes on the hind feet, and the tail is not constricted at the base, but is laterally compressed and sharp-edged above. As in the closely allied Dusky Salamanders, the Shovel-nosed have the lower jaw fixed and immovable, to serve as a shovel in burrowing under debris. The upper part of the head must be lifted in order to open the mouth. The tongue is attached in front, free at the sides and behind. The openings of the internal nares are hidden in a fold of skin at the side of the mouth. These aquatic salamanders prefer mountain brooks where they can hide under larger stones on the bottom. This is the only species in the genus and it is found only in the mountains of eastern United States from southeastern Virginia to northeastern Georgia. Five races have been described, each more or less confined to a different watershed.

Northern Shovel-nosed Salamander, *Leurognathus m. marmoratus*

The back is grayish in this race with light markings that form a broad zigzag pattern. The top of the head and limbs are not reticulated, and the snout is usually not lighter than the rest of the body. The belly usually has a large, light-colored central area. The maximum size is 5¾ inches. Although usually found in water, occasionally one comes out on the wet rocks beside a large stream. Females taken in the autumn contained twenty-six to thirty-four eggs. These are later attached in clusters by means of an extension of the outer egg envelope to the edge of a stone in the water. The larvae may grow to a length of 2⅝ inches before metamorphosing. These salamanders live at elevations of 2,000 to 4,000 feet in the area east and north of French Broad River in southwestern Virginia, western North Carolina, and northeastern Tennessee.

Golden Shovel-nosed Salamander, *Leurognathus m. auratus*

This is similar to the northern race, but the color of the back is lighter and more yellowish, and the light markings usually have bright-yellow centers. The top of the head and limbs are reticulated, and the snout tends to be darker than the rest of the body. This race is found in the headwaters of the Chattahoochee and Tallulah river systems in extreme southwestern North Carolina and northeastern Georgia.

Husky Shovel-nosed Salamander, *Leurognathus m. roboratus*

This is a large, stocky, dark race with the light markings on the back small spots. It is found in the headwaters of the Chattooga River system in extreme northeastern Georgia, western South Carolina, and southwestern North Carolina.

Southern Shovel-nosed Salamander, *Leurognathus m. intermedius*

In this race the light markings on the back are seven or more rounded spots on each side, which are opposite one another, rather than arranged in a zigzag pattern. The back is usually brown, and the belly is dark, sometimes with small, light flecks. As this salamander is more tolerant of small streams, it can live higher in the mountains where these streams have their sources than the Northern Shovel-nosed. It has been captured between 1,700 and 5,500 feet. A female taken in October had large eggs nearly ready for laying. More life history studies are needed on this and the other races. It is found in streams immediately south and west of the French Broad River in extreme southwestern North Carolina and eastern Tennessee.

Black Shovel-nosed Salamander, *Leurognathus m. melanius*

The back is without light markings (except in the very young), and the general body color is blackish. This race is found in streams of extreme western North Carolina and eastern Tennessee.

Dwarf Salamander, *Manculus quadridigitatus*

This creature has only four toes on its hind foot, instead of the usual five. The tail is compressed and slightly keeled above. Males have tubular projections, the cirri, pointing downward below the nostrils, like those in *Eurycea*. It has a bronze middorsal stripe bordered on each side by a narrower brown one extending part way along the tail. The belly is bright-yellow, the tail tip dull-yellow, and the throat and lower parts of legs flesh color. Again, variation is often apparent, as some individuals are much darker than others; some have a row of small, irregular dark spots down the middorsal stripe; and some have narrow, light longitudinal or oblique stripes on the sides. The maximum known size is just over $3\frac{1}{2}$ inches. It lives in swampy areas under logs and other debris. Eggs are laid in midwinter in shallow water, usually attached to pond debris. Larvae appear in March and transform in two or three months. Newly metamorphosed young are found sometimes at a size of $1\frac{1}{4}$ inches but often are considerably larger. This is the only member of the genus. It is found mostly on the coastal plain from North Carolina, south through central Florida and west to eastern Texas. Isolated populations have been reported north to southern Missouri.

Hubricht's Salamander, *Phaeognathus hubrichti*

The first new genus of salamander to be described from the United States in twenty-two years, this striking salamander was first found among dead leaves in a ravine in Butler County, Alabama, in 1960. Its specific name honors its collector, and we may do the same in coining a popular name for this most interesting creature. A very elongate body and tail, with very short legs, indicate that it burrows habitually. Like the related Dusky Salamanders and Shovel-nosed Salamanders, it opens its mouth by raising the upper part of the head while the lower jaw remains fixed in position. It has 21 costal grooves, while its shorter relatives have approximately 14. It is dark-brown in color, with a few lighter spots on the sides and feet. The tail is slightly keeled and is prehensile. The total length of the adult is nearly 9 inches. All specimens except the first have been taken at night at the mouths of burrows, and all come from the same area as the first.

Woodland Salamanders, Genus *Plethodon*

These salamanders have five toes on the hind feet, but the fifth may be reduced so that it is hardly evident. The hind legs are not markedly longer than the front legs. The tail is round, or nearly so, and is not set off from the body by a constriction at the base. The body is usually long and slender, the costal grooves well-defined, the legs short. The tongue is attached in front, free at the sides and behind. There is no light line from behind the eye to the angle of the jaw.

Identifying Woodland Salamanders is made more difficult by the fact that some species show a great deal of variation in color pattern and may occur in a number of distinct phases. Woodland Salamanders move about by night or during heavy rain, seeking worms, small insects, and spiders. By day they hide in damp spots under logs or stones. Most of them thrive in captivity when their natural living conditions are imitated. All of them lay their eggs on land and have no aquatic larval stage. This genus has eighteen full species, more than any other salamander found in the United States. Its total range includes parts of every state except Nevada, Utah, Arizona, Colorado, Wyoming, the Dakotas, Alaska, and Hawaii. Six species are found in the northwestern United States, one in New Mexico, and eleven in the eastern and central United States. They fall into three natural groups: the western, the eastern small, and the eastern large. The very isolated species in New Mexico is apparently more closely related to the eastern small group than it is to the western.

Western Woodland Salamanders

The Woodland Salamanders of the Northwest usually have a broad, light middorsal stripe. There may be a little webbing between the toes, but it is not so extensive as in the Web-footed Salamanders.

Van Dyke's Salamander, *Plethodon vandykei*

These salamanders have a broad stripe down the back of yellowish, tan or reddish, usually contrasting sharply with the dark color of the sides and belly (sides and belly not much darker in some adults). The throat is pale-yellow. There are usually 14, occasionally 15, costal grooves. Maximum total length is about 4⅗ inches. Two races are known.

Washington Salamander, *Plethodon v. vandykei*

The light stripe on the back is broad and usually has straight edges, and the upper surfaces of the limbs are the same color as the stripe. The sides and belly are usually dark, but some adults are nearly plain-yellowish or pinkish-rose. These salamanders live in moist retreats under bark and stones usually near running water. Females taken in April and July contained fourteen and eleven eggs respectively. The eggs after laying are fastened together and attached to a stone by an elastic substance secreted with them. This race is found in western Washington.

Coeur d'Alene Salamander, *Plethodon v. idahoensis*

The dorsal stripe is narrower and usually has irregular borders, and the sides and belly are dark, contrasting sharply with the yellow throat patch. The tops of the legs are also dark. This race is known from northern Idaho and extreme northwestern Montana.

Larch Mountain Salamander, *Plethodon larselli*

This is the smallest of the western Woodland Salamanders. Adults are about 3 inches, only about two-thirds as long as Van Dyke's

Salamander. There are usually 15 costal grooves. The fifth toe is reduced. The dorsal stripe is yellowish, tan or reddish, dark-edged, and often sprinkled with dark flecks. The undersides, including the underside of the tail, are reddish except for the throat, which is cream. So far it has been found only in Multnomah and Hood River counties, Oregon, and in Skamania County, Washington, but special search may bring it to light from adjacent counties.

Dunn's Salamander, *Plethodon dunni*

This is one of the most aquatic of the Woodland Salamanders, usually occurring in water-saturated spots and taking to deeper water to escape from danger. It is closely related to the Western Red-backed but is larger and differs in color. The tan or greenish-yellow dorsal stripe is heavily flecked and does not reach to the tip of the tail. The dark sides are spotted with tan, and the belly is dark, with small yellow or orange spots. Some individuals are dark all over. There are usually 15 costal grooves. Adults may be 5¼ inches long. This species occurs west of the Cascade crest from the northern border of California to Pacific County, Washington.

Western Red-backed Salamander, *Plethodon vehiculum*

Next to the Larch Mountain Salamander, this is the smallest of the western Woodland Salamanders. Adults seldom exceed 4 inches in length. In spite of the common name, the dorsal stripe may be yellow or tan, as well as red. It has straight edges and extends to the tip of the tail. Sometimes unstriped individuals are found. The sides are dusky, with small white specks, the undersides mottled with blue-gray, reddish, or yellowish and white. There are usually 16 costal grooves. This species has a wider range than the others of the group, occurring in western Oregon, western Washington, southwestern Canada, and Vancouver Island.

Del Norte Salamander, *Plethodon elongatus*

As its scientific name indicates, this is more elongated than other western Woodland Salamanders, with a correspondingly greater number of body segments. There are usually 18 costal grooves, with 6 to 8 costal folds between the tips of the toes of the adpressed limbs. The light dorsal stripe, present in the young, is usually lost in the adult, which then appears plain dark-brown or black. There are small, light flecks on the sides and belly. Adults may reach 4¾ inches. This species is found along the coast of extreme northwestern California and southwestern Oregon.

Siskiyou Mountain Salamander, *Plethodon stormi*

This is closely related to the Del Norte Salamander and is very similar to it but is never striped and has the back sprinkled with small whitish flecks. It is known only from Jackson and Jefferson counties, Oregon, and Siskiyou County, California.

Eastern Small Woodland Salamanders

The difference in size between the small and large Woodland Salamanders is not absolute since the two groups do overlap in size. In general, though, members of this group are not only shorter, but more slimly built, with shorter legs and usually with more webbing on the toes. Frequently they have a broad red or yellow dorsal stripe, as so many of the western species have.

Jemez Mountains Salamander, *Plethodon neomexicanus*

Separated by many miles from all other members of the genus, the Jemez Mountains Salamander is found only in the Jemez Mountains of New Mexico, at an elevation of nearly 9,000 feet. It usually has 19 costal grooves, and the fifth toe is very short. The back is brown, with brassy stippling. It is the largest member of the group. Adults may reach 5⅔ inches. It lives under rotting logs, lichens, mosses, and similar moisture-retaining litter on wooded slopes.

Weller's Salamander, *Plethodon welleri*

These small salamanders at maximum size do not exceed 3⅛ inches. The back is black, heavily sprinkled with dull-gold or silver blotches, and the belly is nearly uniform black, sometimes spotted with white. There are usually 16 costal grooves. This species occurs in the mountains from Mount Rogers and White Top Mountain, Virginia, south to Yancey County, North Carolina. It is most often found at higher elevations.

Zigzag Salamander, *Plethodon dorsalis*

This little salamander usually has a red, orange, or yellow dorsal stripe, typically with wavy, irregular edges for at least part of its length (may be straight in race found on Ozark Plateau). The stripe continues broadly onto the tail. The belly is mottled with red, black, and yellow or white. Occasional unstriped individuals are found, but the red on the belly will separate them from unstriped Red-backed and Ravine Salamanders. There are usually 18 costal grooves. The maximum size is 3⅝ inches. The two races both live in and near caves, rock piles, and wooded areas.

Zigzag Salamander, *Plethodon d. dorsalis*

The dorsal stripe is broad, much more than a third the width of the body; it is sinuous, with clear-cut borders. This race is found from southern Ohio and southern and central Indiana and Illinois to central Georgia, Alabama, and Mississippi.

Ozark Salamander, *Plethodon d. angusticlavius*

In this race the dorsal stripe is narrower; its edges are not clear-cut; and it is much less wavy in appearance. The race is found in southwestern Missouri, northern Arkansas, and adjacent Oklahoma.

Red-backed and Lead-backed Salamanders,
Plethodon cinereus

Some individuals of this common and very variable salamander have a wide pink or brick-red, sometimes yellow, dorsal stripe; some are gray or lead-colored above. In parts of New England specimens that are entirely coral-red may be found, without any of the dark lateral or ventral color. These are among the most beautiful of their kind, as their dark, beady eyes emphasize the brilliant tone and slender delicate proportions of the body. Intermediates between the red-backed and lead-backed phases are also occasionally encountered, and in broods hatched in laboratories from single clutches of eggs, both colors are found. In certain areas the red-backed form is more numerous, while in other parts of the range the lead-backed ones predominate. The belly color is more characteristic—the undersides are sprinkled with black and white in equal amounts, giving a salt-and-pepper effect. There may be a little red pigment between the front legs, but it is never so extensive as the red belly markings of the Zigzag Salamander. Ravine Salamanders, on the other hand, have the belly mostly dark. Adults may reach 5 inches. Three races are recognized.

Red-backed and Lead-backed Salamander, Plethodon c. cinereus

In this race, when the dorsal stripe is present, it is straight-edged and bordered by dark pigment. The lead-backed phase is darker than the unstriped phase of the Zigzag Salamander and has little or no red underneath. There are 18 to 20 costal grooves, usually 19. This race is found from Maine to Minnesota, south through North Carolina and eastern Missouri.

Georgia Red-backed Salamander, Plethodon c. polycentratus

This race looks like the former one and has a similar lead-backed phase, but it usually has 20 or 21 costal grooves. There is also usually more red between the front legs. Unstriped ones have red on the legs and sides of the body and head. This race is found in northwestern Georgia.

Ouachita Red-backed Salamander, Plethodon c. serratus

The orange or reddish middorsal stripe has saw-tooth edges, with an occasional dark, unpatterned individual indicating a tendency to the lead color even in this form. There are usually 19 costal grooves. It is somewhat smaller than the other two races—adults may reach 4 inches. It is found in mountains of west central Arkansas and adjacent Oklahoma.

Ravine Salamander, Plethodon richmondi

These are slender, elongate salamanders with very short legs. They are seal-brown to black above, sprinkled with brassy flecks which are sometimes numerous enough to form an irregular stripe. Some very small white blotches are found on the lower sides. The belly is dark, sometimes with small, scattered white dots. A red dorsal stripe is usually present only in the young but has been reported in adults. It is narrower and shorter than in the Red-backed Salamander and does not extend out along the tail. There are three races.

Ravine Salamander, *Plethodon r. richmondi*

The brassy flecks are smaller and fewer in number in this race. It has 19 to 22 costal grooves. Adults may reach $5\frac{1}{2}$ inches. This race is usually not found on hilltops, but stays on valley slopes and in ravines. It is found from central Pennsylvania to southeastern Indiana and south to northwestern North Carolina and northeastern Tennessee.

Cheat Mountain Salamander, *Plethodon r. nettingi*

This race is shorter, $4\frac{3}{8}$ inches, has only 18 costal grooves, and has larger and more numerous brassy flecks than the Ravine Salamander. It likes high elevations in ravines and spruce forests. It is known from altitudes above 3,600 feet in the Cheat Mountains of West Virginia.

Peaks of Otter Salamander, *Plethodon r. hubrichti*

There is more dorsal color, which appears as spots or an irregular dorsal stripe. There are usually 19 costal grooves. They may reach $4\frac{3}{4}$ inches when fully grown. This race is known only from Bedford and Rockbridge counties, Virginia.

Eastern Large Woodland Salamanders

It is only by comparison with the eastern small group that these can be called large, for the largest does not reach 9 inches. In general, they are more stoutly built, with longer legs, less webbing between the toes, and a smaller number of costal grooves, usually 16. Most species lack the broad, light dorsal stripe so common in the other groups.

Bluerock Mountain Salamander, *Plethoden longicrus*

This large salamander can be distinguished from the other large plethodons of the region by the fact that the back is covered with distinct chestnut-brown blotches. The soles of the hands and feet are reddish-brown. It is the largest of the group, reaching a length of $8\frac{3}{4}$ inches. It lives in crevices and fissures in rocky cliffs and seems to feed primarily on ants, spiders, and millipedes, although other small invertebrates are also taken. It is apparently confined to Bluerock Mountain in Rutherford County, North Carolina.

Wehrle's Salamander, *Plethodon wehrlei*

Wehrle's Salamander has more webbing between the toes than others in the group and usually has 17 rather than 16 costal grooves. It is black or dark-brown, with white or bluish dots along each side. In the southern part of its range it tends to have middorsal rows of reddish spots, often paired. The throat is white-spotted or entirely white. It attains a maximum length of $6\frac{5}{16}$ inches. It lives in forests, under stones, and at the mouth of caves from southwestern New York to southeastern Virginia and west to Washington and Monroe counties, Ohio.

Yonahlossee Salamander, *Plethodon yonahlossee*

This striking salamander has a broad chestnut stripe extending down the back and well onto the tail, bordered by white or light-gray. The head and belly are black, more or less spotted with white. There are usually 16 costal grooves. The Yonahlossee Salamander is extremely agile and difficult to catch when disturbed. Since it burrows out of sight under dead leaves for shelter, it is not easy to find at any time. The largest one recorded was 7 inches. It is found in the Blue Ridge Mountains of northwestern North Carolina, southwestern Virginia, and northeastern Tennessee.

Rich Mountain Salamander, *Plethodon ouachitae*

The Rich Mountain and Caddo Mountain Salamanders are found on neighboring mountain ridges, and the two are much alike at first sight, since both are dark above. The Rich Mountain Salamander may have a highly variable pattern of dark-red or chocolate, with many light dots or a metallic frosting. The belly is dark, the throat often light. There are usually 16 costal grooves. Adults may reach $5\frac{1}{2}$ inches. It is rather common in its restricted range, living under rotting logs and other debris on forested slopes from 1,700 to 2,800 feet. It is known only from Rich Mountain in Polk County, Arkansas, and LeFlore County, Oklahoma.

Caddo Mountain Salamander, *Plethodon caddoensis*

This species never has a reddish tone or frosted appearance, but instead is black with white spots and with a white stripe along each side. The throat is light. There are 16 costal grooves. Adults may reach $4\frac{1}{2}$ inches. This species has been taken at lower elevations of 950 to 1,200 feet in the Caddo Mountains of western Arkansas.

Slimy Salamander, *Plethodon glutinosus* (Plate 2f)

These salamanders are shiny-black above, usually well sprinkled with silvery white flecks and spots, slate-colored below. The amount of spotting varies enormously from population to population. There are usually 16 costal grooves. In spite of the common name, the skin secretions of these salamanders are gluelike, so that they feel sticky to handle, not slimy. They live under stones or logs on wooded hillsides or in ravines, appearing to need more moisture than some others of the genus. Only two races are recognized at present.

Slimy Salamander, *Plethodon g. glutinosus*

The throat is usually dark in this race. The maximum recorded length is 7⅜ inches. It is found from extreme southwestern New Hampshire to central Florida and west to eastern Oklahoma and central Texas.

White-throated Slimy Salamander, *Plethodon g. albagula*

A series of populations along the Balcones Escarpment in Bexar, Comal, Hays, and Travis counties, Texas, have light throats, and the spots along the sides are yellowish.

Jordon's Salamander, *Plethodon jordani*

This is another very variable species of salamander. The ground color of the back is black or nearly so. It is usually plain but occasionally marked with small white spots (smaller than those of the Slimy Salamander) or with brassy flecks. The chin is light, and the belly varies from light- to dark-gray. Red is not found on the back except for occasional red spots in the young ones, and there is never a light dorsal stripe. There may be small white spots along the sides. In the Great Smoky Mountains of North Carolina and Tennessee most specimens have bright-red cheek patches, and in the Nantahala Mountains of southwestern North Carolina specimens with red legs are found. (In these same regions, some Blue Ridge Mountain Salamanders also show red cheeks and/or red legs. They usually show some trace of a dorsal stripe and of the light line from eye to jaw and have hind legs longer than the front legs.) Size varies with geography—those in the south are larger than those in the northern part of the range. The greatest length reported is 6⅞ inches. Populations showing various combinations of characters have been named as separate races, but until we know more about them it seems better to include them all in a single form. This is a forest form not usually found near water. While eggs are probably laid in small clusters in hollow logs or under moss and complete development takes place within the egg as in other members of the genus, very few actual observations have been recorded on the breeding habits in this species. It is found from western Virginia and extreme southern West Virginia through western North Carolina and extreme eastern Tennessee to northwestern South Carolina and northeastern Georgia.

Red and Mud Salamanders, Genus *Pseudotriton*

These salamanders are rather uniform in appearance, with elongated, slippery bodies, often reddish in color, and with a preference for cool

Fig. 13. Mud Salamander, *Pseudotriton montanus*

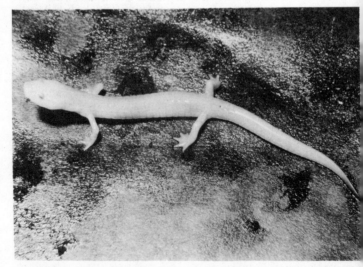

Fig. 14. Grotto Salamander, *Typhlotriton spelaeus*

seepage areas around springs, both facts giving them their popular names. They have five toes on the hind feet, and the tongue is attached by a central stalk and free at the edges. They are very like the Spring Salamanders, but they lack a well-marked light line running from the eye to the nostril. The two species are both found only east of the Mississippi.

Mud Salamanders, *Pseudotriton montanus* (Figure 13)

Mud Salamanders are clear red to chocolate-brown, usually with round black spots on the back and sides (except in the Rusty Mud Salamander). The spots do not tend to fuse in the adult. The eye is usually brown in the Mud, yellow in the Red Salamander. There are four races.

Eastern Mud Salamander, *Pseudotriton m. montanus*

The back is light reddish-brown to dull chocolate-brown, and the dorsal and lateral dark spots extend well down onto the lower sides of the body. The belly is marked with a few to many small, dark dots. There are 16 or 17 costal grooves. This is a large race, reaching a maximum size of 7 inches. It is more aquatic than the Red Salamander, living in and near muddy springs or under logs and bark bordering a stream. Eggs are found in late autumn and winter attached to dead leaves in the runoff from small springs. They are white and have a stalk for their attachment. Larvae may grow to a length of $2\frac{3}{4}$ inches before metamorphosing but sometimes do so when somewhat smaller. It ranges from southern New Jersey south to northeastern Georgia.

Midland Mud Salamander, *Pseudotriton m. diasticus*

The back is bright coral-pink to brilliant red, and the dark spots on the back are usually large and well separated and do not reach below the dorsal insertion of the legs. The belly is unspotted. There are usually 17 costal grooves. Adults may reach $6\frac{1}{8}$ inches. This race seems to be less aquatic than the Eastern Mud, sometimes living at the entrance of a cave under debris. It ranges from southern Ohio to northern Alabama.

Gulf Coast Mud Salamander, *Pseudotriton m. flavissimus*

Adults of this form are smaller and more slender than are those of its near relatives. The back is light brownish-salmon, and the dark spots on the back and sides are small. The sides of the head, body, and tail are light-salmon, and the belly is unspotted. There are usually 16 costal grooves. Adults reach $4\frac{1}{8}$ inches. They appear to live near small streams, in bogs, and in seepage from springs. The race is found from southern South Carolina to eastern Louisiana.

Rusty Mud Salamander, *Pseudotriton m. floridanus*

The back is purplish-brown clouded with dull-yellow and practically unspotted. The sides are marked with short dull-yellow marks, sometimes in irregular lines. There are 18 costal grooves. Adults may reach $4\frac{5}{8}$ inches. This little creature, while not as small as the Gulf Coast Mud Salamander, takes good care not to be observed easily, for it, too, hides in bogs among sphagnum and begonias in pine woods or in small streams flowing through hardwood hammocks or mixed forests. It is found in southeastern Georgia and northern Florida, except in the western panhandle, where the Gulf Coast race is found.

Red Salamander, *Pseudotriton ruber* (Plate 3a)

In Red Salamanders the spots on the back and sides are smaller and more irregular in shape than in the Mud Salamanders. The back is coral-red to dark purplish-brown, and the eye is usually yellowish. There are four races.

Northern Red Salamander, *Pseudotriton r. ruber*

Young adults are coral-red, old ones dark purplish-brown, with the dark dorsal spots tending to fuse. The belly is salmon-red with small, dark spots. The lower sides of the legs and tail are usually without spots. There are no whitish flecks on the snout and head. The maximum size is $7\frac{1}{8}$ inches. Rather frequently collected under moss near springs or in cool, clear streams, this beautiful salamander is sometimes terrestrial in summer, hiding under bark or stones or similar moist places not very close to water. It adapts well to captivity, accepting small earthworms or finely minced hamburger quite readily, and for this reason, its life history has been thoroughly studied. Eggs are laid at the approach of cold weather—October and November—attached in small clusters to flat stones in springs or streams. A single female lays some seventy-two or more eggs, but several females may attach their eggs to the same stone. The larvae, when hatched, are about $\frac{1}{2}$ inch long and usually transform when 3 inches or more in length. This form ranges from southern New York, west to Ohio and south to central Georgia and Alabama. It surrounds the ranges of the Blue Ridge Red and Black-chinned Red in the southern Blue Ridge Mountains.

Southern Red Salamander, *Pseudotriton r. vioscae*

This race resembles the Northern Red, but the dark dorsal spots are usually distinct, the belly is usually strongly spotted, and there are spots on the undersurfaces of the legs and tail and many whitish flecks on the snout and head. This one also likes to stray on the hillsides, hiding by day under damp logs, but is most frequently found in spring-fed streams. Apparently the larvae hatch in March and are slightly less than 1 inch in length. Adults may reach $6\frac{3}{8}$ inches. It occurs from extreme south central South Carolina, south to the Florida panhandle, west to southeastern Louisiana and north to western Tennessee.

Black-chinned Red Salamander, *Pseudotriton r. schencki*

It is easier to identify this salamander than its relatives because of the heavy concentration of black on both jaws. The sides and top of the tail are spotted nearly or quite to the tip, and the throat and chest are usually dotted. The larvae transform when between $2\frac{1}{4}$ and 3 inches. Adults may reach 5 inches. It lives in the southern Blue Ridge Mountains west and south of the French Broad River up to an elevation of over 5,000 feet, usually under logs in fields or forests, occasionally in swampy springs.

Blue Ridge Salamander, *Pseudotriton r. nitidus*

Another mountain dweller, this is the smallest of the Reds, adults not exceeding $4\frac{5}{8}$ inches. The back is clear red, even in old adults, and there is little or no black on the chin. The undersides are unspotted, and the tip half of the tail also usually lacks spots. It seems to be equally at home away from streams in wooded areas and in or near springs and streams. It is found north and east of the French Broad River in the southern Blue Ridge.

Many-lined Salamander, *Stereochilus marginatus*

Only one species is known in this genus. It is a dull-colored little creature, primarily aquatic, as its small legs do not carry it far from its chosen pool or sluggish stream, although it sometimes conceals itself in damp litter under logs on land. Its common name comes from the fine, dark lines along its sides, although sometimes these lines are indistinct or reduced to a few dark spots. Its dorsal tone is brown to dull-yellow, and the belly is yellow with small dark dots. There are five toes on the hind feet, and the tongue is attached in front, free at the sides and behind. Adults may reach $4\frac{1}{2}$ inches. They feed on the many small freshwater invertebrates living among the dead leaves at the bottom of ponds. Egg laying has been induced in captive females by pituitary implants. Before laying, each female turned on her back under a strand of water weed, and as the egg emerged from her cloaca, she pushed it until it adhered to the selected place on the plant by its very adhesive outer capsule. Some females were given flat rocks forming little "bridges," and these gripped the edge of the rock with the front legs while depositing the eggs one by one, each in a chosen spot on the under surface of the rock. Between 16 and 121 eggs were laid in the group of twenty females under observation. The gills of the larvae are long and compressed, and the young salamanders are more mottled than the adults and have irregular light streaks on the sides. They grow to about $3\frac{1}{2}$ inches before beginning to metamorphose. Restricted to the coastal plain of Virginia and the Carolinas, these salamanders are not well known even to persons living within their range.

Grotto Salamander, *Typhlotriton spelaeus* (Figure 14)

When the Grotto Salamander was discovered in underground streams of caves in the Ozarks, it occasioned great curiosity, as it was the first subterranean form to be found in the New World. The larvae live outside the cave in mountain brooks, with functional eyes and a definite color pattern of yellow, longitudinal flecks or dark streaks on a brownish or purplish-gray ground color. The tail fin is high. After metamorphosing and losing the gills and tail fins, the adults find their way into caves; the eyes cease to function, being no longer needed in total darkness; the eyelids grow shut; and most of the pigment is lost. Sometimes the body is pinkish, with faint orange tones on the tail, feet, and belly. Its sensitive skin receptors allow it to find the small blind crustaceans on which it feeds. The maximum length reported is $5\frac{5}{16}$ inches. It is found on the Ozark Plateau in southern Missouri, northern Arkansas, extreme southeastern Kansas, and northeastern Oklahoma.

Texas Blind Salamander, *Typhlomolge rathbuni*

A few years after the discovery of the Grotto Salamander, a second subterranean form was pumped up from an artesian well on the Balcones Escarpment in Texas. It is even more a creature of darkness, for not even the larvae are ever found in streams flowing in the open. The functionless eyes remain only as small, dark spots deep under the skin. The head is ridiculously flattened, and the legs are so attenuated that they could not bear the animal's weight out of water. The red or pink gills remain throughout life and are large and plumelike. The rest of the skin is colorless. The maximum size is $5\frac{3}{8}$ inches. It is known only from the Balcones Escarpment of central Texas.

Frogs and Toads

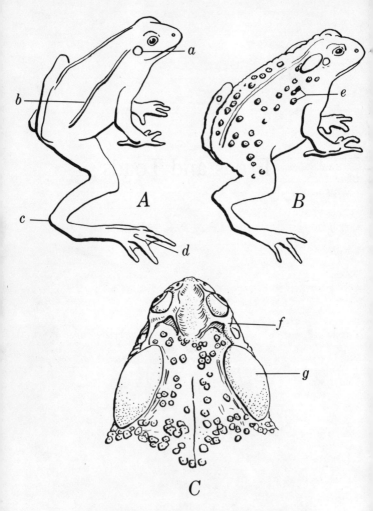

ANATOMICAL PARTS OF THE FROG

A. View of frog showing (a) eardrum, or tympanic membrane, (b) dorsolateral fold, (c) heel, and (d) the toe webs.

B. View of toad showing (e) warts on back.

C. Dorsal view of toad head showing (f) cranial crests and (g) parotoid glands.

FROG GLOSSARY

Anal warts: Small, white warts on each side of the vent in some frogs.

Boss: A rounded, mesa-like bony knob on the top of the skull in some spadefoot toads.

Cloaca: A common chamber into which the digestive, excretory, and reproductive tracts empty. It opens to the outside through the vent.

Cranial crests: Knobby protuberances on the top of the head of toads.

Digital disks: Round, adhesive pads on the tips of the fingers and toes of some frogs.

Dorsolateral folds: Glandular folds of skin running from behind the eye to the region of the base of the hind leg in some frogs.

Nares: Nostrils.

Palatine teeth: Teeth on the roof of the mouth.

Parotoid glands: Rounded or oval glandular protuberances on the back of the head in toads.

Postfemoral: The back of the thigh.

Tympanum: The eardrum of frogs, usually level with the surface of the head.

Vent: The posterior opening of the digestive, excretory, and reproductive systems.

Vocal pouch: Skin sac underneath or at the side of the throat in some male frogs.

Vomerine teeth: Teeth on the roof of the mouth between or just behind the internal nares, usually arranged in rounded patches or in transverse series.

Frogs and Toads

ALL toads are frogs, but not all frogs are toads. This statement sounds like one of the riddles of the medieval schoolmen, but in reality it means only that there are not enough English words for all amphibian species. The entire order of *Salientia* receives the common name of "frog," although this name also is used more strictly to apply to the genus *Rana*.

There is no mistaking a frog. The lack of a tail and the elongated hind legs are enough to distinguish one at a glance. (Tailed Frogs have a posterior extension of the hind end of the digestive tract, but this is not a true tail.) The skin may be smooth or rough and warty but never has scales. Part of the lengthening of the hind leg comes from an elongation of the bones in the ankle region, which makes it look as if the frog had an extra section to its leg. The thigh is the part closest to the body; the shank is next to this; and the heel is the joint separating the shank from the ankle. The toes are usually long and are sometimes joined by a thin sheet of skin, the web. The external ear opening is covered by a membrane, the *tympanic membrane*, or eardrum, which is sometimes very large and conspicuous.

Frogs live in a wider variety of habitats than salamanders. Many of them are arboreal and some have adapted to very arid country, breeding in the temporary ponds formed after rains and burrowing in the ground or hiding in crevices in rocks to avoid desiccation in times of drought.

Most frogs are rather small creatures, inconspicuous except at the breeding season. Then the males gather at the breeding ponds, sometimes in enormous numbers, and amply display their vocal powers. They are the first vertebrates to have true voices. Each species has its own particular call, and the females are able to recognize the calls and move toward the males of their own species, so that even when a number of different kinds are calling from the same pond, mixups are relatively rare. The male clasps any female that approaches him and fertilizes the eggs as she lays them.

Most of our frogs pass through an aquatic tadpole stage. The tadpole is very different from the larva of a salamander. It has external gills at first, but these are soon covered over by a fold of skin. At first it lacks legs; then the hind legs develop, and the front legs appear just shortly before metamorphosis. The tail is long, with a high fin. It is resorbed during metamorphosis, though a remnant remains when the froglet first emerges from the water. Unlike salamanders, frogs always undergo metamorphosis.

TAILED FROGS, FAMILY LEIOPELMIDAE

One of the vagaries of popular naming is the fact that frogs of this family are called Tailed Frogs, although they have no actual tail. The large appendage at the rear end of the males is used as an external copulatory organ, for this is our only frog in which fertilization of the eggs is internal. (Females have a similar, though much smaller, appendage.) But vestigial tail-wagging muscles are present in frogs of this family, which includes also only the New Zealand *Leiopelma*. The presence of these tail-wagging muscles marks *Ascaphus* as one of the most primitive frogs, since not even the earliest known fossil having the highly developed hind legs characteristic of frogs shows any skeletal evidence of having possessed a tail. These muscles, therefore, date very far back indeed in the prehistory of the frogs. This genus includes a single species.

Tailed Frog, *Ascaphus truei* (Plate 3b)

These small, flat-bodied, rather rough-skinned frogs have the outer toe on the hind foot broader than the other toes, and the pupil of the eye is vertical. A considerable color variation has been noted, the upper parts ranging from mottled cinnamon to cocoa-brown and the undersides from pink to gray or almost black. There is usually a light triangle on the snout and a dark line passing backward through the eye. Adults may reach 2 inches. They live in extremely cold mountain streams and in order to carry one alive from its frigid home, its container must be kept no warmer than 40° F. It is often difficult to see these small, inconspicuous frogs as they nestle among the rocks at the bottom of a mountain brook. Seldom do they come out on shore, except on cold, rainy days, and even then do not stray very far from the safety of the turbulent waters.

At mating time the male searches busily among the rocks until he finds a female. He climbs upon her back, and his "tail" is bent underneath her body and inserted well into her vent so that his sperm enter her oviduct. Sometime afterward, the female lays her eggs alone. She attaches them to the downstream side of a rock, where they adhere firmly in the foaming waters. The tadpoles have very effective sucking disks around their mouths, with which they cling to the rock to avoid being carried away by the current. Their food consists of the algae and small invertebrates that they can scrape from the rocks. They may not complete metamorphosis until one to three years after they have hatched. The animal voice apparently first came into existence in the frogs, but the very primitive *Ascaphus* cannot hear sound traveling through the air and therefore has no need for a voice. In the noisy cascades near which it lives, a mating call would probably go unheard; hence the search by the male for a mate. The Tailed Frog is found from southern British Columbia, south through western Washington and Oregon into northwestern California and in the Rocky Mountains of southeastern Washington, northeastern Oregon, northern Idaho, and northwestern Montana.

SPADEFOOT TOADS, FAMILY PELOBATIDAE

Members of this family in the United States are toadlike in form, squat-bodied and short-legged, but they usually lack the large, conspicuous parotoid glands present in the shoulder region of the toads and always have a broad, black, sharp-edged projection on the inner side of the hind foot—the "spade" which the animal uses in digging. The pupil of the eye is normally round at night, but in a bright light it contracts like a cat's into a narrow, vertical slit. This is a small family, though widely distributed. One genus extends from Canada to southern Mexico; one is present in southern Europe and northern Africa; others are found in southeastern Asia and the East Indies.

Spadefoot Toads, Genus *Scaphiopus*

These amphibians are adept at burrowing into loose soil for quick concealment from enemies. This is done with the spade on the inner side of the hind foot, with which the soil is kicked to one side so that the creature's body sinks down into the excavation in a surprisingly short time. Spadefoots remain hidden during the day and come out to feed only late at night, especially after heavy rains. They are not so warty as toads but do have the back sprinkled with small, knoblike tubercles. There are six species in the United States.

Plains Spadefoot, *Scaphiopus bombifrons*

The hard, elevated bump (boss) between the eyes and the short, rounded, sometimes wedge-shaped spade easily separate this species from the others. The Great Basin Spadefoot is the only other one with both a wedge-shaped spade and a boss between the eyes, but its boss is glandular and soft, not underlaid by bone. The two can usually be separated by range alone. The Plains Spadefoot is gray or brown on the back, often suffused with greenish and marked with four irregular light lines, while the small tubercles may be yellow or reddish. Adults may reach 2¼ inches. The loud chorus from the mating pond is not musical, but sounds like hoarse squawking. Breeding occurs from May to August after heavy rains. Masses of eggs are submerged in shallow ponds and attached to vegetation, and hatching takes place in less than two days. The tadpoles scrape the algae for food and also take any animal matter they may find. They transform in five to seven weeks. They are found in the Great Plains from extreme western Missouri, west to western Montana and eastern Arizona and from Canada south into Mexico.

Couch's Spadefoot, *Scaphiopus couchi* (Figure 15)

The spade is elongate and usually sickle-shaped in Couch's Spadefoot, and the top of the head is flat, the eyes widely separated. Its color varies from bright-chartreuse to dull-tan, with a darker marbling which sometimes fades out at breeding time. Adults may reach 3½ inches.

g. 15. Couch's Spadefoot, *Scaphiopus couchi*

g. 16. Pig Frog, *Rana grylio*

The Eastern Spadefoot, the only other one that lacks a boss and has an elongate spade, has light lines on the back. The two can be separated by range alone. The voice is like that of a goat or sheep, harsh and noisy. This species also breeds in the warm months, and eggs may hatch in $1\frac{1}{2}$ days, and tadpoles metamorphose when they are only $\frac{1}{4}$ to $\frac{1}{2}$ inch long. It ranges from southern Oklahoma, south through central and southern Texas into Mexico and west through central and southern New Mexico and Arizona to extreme southeastern California.

Hammond's Spadefoot, *Scaphiopus hammondi*

This frog has a short, wedge-shaped spade and no boss between the eyes. It is greenish, dull-brown, or gray, with darker blotches and often with four irregular light stripes along the back. The dorsal tubercles are tipped with orangish. Adults may reach $2\frac{1}{2}$ inches. The call is rather like the croaking of a *Rana* and is uttered by the male in the breeding pond. Eggs are laid in cylindrical masses and hatch in two days or less. Metamorphosis occurs in four to six weeks at $\frac{1}{2}$ to $1\frac{1}{4}$ inches. Tadpoles are carnivorous, devouring the weak ones of their own species but also preying on mosquito larvae. It is found from western Oklahoma to central Arizona and south into Mexico and also in the Great Valley, foothills, and coast ranges south of San Francisco Bay in California and south into Lower California.

Eastern Spadefoot, *Scaphiopus holbrooki* (Plate 3c)

Like Couch's Spadefoot, this one has an elongate, sickle-shaped spade and lacks a boss, but as the ranges of the two do not overlap, they will not be confused in the field. The Eastern Spadefoot has two yellowish dorsolateral lines on a dull-brown background, although some examples are nearly black. The maximum size recorded is $2\frac{7}{8}$ inches. The voice is harsh, almost like that of a crow, and when many sing in chorus, the sound is very loud and audible for half a mile. Heavy rains incite breeding activities, and the eggs are laid in irregular strings along stems of aquatic plants. They hatch very quickly, and the tadpoles transform in two to seven weeks at $\frac{1}{2}$ inch. After egg laying, the adults hide in the ground and are hardly ever found until the next breeding. It ranges from southern New England to southern Florida, west to eastern Missouri, Arkansas, and Louisiana.

Hurter's Spadefoot, *Scaphiopus hurteri*

This frog has both a sickle-shaped, elongate spade and a boss on the head just behind the level of the eyes. The parotoid gland and the tympanum are distinct. The back is grayish-green, brown, or almost black, and light dorsolateral stripes are prominent. Adults may reach $3\frac{1}{8}$ inches. The call is a single note, less harsh than that of the other species. The eggs are laid singly, but as they tend to adhere by their gelatinous casings, they often form irregular strings in the water. This form ranges from southwestern Missouri, south through western Louisiana and to extreme southeastern Kansas, central Oklahoma, and eastern and southern Texas and south into Mexico.

Great Basin Spadefoot, *Scaphiopus intermontanus*

This Spadefoot has a wedge-shaped spade and a boss between the eyes that is glandular, not bony. There is usually a gray or olive hourglass-shaped marking, set off by grayish streaks, on the back. Adults may reach 2 inches. The voice is a series of short, hoarse, rapid calls. Like other Spadefoots, it burrows in the ground in dry weather. It is found from southern Canada, south through central Washington and Oregon to western California, east to northwestern Arizona, western Colorado, and southwestern Wyoming.

TRUE FROGS, FAMILY RANIDAE

Members of this large and diverse family are called True Frogs, because the most common and conspicuous frogs in Europe, where the early work of classification was done, belong to it. Actually the family is centered in Africa; from there a single genus, *Rana*, has spread to all continents. All the True Frogs of the continental United States belong here, as well as four of the eight frogs that have been introduced into Hawaii. Other members of the family are found in southeast Asia. A small group of South American frogs, the dendrobatids, is also placed in the family, and one of these, the Gold and Black Poison Frog, has also been introduced into Hawaii.

True Frogs, Genus *Rana*

Frogs of this genus are usually streamlined, with slim bodies and long legs. They are built for speed on land and in water, and on this they mostly depend for escape from their enemies, since they usually lack the acrid skin secretions of toads and do not possess much burrowing ability. Their toes are pointed, and those of the hind foot are connected by webbing. During the breeding season, males have the forearm and base of the thumb enlarged. True Frogs lack the enlarged parotoid glands of the toads, the "spade" of the Spadefoots, the fold of skin across the back of the head found in narrow-mouth toads, and the expanded pads at the tips of the toes found in the tree frogs. Their skins are rather thin as a rule and subject to great evaporation, so they tend to live on the margins of ponds or float in the shallow water when at rest. They have a host of enemies, such as fish, wading birds, water turtles, and small mammals, and are alert at all times; if you walk around any sheltered pond, a sudden splash will announce that a frog almost at your feet has finally taken off for safety. As the insects on which most of them feed are diurnal, so are most True Frogs except at the breeding season. In spite of their precarious existence, True Frogs are very numerous both as to individuals and as to species. Nineteen species are here recognized for the continental United States; two of these are also found in Hawaii; and two Asiatic forms have also been introduced there.

Characters important in identifying True Frogs include color and pattern, size of the eardrum (tympanum), extent of webbing between the toes, and whether or not there are raised glandular ridges, called dorsolateral folds, along the back. As usual, geographic distribution must be taken into account. In dealing with such a large number of species, it makes identification easier if we divide them into groups.

In the two following species, there are no dorsolateral folds, and the tympanum is larger than the eye in breeding males, about the same size in females and young (sometimes smaller in the Carpenter Frog). The rear of the thigh is marked with conspicuous dark and light horizontal bands. Both are found on the southeastern coastal plain.

Carpenter Frog, *Rana virgatipes*

This small species is sometimes called the Sphagnum Frog because it frequents sphagnum bogs and swamps, as well as matted vegetation around ponds. It lacks dorsolateral folds and has four yellowish stripes on the back, differing thus from any other frog in the same region. The lower surfaces are light-yellow, with scattered dark spots. The voice sounds like a hammer blow on a board, given rapidly three to six times in succession, and the chorus at the breeding pond starts about dusk and continues until dawn any time between late April and August. Some 600 eggs are laid by a single female, usually in a mass. The tadpole does not metamorphose until the following spring, when it is around $1\frac{1}{4}$ inches in length. Adults may reach $2\frac{5}{8}$ inches. This species is found from southern New Jersey to eastern Georgia.

Pig Frog, *Rana grylio* (Figure 16)

This is much larger and more heavily built than the Carpenter Frog; the rear of the thigh has very sharp dark and light bands. The fourth toe is only a little longer than the third and fifth, and the web extends to the tips of the toes. The Pig Frog varies from olive to blackish-brown above, with scattered dark spots, and the underparts are sometimes heavily mottled. The harsh grunting call gives it its popular name. It breeds from March through September, but calls every month in the year. The tadpoles are large, up to 4 inches, and may not metamorphose for two years. It stays in the water most of the time. Adults may reach $6\frac{3}{8}$ inches. It is found from southern South Carolina, south throughout Florida and west to southeastern Texas.

The four following species do not have the rear of the thigh marked with conspicuous dark and light horizontal bands. The tympanum is larger than the eye in adult males, about the same size in females and young. These frogs occur naturally in the eastern and central states, but both the Bullfrog and the Green Frog have been introduced into the West and Hawaii.

Bullfrog, *Rana catesbeiana* (Plate 3d)

The Bullfrog is the largest in the United States and is much hunted for eating. It is aquatic by choice, hiding under debris at the water's edge. It lacks dorsolateral folds along the back, though there are glandular ridges around the tympanum. It is green above, sometimes with gray or brown markings, and the belly is white or yellowish, often mottled with gray. In the Southeast it may be as dark as the River Frog; the latter has small, light spots along the edges of the jaw. The fourth toe is considerably longer than the third and fifth and extends out beyond the webbing. Bullfrogs emerge later from hibernation than most others and breed in the northern part of the range in June and July, although in Texas its eggs have been found in February. Like the Pig Frog, it may spend two winters as a tadpole, which may sometimes reach a length of over 6 inches. Adults may reach 8 inches. It is found from Nova Scotia to central Florida, west in the North through Wisconsin and to extreme southern South Dakota, southeastern Wyoming, eastern Colorado, and New Mexico, and south through Texas into Mexico. It has been introduced into many places in the West and also onto many of the Hawaiian Islands.

River Frog, *Rana heckscheri* (Figure 17)

This frog has no dorsolateral folds. The back is rough, blackish green, and the belly spotted with dark-gray. The back of the thigh is mottled or has light spots, and there are small light spots along the edges of the jaws. Two different calls are given, neither of them musical. One is a snore or snort, the other an explosive grunt. Apparently they breed from April to July. Like the Bullfrog, the young of the River Frog pass the winter as tadpoles and apparently do not metamorphose until the following April or May, when they are 6 to 7 inches long. The young are said to have reddish eyes. Adults may reach 6 inches. The River Frog is found from southern South Carolina to northern Florida, west to southern Mississippi.

Green Frog, *Rana clamitans*

In spite of the common name, these frogs may be bronze or brown rather than green. As in other members of this group, the tympanum is as large as, or larger than, the eye. Dorsolateral folds extend about halfway down the back. There is no light line along the upper jaw. These eastern frogs have been introduced into northwestern Washington and near Ogden, Utah, and also into Hawaii, where they are presently on Oahu. Which of the two races is represented by these introductions has not been reported.

Bronze Frog, *Rana c. clamitans*

This variety is brown or bronze above, usually not spotted, and often lacks the green color on the upper lip. Its belly is white with dark vermiculations. Males have yellow throats at breeding time, which is

Fig. 17. River Frog, *Rana heckscheri*

Fig. 18. Mink Frog, *Rana septentrionalis*

from April to August. The voice consists of several deep twanging notes like those of a plucked cello string. Adults reach 3⅜ inches. The Bronze Frog is found on the coastal plain from North Carolina to central Florida, west to Texas and north in the Mississippi Valley to the southern tip of Illinois.

Green Frog, *Rana c. melanota* (Plate 3e)

This frog is green to greenish-brown above, usually with dark-brown or gray spots present. The belly is white, but often some dark spots occur on the chin and beneath the legs. The upper lips are usually bright-green. In the northern part of its range, it may be confused with the Mink Frog, which has a strong musky smell and more webbing on the toes. The call is rather similar to that of the Bronze Frog. Adults may reach 4 inches. It is found from the Maritime Provinces of Canada, south to northwestern South Carolina, northern Georgia and Alabama, and northeastern Mississippi, west to Minnesota and Oklahoma.

Mink Frog, *Rana septentrionalis* (Figure 18)

This species often lacks dorsolateral folds; when they are present, they may be indistinct or prominent. The popular name comes from the fetid odor given off by the frog's skin when it is roughly treated. Its back is buff or olive, sometimes with large, dark spots. The webbing between the toes extends to the last joint of the fourth and to the tip of the fifth. Water lily ponds are especially preferred, as the frog can hunt its insect prey by keeping above the floating leaves and consequently remaining safe from predacious fish. Its call is a rapid metallic croak. Breeding occurs from late in June perhaps to mid-August, and the tadpoles do not metamorphose until the following year. Adults may reach 3 inches. It is primarily a Canadian species, ranging south to northern New England and New York, the Upper Peninsula of Michigan, northern Wisconsin, and northern Minnesota.

In the remaining frogs the tympanum of the male is not conspicuously enlarged and is smaller than the eye. The following three have the dorsolateral folds indistinct or absent. They are western in distribution.

Tarahumara Frog, *Rana tarahumarae*

This frog has prominent dark bands on the hind legs. The throat is uniform white or clouded, but not spotted, and there is no light stripe on the upper jaw. The back is rust, olive, or brown, with a few dark spots which often have light centers. It is heavily built, with a broad head and rounded snout. It stays near potholes and pools along the bottom of canyons. Breeding apparently takes place after the heavy July rains. Adults may reach 4½ inches. This Mexican species enters the United States only in the Pajarito Mountains of southern Arizona.

Foothill Yellow-legged Frog, *Rana boylei*

The two Yellow-legged Frogs resemble the Tarahumara Frog but are much smaller and usually have the throat spotted. The Foothill

Yellow-legged has a light patch on top of its head. The back is greenish-brown, reddish or gray, usually with indistinct dark mottling. The undersides of the legs are yellow, with the yellow extending onto the belly. The throat and sides are often mottled with black. It breeds from late March to early May, the egg cluster being attached to stems in shallow water. The tadpole transforms after three or four months, and probably is about ¾ inch long. Adults may reach 2¾ inches. It is found west of the crest of the Cascade Mountains in Oregon, south in California in the coast ranges to Los Angeles County, and in the foothills of the Sierra Nevada to an altitude of 6,000 feet.

Mountain Yellow-legged Frog, *Rana muscosa*

The black or brown markings on the back are more prominent than in the Foothills Yellow-legged Frog, and the tips of the toes are dusky. The light patch on the head is often absent, and the yellow or orange on the belly is more extensive. Adults reach 3⅜ inches. It breeds as soon as the ice melts in the mountain lakes in June and July and remains a tadpole until the following year. This species is found in the Sierra Nevada of California from 6,000 to over 12,000 feet, in the Lake Tahoe region of Nevada, and in the mountains of southern California in Los Angeles, San Bernardino, Riverside, and San Diego counties.

In all the remaining True Frogs of the continental United States, the dorsolateral folds extend the length of the body, and the tympanum is not conspicuously enlarged. The next four species usually have a broad, dark, horizontal stripe running backward through the eye, as though the animal were wearing a face mask. There is a light line along the upper lip and crossbars on the legs. The Wood Frog has a wide range in eastern and northern North America; the other three are confined to the West.

Wood Frog, *Rana sylvatica* (Plate 3f)

This frog shows considerable color variation, as it may be pink, coppery, brown, or nearly black above. There may be broad, light dorsolateral stripes and/or a narrow, light middorsal stripe. The dark mask is always present. It is white below, sometimes speckled with dark, especially on the throat and chest, and the lower surfaces of the thighs may be washed with yellow. As one would expect with such a wide-ranging form, there is a great deal of local variation. Populations toward the north are shorter-legged and more apt to show the light middorsal stripe. A population in North Carolina appears to be large and uniformly bright-coppery in color. Several races have been named, but there is much overlap in characters, and even the authorities cannot agree as to how the species should be divided. We shall not attempt it here, but simply retain them all in one variable form.

They breed earlier in the spring than others in the genus, from mid-March throughout April in the northern United States, the voice being rather like the quacking of a duck. Eggs hatch in ten to fourteen days when the weather becomes warmer but less rapidly from the earliest layings. Tadpoles metamorphose in six to twelve weeks, the froglets being about $\frac{3}{4}$ inch long. Adults reach $3\frac{1}{4}$ inches. This species ranges farther north than any of our other amphibians. It is found throughout most of Alaska and Canada, south in the eastern United States to extreme northwestern South Carolina and northeastern Georgia. There are isolated colonies in the Ozarks, in eastern Kansas, north central Colorado and south central Wyoming, and northern Idaho.

Spotted Frog, *Rana pretiosa* (Figure 19)

The dark mask is present, but not always well marked, and there is a white stripe from the eye to the shoulder. The brown, olive, or gray back has many black, irregular blotches, sometimes light-centered, and the skin is usually covered with small tubercles. The lower parts are red or salmon, sometimes yellowish, and may be white in the young. The throat and sometimes the rest of the underparts are mottled with dusky. The hind leg is rather short—when it is adpressed, the heel usually does not reach beyond the nostril. Dorsolateral folds are usually apparent. These frogs prefer cold mountain streams and nearby marshes. The call is a series of short bass notes audible for some distance. Breeding begins in February, continuing to July in the north. The eggs hatch in about four days. Adults may reach 4 inches. There are two races.

Western Spotted Frog, *Rana p. pretiosa*

The undersides are red or orange in this race. It ranges from southeastern Alaska, south through western Montana, northern Idaho, Washington, northern and western Oregon, and extreme northern California.

Great Basin Spotted Frog, *Rana p. luteiventris*

This form has straw-yellow underparts and tends to be paler above. It is found in northern Nevada, northern Utah, southern Idaho, southeastern Oregon, and western Wyoming. Adults may reach $3\frac{1}{2}$ inches.

Red-legged Frog, *Rana aurora*

This is the largest True Frog that is native to western North America. The back is brown, gray, or reddish, marked with dark flecks and spots. The dark mask and light jaw stripe are usually present but may be rather hard to make out. There is yellow overlaid by red on the belly and undersides of the hind legs and a coarse red, yellow, and black mottling in the groin. The hind leg is long—when it is adpressed, the heel reaches to or beyond the nostril. These frogs are quite wary and stay in quiet ponds and creeks throughout the year. Breeding lasts from January to July, and eggs are usually deposited in clusters. The tadpoles transform in a year or more to froglets about 1 inch long. There are two races.

Fig. 19. Spotted Frog, *Rana pretiosa*

Fig. 20. California Red-legged Frog, *Rana a. draytoni*

Northern Red-legged Frog, *Rana a. aurora*

This race is smaller, adults reaching about 3 inches, and the dark spots on the back usually do not have light centers. It ranges from Canada through western Washington and Oregon into northwestern California.

California Red-legged Frog, *Rana a. draytoni* (Figure 20)

The dark dorsal spots, when present, are usually more distinct and they usually have light centers. The skin is rougher and thicker, the legs shorter, the eyes smaller. Adults may reach 5 inches. It is found throughout western California except the northwestern part, in the Sierras, and has been introduced into Nevada.

Cascades Frog, *Rana cascadae*

The back is greenish-brown with numerous very distinct black spots, while the lower surfaces are pale-yellow or orange. The mask and light jaw stripe are present. The mottling in the groin is slight compared to the Red-legged Frog. The call is a low-pitched croak. Eggs are laid from late May to early July and hatch in eight to twenty days. The tadpoles metamorphose in eleven to fourteen weeks, the froglets being tiny—about ½ inch long. They do not reach sexual maturity for at least three years, possibly four. As they seem to prefer cold temperatures, they stay at elevations from 3,000 to 9,000 feet. Adults may reach 3 inches. They are found in the Cascade Mountains of Washington, Oregon, and northern California and the Olympic Mountains of Washington.

The next three species are slim-bodied, long-legged frogs, with the tympanum smaller than the eye and with the dorsolateral folds extending the length of the body. They lack a dark face mask and are almost always conspicuously marked with large dark spots. The Southern Leopard Frog and Pickerel Frog are confined to the eastern and central United States. The Leopard Frog is our most widely distributed amphibian. It is found from northern Canada to Panama and from the Atlantic Coast to eastern California, Oregon, and Washington.

Leopard Frog, *Rana pipiens*

This frog is probably the most widely used animal in biology classes and experimental laboratories throughout the country. It is also the most confusing. The Southern Leopard Frog was formerly considered a race of this, but recent work indicates that it is a distinct species and some competent workers believe that several of the forms now considered races will also eventually prove to be separate species. On the other hand, some do not recognize one or more of the races. Nor is there any general agreement about the geographic distribution of the named forms. The problem is further complicated by the fact that Leopard Frogs have apparently been widely introduced from one part of the country to another. We are recognizing four races, but the ranges suggested are very tentative, and it will often be best not to attempt to put a race name on your specimen.

Most have a metallic bronzy or green back, with scattered, dark, oval spots. The dorsolateral folds are very prominent and often much lighter in color than the rest of the upper surface. The body is slender and streamlined, medium-sized, and with long, powerful legs for leaping. Leopard Frogs stay in the short grass of meadows or around ponds, where a rich harvest of insects may be taken.

Northern Leopard Frog, *Rana p. pipiens*

Two or three rather irregular rows of light-edged, rounded, dark spots on the brown or green back mark most examples. The undersides are white. A light line runs along the upper jaw. In our north central states some Leopard Frogs have very few dark dorsal spots and sometimes lack them altogether. Another "variety" has the ground color of the back mottled and much darker all over. The voice is a long, low gutteral croak alternating with several short, sharp notes. Breeding takes place during April and early May; eggs are deposited in masses in shallow water. Metamorphosis occurs in eight to twelve weeks, the froglet being $\frac{3}{4}$ to $1\frac{1}{4}$ inches in length at that time. Adults may reach $4\frac{1}{8}$ inches. This race is found from Canada south to the uplands of northern Georgia and Alabama, west to Minnesota, Iowa, and northeastern Missouri.

Rio Grande Leopard Frog, *Rana p. berlandieri*

The skin is pale greenish-olive above and is rougher and more warty than that of other Leopard Frogs, while the toes are more fully webbed. The dark dorsal spots are wider and more transverse. It prefers dry areas, but when the rains come, it may breed at any time of the year. During dry seasons it stays underground, being thus more toadlike than most True Frogs. It is very alert and cannot easily be captured. Adults may reach 4 inches. It is found from southern Nebraska south through Kansas, Oklahoma and Texas and into Mexico.

Western Leopard Frog, *Rana p. brachycephala*

This short-headed race is very variable. In arid regions it is light in color, and the dark spots may lack the light borders, be faint, or almost absent. The dorsolateral folds are usually light. Below it is creamy, sometimes yellowish. Adults may reach 5 inches. It occurs west of the ranges of the Northern and Rio Grande Leopard Frogs to the eastern parts of California, Oregon, and Washington.

Vegas Valley Leopard Frog, *Rana p. fisheri*

The legs are said to be shorter and the eardrum of the males enlarged in this form. The dorsal spots are small, pale, and without sharp outlines. Adults may reach 3 inches. It is known only from springs near Las Vegas, Nevada, and is probably now extinct.

Southern Leopard Frog, *Rana sphenocephala* (Figure 21)

This frog has a whitish spot on the eardrum and a long, pointed head, differing thus from the Northern Leopard Frog. It also has fewer dark spots on the sides and the dark dorsal spots are sometimes absent. It is greenish or brownish above, usually white below. Its voice is a combination of snore and cluck. A maximum size of 5 inches has been reported, but most adults are smaller and decidedly more slenderly built than the Northern Leopard Frogs. It is found from southern New Jersey south east of the mountains through Florida, west to Texas and north in the Mississippi Valley to Missouri, Illinois, and Indiana.

Pickerel Frog, *Rana palustris* (Figure 22)

This frog is rather easily told by the two regular rows of dark, rectangular spots down its back and by the orange or yellow on the concealed surfaces of its hind legs. It stays in cool bogs and along streams, but also comes out into meadows or weed patches to feed upon insects found there. The mouths of caves are also favorite hiding places. Its skin secretes a substance distasteful to snakes and actually lethal to other frogs kept in close confinement with it. The call, like a heavy snore, is sometimes given while the frog is under water. Eggs are laid from late April into May, about 3,000 in a round mass attached to aquatic plants. Adults may reach $3\frac{1}{8}$ inches. It is found from Canada to South Carolina, west to Wisconsin and south to Texas.

The two remaining species of True Frogs found in the United States are squat-bodied and short-legged, looking more like toads in build. However, they lack parotoid glands. The dorsolateral folds extend the length of the body, and the tympanum is not enlarged. They lack a white line on the upper jaw, instead having a mottled pattern there. Unlike other True Frogs, they usually spend the day in burrows, using ones dug by crayfish, Gopher Tortoises, or small mammals.

Crawfish Frog, *Rana areolata*

The dorsal spots are large, round, and light-bordered. The belly is whitish, the chin and throat unspotted except at the sides. There are two races.

Southern Crawfish Frog, *Rana a. areolata* (Figure 23)

This one has a U-shaped snout when viewed from above, and its back is often smooth or nearly so. While the color is variable, males sometimes have yellow or greenish dorsolateral ridges, this color appearing also on concealed surfaces of the hind legs. The popular name comes from their habit of hiding in crawfish burrows, but they also occupy holes in banks or sewers. The voice is a deep, loud trill, and a chorus is said to sound like a drove of hogs at feeding time. Breeding occurs from February to June. Adults may reach $3\frac{5}{8}$ inches. This race

Fig. 21. Southern Leopard Frog, *Rana sphenocephala*

Fig. 22. Pickerel Frog, *Rana palustris*

is found on the Gulf Coast plain of Texas and Louisiana, also in the Red and Arkansas river valleys in northern Louisiana, southwestern Arkansas, and southeastern Oklahoma.

Northern Crawfish Frog, *Rana a. circulosa*

The head is shorter and broader, the back is rougher, and the dorsolateral folds are more prominent than in the southern race. It has the same preference for old crawfish burrows. It breeds from March to the middle of May, and the tadpole transforms in July. Sexual maturity is probably reached when it is three years old. Adults may reach 4½ inches. This race ranges from Indiana to northeastern Oklahoma and south central Mississippi.

Gopher Frog, *Rana capito*

Gopher Frogs resemble Crawfish Frogs in body build, but the dark markings on the back are not edged with light, and the chin and throat are spotted. There are three races.

Carolina Gopher Frog, *Rana c. capito*

The back is covered with numerous small warts so close together as to give a tessellated effect. The belly is heavily marbled or clouded with dark flecks. The call is raucous and strong, between a snore and a groan. Adults reach 3⅞ inches. This race is found on the Atlantic coastal plain from North Carolina to central Georgia.

Florida Gopher Frog, *Rana c. aesopus* (Plate 4a)

This race is pale-colored, and the dark markings are irregular in shape. The back is smooth or slightly warty. The chin and throat are spotted, but the belly is usually unmarked posteriorly. The call is a deep, roaring snore. This frog breeds throughout the year. Eggs hatch in about four days, and the tadpoles are large, up to 3⅜ inches. They metamorphose in twelve to fourteen weeks into 1- or 1½-inch froglets. Adults may reach 4¼ inches. It is found from central Georgia to southern Florida.

Dusky Gopher Frog, *Rana c. sevosa*

Warts are always present on the back of this frog—round, oval, or in long ridges. The skin is always dark—gray or brown, with dark-brown spots or uniform black. The belly is spotted from the chin to at least midbody. Its voice is a hoarse, very loud snore. The frog is wary, diving to the bottom of the pond if disturbed. In winter it stays at the bottom of a gopher tortoise hole or similar natural tunnel. Adults may reach 3⅞ inches. It is found from the Florida panhandle to extreme eastern Louisiana, north in Alabama to Shelby County.

In addition to the Bullfrog and Green Frog, two Asiatic species have been introduced into Hawaii.

Fig. 23. Southern Crawfish Frog, *Rana a. areolata*

Fig. 24. Sheep Frog, *Hypopachus variolosus*

Black Spotted Frog, *Rana nigromaculata*

This frog was introduced into Oahu, presumably to be used as food, but it has not become common. It can be told from the other True Frogs in Hawaii by its light middorsal stripe and the light stripe along each dorsolateral fold. There are many distinct, short, glandular ridges between the folds, but the eyelids are smooth. Adults may exceed 3 inches in length.

Wrinkled Frog, *Rana rugosa*

One of the most successful introductions into Hawaii has been the Wrinkled Frog, now known from the islands of Hawaii, Maui, and Oahu and possibly Kauai. It lacks distinct dorsolateral folds but has many short glandular ridges on the back and sides, and the eyelids are warty. It has altogether a warty, toadlike appearance but lacks enlarged parotoid glands. Analysis of its stomach contents have shown that the food of the species consists of about ninety-eight percent beetles, two-thirds of these belonging to destructive species. The heavy leg muscles are relished as human food by the Japanese, although the maximum length of an adult is less than 2 inches.

Gold and Black Poison Frog, *Dendrobates auratus* (Plate 4b)

This beautiful little frog, measuring only $1\frac{1}{4}$ inches in length, is the most attractive in color of the several kinds of frogs and toads that have been brought into Hawaii. The light golden-green, rounded markings on a jet-black background easily separate it from all other frogs on Hawaii. The name "Poison Frog" is given to members of this genus because Indians of Panama use extractions from their skin to poison the tips of darts. The life history is most unusual. The eggs are laid on land and are guarded by the male. When they hatch, the tadpoles adhere to his back and are carried by him to water. With a vast appetite for small insects, this frog is a useful ally in controlling insect pests. It is known only from Oahu, where it lives on the ground or in low shrubbery.

NARROW-MOUTHED TOADS, FAMILY MICROHYLIDAE

This family is widely distributed in the southern land masses, in South America, Africa, southern Asia, and the East Indies. Only two genera reach the United States. They are small, plump, short-legged, rather dull-colored frogs with smooth skins, small, pointed heads, and tiny eyes. They have a fold of skin across the back of the head. These secretive little frogs remain hidden during the day and become active only at night.

Sheep Frog, *Hypopachus variolosus* (Figure 24)

The look of the head alone is enough to identify members of this family. The narrow pointed snout and tiny eyes remind one more of a turtle than of a frog. Pattern will separate the Sheep Frog from the Narrow-mouthed Toads. The back of the adult is brown to olive, with a narrow light middorsal line from tip of snout to vent. The spotted belly shows a similar light line. The thighs may be cinnamon to salmon. Hiding by day under debris, in burrows, and even in nests of pack rats, this frog is secretive except at breeding time—March to September— when its bleating call, reminding one of a sheep, is heard in the pond. The eggs may hatch in twelve hours, and the tadpole is ready to transform in thirty days. Adults may reach 1¾ inches. This is a Mexican species which ranges into southeastern Texas.

Narrow-mouthed Toads, Genus *Gastrophryne*

These frogs resemble the Sheep Frog in build but lack the narrow light line on the back and belly. There are two species in the United States.

Eastern Narrow-mouthed Toad, *Gastrophryne carolinensis* (Plate 4c)

The gray, brown, or reddish back often has an irregular, dark triangle bordered by broad, light lateral stripes; the pattern is sometimes obscured by dark or light mottlings. The belly is heavily mottled with dark-gray, and the throat is darker in the male. The voice sounds like the bleating of a lamb, very loud when heard close, but not carrying far. Breeding occurs from May to September after a heavy rain. Eggs float in a film on the surface of the pond or sometimes in small clusters in ponds and ditches. Tadpoles transform at a length of around ½ inch. Adults may reach about 1½ inches. It ranges from southern Maryland, south through Florida and west to eastern Oklahoma and Texas, with a colony in Iowa.

Great Plains Narrow-mouthed Toad, *Gastrophryne olivacea*

These are similar to the Eastern Narrow-mouthed Toads but have the belly pale, without dark mottlings, though the throat is darker in the males. There are two races in the United States.

Great Plains Narrow-mouthed Toad, *Gastrophryne o. olivacea*

The back of this toad varies from gray to greenish, depending on temperature and humidity. Young ones have a dark, irregular pattern, that almost disappears in the adult. The belly is pinkish to light-gray, unspotted or nearly so. The call begins as a whistle, ends as a bleat, and has a peculiar buzzing quality. From mid-March to September, eggs are deposited as a floating film on the water. Adults may reach

1⅝ inches. It ranges from southeastern Nebraska and western Missouri, south into northern Mexico. It narrowly overlaps the range of the Eastern Narrow-mouthed Toad and includes that of the Sheep Frog in this country.

Sinaloa Narrow-mouthed Toad, *Gastrophryne o. mazatlanensis*

This frog has dark spots on the back and an unspotted cream belly. There is a dark crossbar across the upper sides of the thighs and shanks, making a continuous mark when the legs are folded. It has a noisy, shrill call and is not easy to capture along the edges of shallow ponds among rocks and vegetation. Adults reach 1⅜ inches. This is essentially a Mexican form, extending to south central Arizona.

TOADS, FAMILY BUFONIDAE

The True Toads belong to the family Bufonidae. Like the True Frogs, this family is represented by a number of genera in the southern land masses and has a single genus that has spread practically throughout the world. The True Toads of the genus *Bufo* are found on all continents except Australia. The sixteen species of toads native to the United States all belong to it. Two of these have been introduced into Hawaii, as has one Asiatic species.

True Toads, Genus *Bufo*

True toads are squat, short-bodied animals with a pair of enlarged glands, the parotoids, one on each side in the shoulder region (not present in the very young). Other smaller glands are scattered over the body. It is these glands, the so-called warts, that give toads their rough, bumpy appearance. They are most likely to be confused with Spadefoot Toads, which they resemble in body shape. True Toads have the pupil of the eye a horizontal oval (round or vertical slit in Spadefoots) and have two brownish or blackish tubercles on the underside of the foot, one of which may be enlarged for digging (a single black "spade" in Spadefoots). Parotoid glands may be present in Spadefoots but they are small and usually indistinct. Toads usually have bony ridges, called cranial crests, on the head between and behind the eyes.

Toads were never built for speed, as their short legs propel their thick bodies only a few inches at each leap. They do escape predators, however, by secreting a thick whitish fluid from the parotoid and other skin glands which is very caustic to the mucous membranes of most other creatures, so that a wolf or fox that has once seized a toad in its mouth will stay clear of them forever after. (If you pick up a toad, keep your hands away from your eyes and mouth until you have washed them.) Another protection for toads is their ability to conceal themselves, which they do by slipping into a crevice, hiding under fallen leaves, or burrowing in soft earth, which some can do very rapidly because of a big "shovel" on the hind foot. After covering the body with soil, the toad becomes invisible to a hunting enemy. Toads also bury themselves more deeply to escape the effects of low winter temperatures or long-continued drought in summer.

Mating occurs in spring and summer, the chorus of the males attracting the females to the breeding pond. Eggs are laid in long strings, never in jellylike masses, as in the True Frogs. The tadpoles, when they emerge, are very small, and nearly all are black in color. They transform into miniature toadlets after a few weeks and then swarm from the water up the bank, often in vast numbers. The discovery of such a migration, especially after a summer rain, has given rise to the idea of a "rain of frogs." It actually can rain frogs during a windstorm, when the entire contents of a small pond may be sucked up by the wind and deposited at some other spot, but this rarely happens. This migration of baby toads, all of them much the same size, is an annual spectacle for those who are observant, while the wind-borne water may contain large and small frogs, fish, and water plants sucked from the pond as well.

The existence of toads on dry land, instead of in or near water, is possible because of their heavy, dry skins, which prevent the rapid evaporation of water. Human beings do not get warts from handling toads, contrary to popular belief.

The first three species have one or more enlarged glands on the hind legs and usually one or two enlarged, light tubercles at the angle of the jaw. The skin is often smooth between the warts, and the cranial crests are low or absent. There is a fold of skin on the inner side of the hind foot near the heel. The throat is pale in males as well as females. These three are found only in the western states (one introduced into Hawaii).

Colorado River Toad, *Bufo alvarius* (Figure 25)

This is our largest toad—up to 7 inches—except for the Giant Toad, which equals it in the United States and exceeds it in tropical America. The two cannot be confused, because only the Colorado River Toad has heavy glands along the outer surfaces of both the thigh and the shank. These toads are olive or brown above, cream-colored below. The cranial crests are low and broad, the parotoid glands elongate, the skin smooth between the warts. The Colorado River Toad is nocturnal, and more aquatic than most other toads, although it lives in dry regions. It always chooses the wet areas near permanent springs, and may be found around watering troughs on cattle ranches. It feeds on spiders, insects, and even small lizards. The call is a low-pitched hoot, rather weak for such a big toad. Colorado River Toads probably mate from May to July, laying eggs in long strings, each containing up to 8,000 eggs. Metamorphosis is said to be rapid, taking place in a month. The poison from the skin glands is evidently very effective in protecting this toad against marauding mammals. It is found in southern Arizona, extreme southwestern New Mexico, and southeastern California, ranging south into Mexico.

Fig. 25. Colorado River Toad, *Bufo alvarius*

Fig. 26. Great Plains Toad, *Bufo cognatus*

Yosemite Toad, *Bufo canorus*

In this toad the parotoid glands are large and flat and close to each other, the space between them being less than the width of one parotoid. The cranial crests are absent or very small. Although a few large warts occur over the back, the skin between them is relatively smooth. Enlarged glands are lacking on the thigh, and those on the shank are not so large as in the Colorado River Toad. The adult male has almost no pattern, being dull olive-yellow to almost black above, sometimes with a narrow yellowish middorsal line or traces of dark spots. The female has the warts encircled by black. The voice of the calling male is a rapid, melodious trill. Breeding occurs from May to July, as soon as the snow melts. Adults may reach 3 inches. It is found in the high Sierra Nevadas, from 6,400 to 11,300 feet, from Alpine County to Fresno County, California.

Western Toad, *Bufo boreas*

These toads have a conspicuous white or cream-colored dorsal stripe, oval, well-separated parotoid glands, and lack cranial crests (except occasionally in old adults). The glands on the shanks are pronounced but not so large or prominent as in the Colorado River Toad. The thighs lack enlarged glands. The back is dusky, gray or greenish, with dark blotches around the warts, which are often tinged with rust. The voice sounds like the calling of baby chicks. Four subspecies are known.

Boreal Toad, *Bufo b. boreas*

The dark mottlings on the back and belly are usually more pronounced than in the California Toad. Those on the back tend to form dark borders to the middorsal light stripe. The eyes are a little smaller and the head narrower than in the other races. The skin between the warts is often rough. Breeding occurs from March to July. Adults may reach 5 inches. This toad is found from southeastern Alaska, south into northern California in the west, and through central Colorado in the east.

California Toad, *Bufo b. halophilus*

This toad is generally lighter than the Boreal Toad, with less ventral blotching, and the eyes are larger. It breeds from January to July. Adults reach $4\frac{5}{8}$ inches. It is found in central and southern California, south into Lower California and east to Pyramid Lake, Nevada. It is apparently the race that has been introduced into Hawaii.

Black Toad, *Bufo b. exsul*

This little toad is sometimes solid-black above and sometimes mottled with white, while the belly is whitish with heavy black blotches. The skin is smooth. Its color makes it the most distinctive of any of the Western Toads. Adults may reach 2 inches. It is found over a relatively small range in Inyo County, California, where it was once quite abundant during the spring breeding season, emerging by day, as well as by night. Today the onrush of civilization has almost destroyed its habitat, and it has grown very rare.

Amargosa Toad, *Bufo b. nelsoni*

The snout is rather pointed and elongate, while the head is narrow and wedge-shaped. The light middorsal stripe is pale-yellow and the rest of the back is yellowish-olive. The tubercles are cinnamon-brown in the center. These toads are nocturnal and breed in rather shallow ponds in May. Adults may reach 3⅝ inches. They are found in Nye and Lincoln counties, Nevada.

The next two species have no enlarged glands on the legs and lack the skinfold along the outer side of the foot. The skin of the body is loose and encloses nearly the whole thigh. The parotoid glands are oval in shape and the tubercles on the hind foot are sharp-edged. There is a dark spot on the throat of the male which may be partly hidden by an overlapping flap of loose skin.

Great Plains Toad, *Bufo cognatus* (Figure 26)

This is a beautiful creature, its dorsal tones of gray, green, yellowish, or brown being emphasized by very large dark-green or olive blotches set off by pale margins. Its cranial crests extend diagonally forward, meeting on the snout in an enlarged boss. It can burrow readily in sandy soil and moves around usually at night. At mating time (April to September) the din made by several males is very loud as the individual call is a high metallic trill of several seconds' duration. Adults may reach 4½ inches. It is found from southeastern California through the Great Plains to Canada, south through western Texas and into Mexico.

Texas Toad, *Bufo speciosus*

One of the most skillful burrowers, this toad has both tubercles of the hind foot sharp-edged, the inner one being sickle-shaped and therefore ideal for digging. Its cranial crests are lacking, or at most are indistinct, while its parotoids are oval and not very large. It is gray with greenish spots containing the pink or greenish warts. Its call is a series of short, high-pitched trills. It breeds in cattle tanks and irrigation ditches, as well as in natural rain pools. Adults may reach 3⅝ inches. It ranges from southwestern Kansas to northern Mexico.

The following two species also lack the skin fold on the foot and the enlarged glands on the hind legs. They differ from the Texas and Great Plains Toads in having at least half the upper leg free of the encasing body skin. The outer foot tubercle is blunt. The cranial crests are absent or inconspicuous. The parotoid glands are oval.

Southwestern Toad, *Bufo microscaphus*

The cranial crests are usually absent in this species. The color of the back is greenish, brownish, or salmon; the underparts are buffy. There is a light stripe across the head. The throat is pale in both males and females. The voice is a long musical trill. Adults may reach 3½ inches. Two races are known.

Arizona Toad, *Bufo m. microscaphus*

The parotoids are rather elongate and nearly parallel; the skin is relatively smooth; and the back has few or no dark spots. This toad is active both by day and by night and can be found along irrigation ditches or in marshy spots within its range. It feeds on insects and snails, also accidentally on plant fragments. It jumps as much as eighteen inches at a time and hops instead of walking. It is found in scattered localities along tributaries of the Colorado River in southwestern Utah, southern Nevada, central Arizona, and southwestern New Mexico.

Arroyo Toad, *Bufo m. californicus*

The parotoids are broadly oval and divergent; the skin is rougher; and the back has dark spots. The life history is well known. Breeding takes place from March to June, and eggs are laid among debris at the bottom of a pool in long strings. The tadpoles have a heavier concentration of white coloring on the belly than do those of the Arizona Toad. It is found in southwestern California and Lower California.

Oak Toad, *Bufo quercicus* (Plate 4d)

The smallest toad in our country, it does not exceed 1¼ inches in length. Its varied colors of spots, stripes and warts render it nearly invisible on the floor of the pine woods, where it seeks its food mostly by day, unlike many toads which are crepuscular or nocturnal. It always shows a light middorsal stripe and four or five pairs of dark spots on the back, though in very dark individuals the spots may be obscured. The cranial crests are inconspicuous. Its voice is like the peep of a young bird, and when many call in chorus, the loud sound seems out of proportion to the small singers. It is found in the coastal plain from North Carolina to Louisiana, including all of Florida. It has been reported as far north as Shelby County in Alabama.

The next five species lack the enlarged glands on the hind legs. Most of the upper part of the leg is not enclosed in the body skin. The cranial crests are well developed and conspicuous. The parotoid glands are oval or rather elongate, sometimes kidney-shaped, not extending down on the sides or forward almost to the eyes.

Southern Toad, *Bufo terrestris* (Figure 27)

The high cranial crests terminate in heavy knobs. These toads are usually some shade of brown. They may have dark spots surrounding one or more warts, and there may be a rather inconspicuous middorsal light stripe. They are grayish or buffy below, with the throat of the male dark. Young ones of this species have the crests and knobs less developed and are hard to distinguish from young of the American Toad. Backward extensions of the crests show where the knobs will develop in young Southern Toads, while American Toads show little backward extension of the crests. The two are actually separated in range, however, except on the borders of our southeastern coastal plain, where they may occur together. Southern Toads are active at dusk and at night and by day hide in burrows. The voice is a high, musical trill and in chorus the sound is quite deafening. Breeding takes place from March to September, often in very shallow puddles. Adults may reach $2\frac{5}{8}$ inches. It is found on the coastal plain from southeastern Virginia to the Mississippi River, including Florida. In Mississippi it has been reported as far north as Leake County.

American Toad, *Bufo americanus*

This toad is easily confused with Fowler's Toad which occupies somewhat the same territory. They can be distinguished by the crests behind the eyes; in the American Toad there is a little space between the crests and the parotoids (occasionally they are joined by a short backward spur of the crest), while in Fowler's Toad the parotoids and crests are in contact behind the eyes. There are only one or two large warts in each of the large dark dorsal spots in the American Toad, three or more in Fowler's Toad. There are two races in the United States.

American Toad, *Bufo a. americanus* (Plate 4e)

These toads vary greatly in color—they may be brown, brick-red, olive, or gray, marked with dark spots and sometimes light blotches as well. There may be a light middorsal stripe. The undersides are usually spotted with dark. The American Toad is common wherever it occurs. Its call is a long musical trill sometimes lasting a half minute and rather ventriloquistic, so that one is not always sure from which direction a single call is coming. Breeding takes place from March to July. Adults may reach $4\frac{1}{4}$ inches. It is found from Canada throughout the eastern United States except the southern coastal plain, west to South Dakota and northeastern Kansas.

Dwarf American Toad, *Bufo a. charlesmithi*

This little fellow is usually reddish in color, while its belly has only a few faint spots, if any. As its name indicates, it is much smaller than its near relatives, reaching a length of $2\frac{1}{2}$ inches. It is found from southwestern Indiana and southern Illinois to eastern Oklahoma and northeastern Louisiana.

Fig. 27. Southern Toad, *Bufo terrestris*

Fig. 28. Southwestern Woodhouse's Toad, *Bufo w. australis*

Houston Toad, *Bufo houstonensis*

This toad is apparently related to the American and Southern Toads. The cranial crests behind the eyes are much thicker in the Houston Toad, however, and come quite close to the parotoid glands. A light middorsal stripe is often present, while the dark, mottled pattern on the back often suggests a herringbone weave. The belly has many small dark, spots. The call is a high, piercing, and rather musical trill. Adults reach 2⅝ inches. It is found in southeastern Texas.

Woodhouse's Toad, *Bufo woodhousei*

This is the most widely distributed species of toad in the United States, ranging from southern New England to California. The cranial crests are well developed, the parotoid glands elongate. There is a light middorsal stripe. Breeding males have a black throat. There are four races.

Rocky Mountain Toad, *Bufo w. woodhousei*

The light middorsal stripe, prominent cranial crests, and elongate parotoids characterize this form. The dark dorsal spots are irregular and not always prominent. The belly is white or yellow, usually without spots but sometimes with a dark spot on the breast. The back is yellowish, brown to gray, sometimes slightly greenish. Adults may reach 5 inches. It is very abundant, and in spite of its common name is not confined to the Rockies, but occurs over a wide range, from the Dakotas to southern Washington and south into Mexico.

East Texas Toad, *Bufo w. velatus*

The dark mottling of the chest may be continued onto the belly in numerous black spots. The light middorsal stripe is narrow, becoming more prominent posteriorly. There is sometimes an indistinct light stripe paralleling it on each side. The back is dark brown, reddish, or gray, without distinct spots. Adults reach 3¼ inches. It is found in northeastern Texas and intergrades between it and Fowler's Toad occur in Oklahoma, Arkansas, Louisiana, and parts of Texas.

Fowler's Toad, *Bufo w. fowleri*

This toad and the American Toad are the commonest ones in the eastern United States and are often confused. Hybrids do occur in some areas, although Fowler's Toad tends to breed later than the American Toad in a given locality. A typical Fowler's Toad has the cranial crest and the parotoid in contact, instead of having a space between them as in the American Toad. There are three or more warts in each of the largest dark dorsal spots in Fowler's Toad, while the chest and belly are usually unspotted, although some have a single dark spot on the breast. The back is brown or gray, sometimes greenish or brick-red, and a light middorsal stripe is usually present. The call is a rather discordant nasal bleat. Breeding takes place from the middle of April to August, some 8,000 eggs being laid by a single female. In forty to sixty days the tadpoles transform into $\frac{1}{2}$-inch-long young. Needless to say, the survival rate of these infants is very low. Adults may reach $3\frac{1}{4}$ inches. It ranges from central New England to eastern Louisiana, west to Michigan and eastern Oklahoma. It is not found in the southern part of the Atlantic coastal plain or in most of Florida.

Southwestern Woodhouse's Toad, *Bufo w. australis* (Figure 28)

In their restricted range these toads are quite uniform in appearance and structure. There are well-developed black markings on the sides of the chest, and the dorsal light stripe usually does not continue onto the snout. Adults reach 4 inches. It is found in southwestern Texas, southern New Mexico, and southeastern Arizona.

Dakota Toad, *Bufo hemiophrys*

Adults can be told by a heavy swelling or boss on top of the head, sometimes grooved down the center, and extending from the end of the snout to the level of the posterior end of the eyelids. The ground color is brownish or greenish, and the red or brown warts in the dark spots along the back make it a very handsome creature. A pale mid-dorsal stripe is usually present. Adults reach $3\frac{1}{4}$ inches. It is found in northwestern Minnesota, northeastern South Dakota, North Dakota, and northern Montana. An isolated population in southern Wyoming has been reported.

The following forms have the parotoid glands round, triangular, or enlarged and extending down the sides of the body or forward almost to the eyes.

Giant Toad, *Bufo marinus*

Its large size—over 9 inches—rough brown skin and huge, triangular parotoids which extend down the sides of the body make the recognition of adult males easy. The absence of enlarged glands on the hind legs will separate it from the Colorado River Toad. The female and young are light yellowish, with several brown spots down each side of the back. As in many frogs, a full-grown female is appreciably larger than an adult male. The cranial crests are well developed. Because of its large size and consequently great appetite for insects, it has been introduced into most tropical countries where sugar cane is grown, as it patrols the plantations and devours harmful sugar beetles in vast numbers. It barely crosses the border of Texas from Mexico, from which country its range extends south through Central America and most of South America. It has also been introduced into southern Florida and into Hawaii.

Gulf Coast Toad, *Bufo valliceps* (Figure 29)

This is one of our handsomest toads, with the back varying from nearly black with spots of orange to bright-brown with whitish spots. There are a light middorsal and two dorsolateral stripes, the dorsolaterals bordering wide dark-brown stripes on the sides, not like the pattern of any other United States species. The cranial crests are high, the area between them along the top of the head appearing concave. The parotoids are triangular or round. The call is a short rattle or trill. It mates from March to August, the eggs often being in double strings. The tadpoles transform in twenty to thirty days into toadlets ½ inch long. Adults reach 5 inches. It is found from southern Louisiana and southern Arkansas south to Costa Rica.

Red-spotted Toad, *Bufo punctatus*

This species is quite readily told from our other toads by its small, round parotoids. It is gray or brown above, the warts often reddish or orange. The cranial crests are indistinct or absent. It inhabits dry country but chooses a home area near a spring, pool, or cattle tank. Its voice is a high trill lasting four to ten seconds, birdlike and pleasing. It mates from April to September; the eggs are laid singly, not in long strings as in other toads, and the young after forty to sixty days as tadpoles transform at ⅖ inch. Adults reach 3 inches. It is found from southwestern Kansas to southern California and south into Mexico.

Green Toad, *Bufo debilis*

These toads are bright-green or yellow-green on the back, with black spots or bars which sometimes fuse to form a broken network. The cranial crests are reduced or absent. The parotoids are large, rather flat, and extend down on the sides of the body. The belly is light, the throat dark in males. The brilliant color on the back is enough to separate it from any of our other toads except the Sonoran Green Toad, in which the black markings form a bold network surrounding large patches of greenish-yellow. There are two races.

Eastern Green Toad, *Bufo d. debilis*

The nostrils are set a little back from the tip of the snout, and the parotoid is as large as the side of the head in this race. This toad is more brilliantly green than any other in our country. It lives in dry areas under rocks, where it can enjoy the moisture, and comes out to hunt only after a rainfall. If rains occur during spring and summer it will come out to breed; if not, it postpones breeding until the next year. Its voice is a shrill whistle lasting for several seconds. Adults reach 1⅞ inches. It ranges from south central Kansas into northeastern Mexico.

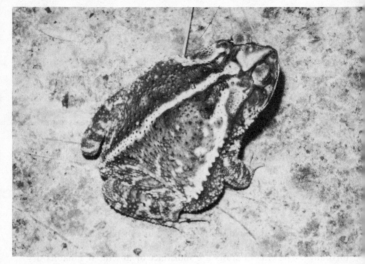

Fig. 29. Gulf Coast Toad, *Bufo valliceps*

Fig. 30. Squirrel Tree Frog, *Hyla squirella*

Western Green Toad, *Bufo d. insidior*

The nostrils are at the extreme tip of the snout, and the parotoids are even larger than the side of the head. The greenish color of this toad offers it good concealment in the grass near ponds. It is rather abundant, and comes out to feed in rainy weather. Adults reach $2\frac{1}{8}$ inches. It is found from southeastern Colorado and western Kansas through western Oklahoma and Texas, west through eastern and southern New Mexico and southeastern Arizona and south into Mexico.

Sonora Green Toad, *Bufo retiformis*

This species is built like the Green Toad, with large parotoids extending well down on the sides. The back is covered by a network of broad dark lines surrounding large, oval, greenish-yellow spots, this pattern continued on the parotoids and upper surfaces of the limbs. The belly is unspotted, and a dull bluish spot extends across the posterior body and onto the lower surface of the thigh. Adults reach $2\frac{1}{4}$ inches. It is found in south central Arizona and south into Mexico.

Asiatic Toad, *Bufo gargarizans gargarizans*

The Asiatic Toad has poorly developed crests on the head, while its parotoid gland extends anteriorly above the ear and nearly to the eye; the other large toad on Hawaii, the Marine Toad, has prominent cranial crests and parotoids well behind the eyes. The Asiatic Toad was introduced into Kauai around 1895 to assist in controlling insect pests, especially the destructive beetles. It reaches a 9-inch maximum size, about the same as the Marine Toad, which was also introduced into Hawaii because of its voracious appetite for beetles.

TREE FROGS AND THEIR ALLIES, FAMILY HYLIDAE

This very large and diverse family is centered in the American tropics. Five genera are found in the United States and one, *Hyla*, has spread to all other continents. Most members of the family have enlarged sucking disks on the tips of the toes, but this is not an infallible clue, since sometimes the disks are so small as to be hardly noticeable or are absent entirely. And some leptodactylids have similar toe disks These enter the United States only in Florida, Texas, and extreme southern New Mexico and Arizona. Any place else in the country a frog with disks on the toes will belong to the Hylidae. Perhaps the most constant characteristic of members of the family is the skinniness of the hind legs. The thighs in particular seem to be only a little thicker than the shanks and are usually long (may be short in Chorus Frogs). The legs are very different in appearance from the short, plump legs of True Toads, Spadefoots and Narrow-mouthed Toads. True Frogs have long legs, but their thighs are heavy and muscular. It is hard to see how Tree Frogs can accomplish the tremendous leaps that they do with so little muscular equipment.

Many Tree Frogs are nearly as versatile as chameleons when it comes to changing their colors and patterns.

Of the genera found in this country, toe disks are present in the Tree Frogs and Mexican Tree Frogs. The latter enters the United States only in extreme southeastern Texas. Chorus Frogs have small disks which may be hardly evident. They have only a little webbing between the toes, less than in the Tree Frogs. Cricket Frogs lack toe disks and have more webbing between the toes than Chorus Frogs. They always have black and white stripes on the hind surfaces of the thighs and usually a triangular mark between the eyes. Burrowing Tree Frogs also lack toe pads. They have a fold of skin across the back of the head, and the skin of the head is firmly attached to the skull, which is very hard and bony.

Tree Frogs, Genus *Hyla*

This genus includes some of our most beautiful frogs. They are frequently some shade of green or brown, and many are capable of a bewildering variety of changes. If your frog doesn't seem to fit any of the pictures or descriptions, let it sit in a jar or terrarium for awhile. It may change into something you can recognize. The throat is dark in the males. The toe disks are typically well developed, and there is more or less webbing between the toes. Most are rather small frogs, seldom exceeding 2 inches in length, and one, the Little Grass Frog, is the smallest frog in this country and one of the smallest in the world. Only the Cuban Tree Frog, introduced into South Florida, could be called large—it has a maximum recorded length of $5\frac{1}{2}$ inches.

Cuban Tree Frog, *Hyla septentrionalis*

This is a large, rather rough-skinned Tree Frog with large disks on the fingers and toes. The color variation is enormous. A very dark-brown frog may change in a few minutes to a pale sandy-gray or greenish, sometimes elaborately marked with spots or reticulations. The skin on top of the head is firmly fused to the underlying bony skull. This frog, now well established in southern Florida, was probably brought in from the West Indies as a stowaway on cargo. Near houses it "domesticates" itself, preferring to spend the heat of the day on the sides of water jars on cool verandahs or in cisterns. In wilder areas it stays in leaf axils on trees. It climbs well using its large toe disks. Its appetite is voracious, and it devours any living creature of suitable size, including other frogs and even its own young. Its voice is a snoring rasp. The maximum size is $5\frac{1}{2}$ inches. It is found in extreme southern Florida and the Keys.

Green Tree Frog, *Hyla cinerea*

This graceful and elegant creature usually has a brilliant green, smooth back, although in cool weather it may be dark-olive or slate-gray, and when it is calling it may be silvery or yellowish. There are frequently scattered, pin-head-size, golden, black-bordered spots on the back. The undersides are white or yellowish. Adults may reach 2½ inches. There are two races.

Green Tree Frog, *Hyla c. cinerea* (plate 4f)

This race usually has a light stripe beginning on the upper lip and continuing at least halfway along the side and often to the region of the hind leg. The stripe may be black-edged, and its borders are very clear-cut; the green color of the back continues for a little way below the stripe before fading into the light color of the belly. There are also light stripes on the backs of the forearms and shanks. Squirrel Tree Frogs often are similar in color and also have light stripes on the sides, but the edges of the stripes are not so clearly defined. They may have gold flecks on the back, but not small, round, black-bordered gold spots. The Pine Barrens Tree Frog has a lavender stripe bordered by white on the side. The Barking Frog is much stouter in build and almost always is marked with profuse, large, dark spots. The Green Tree Frog may be found climbing on stalks of cat-tails and other vegetation near water. In winter it may be found on bushes some distance from water. It does not seem to climb so high in the trees as some of our other Tree Frogs. In captivity it easily learns to take flies and other insects from its captor's fingers. It breeds during the summer months, the males often forming very large choruses. Such choruses seem to be made up of groups of two frogs answering each other—"*bo-bep, bo-bep.*" It is found from Delaware throughout Florida, west in the Gulf coastal plain to central and southern Texas and north in the Mississippi Valley to southern Missouri and Illinois.

Northern Green Tree Frog, *Hyla c. evittata*

This race has the lateral white stripes reduced or absent. (Some populations of *Hyla c. cinerea* occasionally contain a stripeless frog or one which has a stripe on one side of the body and none on the other.) A chorus of breeding males sounds like a bevy of ducks and is extremely loud. This race occurs in a limited area in the radius of a few miles from the Potomac River between Washington, D.C., and Alexandria, Virginia.

Barking Tree Frog, *Hyla gratiosa* (Plate 5a)

This handsome green, brown, or gray, dark-spotted Tree Frog, with a granular skin above, makes an attractive pet, soon learning to accept moths and other soft-bodied insects from its captor's hands. The ear-drum is about the same size as the eye. It is rather stout-bodied for a Tree Frog, and the spots are round or oval and edged with black. (They may disappear in some of the color phases.) There is a light stripe running from the upper jaw along the side. The throat of the male is green or yellow with dark spots just back of the chin. In the female the throat is light in the center with yellow at the sides and on the chest. In its native haunts it may stay in tall trees, but in times of drought it descends to burrow in soil, beneath grass clumps, or in other moisture-conserving vegetation. Males may give a barking call from trees, repeated several times. In the breeding ponds they call in quite a different manner—an explosive sound repeated at short intervals. They breed during the spring and summer. Adults may reach 2¾ inches. Barking Tree Frogs are found along the coastal plain from North Carolina to southern Florida and eastern Louisiana. They have been introduced into New Jersey.

Squirrel Tree Frog, *Hyla squirella* (Figure 30)

This frog's skin changes with varying conditions, becoming green, brown, spotted, or plain, so that its identification by color is difficult. There may be a dark bar between the eyes and a white stripe along the side. The thigh is yellowish behind and unspotted. It may be easier to identify one by deciding what it is not. In its green phase it looks very much like a small Green Tree Frog, but the light stripe on the side has a more indefinite border and the animal is more chubby in build. It may have gold flecks on the back, but not tiny, black-bordered, gold dots. Green Tree Frogs never turn a real dead leaf brown as Squirrel Tree Frogs may. Pine Woods Tree Frogs have definite yellow or orange spots on the back of the thigh, not just a yellowish wash. Spring Peepers have a dark X-shaped mark on the back and are never bright-green in color. Gray and Bird-voiced Tree Frogs have a light spot below the eye but not a light stripe. The Pine Barrens Tree Frog has a lavender stripe on the side. The skin of the Barking Tree Frog is granular, that of the Squirrel Tree Frog smooth. Squirrel Tree Frogs seem to climb higher in trees than Green Tree Frogs and are frequently found around houses. They often give a nasal quacking call before a rain or rasp like scolding squirrels (from which comes the popular name). The breeding call is a harsh, rapid trill. They breed during the summer months, and the eggs are laid singly on the bottom of the pond. Adults may reach 1½ inches. Squirrel Tree Frogs are found from southern Virginia south throughout Florida and west to the central coastal area of Texas.

Canyon Tree Frog, *Hyla arenicolor*

This frog has a thick, rough skin, rather suggestive of that of a toad and probably for the same purpose—to protect the body from desiccation in times of extreme drought. It is brown or olive-gray above, usually with darker spots or blotches, and the rear of the thigh is yellow or orange. There is no dark stripe through the eye. While few Tree Frogs have external parasites, this one sometimes has small encysted mites on the belly skin. It lives in dry desert lands of the southwestern United States around the infrequent freshwater springs and in canyons along which rivers flow in rainy seasons. It breeds from

May through July. The call is an explosive trill. Adults may reach 2 inches. It ranges from southern Utah and southern Colorado south through Arizona, western New Mexico, and western Texas into Mexico.

California Tree Frog, *Hyla californiae*

This is very similar to the Canyon Tree Frog but is grayer in color, the dorsal blotches are usually larger, and there is more webbing between the toes. California Tree Frogs are found among rocks near streams and ponds in arid and semiarid country. The adults are seldom more than a few feet from water, though the young may range farther. Breeding takes place during the spring and summer months. The call is a short, low-pitched quack. Adults may reach 2 inches. They are found in southwestern California and Lower California.

Pine Barrens Tree Frog, *Hyla andersoni*

This frog is a beautiful creature, looking like a piece of costume jewelry with its lavender, white, and green colors and shining eyes. It is a stout-bodied little Tree Frog, with the green of the back separated from the white of the belly by a white-bordered, plum-colored band. It frequents swamps in pine barrens, where it remains well hidden except at mating time, when the males give a honking call to summon the females to the breeding pond. Adults may reach $1\frac{7}{8}$ inches. The range is discontinuous; it is known from southern New Jersey, a small area of southern North Carolina, and another in northeastern Georgia.

Pine Woods Tree Frog, *Hyla femoralis*

This frog is difficult to identify without a close view, as the large, roundish, bright-orange or yellow (rarely whitish) spots on the dark hind surface of the thigh are usually concealed. Its back may be gray, greenish, or reddish-brown, with dark mottlings, blending well with the bark of the pine trees on which it lives. The mating call is a series of harsh, rattling notes suggesting that of a cicada, and continues all night during the breeding season, from late April to September. The eggs float in small groups on or just below the surface of the pond. They hatch in three days and metamorphosis takes place seven to eleven weeks later when tadpoles reach $\frac{1}{2}$ inch. As these frogs do not always lay in permanent ponds, many eggs and tadpoles are killed by desiccation. Adults may reach $1\frac{5}{8}$ inches. They are found mostly in the coastal lowlands from Maryland to eastern Louisiana, including all but southern Florida.

Gray Tree Frogs, *Hyla versicolor* and *Hyla chrysoscelis* (Figure 31)

These two frogs are very similar in appearance and apparently have been thoroughly confused in the literature—so confused that until someone makes a thorough study of the whole group in all parts of its range it is probably impossible to identify individual specimens. In spite of the common name, they may be green, brown, or almost white, as well as gray, usually with a large, dark, irregular star-shaped mark on the back and with a dark-bordered light spot below the eye. The back side of the thigh is orange, sometimes mottled with black so that the orange is reduced to spots about the size of a toe disk, sometimes flecked with white. The skin is usually rough and warty but may be smooth. Adults may reach 2⅜ inches. It has been shown that the two species differ in the voice of the calling males. In both the call is a loud resonant trill, but in *versicolor* the trill is decidedly lower in pitch than in *chrysoscelis*. The females are well able to distinguish between the calls. *Versicolor* is more northern and eastern in distribution, while *chrysoscelis* is more southern and western, but there is apparently considerable overlap. They have been found together in Minnesota and also in Texas. It is possible that either or both species may be represented by several races, but until we can tell the species apart it seems foolhardy to name races. Adults may reach 2⅜ inches. The whole complex ranges from Maine to northern Florida and from eastern North Dakota through central Texas to the Gulf Coast.

Bird-voiced Tree Frog, *Hyla avivoca*

This is like a small version of the Gray Tree Frog, with the same variable color and markings and light spot below the eye, but the hind surfaces of the thighs are greenish or yellowish-white, not orange. There are two races.

Western Bird-voiced Tree Frog, *Hyla a. avivoca*

The concealed surfaces of the legs are bright-green or yellowish-green. The vibrant, birdlike whistle rapidly repeated gives this little frog its popular name. It is larger than the other race—adults may reach 2 1/16 inches. It lives in swamps near streams draining into the Gulf of Mexico from southwestern Georgia to eastern Louisiana and in the Mississippi Valley, mostly east of the river, to southern Illinois.

Eastern Bird-voiced Tree Frog, *Hyla a. ogechiensis*

This is a paler race with the concealed surfaces of the thighs pale-greenish or yellowish-white. Adults may reach 1½ inches. It is found in streams of the Atlantic drainage in Georgia and southern South Carolina.

Spring Peeper, *Hyla crucifer*

These small Tree Frogs are usually some shade of tan or brown, occasionally olive, with a darker mark on the back in the shape of an irregular cross. This mark suggests the scientific name which means "bearing a cross." Peepers are much less versatile than many other Tree Frogs—they may change from light to dark but are never bright-

31. Gray Tree Frog, *Hyla versicolor*

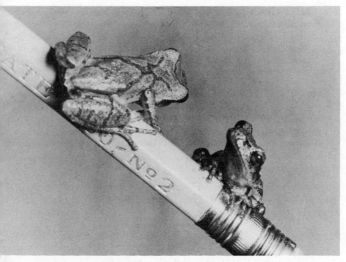

32. Northern Spring Peeper, *Hyla c. crucifer*

green, and the pattern is constant. They are also more terrestrial than most Tree Frogs—they may be found on low bushes or on the ground but apparently do not climb high in the trees as some others do. Adults may reach $1\frac{3}{8}$ inches. There are two races.

Northern Spring Peeper, *Hyla c. crucifer* (Figure 32)

This race is usually immaculate pinkish below, and the arms of the cross are usually narrower than in the southern race. Its delicate body seems as translucent as wax. The shrill, loud whistle of this little frog is heard during mild rains even before the snow melts. It is one of the earliest breeders, and its tadpoles develop before many of our other frogs come out of hibernation. It is found from Canada south throughout eastern United States to the panhandle of Florida and to eastern Texas.

Southern Spring Peeper, *Hyla c. bartramiana*

It closely resembles the northern race, but it is heavily patterned with dark spots below. In Florida it should be called a Winter Peeper, for it starts breeding in December. It is found in southern Georgia and northern Florida.

Little Grass Frog, *Hyla ocularis*

A full-grown adult Little Grass Frog measures less than $\frac{3}{4}$ inch in length—our smallest frog. It may be grayish or greenish above but is usually reddish-brown. The dark line that runs through the eye back to or beyond the shoulder distinguishes it from the young of other Tree Frogs, with which it might be confused. Sometimes a middorsal stripe is present. These midget frogs are able to turn the head from side to side or tip it up, a most unusual ability in a frog. They stay on low bushes or in grass near ponds and cypress swamps. The shrill chirping call, suggesting that of an insect, is so high-pitched that some people are unable to hear it. In Florida breeding may take place any month of the year; further north, from January to September. It is found from southeastern Virginia south throughout Florida and west to southeastern Alabama.

Pacific Tree Frog, *Hyla regilla*

This is a very variable Tree Frog—the color of the back may be green, tan, brown, reddish, gray or almost black, and an individual may change from light to dark in a few minutes. There is a dark stripe running from the snout through the eye at least to the shoulder, sometimes continuing along the side, though it may break up into a series of spots. There may be dark markings on the back and legs and a dark triangle on the head. Most have a dark line along the upper lip, bordered above by cream. The combination of toe pads and dark eyestripe should separate it from other western members of the family. Adults may reach $1\frac{7}{8}$ inches. A number of races have been described, based on combinations of minor structural differences. In order to evaluate them, you would need to have series of specimens of several different races on hand for comparison. Until we know more about them, we will continue to include all but one of these races in *Hyla r. regilla*.

Pacific Tree Frog, *Hyla r. regilla*

The Pacific Tree Frog is active at night and also sometimes in the daytime during the entire year where winters are not severe. Its food consists mostly of small insects which abound near ponds and springs. The frog has been found some distance away from water and survives up to an elevation of 11,000 feet. In the southern part of its range mating and egg laying take place from January to May but in the north, probably in June and July. Eggs are deposited in clusters in shallow water, attached to vegetation, and hatch in one to two weeks. The tadpoles metamorphose when they are $\frac{5}{8}$ inch or less in length, and about two years are required for the frog to attain maturity. These frogs are found from Canada to Lower California, east to western Montana, and extreme western Arizona.

Arizona Tree Frog, *Hyla r. wrightorum*

In this race the dark eyestripe extends along the side, sometimes to the region of the hind leg, though it may break up into spots posteriorly. The spotting on the head and upper part of the back is reduced or absent, but there may be dark bars on the lower back and there are dark spots on the legs. There is less webbing between the toes. Breeding takes place in temporary or permanent ponds, brooks, and sometimes wells. Its call, like that of many Tree Frogs, is ventriloquistic, so it is able to escape detection even during the mating period which is usually from June to August. It lives in the mountains of central and southern Arizona and west central New Mexico, from 5,000 to over 7,000 feet above sea level.

Mexican Tree Frog, *Smilisca baudini* (Figure 33)

This is a rather large Tree Frog with large toe disks and with a light spot below the eye, another at the base of the arm, and a dark patch in the shoulder region. Like many Tree Frogs, its skin changes color under different conditions of humidity and temperature, varying from dark-gray to greenish to yellowish to pale-gray. Various irregular dark markings may be present. The voice is a blurred *keck-keck-keck*, with sometimes a chuckling note. Adults may reach $3\frac{1}{2}$ inches. It is found from extreme southeastern Texas to Honduras.

Burrowing Tree Frog, *Pternohyla fodiens* (Figure 34)

This is a pale-yellow to brown frog marked with large, dark, black-bordered spots. The skin on top of the head is fused to the hard, bony

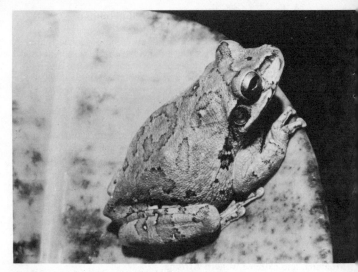

Fig. 33. Mexican Tree Frog, *Smilisca baudini*

Fig. 34. Burrowing Tree Frog, *Pternohyla fodiens*

skull. There is a fold of skin across the back of the head. Although it is related to the Tree Frogs, it is a burrowing, terrestrial form and lacks suction disks on the toes. The breeding call is loud and low-pitched— "*wak-wak-wak*." It breeds in July and August. Adults may reach 2 inches. It is a Mexican form, found in the United States only in open grasslands of extreme south central Arizona.

Cricket Frogs, Genus *Acris*

These miniscule frogs remind one more of miniature True Frogs than they do of Tree Frogs. Their backs are rather rough-skinned; their toes are long, more or less webbed, and without well-developed disks. Cricket Frogs come in a bewildering variety of colors, but two elements of the pattern are quite constant. There are one or more black longitudinal stripes on the rear surface of the thigh and almost always there is a dark triangle on the head with its base between the eyes and its apex pointing backward. Frequently in front of this triangle is a light triangle with its apex on the snout. This triangle may be red, green, or straw-colored, with the color carried back as a margin to the dark triangle and continuing along the back as a middorsal stripe. The basic ground color of the back is some shade of brown, green, or gray. There are often oblique dark bars on the sides. The two species are separate for much of their range but overlap broadly in the Southeastern states.

Southern Cricket Frog, *Acris gryllus*

This is a small species, with a more pointed head, longer legs, and less webbing between the toes than in the Northern Cricket Frogs. The web does not reach to the tip of the first toe. Two races are known.

Southern Cricket Frog, *Acris g. gryllus*

On the rear of the thigh the single dark stripe is clear-cut and bordered above and below by a well-defined light stripe. It lives in meadows near ponds or creeks where it can hide in vegetation, feeding on small flying insects so common in such a habitat. It is one of the most abundant frogs wherever it is found, and one of the hardiest, as it emerges on mild days even in midwinter and begins its mating call, which is a series of short, explosive, rasping notes. Breeding is known to take place from February to October. Eggs are laid singly, attached to plants or stones on the pond bottom. Tadpoles transform in seven to thirteen weeks when just over $\frac{1}{2}$ inch long. Adults may reach $1\frac{1}{4}$ inches. It is found from southeastern Virginia to the Gulf Coast (except coastal Georgia and peninsular Florida) and west to the Mississippi.

Florida Cricket Frog, *Acris g. dorsalis*

This frog has two dark stripes on the rear of the thigh, the lower one narrower than the upper. It may breed at any time of the year. Its call is a metallic click repeated several times. Adults reach $\frac{3}{4}$ inch. It is found from southeastern Georgia south throughout peninsular Florida.

Northern Cricket Frog, *Acris crepitans*

This species is slightly larger than the Southern species, has a blunter head, shorter legs, and the webbing reaches to the tip of the first toe. The dark stripe on the rear of the thigh is ragged in outline, not clear-cut. This species ranges farther north than the Southern Cricket Frog, but it also ranges farther south in Texas. There are two races.

Northern Cricket Frog, *Acris c. crepitans* (Plate 5b)

Over the eastern and central United States the shrill voices of these little frogs announce the earliest coming of spring. Individual voices have a ticking sound, almost like that of winding a watch. They are usually found in company with Spring Peepers, the earliest of the Tree Frogs to appear, and also with the Chorus Frogs. The breeding period is from April to July, the eggs being deposited separately or in small groups. Adults may reach $1\frac{3}{8}$ inches. They are found from southern New York to eastern Texas, excepting peninsular Florida and the southeastern coastal areas.

Blanchard's Cricket Frog, *Acris c. blanchardi*

This frog has more warts and is heavier in build than the others. The dark stripe on the thigh has irregular edges which blend into the dark ground color above it, and the back is more or less uniformly gray or tan, lacking the darker spots and bars found in the others. Variation in color is much less marked than in other Cricket Frogs. It breeds from February to late July. Adults reach $1\frac{3}{8}$ inches. It is found from Michigan to northern Tennessee, west to Colorado, and south through Texas to Mexico.

Chorus Frogs, Genus *Pseudacris*

These little songsters are related to the Tree Frogs but have short toe webs and small disks so that their climbing is limited to the small shrubbery bordering the ponds near which they live. A dark stripe passes through the eye, and the upper jaw is light (except in the Florida Chorus Frog). They often have a dark triangle on the head, as Cricket Frogs do, but never black longitudinal lines on the backs of the thighs. The pattern on the back is frequently one of dark stripes, though the stripes may be broken into rows of spots. There may be a middorsal stripe with a dorsolateral stripe on either side of it and below that a lateral stripe. In some forms the middorsal stripe is absent, and occasionally all three of the dorsal stripes are faint or absent. The Spotted Chorus Frog and Strecker's Chorus Frog appear more spotted or blotched than striped. Chorus Frogs make up for their climbing inabilities by agility in leaping and in diving and swimming to get away from real or apparent danger. They are hardy and call on mild winter nights in the same ponds with Cricket Frogs and Spring Peepers.

Mountain Chorus Frog, *Pseudacris brachyphona*

The middorsal stripe is lacking or represented only by a blotch on the hind part of the back, while the dorsolateral stripes are broad and curved in like a pair of reverse parentheses. The lateral stripes are also broad. Sometimes the dorsolateral stripes meet to form an X-shaped figure. (Spring Peepers with a similar X lack the white upper lip.) The general color is brown or grayish. The high-pitched call is not continuous, but is given as a series of single notes at intervals of about a second, the entire call lasting from a quarter of a minute to several times as long. Breeding occurs from March to July, and eggs from one female may number 1,500 a season. They are laid in small masses attached to water plants. They hatch in three or four days in mild temperature, but not for ten days when the water is cold. The tadpole stage lasts two months or a little less. After metamorphosis, the froglet is about $\frac{1}{3}$ inch long. Adults may reach $1\frac{1}{2}$ inches. This species ranges from southern Pennsylvania and Ohio to central Alabama.

Brimley's Chorus Frog, *Pseudacris brimleyi* (Figure 35)

The middorsal and dorsolateral stripes are weak in this frog, sometimes hardly evident, while the lateral black stripe is prominent. The markings on the legs tend to be longitudinal, and a narrow dark line occurs on the outer border of the shank. The lower surfaces are yellow, and usually there are dark spots on the chest. The call is a short, rasping trill. Adults may reach $1\frac{1}{4}$ inches. It is found in the lowlands from southeastern Virginia to Georgia.

Spotted Chorus Frog, *Pseudacris clarki* (Figure 36)

This is the only Chorus Frog with black-edged green patches, the spots usually numerous and scattered, not often arranged in rows. There is a green triangle between the eyes, and the belly is white. Its beautiful colors are seldom seen by day, as it is primarily nocturnal. The voice is not musical, but has been compared to the noise made by a saw. Breeding may occur any time in the southern part of its range but mostly in April and May in the north. Adults reach $1\frac{1}{4}$ inches. It is found from central Kansas to southern Texas.

Southern Chorus Frog, *Pseudacris nigrita*

The markings are usually black in the Southern Chorus Frog, standing out strongly when the ground color is light-tan or grayish but less evident when it is dark. The stripes are broad but tend to be broken and in the Florida race are usually rows of spots. The underparts are light, and the dark marks on the legs are transverse bars. The skin on the back is rather rough. There are two races.

Southern Chorus Frog, *Pseudacris n. nigrita*

The lateral stripes are continuous, but the three dorsal ones are often broken. The middorsal one may fork posteriorly. This form has a

Fig. 35. Brimley's Chorus Frog, *Pseudacris brimleyi*

Fig. 36. Spotted Chorus Frog, *Pseudacris clarki*

prominent white line bordering the upper lip. The voice is a musical trill. It breeds in ditches or ponds in the pine barrens from November to April. Adults reach 1¼ inches. It is found in the lowlands from eastern North Carolina to northern Florida and west into southern Mississippi.

Florida Chorus Frog, *Pseudacris n. verrucosa* (Figure 37)

This little frog has its upper lip mostly black instead of pale-yellowish or white, the black appearing usually as a series of spots but sometimes fused so that very little of the light color shows. The dark spots on the back are usually separated from one another. The voice is a rasping trill, often repeated. Breeding takes place from December through March, though they may call sporadically after heavy rains at other times of the year. Adults may reach 1¼ inches. It is found throughout peninsular Florida.

Chorus Frog, *Pseudacris triseriata*

The light line along the upper lip and dark lateral stripes are the most constant markings in this species. The middorsal and dorsolateral stripes are usually present but may be broken or occasionally absent. The stripes are brown or gray, not black as in the Southern Chorus Frogs, nor green as in the Spotted Chorus Frog, and the dorsolateral stripes are not strongly curved inward as they are in the Mountain Chorus Frog. The middorsal stripe often forks posteriorly and a dark triangle may be present on the head. The ground color of the back is brown, gray or greenish. The underside is light, though a few dark spots or specks may be present on the throat and chest. This is the most widespread of the Chorus Frogs; four races have been described.

Western Chorus Frog, *Pseudacris t. triseriata*

The three dark dorsal stripes are broad and usually as strong as the lateral stripe in the Western Chorus Frog, but may be reduced to series of dark spots or lacking. The legs are long. These frogs frequent the shore instead of staying mostly in the water, except at breeding time, which occurs from February to June, the later time in the North. Up to 1,500 eggs are laid by one female in small clusters attached to pond plants. The tadpole measures about 1 inch in length and transforms in six to thirteen weeks into a froglet ¼ to ½ inch long. Adults may reach 1½ inches. This species survives even near large cities, where the loud choruses can be heard at night in early spring. It is found from southern Canada and western New York to Kansas and Oklahoma, with scattered colonies in New Mexico and Arizona.

Upland Chorus Frog, *Pseudacris t. feriarum* (Plate 5c)

The pattern is extremely variable; the middorsal and dorsolateral stripes are sometimes lacking altogether in the Upland Chorus Frog. When they are present, they are narrow and may be broken into streaks

Fig. 37. Florida Chorus Frog, *Pseudacris n. verrucosa*

Fig. 38. Illinois Chorus Frog, *Pseudacris s. illinoensis*

or rows of small spots. The light line along the upper lip is constant, and so is the dark lateral stripe from the snout to the groin. This is one of the earliest frogs to breed throughout its range, beginning to call in February in the North and earlier in winter in the South. Adults may reach 1⅜ inches. It is found from northern New Jersey to the panhandle of Florida and west to eastern Texas and Oklahoma. It intergrades with the Western Chorus Frog in southern Indiana and Illinois.

New Jersey Chorus Frog, *Pseudacris t. kalmi*

More heavily built than the Western form, the New Jersey Chorus Frog has broad, clearly marked dorsal stripes. The middorsal one usually forks posteriorly. Adults may reach 1½ inches. It is found from Staten Island, New York, south through the Delmarva Peninsula. In northern New Jersey and eastern Pennsylvania it intergrades with the Upland Chorus Frog.

Boreal Chorus Frog, *Pseudacris t. maculata*

This has the shortest legs of any of the Chorus Frogs, as the heel barely reaches to the ear when the leg is carried forward. It hops, while other Chorus Frogs jump. Otherwise it is very similar to the Western Chorus Frog. Breeding occurs in May and early June, for metamorphosis must occur before the long winter sets in. Adults may reach 1⅜ inches. It is found from Great Bear Lake in northwestern Canada, south to northern New Mexico and from Idaho and Colorado east to intergrade broadly with the Western Chorus Frog from northern Michigan to Nebraska.

Ornate Chorus Frog, *Pseudacris ornata*

The Ornate Chorus Frog has dark spots on the yellowish or reddish sides, while the concealed surfaces of the legs have yellow spots. There is no middorsal stripe, but traces of the dorsolateral stripes are usually present. A black mask goes along the side of the head from the tip of the snout to behind the eardrum. Ornate Chorus Frogs vary greatly in color from black to silvery-white or green, but usually they are reddish-brown. Young ones have less distinct patterns. The call is rapid and metallic, like two pieces of steel struck together, somewhat like that of the Spring Peeper. It is heard from late fall to early spring. Adults may reach 1 7/16 inches. Ornate Chorus Frogs are found in cypress ponds and flatwoods ditches in the coastal plain from North Carolina to eastern Louisiana.

Strecker's Chorus Frog, *Pseudacris streckeri*

These are large and heavily built for Chorus Frogs, and the forearm is stout; the animals have more of a toadlike appearance. They usually appear more mottled or spotted than striped. The dark stripe through the eye is prominent, and there is a dark spot below the eye. The breeding call is a clear, shrill, bell-like note. They breed from November to June. There are two races.

Strecker's Chorus Frog, *Pseudacris s. streckeri*

This frog is highly variable in color—gray, brown, olive, or green. It can usually be recognized by the black spot below the eye, although this may sometimes merge with the narrow dark line along the upper lip. The dark lateral stripe is often broken into spots. The groin is mottled with strong yellow or orange and dark-brown. Adults may reach $1\frac{7}{8}$ inches. It is found in woodland streams, sand prairies, and even fields from Oklahoma and Arkansas to the Gulf of Mexico in Texas.

Illinois Chorus Frog, *Pseudacris s. illinoensis* (Figure 38)

The dark lateral stripe is weakly developed, so that this frog is distinctly pale in appearance. No yellow or orange occurs in the groin. It may reach $1\frac{1}{2}$ inches. It lives in scattered localities in southeastern Missouri and southwestern and west central Illinois.

SOUTHERN FROGS, FAMILY LEPTODACTYLIDAE

This is a large and diverse family of frogs abundant in tropical America and Australia. Four species reach the United States in Texas, southern New Mexico, and southern Arizona, and a fifth has been introduced into Florida. They differ from all other frogs in the United States in laying their eggs on land, not in water.

Robber Frogs, Genus *Eleutherodactylus*

These frogs have small disks on the digits, but these disks are truncate, not rounded like those of the Tree Frogs. There is no white stripe along the upper jaw. There are teeth on the roof of the mouth. Two species occur in the United States.

Barking Frog, *Eleutherodactylus augusti*

This frog is toadlike in shape but is smooth-skinned, has enlarged disks on the fingers and toes, and a fold of skin across the back of the head. It has definite lateral skinfolds and a ventral disk formed by folds of skin to help it cling to the nearly vertical rocks in the limestone caves from which it hardly ever ventures, even when it is raining. The color of the back is variable, tan, gray, greenish, or rusty with darker mottlings. Young have a broad, light band across the back. When caught a Barking Frog can inflate to an amazing size—an act supposed to confound its enemies. Its common name comes from its call, which resembles the bark of a dog. Two races have been reported from our country.

Eastern Barking Frog, *Eleutherodactylus a. latrans*

This race is large—adults are usually over $2\frac{4}{5}$ inches, and females may reach $3\frac{3}{4}$ inches. The dark bars on the hind legs are poorly defined. It is known from central Texas and southeastern New Mexico.

Western Barking Frog, *Eleutherodactylus a. cactorum*

This race is smaller, the adults usually less than 2⅔ inches, and the dark bars on the legs are more pronounced. Because of its nocturnal and secretive habits, it is easily overlooked even near the white limestone formations enclosing streams around which it lives. The large ventral disk helps it adhere to the vertical sides of rock crevices. Eggs are laid under a rock, and the male remains with them to moisten them with his urine if they tend to become dry. Apparently twenty-five to thirty-five days elapse between fertilization and hatching of the eggs. As in other members of the genus, the tadpole stage is completed inside the egg, so that the young one emerges fully metamorphosed. This is a Mexican species that has been reported in the highlands of southern Arizona.

Greenhouse Frog, *Eleutherodactylus ricordi planirostris* (Plate 5d)

These little frogs are dead leaf-brown in color, mottled with reddish, orange, or tan and sometimes with a light longitudinal line on either side of the back. Their ancestors came from the West Indies from whence they could easily have been transferred to the mainland of Florida on fruit or other cargo by the Carib Indians. They seek out a moist crevice or a pile of wet leaves and lay their eggs there. The tadpole stages are completed inside the egg capsule, and when the young one is ready to emerge, it has the front and hind limbs fully developed, while the lungs are adapted for air breathing and only a small vestige of a tail remains as a reminder of the tadpole stages, this being quickly shed. Development within the egg to such a point is very effective in preserving the frog population, as all the dangers from predatory fish and other eaters of frog tadpoles that must develop in water are avoided. Maximum size is 1¼ inches. It is now found throughout peninsular Florida.

Chirping Frogs, Genus *Syrrhophus*

These little frogs also have small truncate disks on the digits. They have no lateral folds, belly disk, or fold of skin across the back of the head. They also lack a dark transverse band between the eyes, which is frequently found in Robber Frogs. There are no teeth on the roof of the mouth. Two species occur in the United States.

Cliff Frog, *Syrrhophus marnocki*

The Cliff Frog is greenish mottled with brown and its skin is smooth. The chirp or trill resembles that of a cricket. Mating usually occurs in April or May. Adults live in caves and crevices in rocks along limestone ledges and their bodies are flattened to fit their narrow quarters. They may reach 1½ inches. They are found from central Texas to the Big Bend region.

Rio Grande Frog, *Syrrhophus campi*

This frog is grayish or dull yellowish without a distinct pattern. It is adept in concealing itself by day, but at night it comes out from its shelter under stones or debris to feed. It is very agile and can leap and hop as well as run, just as the Cliff Frog does. The brief, cricketlike chirp can be heard only for a short distance. Breeding occurs in April and May. Up to twelve quite large eggs are laid, and tiny froglets about $\frac{1}{4}$ inch long eventually emerge, the tadpole stages having been completed within the egg. Adults may reach 1 inch. They are found in extreme southeastern Texas and northeastern Mexico.

Mexican White-lipped Frog, *Leptodactylus labialis* (Figure 39)

The body form of these frogs is rather like that of the True Frogs of the genus *Rana*, but there are no webs between the toes. There are no disks on the toes, but there is a belly disk formed by a fold of skin, and a lateral fold on each side of the back. A white stripe runs along the upper jaw. The back is gray to brown, with some darker spots. Unlike our other members of this family, the Mexican White-lipped Frog lays its eggs in a frothy substance secreted with them, usually near water under a stone or clump of grass roots, and after the heavy rains of May or June. The eggs hatch very quickly, in less than two days, and in about thirty days the tadpoles metamorphose. Adults may reach 2 inches. This frog is found from the Lower Rio Grande Valley in Texas southward to Panama.

Fig. 39. Mexican White-lipped Frog, *Leptodactylus labialis*

Crocodilians

Fig. 40. American Crocodile, *Crocodylus acutus*

Crocodilians

FAMILY CROCODYLIDAE

It is surely unnecessary to define the family of the Crocodiles and Alligators, since there is nothing they can be confused with except some of the very large lizards which do not occur in the United States. They differ from lizards in having the vent, the posterior opening of the digestive tract, a longitudinal slit, while in lizards it is a transverse slit. Only two of these huge reptiles are native to the United States, although young of other species are often imported and sold as "baby alligators."

American Crocodile, *Crocodylus acutus* (Figure 40)

The American Crocodile can be told from the Alligator by its more slender, pointed snout and by the fact that the fourth tooth from the front of the lower jaw fits outside the upper jaw so that it can be seen when the mouth is closed. It is not true that there is a difference in the way the jaws are hinged in the Alligators and Crocodiles. Crocodiles tend to be somewhat lighter in color than Alligators.

The distribution of the Crocodile is very limited in the United States; at the present time it is confined to the Everglades National Park region in south Florida and perhaps adjacent areas around the Keys. It ranges south through the Greater Antilles and southern Mexico into northern South America.

American Alligator, *Alligator mississippiensis* (Plate 5e)

The Alligator can be told from the Crocodile by the broad, blunt snout and by the fourth tooth from the front of the lower jaw, which lies inside the closed mouth, rather than outside, as it does in the Crocodile. In the United States, Alligators grow larger than Crocodiles. Adults usually range from 6 to 12 feet in length, but the maximum is more than 19 feet. The largest recorded specimen of Crocodile from the United States was 15 feet. (They may exceed 20 feet in South America.)

The Alligator is rather widely distributed in the southeastern states, although it is quite scarce in many parts of its range at the present time. Where it is protected it has become fairly common again and, if overprotected, may grow bold and irascible. In public springs, lakes, and rivers where people swim the alligators have to be removed from time to time, because they may attack humans. The Alligator is found in the coastal plain from about the region of Cape Hatteras, North Carolina, southward throughout Florida and westward to the southern tip of Texas.

Turtles

ANATOMICAL PARTS OF THE TURTLE

A. View of turtle with smooth jaws.

B. View of turtle with cusps on jaws.

C. View of carapace of turtle showing (c) central laminae, (l) lateral laminae, (m) marginal laminae, (x) precentral, and (y) postcentrals.

D. View of plastron of turtle showing (g) gular laminae, (h) humeral laminae, (p) pectoral laminae, (a) abdominal laminae, (f) femoral laminae, and (an) anal laminae.

E. Dorsal view of head of Sea Turtle with two pairs of scales between the eyes.

F. Dorsal view of head of Sea Turtle with a single pair of scales between the eyes.

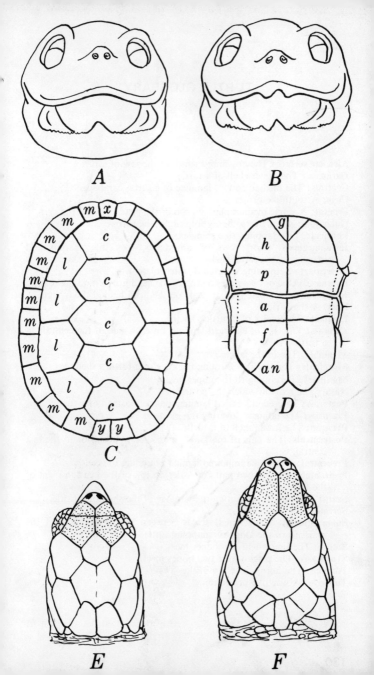

A

B

C

D

E

F

TURTLE GLOSSARY

Alveolar surface: The crushing surface of the jaw of a turtle.
Carapace: The upper shell of a turtle.
Centrals: The median row of laminae of a turtle carapace.
Cusp: A toothlike projection.
Frontal: A single median plate on top of the head between the eyes.
Gular fold: A transverse fleshy fold under the throat.
Imbricate: Overlapping, like shingles.
Inframarginals: Short rows of laminae between the plastrals and marginals in a turtle shell.
Intercalary: Something inserted or interpolated.
Internasal: One or two scales on top of the head just behind the rostral.
Interparietal: A single median scale on the head behind the frontal.
Keel: A sharp ridge.
Laminae: The scales of a turtle's shell.
Laterals: The row of enlarged laminae on each side of the centrals in a turtle's shell.
Mandible: The lower jaw.
Marginals: The laminae forming the edge of a turtle's shell.
Maxillary: Pertaining to the upper jaw.
Nasal: The scale in which the nostril lies.
Pectorals: The second paired laminae on the plastron of a turtle.
Plastrals: The laminae covering the plastron.
Plastron: The lower shell of a turtle.
Postcentrals: The pair of marginals immediately posterior to the last central.
Precentral: The single unpaired lamina preceding the centrals.
Prefrontals: One or two pairs of scales on top of the head in front of the frontal.
Seam: The furrow separating the laminae of the shell of a turtle.
Serrate: Saw-toothed.
Submarginals: A few small scales between the marginals and the plastrals of the alligator snapping turtle.
Suture: The line where two bones meet.
Symphysis: The place where two bones meet.
Tomium: The horny covering of the jaws.
Tubercle: A wartlike projection.

Turtles

THERE is never any room for doubt about whether a given animal is a turtle. The shell in which the body is encased is a complete giveaway. The upper shell is called the carapace, the lower shell the plastron. Usually each consists of two parts; an inner series of bony plates is covered by an outer series of horny laminae (sing. lamina). In Softshell Turtles and Leatherbacks, the laminae are lacking, and the shell is covered by a leathery skin. The carapace and plastron are united between the front and hind legs by a bony or ligamentous bridge. The carapace may be rather flat and low, smoothly rounded, or high and arched. There may be one or more sharp ridges running the length of the carapace, which is then said to be keeled. The parts of the plastron may be reduced so that more or less of the soft underparts of the turtle are exposed, or the plastron may form a complete plate covering the underside. In either case the plastron may be crossed from side to side by one or two hinges, dividing it into lobes which are more or less movable on each other. Most turtles can draw the head and legs back into the protection of the shell, but only the Box Turtles, with their hinged plastron, can close up the shell completely.

The individual laminae are given names. Since they may differ in number and shape from species to species, and since these differences may be helpful in identification, the typical laminae of a carapace and plastron are illustrated here. The laminae do not correspond to the underlying bony plates, so do not try to use them to identify a bony shell picked up in the woods.

In measuring the length of a turtle, it is customary to measure only the length of the carapace. This is a straight-line measurement, not over the curve of the shell. In comparing the size of your specimen with the figures given here, do not include the head and tail.

All turtles lack teeth. Instead, the jaws are covered with a sharp-edged horny sheath. The jaws may be smooth-edged or serrate. The upper jaw may have a notch in front, with or without cusps on either side. It may be smoothly rounded, or it may turn down in a decided hook. Inside the cutting edge of the jaw is a more or less flattened, broad, or narrow chewing surface, which may be marked with grooves and ridges. Some turtles have fleshy projections, barbels, on the underside of the chin and throat.

Most turtles are more or less aquatic, but some are terrestrial. Even very aquatic ones may come out of the water to bask in the sun, and in all turtles, without exception, the female must come to land to lay her eggs. Generally she digs a hole, deposits the eggs in it, and then fills up the hole before departing. The young, when they hatch, must dig their way out and, if aquatic, find their way to the water.

You should not have much difficulty deciding what family your turtle belongs to. Identification of species is more difficult. Partly this is due to the enormous amount of variation within the species. In the first place, young turtles are often very different from their parents. They usually have bright, characteristic color patterns which are obscured in the adults, particularly the females. The carapace may be keeled in the young, rounded in the adults. Males and females may differ in pattern, in shell shape, in size of the head, in length of the claws. Even two animals of the same sex and age may differ strikingly in pattern. However, there are not so many different kinds of turtles as there are of snakes and lizards and some of them have very restricted ranges. Locality is a big help in identifying turtles.

SNAPPING TURTLES, FAMILY CHELYDRIDAE

These are large, unpleasant-looking turtles with big heads, chin barbels, and hooked upper jaws. The carapace is keeled, knobby, and saw-toothed behind. The plastron is small, cross-shaped, and loosely joined to the carapace by a narrow bridge. The tail is long and armed with bony tubercles.

Snapping Turtles, Genus *Chelydra*

These large, pugnacious, aquatic turtles are noted both for their tendency to eat everything they can get into their mouths, including young ducklings and game fish, and for their own succulence. The only other turtle in the United States with which they might be confused is the Alligator Snapping Turtle, from which they can be distinguished by the position of the eyes. In *Chelydra* the eyes can be seen from directly above the head, in the Alligator Snapping Turtle the top of the head is flat, and the eyes are on the side of the head so that they are not visible from directly above. There are two species of Snapping Turtles in the United States.

Common Snapping Turtle, *Chelydra serpentina* (Plate 5f)

This large, ugly, belligerent turtle differs from its near relative, the Florida Snapping Turtle, in having the upper side of the neck thickly dotted with round, wartlike tubercles; in the Florida Snapping Turtle the tubercles on the upper side of the neck are long and pointed. There are characters in the skeleton that readily separate the two species, but they are difficult to tell apart in life, and if there is doubt, range should be considered. Large adults probably average about 30 pounds, though occasional specimens may more than double this. Probably about 70 pounds is the maximum ever reached by an individual in nature. The maximum length recorded is $18\frac{1}{2}$ inches.

Mating occurs from early summer to late fall, and the number of eggs in a clutch ranges from eight to more than thirty. The eggs hatch in about eighty to ninety days. Unlike most other aquatic turtles, Snapping Turtles seldom bask in the sun; usually they lie quietly under water or with just the tip of the snout protruding. Occasionally, though, they wander out on land.

The Common Snapping Turtle ranges from southern Canada southward throughout the eastern United States to north Florida, west to Montana, and south through eastern Wyoming, Colorado, and New Mexico through most of Texas except the Trans–Pecos region and extreme southern Texas.

Florida Snapping Turtle, *Chelydra osceola*

This species is very similar to the preceding in general appearance. Living specimens are best distinguished by the shape of the tubercles on the back of the neck; they are spiny in the Florida Snapping Turtle, rounded and wartlike in the Common Snapping Turtle. The Florida species does not seem to be too different from its northern relative in size, although probably an occasional specimen may be somewhat larger. In general habits and behavior the two are very similar, but the Florida Snapping Turtle is not as favored as an item of food, as is the Common Snapping Turtle. It is very seldom eaten by Floridians and has never appeared in the markets as the Common Snapping Turtle does in some places in the North.

The Florida Snapping Turtle ranges from north Florida southward throughout the peninsula.

Alligator Snapping Turtle, *Macrochelys temmincki*
(Plate 6a)

This is a very large turtle of the rivers of the Southern states. Its large size, the presence on the carapace of three sharply elevated longitudinal keels, the flatness of the top of the head, and the fact that the eyes cannot be seen from above will distinguish it from the Snapping Turtles. The actual maximum size of this turtle is not known, but it probably reaches a length of 26 inches and a weight of 200 pounds; a specimen of over 400 pounds has been reported, but this figure seems dubious.

This enormous turtle rests on the bottom of a stream and feeds by leaving its mouth open and waving a little pink "bait" on its tongue. When fish and other animals misguidedly approach the wiggling "bait," perhaps under the delusion that it is a succulent worm, the Alligator Snapping Turtle simply closes down on its prey. This bait fishing is not the only method of feeding apparently, for an Alligator Snapping Turtle will approach a baited hook resting on the bottom along the edge of a stream at night.

These turtles seem to be restricted to rivers and to bodies of water, such as oxbows, canals, and dead lakes, that were once connected with rivers. Almost nothing is known of the breeding habits in nature; however, they have been observed breeding in captivity, and the females have been seen digging their nests and depositing eggs. The number of eggs ranges from a little over a dozen to four dozen. They are laid in early summer, and the young appear in fall.

Alligator Snapping Turtles are found in large streams entering the Gulf of Mexico, from the Suwannee River drainage of Florida westward through southern Georgia, Alabama, and most of Mississippi, northward in the Mississippi basin through western Tennessee and Kentucky to southern Illinois and Indiana, westward to southeastern Kansas, and south through much of eastern Texas.

MUD AND MUSK TURTLES, FAMILY KINOSTERNIDAE

The Mud and Musk Turtles are much smaller than the Snapping Turtles, the largest hardly reaching 6 inches in length. The carapace is long and smooth; it may have longitudinal keels but is not knobby nor markedly saw-toothed behind. There are eleven marginal laminae on each side (most other turtles have twelve) and ten or eleven laminae on the hinged plastron. There are barbels on the under side of the chin.

Mud Turtles, Genus *Kinosternon*

These small aquatic turtles look a good bit like baby snappers, from which they can be told by their short tails and by the nearly smooth, rather than strongly saw-toothed, rear edge of the carapace. They differ from the similar and closely related Musk Turtles in having a larger, more complete plastron which covers more of the undersurface of the soft parts of the body. The plastron has two hinges (not evident in the babies), and the front lobe is more movable than in the Musk Turtles. The pectoral laminae on the anterior lobe of the plastron are nearly triangular in shape, without a well-developed inner edge (in the Musk Turtles the pectoral laminae are more rectangular and have well-developed median margins).

These small turtles are quite aquatic and rather inconspicuous. Since they are of no economic value and are not eaten as food, they are probably best known to fishermen, for they will take worms or other bait and, when caught, are quite difficult to take from the hook. There are five species in the United States.

Striped Mud Turtle, *Kinosternon bauri*

This turtle, which measures 3 to 4 inches in carapace length, is one of the smallest found in the United States and indeed anywhere in the world. It can be recognized by the presence of three longitudinal light lines down the back and two light stripes on either side of the head. It is the least aquatic of all the Mud Turtles; it is not at all uncommon to find one on land, particularly in wet meadows or under moist debris. Striped Mud Turtles also tend to be less pugnacious than most Mud Turtles. There are two races of this species.

Key Mud Turtle, *Kinosternon b. bauri*

This race, which is found only on the lower Florida Keys, is darker and has less striping on the chin.

Striped Mud Turtle, *Kinosternon b. palmarum*

The chin is more heavily streaked below, and the general color is lighter in the Striped Mud Turtle of the upper Keys and peninsular Florida.

Yellow Mud Turtle, *Kinosternon flavescens*

The Yellow Mud Turtle has both the ninth and the tenth marginal laminae higher than the other marginals. It is larger than the Striped Mud Turtle, adults being about 4 to 5 inches in length.

This Mud Turtle seems to prefer ponds and certainly the Illinois race is practically restricted to ponds. As with most Mud Turtles, its life history is poorly known. Like the others, it presumably lays very few eggs—probably two is the normal complement for this species. There are three races of the Yellow Mud Turtle.

Yellow Mud Turtle, *Kinosternon f. flavescens*

Yellow coloring on the chin and throat mark this southwestern race which ranges from southern Nebraska and southeastern Colorado through most of Kansas and Oklahoma, central and western Texas, eastern and southwestern New Mexico, and into southern Arizona.

Illinois Mud Turtle, *Kinosternon f. spooneri*

Darker than the southwestern race and with the yellow under the chin restricted to the barbels and front half of the lower jaw, this isolated race is found in ponds of western Illinois and adjacent Iowa and Missouri.

Stejneger's Mud Turtle, *Kinosternon f. stejnegeri*

This Mexican race has been reported in the United States only from extreme southern Arizona.

Mexican Mud Turtle, *Kinosternon hirtipes murrayi*

This Mud Turtle can be told from all except the Sonora Mud Turtle by the lack of light lines down the back and by the fact that the tenth marginal lamina is much higher than the ninth. It differs from the Sonora Mud Turtle in having a light line running from the angle of the jaw to the region of the ear. Adults are from 5 to 6 inches in length. Two races of this species are known, but only one extends into the United States in western Texas and southern Arizona.

Sonora Mud Turtle, *Kinosternon sonoriense*

This is the common Mud Turtle of the Mexican–United States border. It differs from all other United States Mud Turtles in having the tenth marginal lamina higher than the ninth and in lacking a light line from the angle of the jaw to the ear. Adults range from 4 to 6½ inches in shell length. As with most Mud Turtles, its life history is poorly known.

The Sonora Mud Turtle ranges from southwestern Texas through southern New Mexico and Arizona into southeastern California east of the San Fernando Mountains. It also occurs in adjacent states of Mexico.

Common Mud Turtle, *Kinosternon subrubrum*

This is the common Mud Turtle of the eastern United States. It can be told from the other Mud Turtles of this region by the fact that neither the ninth nor the tenth marginal lamina is higher than the others and by the absence of three longitudinal light lines down the back. The largest specimens approach 5 inches in length, although most adults are 3 to 4 inches. They are a little smaller than Yellow Mud Turtles and a little larger than striped Mud Turtles.

This species occupies both large and small bodies of still or running water. It is commonly found in ditches where there is a great deal of aquatic vegetation and sometimes it comes out on land. Its life history is better known than that of most Mud Turtles. In the North, Common Mud Turtles hibernate in mud and rotten wood from November to early April. Apparently the southern races do not hibernate. Eggs are laid throughout the spring months although some individuals may nest in late summer or early autumn. The number of eggs is small (as in most Mud Turtles) ranging from two to five. They hatch in late summer or early autumn. Apparently this turtle will eat any small item of animal food it can get—insects, other soft-bodied invertebrates, and vertebrates small enough for it to handle.

There are three races of this species.

Eastern Mud Turtle, *Kinosternon s. subrubrum*

The Eastern Mud Turtle lacks light stripes on the sides of the head. It ranges from southern New York and western Connecticut southward to northern Florida, then westward to Mississippi and northward in the Mississippi Basin to the southern tip of Lake Michigan in Indiana and Illinois.

Mississippi Mud Turtle, *Kinosternon s. hippocrepis*

Two light stripes on the side of the head separate this race from the Eastern Mud Turtle. It is found in the Mississippi Valley, for the most part west of the Mississippi River. It occurs from southern Alabama and southern and western Mississippi northward into southern Missouri, westward into eastern Oklahoma and eastern Texas and southward along the Gulf coast.

Florida Mud Turtle, *Kinosternon s. steindachneri*

This race has the smallest plastron of any Mud Turtle. It occupies practically all the peninsula of Florida.

Musk Turtles, Genus *Sternothaerus*

These small turtles are related to the Mud Turtles and are very similar to them in many ways. They can be told from the Mud Turtles by the pectoral laminae, which are rectangular or nearly so, rather than triangular, and which meet along the midline with a broad margin, rather than a point. Also, the plastron is smaller, leaving much more of the soft underparts exposed and is crossed by only one hinge. They are small turtles, averaging around 3 or 4 inches in length; the Flattened Musk Turtle has the smallest reported maximum length of any turtle known from the United States. Their name is derived from the foul-smelling glandular material they secrete when captured.

Musk Turtles are among the most aquatic of all North American turtles. They are often aggravating to fishermen, for they take a worm on a baited hook readily and it is extremely difficult to release a hooked specimen. They apparently eat any kind of animal food they are capable of handling and can find along the bottom of the waters in which they live. They are essentially bottom crawlers, although they do bask in the sun. Some of the species are quite capable climbers and can be seen sunning on tree limbs well above the water.

There are four species of this group. One of them, the Stinkpot, is easily recognized by the presence of barbels on the underside of the throat, as well as on the underside of the chin. Identification of the other forms is difficult and even the experts do not agree on the limitations of the different species and races. Check the range—it may be your best cue.

Stinkpot, *Sternothaerus odoratus* (Figure 41)

The barbels on the throat as well as on the chin will distinguish the Stinkpot from the other Musk Turtles in its range. Also, it usually has a pair of light stripes, one above and one below the eye, on the side of the head. The Stinkpot is the only Musk Turtle whose life history is at all well known. Mating takes place in the spring and early summer, although some years it may occur in late fall. Egg laying occurs from April to June in Florida while in the North it is later, running from May until August. The hatchlings are found in late fall in the North and late summer in the South. The number of eggs ranges from one to five in each clutch. The Stinkpot is widespread, ranging from central Maine southward throughout Florida and westward into southern Wisconsin, Illinois, Missouri, southeastern Kansas, eastern Oklahoma, and eastern and central Texas.

Fig. 41. Stinkpot, *Sternothaerus odoratus*

Fig. 42. Loggerhead Musk Turtle, *Sternothaerus m. minor*

Keel-backed Musk Turtle, *Sternothaerus carinatus*

This Musk Turtle has a sharp keel down the middle of the back. (Juveniles of other forms may also have keels.) The sides of the carapace are rather steep-sloped from the keel to the marginal laminae. In general, this turtle is more brightly colored than the Stinkpot, ranging from light-tan or orangish to dark-brown or blackish-brown in large old adults. The head is marked with light spots on a dark background. The gular lamina is absent. The Keel-backed Musk Turtle is found in Louisiana, western Mississippi, southern Arkansas, southeastern Oklahoma, and eastern Texas.

Loggerhead Musk Turtle, *Sternothaerus minor*

The gular lamina is usually present in this species. The head is marked with dark spots or stripes on a light background. Young have dorsal keels, but they are not as high as those of the Keel-backed Musk Turtles and in adults the shell is arched, without a keel. There are two races.

Loggerhead Musk Turtle, *Sternothaerus m. minor* (Figure 42)

This race has three dorsal keels (lost in old adults) and dark spots on the head. The head is enormous in old males. The Loggerhead Musk Turtle ranges from the South Carolina–Georgia boundary in the coastal plain southward to central Florida and westward through southern Alabama to the vicinity of Mobile Bay.

Stripe-necked Musk Turtle, *Sternothaerus m. peltifer*

There is only one well-developed dorsal keel, and the sides of the neck are striped in this race. It occurs in western South Carolina, northern Georgia and Alabama, extreme western North Carolina, southeastern Tennessee, and eastern Mississippi.

Flattened Musk Turtle, *Sternothaerus depressus*

This species is rather similar to the Keel-backed Musk Turtle, though as the name indicates it tends to be lower and flatter. The head pattern consists of thin, dark reticulations on a greenish background. A gular lamina is present. The maximum reported length is $4\frac{3}{16}$ inches. The Flattened Musk Turtle is restricted to the Black Warrior drainage of Alabama.

FRESH WATER, MARSH AND BOX TURTLES, FAMILY EMYDIDAE

This is the largest and most varied of the families of turtles. Most of the species are more or less aquatic, but some are terrestrial. They range in size from small (though not so small as the smallest Mud and

Musk Turtles) to large (though not so large as the Snapping Turtles). The plastron is always well developed. It may be unhinged and joined to the carapace by a bony bridge or have a single hinge and be joined to the carapace by ligaments. There are twelve plastral laminae. The feet are neither elephantine nor paddle-shaped and the toes are more or less webbed.

Pond Turtles, Genus *Clemmys*

Pond Turtles are mostly small turtles; the plastron is a single plate, not hinged, and is firmly joined to the carapace. The neck is not unusually long for a turtle, and there is no central ridge along the crushing surface of the upper jaw. It is difficult to differentiate the entire group from all other groups of turtles, but most of our individual species are rather easy to separate from other turtles found within their ranges. Some Pond Turtles are aquatic; others are quite terrestrial; and indeed the Wood Turtle of the northeastern States is the most terrestrial turtle of the United States except the Box Turtles and the Gopher Tortoises. There are three species in the eastern United States and one in the West.

Spotted Turtle, *Clemmys guttata*

This little turtle can be recognized by the scattered, round, distinct yellow spots on the dark-brown or black laminae of the back. Rarely, the spots are lacking from the carapace, but even then they can generally be seen around the head and neck. It is small, less than 5 inches, and smooth-shelled, with no strong keel down the back.

The female lays from one to four eggs in early summer, and hatchlings have been found in early fall. Spotted Turtles show a strong tendency to be carnivorous but will occasionally eat vegetable matter. Like most of the Pond Turtles, they make nice pets provided they are furnished with both a place to hide in the water and a place to crawl around and hide on land.

The Spotted Turtle is found in the eastern United States from southern Maine along the east coast southward to Georgia, east of the mountains and westward through Pennsylvania and New York into northern Ohio, Indiana, southern Michigan, and southern Canada. In the southern part of its range it is restricted to the Atlantic coastal plain.

Wood Turtle, *Clemmys insculpta* (Plate 6b)

This keeled, rough shelled turtle is the largest of the Pond Turtles, reaching a carapace length of about 9 inches. It can be told from the Spotted Turtle by the absence of round, bright-yellow spots on the carapace and from the Bog Turtle by its larger size and by the absence of bright-orange blotches on the sides of the head, though the throat and legs are frequently marked with orange. It is the most terrestrial of the turtles in the northeastern states, with the exception of the Box Turtles; it differs from them in lacking a hinge on the plastron.

From four to twelve eggs are deposited in June, and hatchlings may be found in late September and October. Wood Turtles are omnivorous and are easy to keep in captivity since they will feed on all sorts of vegetable matter such as melon rinds, lettuce, and spinach.

The Wood Turtle ranges from extreme southeastern Canada southward through Maine into northern Maryland and West Virginia, westward through most of Pennsylvania and in the lake region in the northern half of Michigan, including all of the Upper Peninsula, northern Wisconsin, southeastern Minnesota, and extreme northeastern Iowa.

Bog Turtle, *Clemmys muhlenbergi*

This is the smallest of the Pond Turtles, not exceeding 4¼ inches in length. Like the Wood Turtle it is brownish and has a rough shell with a keel down the back which will at once distinguish it from the smooth-shelled Spotted Turtle. It can be told from a small Wood Turtle by the bright-orange (sometimes yellow) blotch on each side of the head.

Very little is known of the habits of this turtle. It has a rather spotty distribution and may be extremely abundant in some places and extremely rare in others. Its disjunct distribution suggests that it once occupied a wider range and may now be on the way to extinction. Isolated populations are known in New York, northwestern Pennsylvania, a region through southern New York, New Jersey, Maryland, southeastern Pennsylvania and Virginia, and in an area in western North Carolina and eastern Tennessee.

Western Pond Turtle, *Clemmys marmorata*

The Pacific Coast representative of the Pond Turtles has a low, wide, nearly smooth shell. It is usually dark above, the laminae often marked with spots, dashes, or a network of fine lines. It is moderate in size for a Pond Turtle, individuals seldom exceeding 7 inches in length.

Western Pond Turtles are very aquatic; they are found most often in ponds but are also sometimes seen in streams and rivers and have occasionally been taken in brackish water. Like many turtles, they eat both plant and animal food and can be taken on a baited hook. The female lays from 5 to 11 eggs in a pit dug in a sandy bank or open slope above a stream or pond. Two races of this species are known.

Northwestern Pond Turtle, *Clemmys m. marmorata*

The throat is usually lighter than the sides of the head in this race. It occurs from southwestern British Columbia to the San Francisco Bay area, where it intergrades with the southwestern form. It has also been reported from extreme western Nevada.

Southwestern Pond Turtle, *Clemmys m. pallida*

The throat and sides of the head are about the same color. This race ranges southward from the Monterey Bay area into Lower California.

Blanding's Turtle, *Emydoidea blandingi* (Plate 6c)

Blanding's Turtle has a hinged plastron like the Box Turtles but cannot close its shell completely. There is a notch at the tip of the upper jaw. The chin and throat are bright-yellow and the adults have many small light spots and streaks on the carapace. The only other turtle with light spots on the back found in the range of Blanding's Turtle is the Spotted Turtle but in that species the spots are larger and round, not streaked. Also, the Spotted Turtle lacks the hinged plastron. Blanding's Turtle has an elongated shell and may reach a length of over 10 inches.

This turtle is rather aquatic but does come out on land to wander and bask from time to time. From 6 to 12 eggs are laid in June and July, and hatchlings have been found in late September. Blanding's Turtle apparently feeds on practically anything it can get.

The range of this turtle, like that of the Bog Turtle, is discontinuous at the present time. Isolated populations are found in Massachusetts and New Hampshire, while the main population is found in southern Canada, Michigan, extreme northern Ohio and Indiana, northern Illinois, Wisconsin, eastern Minnesota, eastern South Dakota, Iowa, and eastern Nebraska.

Box Turtles, Genus *Terrapene*

Every country child in the eastern and central United States knows the Box Turtle, so called because the hinge across the plastron allows the shell to be closed up into a tight box (except in very young or very fat individuals). None of our other turtles are able to withdraw so completely from the world. The upper jaw ends in a down-turned hook.

Box Turtles make charming pets, clean, gentle, and easy to feed, for they will eat almost anything. In nature the adults are probably largely vegetarians, and some of them have even been known to eat the poisonous toadstool, *Amanita*, with impunity. Box Turtles are found only in North America; there are two rather closely related species in our area.

Box Turtle, *Terrapene carolina*

The Box Turtles of the eastern United States are basically woodland animals. They seldom enter water but are apt to be found stalking gravely through open wooded areas. They differ from the Western Box Turtles in having a higher, more domed shell, with at least some trace of a median keel on the back. The pattern of the plastron is rather pale or even lacking.

The Gulf Coast race of this species is the largest of our Box Turtles, attaining a maximum shell length of about 7 inches.

These turtles nest in June and July, laying from two to seven eggs, and hatchlings may be found in early fall, although many times the hatchlings do not emerge in the fall but apparently stay in the nest until the next spring.

There are four subspecies of this turtle.

Eastern Box Turtle, *Terrapene c. carolina* (Plate 6d)

The rear margin of the carapace extends almost straight downward (flares outward in other races). This is the common Box Turtle of the eastern United States, ranging from southern Maine to extreme northern Florida and westward through northern Alabama and Mississippi in the South and to Illinois and southern Michigan in the North.

Florida Box Turtle, *Terrapene c. bauri* (Figure 43)

There are two yellow stripes on the side of the head in this Box Turtle. It occupies practically all peninsular Florida except the Glades areas in southern Florida.

Gulf Coast Box Turtle, *Terrapene c. major*

With its maximum shell length of about 7 inches, this is the largest of the Box Turtles. It is restricted to a narrow strip along the Gulf coast from the Suwannee River region of Florida westward through southern Alabama, Louisiana, and southeastern Texas.

Three-toed Box Turtle, *Terrapene c. triunguis*

In spite of the name, don't rely on the number of toes on the hind foot. It may have four, or a member of one of the other races may have three. The shell is narrow, keeled, and flaring behind, and there are usually bright-orange or yellow spots on the head and neck. It is found north of the range of the Gulf Coast Box Turtle, extending from extreme southwestern Georgia through southern Alabama, most of Mississippi, northern Louisiana, eastern Texas, eastern Oklahoma, eastern Kansas, all of Arkansas, and most of Missouri.

Western Box Turtle, *Terrapene ornata*

Western Box Turtles differ from their Eastern relatives in having a lower, less domed carapace without a trace of a median keel. The ground color of the plastron is usually dark, and there is a bright conspicuous pattern of light lines and vermiculations. Maximum size is about $5\frac{3}{4}$ inches. Western Box Turtles are typically animals of the open prairies although they may also occur in woods and swamps.

There are two races recognized in this species.

Fig. 43. Florida Box Turtle, *Terrapene c. bauri*

Fig. 44. Mississippi Map Turtle, *Malaclemys kohni*

Ornate Box Turtle, *Terrapene o. ornata*

The bright pattern shows on both carapace and plastron. The range of this form overlaps that of the Box Turtles of the eastern United States. It is found from the Gulf Coast of Texas and western Louisiana, northward into southern South Dakota, eastward to Illinois and western Indiana, and westward through eastern New Mexico, Colorado, and southeastern Wyoming.

Salt Basin Box Turtle, *Terrapene o. luteola*

The pattern on the carapace is obscure in this race, which is found in the extreme southwestern United States in the Trans–Pecos region of Texas, southern New Mexico, and extreme southeastern Arizona and ranges into northern Mexico.

Chicken Turtle, *Deirochelys reticularia*

The Chicken Turtle has a long, narrow shell, narrow vertical stripes on the hind legs, and a single broad yellow stripe down the front of each foreleg. Its most characteristic feature, though, is its long, striped neck, which is about as long as the plastron. This moderate-sized (up to 10 inches but most are smaller), hard-shelled pond turtle is commonly seen basking on logs over water in the southeastern United States. The lack of red in the pattern will distinguish it from the Painted Turtles, and its smaller size, more elongated body, and the single broad yellow stripe on each front leg will separate it from the Cooters and Sliders. Frequently, when it basks, it stretches its long, striped neck out to the fullest extent, and then it is unmistakable. It occurs in all sorts of still water and frequently wanders out on land. Some people esteem it as food, but to most of us the small amount of meat is not worth the effort it takes to dress one out.

There are three rather well-marked races of this turtle.

Eastern Chicken Turtle, *Deirochelys r. reticularia* (Plate 6e)

The network pattern on the carapace is formed of narrow, greenish, or brownish lines. This form ranges along the coastal plain from North Carolina south of Cape Hatteras to north Florida and westward along the Gulf Coast to eastern Louisiana.

Florida Chicken Turtle, *Deirochelys r. chrysea*

This peninsular Florida race has the netlike pattern of the carapace formed of broader yellow or orange lines.

Western Chicken Turtle, *Deirochelys r. miaria*

The carapace pattern is only a little lighter than the ground color in this race, which occurs west of the Mississippi in Louisiana and eastern Texas, ranging northward into Arkansas and southeastern Oklahoma.

Diamondback Terrapins, Map Turtles, and Sawbacks, Genus *Malaclemys*

These turtles have a well-developed but unhinged plastron and a dorsal keel which may be ornamented with knobs or spines. The neck is not conspicuously long as it is in the Chicken Turtle. The crushing surface of the upper jaw is broad and smooth, without a well-marked ridge down the center. The toes are webbed beyond the base of the claws. There are ten species in the genus, all found in the United States.

Diamondback Terrapin, *Malaclemys terrapin* (Plate 6f)

This turtle is the epicure's delight, the famous terrapin from which terrapin soup is made. It is a rather small turtle, the largest females running about 9 inches in carapace length, the largest males about 5 inches, a disparity in size that is characteristic of the genus. The carapace of the Diamondback Terrapin usually appears bumpy, and the laminae of the back are typically marked with concentric rings. Terrapins can generally be told from Map Turtles and Sawbacks by the hind edge of the shell which tends to curl upward rather than flare outward. Also, the side of the neck generally has a light background with dark markings rather than a dark background with light markings. Perhaps one of the best ways to identify this turtle is by its habitat, since it is found in brackish or salt water in coastal marshes, while the other turtles with which it might be confused are freshwater or terrestrial forms.

The Terrapin, living as it does in salt marshes, feeds largely on crustaceans and molluscs but will occasionally eat plant food and in captivity thrives on cut fish. Because of the tremendous economic importance of this species, its life history has been studied in great detail. The eggs are laid in May and June and number about five to twelve in a clutch. They are deposited in nests that are dug in sand in rather open areas. The young hatch and emerge in the fall of the year.

Seven races of this species are now recognized, but there is a good bit of overlap between the characters of the different forms. Geography is safer than structure if you wish to give a subspecific name to your specimen.

Northern Diamondback Terrapin, *Malaclemys t. terrapin*

Seen from above, the carapace looks wedge-shaped in this northern race, which is found from Cape Cod southward to the Cape Hatteras region.

Carolina Diamondback Terrapin, *Malaclemys t. centrata*

The carapace is more oval in this race. It ranges from the Cape Hatteras region of North Carolina along the coast to about the St. Johns River region of Florida.

Florida East Coast Terrapin, *Malaclemys t. tequesta*

The carapace is dark or horn-colored, the pattern not well marked. This race is found along the east coast of Florida from about the mouth of the St. Johns river southward to below Miami.

Mangrove Terrapin, *Malaclemys t. rhizophorarum*

The neck appears streaked in this race of the mangrove swamps of extreme southern Florida and the Keys.

Ornate Diamondback Terrapin, *Malaclemys t. macrospilota*

The centers of the large laminae of the carapace are orange or yellow in the Diamondback of the west coast of Florida. It ranges from southern Florida westward nearly to the Pensacola region.

Mississippi Diamondback Terrapin, *Malaclemys t. pileata*

This large dark form is found along the coastal region from extreme western Florida to about the Louisiana–Texas boundary.

Texas Diamondback Terrapin, *Malaclemys t. littoralis*

The plastron is lighter and the shell higher than in the Mississippi race. The Texas Terrapin ranges from about the Louisiana–Texas border on the coast southward probably into northern Mexico.

The other species of *Malaclemys* were formerly set off from the Diamondback Terrapins as the genus *Graptemys*. Structurally they are very close to the Diamondback Terrapins. The posterior margin of the carapace flares out rather than curls up as it does in the Terrapins, and the ground color of the side of the neck is generally dark with light markings rather than light with dark markings. Map Turtles and Sawbacks do differ markedly from the Terrapins in habitat preference; they are essentially turtles of deep rivers and lakes connected with rivers rather than coastal tidal marshes.

Like the Diamondbacks, these turtles are especially fond of crayfish, snails, and clams, although they will eat other kinds of animal food, sometimes even carrion. They are very aquatic, for the most part staying in the water. They will come out on logs or on shore to bask, but when they do, they are apt to be nervous and generally quite wary, slipping back into the water at the first hint of disturbance. As with the Terrapins, there is a marked disparity in size between the sexes, the males being much smaller than the females. Because they live in deep, often rocky and tree-and-log-cluttered rivers, we know little about the habits of many of them. The life history of the Map Turtle is probably typical for the group. The females lay the eggs from May to June in sandy areas, sometimes as much as a hundred yards from water, and the young hatch in August and September. In regions where they hibernate, the Map Turtles, like other members of the genus, seem to be among the first to come out of hibernation in the spring and among the last to go in the fall.

It is impossible in a book of this size to diagnose adequately all the various species in this group; here, as has been true so many times, geographic distribution should be taken into consideration, since many of these species are restricted to narrow ranges, sometimes to a single river system.

Map Turtle, *Malaclemys geographica*

The Map Turtle is one of the widely distributed species of the group. The young are easy to recognize—the pattern on the back looks like a map of canals and drainage systems—but the dorsal pattern of the adults is obscure. The shell is rather low and flattened, with a central keel. The large head is marked with narrow yellow lines, and there is a triangular yellow patch behind each eye, separated from it by several of the narrow lines. Females may reach 10¾ inches, males are little more than half as big.

The Map Turtle ranges through the north central states from southern Wisconsin and eastern Minnesota southward to Arkansas, northeastern Oklahoma, eastern Kansas, into northern Alabama, through much of Tennessee and Kentucky and northeastward through Ohio, extreme northwestern Pennsylvania to the northern border of New York and into southern Canada. There is an isolated population in south central Pennsylvania.

Barbour's Map Turtle, *Malaclemys barbouri*

This and the following species are very similar. In both the yellow marking on the head are more extensive than in the Map Turtle. The heads of the females are enormous. Light markings on the marginals are narrow in Barbour's Map Turtle, broad in the Alabama Map Turtle. The safest way to identify them is by range. This is a Gulf Coast turtle with a restricted distribution in streams that flow into the Gulf of Mexico from the Florida panhandle and adjacent Georgia and Alabama, from the Apalachicola River westward to the Escambia River.

Alabama Map Turtle, *Malaclemys pulchra*

Both in size and appearance this turtle is very like Barbour's Map Turtle. Adult females reach 8½ inches, males 5 inches. A longitudinal light bar runs back from the point of the chin in the Alabama Map Turtle, across the chin in Barbour's Map Turtle. This turtle ranges from the Escambia River system of extreme western Florida, westward through the Pearl River system of Louisiana.

Mississippi Map Turtle, *Malaclemys kohni* (Figure 44

A yellow crescent behind the eye swings forward under the eye and separates the narrow head stripes from the eye. The claws on the front feet of adult males are very large. This species is found in the western Mississippi River basin from southern Louisiana and eastern Texas northward through Missouri to Illinois, southern Nebraska, eastern Kansas, and Oklahoma.

False Map Turtle, *Malaclemys pseudogeographica*

One or more of the yellow head stripes reach the eye. The claws of the adult males are very long. This wide-ranging species is divided into three races.

False Map Turtle, *Malaclemys p. pseudogeographica* (Figure 45)

The False Map Turtle lacks enlarged light spots on the lower jaw. It occurs in southern Wisconsin and southeastern Minnesota. Southward it intergrades extensively with the Ouachita Map Turtle through Illinois, southern Indiana, and northern Missouri to eastern Nebraska.

Ouachita Map Turtle, *Malaclemys p. ouachitensis*

There is a squarish light spot behind the eye, a smaller spot below the eye and another on the chin. This form ranges from the Ohio River drainage in West Virginia and Ohio westward through eastern Kansas and Oklahoma and south into northeastern Texas and northwestern Louisiana. To the north it intergrades through a wide area with the False Map Turtle.

Sabine Map Turtle, *Malaclemys p. sabinensis*

The light spot behind the eye is rounder. This race is restricted to the Sabine River system in Texas and western Louisiana.

Texas Map Turtle, *Malaclemys versa*

This species is smaller than the other Map Turtles. Adult females may reach 5 inches, males $3\frac{1}{2}$. The laminae of the carapace tend to be humped up in the center. This species is restricted to the Colorado River system in Texas.

The next three species are all spiny, markedly so in the young, less so in large females.

Ringed Sawback, *Malaclemys oculifer*

This species is larger than the Texas Map Turtle, approaching the Alabama Map Turtle in size. There are broad light rings on the dorsal laminae. The Ringed Sawback is restricted to the Pearl River drainage in Mississippi and Louisiana.

Yellow-blotched Sawback, *Malaclemys flavimaculata*

As the name indicates, the light markings are more like blotches than rings. It is smaller than the Ringed Sawback. This is the Sawback of the Pascagoula River system in Mississippi.

Fig. 45. False Map Turtle, *Malaclemys p. pseudogeographica*

Fig. 46. Peninsula Cooter, *Chrysemys f. peninsularis*

Black-knobbed Sawback, *Malaclemys nigrinoda*

The spines are flattened, the rings on the carapace narrow. It is found in the Alabama–Tombigbee–Black Warrior River system in Alabama.

Painted Turtles, Cooters and Sliders, Genus *Chrysemys*

These are the rather small to large, hard-shelled turtles most often seen basking on logs in waters throughout most of the United States. The carapace is smooth or wrinkled but not knobby, the plastron well-developed but without a hinge. The crushing surface of the upper jaw has a ridge down the middle. These turtles lack the long, striped neck of the Chicken Turtle. Adult males have very long claws on the front feet and are smaller, often very much so, than the females. There are eight species recognized in the genus *Chrysemys*, and some of them break up into a number of races. To further confuse things, there is not only a good bit of intergradation between races but hybridization between species. There is also a good bit of variation within each species, between individuals, between the sexes, and between young and adults. Once again geography may be the most helpful cue to identification. The genus is divided into several groups. The first has only one species.

Painted Turtle, *Chrysemys picta*

These are pretty little turtles with bright-yellow or red markings, especially in the young. Smaller than the cooters and sliders, they average about 5 inches, though the Western race is somewhat larger. The hind edge of the carapace is smoothly rounded, not saw-toothed.

Painted Turtles are quiet water turtles, feeding on all sorts of animal and plant material. Egg laying takes place from May to July, earlier in the South than in the North. Usually five or six eggs are laid at a time. They hatch in August and September.

The four races of this turtle are well-marked, but intergrades between them are common.

Eastern Painted Turtle, *Chrysemys p. picta*

The light anterior edges of the large, parallel dorsal laminae form lines across the back. There are bright-yellow spots on the head and red markings around the edge of the shell. This race is found from southern Maine southward to North Carolina and west into northern South Carolina, Alabama, and Mississippi.

Western Painted Turtle, *Chrysemys p. belli*

The carapace is marked with light, irregular lines and there is less red around the edge of the shell in the western race. It ranges from western Illinois, Wisconsin, and the Upper Peninsula of Michigan to the Pacific Coast in the region of Vancouver, British Columbia, and on to Vancouver Island. In the eastern part of its range it extends southward to southern Missouri and Kansas, but in the west its range, except for isolated populations, is more northerly. It is widely distributed in Washington, northern Idaho and northern Wyoming. Isolated populations occur in New Mexico, Arizona, Colorado, and Utah.

Southern Painted Turtle, *Chrysemys p. dorsalis*

The edges of the large laminae on the back are not parallel, so the lines formed by their light edges are more irregular than in the Eastern Painted Turtle. There is a red or yellow stripe down the center of the back. This is the race of the lower Mississippi Valley, ranging from southern Louisiana northward into Arkansas and southeastern Missouri and east of the river in Mississippi, northwestern Alabama, western Tennessee, Kentucky, and the extreme southern tip of Illinois.

Midland Painted Turtle, *Chrysemys p. marginata* (Plate 7a)

This looks very like the eastern race, but resembles the southern race in not having the large dorsal laminae in parallel rows. It ranges from western New York southward through western Pennsylvania, West Virginia, Kentucky and into Tennessee, through southern Illinois, Indiana, Ohio, and Michigan into southern Canada.

The members of the next two groups were formerly separated from the Painted Turtles as the genus *Pseudemys*. They are larger than the Painted Turtles, the chewing surface of the jaws is better developed, the carapace frequently saw-toothed behind.

The *scripta* group (Pond Sliders) includes two species in which the chin is rounded below. The upper jaw has a distinct, V-shaped notch in the middle but does not have pronounced cusps on either side. The young are brightly marked, the adults more somber, with the males in particular showing a strong tendency toward melanism. The head is usually marked with a *broad* yellow or red spot or line behind the eye, but this may hardly show in dark-colored adults. The group extends from the United States into northern South America.

Pond Slider, *Chrysemys scripta*

The undersurface of the chin is rounded in the Pond Sliders.

The carapace is generally lower and flatter than in other cooters and sliders (except the Big Bend Turtle), and there is usually a conspicuous red or yellow patch on the side of the head. There are three races in our region.

Yellow-bellied Turtle, *Chrysemys s. scripta*

The yellow is by no means confined to the belly—there is a yellow blotch behind the eye, vertical yellow bars on the carapace, narrow yellow stripes on the legs. These turtles are shorter than the other cooters and sliders, seldom exceeding 8 inches in length, and the bony shell is very thick. Country people in the Southeast call turtles of the *scripta* group Baptists (hard-shelled), while they name other cooters Methodists. Pond Sliders also seem to be more pugnacious than other members of the genus. This race ranges from the Dismal Swamp region of Virginia into northern Florida, intergrading with the next race along the Gulf Coast.

Red-eared Turtle, *Chrysemys s. elegans* (Plate 7b)

The name indicates the broad, reddish stripe behind the eye, but occasionally the stripe is yellowish, or it may be obliterated in the general darkening of the melanistic males. The young are most often seen swimming in tanks in dime stores, for these are the commonest baby turtles of the pet trade. As a result, they have been widely introduced in parts of the country outside the original range. This is a turtle of the Mississippi Basin and western Gulf drainage, broadly distributed from Ohio westward to Iowa and from New Mexico throughout most of Texas east to western Florida and Georgia.

Cumberland Turtle, *Chrysemys s. troosti*

The Cumberland Turtle resembles the Red-eared Turtle but has a narrower yellow stripe behind the eye and broader stripes on the legs. It is restricted to the upper reaches of the Cumberland and Tennessee rivers.

Big Bend Turtle, *Chrysemys gaigeae*

This turtle is very like the Pond Slider. There is a large, round, black-bordered, yellow spot on the side of the head behind the eye. It is found in south and central Texas and adjacent parts of Mexico.

The other five species of *Chrysemys* have the undersurface of the chin flattened instead of rounded. If there is a light line or spot behind the eye, it is narrower than in the pond sliders, not more than a third the width of the eye.

Red-bellied Turtle, *Chrysemys rubiventris*

These are large turtles, sometimes exceeding 15 inches in length. The notch in the upper jaw has a well-marked cusp on either side. There is a light arrow-shaped mark running between the eyes with the tip of the arrow on the snout. The carapace is not highly arched and is usually marked with red, and there is red or orange coloring around the edge of the plastron. There are two races of this species.

Red-bellied Turtle, *Chrysemys r. rubiventris*

This race is found from southern New Jersey and southeastern Pennsylvania south into eastern North Carolina and west to eastern West Virginia.

Plymouth Turtle, *Chrysemys r. bangsi*

This race is now found only in some ponds around Plymouth, Massachusetts, though it was probably once more widely spread.

Florida Red-bellied Turtle, *Chrysemys nelsoni*

This species is very similar to the Red-bellied Turtle, but is slightly smaller and has a higher, more domed shell. There are few stripes on the head, but the arrow-shaped mark is present. Like other members of the group, it is very good to eat. When the population of Diamond-back Terrapins was reduced by overmarketing, Red-bellied Turtles were frequently substituted. This form is found in the ponds and streams of peninsular Florida.

Alabama Red-bellied Turtle, *Chrysemys alabamensis*

Very like the Florida Red-bellied Turtle, but with more numerous head stripes. It occurs along the Gulf Coast from western Florida to Mobile Bay, Alabama.

Cooter, *Chrysemys floridana*

These may grow as large as the Red-bellied Turtles but have a more highly arched shell and lack the arrow-shaped mark on the head and the red markings on the shell. The plastron is usually light-yellow, with few or no dark markings. There are three races.

Florida Cooter, *Chrysemys f. floridana*

This race has a smooth, unnotched upper jaw. There are dark, doughnut-shaped marks on the undersides of the marginals, but the light plastron is usually unmarked. It ranges from the Dismal Swamp region of Virginia southward in the coastal plain to southern Georgia and northern Florida.

Peninsula Cooter, *Chrysemys f. peninsularis* (Figure 46)

The light lines on the head tend to form loops behind the eyes. These herbivorous turtles are found in all sorts of aquatic places, particularly where there is a good deal of vegetation. Eggs may be laid throughout the winter and early spring but most usually are deposited in late spring. The number of eggs in a nest averages around twenty. Probably the number laid at one time by the female depends on how many times she has laid before since most apparently lay at least twice during the year. The eggs hatch in late summer or early fall, apparently regardless of how early they were laid in the spring. This cooter ranges throughout most of peninsular Florida except the extreme northern and southern parts.

Missouri Slider, *Chrysemys f. hoyi*

This race is somewhat smaller than the others, with a short broad shell. The upper jaw has a median notch but no sharp cusps on either side of it. The Missouri Slider ranges from southern Missouri and southeastern Kansas south to the Gulf Coast of central Texas and east to Alabama.

River Cooter, *Chrysemys concinna*

These again are mostly rather large turtles, the largest reaching a maximum length of over 16 inches, though most adults are smaller. The dark markings on the underside are well-developed, and there is a light, C-shaped mark on the second lateral lamina. Five races of this southeastern species are recognized.

River Cooter, *Chrysemys c. concinna*

The River Cooter has a long, narrow, rather depressed shell and a smooth upper jaw without a notch at the tip. The light color of the plastron and the head stripes are yellow or reddish. This is a form of the piedmont rivers, ranging from Virginia southward to northern Georgia and Alabama.

Slider, *Chrysemys c. hieroglyphica*

The shell is rather long, low and narrow, the upper jaw slightly notched but without cusps. This race is found in the central Mississippi Valley from southern Indiana and Illinois through central Alabama, Mississippi, Louisiana, and extreme eastern Texas. It does not reach the Gulf Coast.

Mobile Cooter, *Chrysemys c. mobilensis*

This race has a high, domed shell, and the light markings have an orange cast. It is found along the Gulf Coast from western Florida to extreme eastern Texas.

Suwannee Cooter, *Chrysemys c. suwanniensis*

Also known as the Suwannee River Chicken and a favorite food of many people. It is the largest and darkest of the cooters, but the light stripes on the head are usually pale greenish-yellow. The shell is deep and high. It is found along the Gulf Coast of Florida from the Apalachacola region to Tampa Bay.

Texas Slider, *Chrysemys c. texana*

This is the smallest member of the species, adults rarely exceeding 10 inches in length. The upper jaw has a notch, but no cusps on either side. It occurs in central and southern Texas, southeastern New Mexico and adjacent parts of Mexico.

TORTOISES, FAMILY TESTUDINIDAE

This family includes the most terrestrial of the turtles. The hind legs are columnar, the toes unwebbed. The plastron is well-developed, unhinged, and firmly joined to the carapace.

Gopher Tortoises, Genus *Gopherus*

These dry land tortoises are unmistakable. The hind legs are round and blunt like an elephant's foot; the forelegs are flattened and heavily scaled in front. The laminae of the domed shell are marked with growth rings. Three species of this genus are known, and all of them occur in the United States. They are basically vegetarians, although they will occasionally eat meat. They are all quite similar, but since their ranges do not overlap, their identification should not present any problem.

Desert Tortoise, *Gopherus agassizi*

The head of this turtle is somewhat narrower, and the hind foot somewhat larger than in the other species. Males may reach a length of 14½ inches, females are smaller.

These are the tortoises of the extreme southwestern deserts. They hibernate in winter (at least in the northern part of the range) in large communal dens or crevices on the slopes and in summer move away from the dens to grassy flats where they can forage. There is thus an annual migration between the feeding grounds and the denning area. While on the feeding grounds they dig small burrows in which to escape from extreme heat and drought. From what little is known of the feeding habits of this species, grass seems to be the great staple in the diet.

The Desert Tortoise is found in southwestern Arizona, southeastern California, southern Nevada, and extreme southwestern Utah, as well as adjacent parts of Mexico.

Texas Tortoise, *Gopherus berlandieri* (Plate 7c)

This is the smallest of the three Gopher Tortoises, the maximum length being about 8½ inches. The head is broad, the jaw rather pointed.

These turtles are inhabitants of well-drained sandy soils, and though they sometimes live in quite arid regions, they are not so tolerant of pure desert conditions as the Desert Tortoises. They do not use communal burrows but dig individual tunnels, sometimes of considerable length, in which to retreat from adverse weather conditions. Apparently though they do not really hibernate. Actually very little is known about these tortoises. They have been seen eating the ripe fruits of the cactus (*Opuntia*), but otherwise their diet is unknown.

The Texas Tortoise occurs in southeastern Texas and adjacent parts of Mexico.

Gopher Tortoise, *Gopherus polyphemus* (Figure 47)

This is the familiar Gopher of the southeastern states. It is as large or larger than the Desert Tortoise, with a broader head and smaller hind feet.

The Gopher Tortoise spends much of the time in its burrow but comes out in the early morning and late evening to browse. The piles of excavated dirt that mark the entrances to the long tunnels are familiar sights in sandy ridges from South Carolina to Louisiana. The flesh is delectable, and this tortoise is widely hunted for its meat.

It is found from southern South Carolina through most of Florida except the extreme southern Everglades and westward along the Gulf coast to Louisiana.

SEA TURTLES, FAMILY CHELONIIDAE

There is little chance of mistaking the members of this family. They are large marine turtles with paddle-shaped limbs and with horny laminae on the carapace. They almost never come to shore except to lay eggs.

Loggerhead Turtle, *Caretta caretta*

These large sea turtles can be told at a glance from all except other sea turtles by their front limbs which are modified into swimming flippers. They can easily be told from the Leatherback Turtles, which have the shell covered with a leathery skin, rather than with large, symmetrically placed horny laminae. Loggerhead Turtles have two pairs of prefrontal scales on top of the head and five or more lateral laminae, while the Green Turtles have only one pair of prefrontal scales and only four pairs of lateral laminae. From the somewhat similar Ridleys, the Loggerhead Turtles differ in having only three enlarged inframarginal laminae (separating the marginals from the typical plastral laminae) on each side of the plastron, rather than four. Hawksbill Turtles have only four pairs of lateral laminae. Although there are unverified records of Loggerheads reaching a weight of half a ton or more, about 300 pounds is probably the largest that is caught nowadays.

Loggerheads are confirmed wanderers. They may be encountered in inshore waters, including small bays and streams, as well as out on the high seas as much as 500 miles from shore. It is not an uncommon sight to see one moving about in shallow, warm, coastal waters, occasionally coming to the surface to blow and breathe and then diving and swimming along under water. In the open sea they are sometimes found floating at the surface. The adults feed on various kinds of shellfish. Loggerheads nest on the beaches of the southern United States throughout the summer months. The number of eggs laid by females of the eastern race probably averages close to ten to twelve dozen, and the eggs hatch in from one to two and a half months.

There are two races of the Loggerhead Turtle within our limits. Range alone is enough to identify them.

Fig. 47. Gopher Tortoise, *Gopherus polyphemus*

Fig. 48. Pacific Loggerhead, *Caretta c. gigas*

Atlantic Loggerhead, *Caretta c. caretta*

This form ranges throughout the Atlantic Ocean and Mediterranean Sea, northward as far as Newfoundland and southward to the Rio de la Plata in Argentina.

Pacific Loggerhead, *Caretta c. gigas* (Figure 48)

This is the race of the Pacific and Indian Oceans. On the coast of the continental United States it is found only in the vicinity of California, and despite the fact that it ranges widely throughout the Pacific Ocean, there seem to be no records of it from Hawaii.

Green Turtles, Genus *Chelonia*

These sea turtles are famous for the excellent steaks and soups that come from them. Like all sea turtles, they have the limbs modified into paddles. They differ from the Leatherback Turtles in having the carapace and plastron covered by the typical large, regularly arranged, horny laminae; from the other sea turtles with a normal shell they can be recognized by the presence of a single pair of prefrontal scales rather than two pairs. In addition, only the Hawksbill Turtles share with them the character of having four pairs of lateral laminae, rather than five or more pairs. There are two species in this genus.

Atlantic Green Turtle, *Chelonia mydas* (Plate 7d)

The Atlantic Green Turtle has a rounded, gently sloping shell and is predominantly brown in color. (The name Green Turtle comes from the color of the fat, not from the color of the shell.) It is not so much a turtle of the open seas as is the Loggerhead; it is found more often in shallow water, particularly where there is an abundance of the submerged vegetation on which it feeds. Places where the grassbeds are from two to four fathoms deep, particularly near areas that have exposed, rocky holes in the bottom in which it may rest and sleep, seem to be the habitat preferred by the Green Turtle. The breeding season of this species depends, to a great extent, on geography; apparently it is early summer in the northern and southern temperate regions, midsummer in the tropics. The female comes up on a sandy beach at night to dig her nest and lay her eggs. The number of eggs ranges from about 75 to 100. This turtle is of considerable economic importance. It has long been regarded as a delicacy; not only is the meat eaten fresh but not long ago there were factories in the West Indies that canned the meat for export. As with so many of the marine turtles, it is difficult to get an accurate measurement of maximum size. Specimens have been recorded at 850 pounds but probably none that are captured by fishermen today exceed 500 pounds in weight.

The Atlantic Green Turtle is found in the Atlantic Ocean, the Gulf of Mexico, and the Mediterranean Sea.

Pacific Green Turtle, *Chelonia agassizi* (Figure 49)

This species is like the Atlantic Green Turtle but is greenish-olive to black in color, rather than brown and has a narrower, more steeply sloping shell. It is apparently not so strict a vegetarian but is more inclined to feed on invertebrates.

This species ranges in the eastern Pacific Ocean from southern California southward to Chile and straggles to Hawaii, where it has been reported to come out on remote beaches to bask, as well as to lay eggs.

Hawksbill Turtle, *Eretmochelys imbricata* (Plate 7e)

These are the turtles from whose shell comes the tortoiseshell once so popular for making combs and brushes, buttons, and other ornaments. In these modern days of economical plastics the commercial value of the Hawksbill Turtle has dropped rapidly. The carapace and plastron are covered by large, distinct, regularly placed horny laminae, which serve to distinguish it from the Leatherback. It differs from the other sea turtles in the possession of two pairs of prefrontal scales on top of the head and only four pairs of lateral laminae; it is the only sea turtle with this particular combination of characters.

Hawksbill Turtles are small as sea turtles go; the heaviest specimen on record weighed 280 pounds but most do not reach 100 pounds. The shell is shield-shaped, brown above and yellowish below. Young ones may be almost black. Usually the "tortoiseshell" ornamentation of the laminae does not show up until after they have been removed and polished.

The life history of this species is very poorly known in spite of its former great economic importance. As with the other sea turtles, the females come to shore to lay their eggs on sandy beaches. Probably most of them lay around 150 eggs at a time. Green Turtles are largely herbivorous, and most of the other sea turtles seem to be mostly carnivorous, but the Hawksbill Turtles apparently eat anything they can get hold of, plant or animal. There are two subspecies.

Atlantic Hawksbill, *Eretmochelys i. imbricata* (Figure 50)

This form occurs along the Atlantic coast of the Americas from Massachusetts to Brazil, with scattered records along the west coast of Europe.

Pacific Hawksbill, *Eretmochelys i. bissa*

This is a race of the Indo–Pacific region. There are no records for the Pacific coast of the continental United States, but next to the Green Turtle it is the commonest turtle in the seas around Hawaii.

Ridleys, Genus *Lepidochelys*

These are the smallest of our sea turtles—adults may reach 28 inches in length and weigh nearly 80 pounds. Like all except the Leatherback,

Fig. 49. Pacific Green Turtle, *Chelonia agassizi*

Fig. 50. Atlantic Hawksbill, *Eretmochelys i. imbricata*

they have horny laminae on the back. From the other sea turtles they differ in having two prefrontal scales on the top of the head, five or more lateral laminae on each side of the back, and four inframarginal laminae under the edge of the lateral side of the carapace. The head is large and the shell nearly as wide as it is long.

Atlantic Ridley, *Lepidochelys kempi* (Figure 51)

Adults of this species are gray in color and usually have five pairs of lateral laminae. Females come ashore to lay their eggs along the western coast of the Gulf of Mexico, but nonbreeding individuals are found along the eastern coast of North America from Newfoundland to the Gulf of Mexico. They are unknown in the Caribbean but straggling specimens sometimes appear on the western coast of Europe.

Pacific Ridley, *Lepidochelys olivacea*

Adults of this species are olive-colored above and have a greenish-yellow or greenish-white plastron. Young are grayish-black. There are five to nine lateral laminae, usually six to eight. This species is found in the warmer parts of the Indian and Pacific oceans. It has been reported once from the coast of Humboldt County, California.

LEATHERBACK TURTLES, FAMILY DERMOCHELIDAE

These huge marine turtles have the shell covered with a smooth skin instead of horny laminae. (Young have a mosaic of small scales that are later shed.) The limbs are paddle-shaped.

Leatherback, *Dermochelys coriacea* (Figure 52)

These are the largest of all turtles, adults ranging from $\frac{1}{4}$ to $\frac{3}{4}$ of a ton; possibly occasional specimens reach a ton in weight. They differ from all turtles except other sea turtles in having paddle-shaped limbs. Unlike all other sea turtles, they lack large, uniformly arranged, horny laminae on the carapace and plastron, but instead are covered by a smooth dark-brown or black skin. There are seven longitudinal ridges down the back and five similar ridges down the belly.

The Leatherback is usually seen far at sea but occasionally comes in near shore and of course the females come to land to lay eggs although records of this event are extremely rare. From the little we know, it is omnivorous in its feeding habits. Apparently it has little economic importance.

The Leatherback is apparently widely distributed in the warm seas of the world. In the western Atlantic it has been reported from as far north as Newfoundland and as far south as Argentina and in the eastern Pacific is found from British Columbia to Chile. It also appears rarely in the vicinity of the Hawaiian Islands.

g. 51. Atlantic Ridley, *Lepidochelys kempi*

j. 52. Leatherback, *Dermochelys coriacea*

SOFTSHELL TURTLES, FAMILY TRIONYCHIDAE

Unlike all other turtles except the Leatherbacks, members of this family have the shell covered with a leathery skin rather than horny laminae. They are freshwater rather than marine and do not have the paddle-shaped limbs of the Leatherbacks.

Softshell Turtles, Genus *Trionyx*

This is a group about which there can be no confusion. These creatures are obviously turtles and just as obviously have soft, leathery backs rather than hard shells as do all the other freshwater turtles. The long, tubular snout and fleshy lips on the upper jaw are also characteristic. Softshell Turtles are found in rivers, ponds, lakes, and some species even in small ditches. Most individuals are irascible and, with their long necks and sharp strong jaws, are animals to be handled with extreme caution. They also are quite palatable if one is willing to go to the effort to dress them out for the meat. From what we know of the food habits of those for which detailed studies are available, the Softshells are quite omnivorous, though they tend to be carnivorous and predatory. Four species of this genus are now recognized in the United States.

Florida Softshell, *Trionyx ferox* (Plate 7f)

The Florida Softshell can be told from the other two species of the continental United States by the little, rounded, hemispherical bumps on the carapace; the Spiny Softshell has cone-shaped or spiny projections on the carapace, and the Smooth Softshell lacks projections, the back being perfectly smooth. Furthermore, the Florida Softshell and Spiny Softshell can both be told from the Smooth Softshell by the presence of a little lateral projection from the nasal septum in each nostril. As one looks directly into the nostrils they do not look like round holes, but rather appear as two kidney-shaped openings. These are big turtles—a large female may reach 18 inches in carapace length (males are smaller).

The female comes to shore from March to July and lays her eggs in a nest excavated in a sandy area. The number of eggs in a clutch may vary from eighteen to twenty-four. Although large and quite palatable, this turtle is seldom seen in the markets and in Florida is mostly eaten by Indians.

The Florida Softshell is restricted in distribution, ranging from the coastal region of southern South Carolina through southern Georgia and all of Florida east of the Apalachicola River basin.

Spiny Softshell, *Trionyx spiniferus*

This wide-ranging Softshell can be recognized by the presence of spiny or conical projections, particularly along the front edge of the carapace, and by the kidney-shaped nostrils. A few individuals of some of the races reach sizes equal to the largest known Florida Softshell, but the average size is smaller.

While the Florida Softshell is quite ubiquitous, occurring in lakes, ponds, and ditches as often as in rivers, the various races of the Spiny Softshell show a strong predilection for rivers. The females lay their eggs in early summer; the size of the clutch ranges from less than a dozen to more than two dozen. The incubation period is not known, and perhaps at least sometime the young do not emerge until the spring following egg laying.

There are four races of this turtle known at the present time. Although there are good pattern differences that can be used to identify young individuals, in old ones the pattern tends to fade; geographic area should be given primary consideration in identifying turtles of this species.

Eastern Spiny Softshell, *Trionyx s. spiniferus*

The light line extending back from the jaw does not meet a similar line extending back from the eye. This race is found in the central and eastern United States, for the most part west of the mountains. It ranges from extreme northern Alabama northward through western North Carolina, West Virginia, Pennsylvania, and New York, and westward through southern Michigan and Wisconsin into the region of the Mississippi River. An isolated, introduced population occurs in the lakes of southern New Jersey.

Gulf Coast Softshell, *Trionyx s. asper*

The light lines extending back from the eye and jaw meet on the side of the head. This form ranges from southern North Carolina southward through most of South Carolina and Georgia and westward into Alabama, the panhandle of Florida, and most of Mississippi and southern Louisiana.

Texas Softshell, *Trionyx s. emoryi*

Males and young usually have small white spots on the carapace. Spines of the female may be less well developed than in other races. This is the race of the Southwest, ranging throughout western Louisiana, southwestern Arkansas, southern Oklahoma, and most of Texas, extending into New Mexico in the Rio Grande and Pecos rivers and southward into northern Mexico; an isolated population is present in the Colorado River Basin of southern California, southern Nevada, southeastern Utah and southern and western Arizona.

Western Softshell, *Trionyx s. hartwegi*

Dark markings on the shell are smaller than in the Eastern Spiny Softshell. This race ranges west of the Mississippi from mid-Arkansas northward to central Minnesota and westward into eastern Colorado, Wyoming, and Montana.

Smooth Softshell, *Trionyx muticus*

This Softshell has no ridges in the nostrils and no bumps or spines on the back. It is the smallest of the Softshells; adult females reach a maximum length of about 14 inches, but the average size is much smaller.

Like the Spiny Softshell, it shows a preference for rivers, rather than lakes and ponds. Although the range of this species extensively overlaps the range of the Spiny Softshell, they seldom overlap in habitat, and where one is found, the other is usually absent. The breeding habits of this turtle are a little better known than are those of most of the Softshells. The eggs are laid in the early summer and range from a dozen and a half to nearly three dozen in the individual clutch. As in the other species, the eggs are laid in a hole dug in an open sandy area. Incubation time varies with temperature and water conditions but generally runs between two and two and a half months.

There are two races of this form.

Mississippi Smooth Softshell, *Trionyx m. muticus*

The pattern of the young consists of small dots and streaks. There are usually stripes on the dorsal surface of the snout. This race occurs in the Mississippi–Missouri River drainage, from Louisiana to central Texas and northeastern New Mexico in the south and from southern South Dakota to extreme western Pennsylvania in the north.

Gulf Coast Smooth Softshell, *Trionyx m. calvatus*

The young are marked with large, circular spots. The dorsal surface of the snout is unstriped. This race is found in the Pearl, Pascagoula, and Escambia river drainages from central Mississippi to extreme western Florida.

Chinese Softshell, *Trionyx sinensis*

This Softshell of eastern Asia is rather small for a Softshell, adults being somewhat less than 10 inches long. The dorsal tubercles tend to form longitudinal rows. It has been introduced into the Hawaiian Islands and is now definitely known to be established on the island of Kauai.

Lizards

ANATOMICAL PARTS OF THE LIZARD

A. Side view of body of lizard with granular scales.

B. Ventral view of foot of a Gecko.

C. Side view of body of a lizard with imbricate scales.

D Dorsal view of head of Gecko.

E. Lateral view of head of Gecko.

F. Ventral view of head of Gecko showing (a) labial scales.

G. Dorsal view of head of Skink showing (b) rostral scale, (c) supranasal scales, (d) supraocular scales, (e) parietal scales, (f) frontonasal scale, (g) prefrontal scales, (h) frontal scale, (i) fronto-parietal scales, and (j) interparietal scale.

H. Lateral view of head of Skink showing (k) labial scales and (1) ciliaries.

I. Ventral view of head of Skink showing (m) mental scale and (n) chin shields.

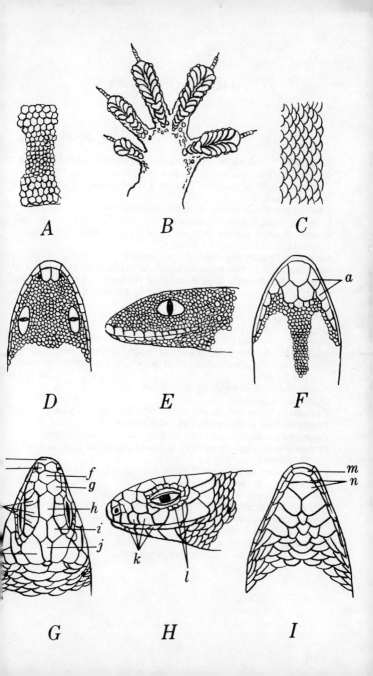

A   B   C

D   E   F

a

f
g
h
i
j
k
l

m
n

G   H   I

LIZARD GLOSSARY

Anal plate: The single or divided scale lying just in front of the vent.

Azygous: Single, not divided, median in position.

Canthals: Scales forming the edge of a ridge extending from the eye to the nostril.

Chin shields: Single or paired scales under the chin.

Ciliaries: A single row of tiny scales that partially surrounds the eye.

Frontal: A single median plate on top of the head between the eyes.

Imbricate: Overlapping, like shingles.

Intercalary: Something inserted or interpolated.

Internasal: One or two scales on top of the head just behind the rostral.

Interparietal: A single median scale on the head behind the frontal. It may be separated from the latter by the paired frontoparietals.

Keel: A sharp ridge.

Labials, upper and lower: Scales bordering the jaw.

Lamellae: The plates forming pads on the feet of some lizards.

Loreal: A small scale between the nasal and preocular.

Lorilabials: An irregular group of scales arranged longitudinally between the loreal and labials or posteriorly between the subocular and labials.

Nasal: The scale in which the nostril lies.

Oviparous: Egg-laying.

Postlabials: Scales behind and in line with the upper labials.

Postnasal: One or two scales just behind the nasal.

Postoculars: One or more small scales directly behind the eye.

Prefrontals: One or two pairs of scales on top of the head in front of the frontal.

Preocular: One or more small scales directly in front of the eye.

Rostral: Plate at the tip of the snout.

Suboculars: Scales between the eye and the labials.

Supraoculars: Scales above the orbits.

Supraorbital semicircles: Scales forming paired arcs on top of the head between the eyes.

Temporals: Scales, lying one above the other, behind the postocular and between the parietals and upper labials.

a. Eastern Lesser Siren
Siren i. intermedia

b. Hellbender
Cryptobranchus a. alleganiensis

c. Spotted Salamander
Ambystoma maculatum

d. Blue-spotted Salamander
Ambystoma laterale

e. Tiger Salamander
Ambystoma tigrinum

f. Pacific Giant Salamander
Dicamptodon ensatus

a. Two-toed Amphiuma
Amphiuma means

b. Red-spotted Newt
Notophthalmus v. viridescens

c. Mudpuppy
Necturus maculosus

d. Mountain Salamander
Desmognathus ochrophaeus

e. Long-tailed Salamander
Eurycea l. longicauda

f. Slimy Salamander
Plethodon glutinosus

a. Red Salamander
Pseudotriton ruber

b. Tailed Frog
Ascaphus truei

c. Eastern Spadefoot
Scaphiopus holbrooki

d. Bullfrog
Rana catesbeiana

e. Green Frog
Rana c. melanota

f. Wood Frog
Rana sylvatica

a. Florida Gopher Frog
Rana c. aesopus

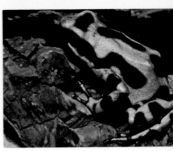

b. Gold and Black Poison Fro
Dendrobates auratus

c. Eastern Narrow-mouthed Toad
Gastrophryne carolinensis

d. Oak Toad
Bufo quercicus

e. American Toad
Bufo a. americanus

f. Green Tree Frog
Hyla c. cinerea

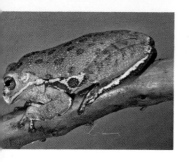

a. Barking Tree Frog
Hyla gratiosa

b. Northern Cricket Frog
Acris c. crepitans

c. Upland Chorus Frog
Pseudacris t. feriarum

d. Greenhouse Frog
Eleutherodactylus ricordi planirostris

e. American Alligator
Alligator mississippiensis

f. Common Snapping Turtle
Chelydra serpentina

a. Alligator Snapping Turtle
Macrochelys temmincki

b. Wood Turtle
Clemmys insculpta

c. Blanding's Turtle
Emydoidea blandingi

d. Eastern Box Turtle
Terrapene c. carolina

e. Eastern Chicken Turtle
Deirochelys r. reticularia

f. Diamondback Terrapin
Malaclemys terrapin

a. Midland Painted Turtle
Chrysemys p. marginata

b. Red-eared Turtle
Chrysemys s. elegans

c. Texas Tortoise
Gopherus berlandieri

d. Atlantic Green Turtle
Chelonia mydas

e. Hawksbill Turtle
Eretmochelys imbricata

f. Florida Softshell
Trionyx ferox

a. Desert Banded Gecko
Coleonyx v. variegatus

b. Mediterranean Gecko
Hemidactylus turcicus turcicus

c. Green Anole
Anolis carolinensis

d. Desert Iguana
Dipsosaurus dorsalis dorsalis

e. Western Chuckwalla
Sauromalus o. obesus

f. Eastern Collared Lizard
Crotaphytus c. collaris

a. Texas Horned Lizard
Phrynosoma cornutum

b. Northern Side-blotched Lizard
Uta s. stansburiana

c. Sonora Spiny Lizard
Sceloporus c. clarki

d. Colorado Desert Fringe-toed Lizard
Uma n. notata

e. Zebra-tailed Lizard
Callisaurus draconoides

f. Eastern Glass Lizard
Ophisaurus ventralis

a. California Alligator Lizard
Gerrhonotus m. multicarinatus

b. Reticulate Gila Monster
Heloderma s. suspectum

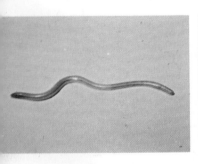

c. California Legless Lizard
Anniella pulchra

d. Common Desert Night Lizard
Xantusia v. vigilis

e. Great Basin Whiptail
Cnemidophorus t. tigris

f. Five-lined Skink
Eumeces fasciatus

a. Ground Skink
Lygosoma laterale

b. Worm Lizard
Rhineura floridana

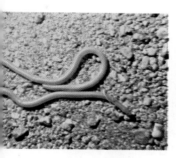

c. Southwestern Blind Snake
Leptotyphlops h. humilis

d. Coastal Rosy Boa
Lichanura t. roseofusca

e. Rubber Boa
Charina bottae

f. Brown Water Snake
Natrix taxispilota

a. Banded Water Snake
Natrix f. fasciata

b. Graham's Water Snake
Regina grahami

c. Striped Swamp Snake
Regina a. alleni

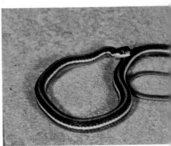

d. Eastern Ribbon Snake
Thamnophis sauritus

e. Northern Lined Snake
Tropidoclonion l. lineatum

f. Eastern Hognose Snake
Heterodon platyrhinos

a. Southern Ringneck Snake
Diadophis p. punctatus

b. Rainbow Snake
Abastor erythrogrammus

c. Northern Black Racer
Coluber c. constrictor

d. Rough Green Snake
Opheodrys aestivus

e. Speckled Racer
mobius margaritiferus margaritiferus

f. Eastern Indigo Snake
Drymarchon c. couperi

a. Corn Snake
Elaphe g. guttata

b. Bull Snake
Pituophis m. sayi

c. Scarlet King Snake
Lampropeltis t. doliata

d. California King Snake
Lampropeltis g. californiae

e. California King Snake
Lampropeltis g. californiae

f. Southeastern Scarlet Snake
Cemophora c. copei

a. Texas Long-nosed Snake
Rhinocheilus l. tessellatus

b. Sharp-tailed Snake
Contia tenuis

Mohave Shovel-nosed Snake
Chionactis o. occipitalis (left) and
Colorado Desert Shovel-nosed Snake
Chionactis o. annulata

d. Banded Sand Snake
Chilomeniscus cinctus

e. California Night Snake
Hypsiglena t. nuchalata

f. Texas Cat-eyed Snake
*Leptodeira septentrionalis
septentrionalis*

a. California Lyre Snake
Trimorphodon vandenburghi

b. Texas Coral Snake
Mircrurus f. tenere

c. Northern Copperhead
Agkistrodon c. mokasen

d. Eastern Massasauga
Sistrurus c. catenatus

e. Eastern Diamondback Rattlesnake
Crotalus adamanteus

f. Timber Rattlesnake
Crotalus h. horridus

Lizards

It is usually easy enough to tell whether a particular animal is a lizard. The dry, scale-covered skin is enough to separate one from the salamanders, which have a similar body build. The difficulty comes with some forms that have lost their legs and look more like snakes than typical lizards. Glass Lizards and California Legless Lizards have movable eyelids, which snakes lack. Worm Lizards really look more like earthworms than snakes. Their scales are arranged in rings around the body, resulting in a segmented appearance. But the head is distinctly lizardlike, even though it lacks eyes and external ear openings.

Many kinds of lizards are apt to break off their tails when attacked. Apparently this is a protective device—the twitching end of the tail distracts the predator while the lizard itself escapes. The animal grows a new tail very readily, but the regenerated tail differs from the original in appearance and is shorter. For this reason we usually give the head and body length of a lizard rather than the total length. Measure in a straight line from the tip of the snout to the vent.

Young lizards often differ strikingly from their parents in color and pattern, and males may differ from females. To further confuse things, breeding individuals may show different colors than nonbreeding ones. In some species, the color of the individual depends very much on the color of the soil where it lives. And finally, some lizards can change color with changing conditions of light, temperature, and their own state of health and excitement. We have tried to mention the chief variations present in each species, but if your lizard does not exactly match the description, remember to allow for the possibility of individual variation.

Some lizard scales are small, rounded, and not overlapping. Such scales are called granules. Other scales overlap like shingles. These scales may be smooth or keeled, and they may have the free edge smoothly rounded or ending in one or more spines. The number, size, and shape of the scales on different parts of the body all are important in identifying lizards.

Lizards may be found on the ground or climbing on trees, bushes, rocks, or buildings, or burrowing in the soil. Most of our species are diurnal, but the Geckos, Night Lizards, and Gila Monster are active at night. Most species lay eggs, and sometimes the egg clutch is guarded by the female. Occasionally the young are born alive. Most are insectivorous, but again there are exceptions. Some of the larger ones feed on other small vertebrates, and a few are vegetarians.

Members of the first three families of lizards are known as geckos.

171

Those in the United States are stoutly built, short-tailed little lizards, mostly nocturnal and well adapted for climbing. The skin is soft, and the scales on top of the head are not enlarged into symmetrical shields. The digits are frequently expanded or have pads at the tips. Many geckos look at the world through a clear "spectacle" in the fused and immovable eyelids. The pupil of the eye is usually a vertical slit. The tail is very easily shed. Unlike other lizards, geckos have voices. Females lay one or two nearly round, white, usually hard-shelled eggs.

GROUND GECKOS, FAMILY EUBLEPHARIDAE

These little lizards have a soft skin with tiny scales on the back and top of the head. They have movable eyelids and vertical pupils, and the toes lack expanded pads. The only genus found in the United States is represented here by a single species.

Banded Gecko, *Coleonyx variegatus*

These brightly banded, agile little lizards can be recognized by their vertical pupils and movable eyelids, the granular scales on top of the head, and the lack of toe pads or expansions under the digits. The brown-and-cream-colored bands of the young tend to become more mottled in the adults. The short tail is constricted at the base and is easily broken off. Adults are about 2½ to 3 inches in head and body length. They are nocturnal ground dwellers of the dry Southwest, where they live under rocks and sometimes in small holes or under detritus on the ground. Like other geckos, they may squeak when caught, and one observer mentions "a long drawn-out rattle." The females lay two eggs, but otherwise very little is known of the life history. There are a number of races of this species, five of which occur in the United States.

Desert Banded Gecko, *Coleonyx v. variegatus* (Plate 8a)

In adults the top of the head is spotted, and the dark body bands have light centers or are broken into spots. This form occurs in southern California, southern Nevada, and western Arizona.

San Diego Banded Gecko, *Coleonyx v. abbotti*

The top of the head is not spotted in adults; there is a clear light collar; and the dark body bands are not wider than the light. This race is found in the coastal strip of southern California, northward to the vicinity of the Santa Barbara County border.

Tucson Banded Gecko, *Coleonyx v. bogerti*

The pattern of the adults is like that of the San Diego race, but the top of the head is spotted in this race, which occurs in southeastern Arizona and extreme southwestern New Mexico.

Texas Banded Gecko, *Coleonyx v. brevis*

Adults of this race are generally more spotted than those of the other races. This form is more eastern in distribution, occurring in central and southern New Mexico and western and southwestern Texas.

Utah Banded Gecko, *Coleonyx v. utahensis*

The dark body bands of the adult are wider than the light. This race is limited in distribution to extreme southwestern Utah, southern Nevada, and northwestern Arizona.

NEW WORLD GECKOS, FAMILY SPHAERODACTYLIDAE

These big-eyed little geckos lack movable eyelids and have "spectacles." The skin is soft; the scales on the top of the head are small. Of the two genera found in the United States, the Dwarf Geckos have a small, round pad at the tip of each toe, with a claw to one side, and the Yellow-headed Geckos lack such pads. Unlike other geckos, the females lay only one egg at a time, instead of two, although several females may lay in one spot.

Dwarf Geckos, Genus *Sphaerodactylus*

These are diminutive, round-bodied geckos with distinctly pointed heads. They can be told from other geckos in the United States by the single, small, round pad at the tip of each toe. They are adept climbers, active at night, hiding in cracks or under debris during the day. There are three species within our limits.

Ocellated Gecko, *Sphaerodactylus argus argus*

These lizards are variable in color. Some are plain brown above, others have rows of dark-bordered light spots. The belly varies from dusky to very dark; the tail may be orange or brown. This small lizard has a head-and-body length of about $1\frac{3}{8}$ inches. The Ocellated Gecko differs from the Reef Gecko in the small size of the dorsal scales; about twenty to twenty-four are contained in a distance equal to that from the tip of the snout to the ear, while in the Reef Gecko only about 10 to 12 dorsal scales would occupy the same distance. It differs from the Ashy Gecko in having the dorsal scales keeled rather than smooth. Little is known of the life history. The species has apparently been introduced into Key West from Jamaica.

Reef Gecko, *Sphaerodactylus notatus*

This is one of the smallest of all geckos and indeed of all lizards. Large individuals have a head-and-body length of only about $1\frac{1}{8}$ inches. The dorsal scales are keeled and are about twice as large as those of the

Ocellated Gecko. Some individuals have two light spots on the neck and three broad, dark, light-centered stripes that narrow to points on the head and fade out about midbody. Others are sprinkled with small, dark spots. Others are plain brownish, without dark markings. Little is known of the life history. This species is known from Cuba and the Bahama Islands and is fairly widespread throughout southernmost Florida and the Keys.

Ashy Gecko, *Sphaerodactylus cinereus* (Figure 53)

This Dwarf Gecko has smooth, granular dorsal scales. Adults have tiny light spots scattered on a brown ground color. Anteriorly the spots may fuse into streaks. The young are marked with dark-reddish crossbands and have a red tail. Adult specimens average about $1\frac{3}{8}$ inches in head-and-body length. These chubby little geckos are fond of settled areas and are usually found around houses, outbuildings, and other manmade structures. The eggs are reported to be laid in August under debris on the ground. The species is found in Haiti, Cuba, and in Florida on Key West. It has also been reported from some of the other Keys.

Yellow-headed Gecko, *Gonatodes albogularis fuscus* (Figure 54)

This species belongs to a group known as Padless Geckos, because they lack expanded pads on the toes. There are many species of Padless Geckos, but this is the only one found in the United States.

Like the Dwarf Geckos, Yellow-headed Geckos have fused eyelids and "spectacles." The top of the head and body are covered with small, tuberculate scales. These geckos are usually mottled grayish-brown in color but may be uniformly dark; the heads of adult males are bright-yellow, which gives the species its name. Females and young usually have a more or less well-developed, narrow, light collar. This is a small lizard with a head-and-body length of about $1\frac{1}{2}$ inches and with the tail about that long again if it hasn't broken off. Hatchlings are about $\frac{3}{4}$ inch long. Yellow-headed Geckos are more diurnal than other geckos. Perhaps this is why the pupil of the eye reportedly changes in shape, being vertical during the day and round at night. They are often found around buildings and are rather gentle but difficult to collect, because they are alert and agile. The Yellow-headed Gecko ranges from Nicaragua, south to Columbia and has apparently been introduced into Jamaica and Cuba as well as Key West in Florida.

TRUE GECKOS, FAMILY GEKKONIDAE

This is a large family widely distributed throughout the warmer parts of the world. Of several hundred species, only six, belonging to five genera, are found in the United States, and of these only one is native. Four species have been introduced into Hawaii and one into the southeastern United States. All of them have immovable eyelids,

Fig. 53. Young Ashy Gecko, *Sphaerodactylus cinereus*

Fig. 54. Yellow-headed Gecko, *Gonatodes albogularis fuscus*

with "spectacles," vertical pupils, and expanded digits. The dorsal scales are granular but may be interspersed with larger scales arranged in more or less regular rows.

Leaf-toed Gecko, *Phyllodactylus xanti nocticolus*
(Figure 55)

The fingers and toes each are widened at the tip, with the underside divided into two large plates, a right and a left, with a groove between, into which the claw can be retracted. Thus the tip of the toe looks something like the hoof of a cloven-hoofed animal. This species is pale-gray, flesh-colored, or brown above, and in life appears somewhat translucent. There are darker markings on the back. These are desert-dwelling geckos, found around boulders on hillsides in arid and semiarid regions. Like so many other geckos, they are creatures of the night, emerging from their daytime hiding places to roam around searching for night-loving insects. As with other geckos, the females lay two eggs; otherwise the breeding habits are not known. They are fairly large for geckos, reaching about $2\frac{1}{2}$ inches in head-and-body length, with the tail somewhat longer if it is complete, although individuals with the original tail are extremely uncommon. Our only native member of the family, this species is restricted to Lower California and southern California, northward as far as Riverside County.

House Geckos, Genus *Hemidactylus*

In this genus the lamellae (scales) under the fingers and toes are expanded and arranged in two rows except on the last joint, which is slender, clawed, and rises at an angle from the expanded part of the digit. The inner digits, corresponding to the thumb and big toe, are well developed and have terminal joints, with claws like those of the other digits. This is a wide-spread genus with many species, of which two have been introduced and become established in the United States.

Mediterranean Gecko, *Hemidactylus turcicus turcicus*
(Plate 8b)

The Mediterranean Gecko has the small, granular scales on the back interspersed with larger, keeled scales arranged in fourteen or sixteen more or less longitudinal rows. The ground color is pinkish to ivory-white, marked with small light and dark spots. This introduced Gecko is the only lizard in the southeastern United States that characteristically climbs about on the walls of houses at night. (The smaller Yellow-headed Gecko can climb but seems to prefer vacant buildings.) In the New World, at least, this species is almost entirely confined to human habitations, feeding on insects attracted to the lights at night. Although there are literature reports that this species does call, the junior author has had them on the walls of his house in Gainesville for many years and has never heard the voice of one. The details of the life history are unknown despite its widespread distribution and common occurrence.

Fig. 55. Leaf-toed Gecko, *Phyllodactylus xanti nocticolus*

Fig. 56. Brown Anole, *Anolis sagrei*

Young individuals in the Gainesville region appear in early April and are preyed on by spiders. Adults are about 2 to 2⅜ inches in head-and-body length. The species is widespread throughout the tropics and subtropics of the world. In the United States it has been introduced and is established in Key West, Miami, and Gainesville, Florida, in New Orleans, and in Brownsville, Texas.

Fox Gecko, *Hemidactylus garnoti*

This species is closely related and very similar to the Mediterranean Gecko. It is a little larger, adults being about 2¾ inches in head-and-body length, and more brightly colored. The dorsal scales are all granular except for a single row of larger, rounded tubercles along each side. Fox Geckos appear to be more inclined to live on natural objects than Mediterranean Geckos. At night they may be found foraging for food on the trunks of trees, as well as on buildings, walls, and fences. They are quite variable in pattern and seem to have the ability to adapt their body coloring to match the general color of the background on which they are resting. The two eggs are laid under slabs of rock and beneath loose bark and in crevices in the trunks of trees. Frequently a number of females lay in the same place. This species is known from about half a dozen of the islands in the Hawaiian group.

Stump-toed Gecko, *Gehyra mutilata*

Like the House and Fox Geckos, this species has the digits broadened at the base, with the lamellae underneath arranged in two rows. The last joint of each of the four outer digits is narrow, clawed, and set at an angle to the expanded part. It differs from the House and Fox Geckos in having the inner digit on each foot, corresponding to the thumb or big toe, well developed, but lacking the narrow, clawlike terminal joint. The dorsal scales are small and granular. This Gecko has a pronounced ability to vary its body coloration in harmony with the background it is resting on. When on a white background, it looks almost albinistic except for its large, dark eyes. These Geckos feed on beetles and moths and can be found at night on tree trunks and on the walls of buildings. As with most Geckos, the female lays two eggs. They are sticky when laid and adhere both to each other and to the surface on which they are placed. They are often found in the bases of the fronds of palm trees and in holes and depressions in the ground. This species is known from about half a dozen of the islands in the Hawaiian group.

Mourning Gecko, *Lepidodactylus lugubris*

Like the other geckos found in Hawaii, this species has the basal part of each digit expanded, with a double row of lamellae below. It differs from the others in having the narrow terminal joint not set at an angle to the expanded part. The inner digit on each foot is well developed but lacks a claw. The dorsal scales are small and granular.

These geckos are light pinkish-gray or brownish above, frequently with small, paired blackish spots down the back. The young frequently have dark lateral stripes. They are the smallest of all the Hawaiian geckos, the adults having a head-and-body length of less than 2 inches. They are gregarious, living in rather open, nonforested areas and around human habitations, and are also rather noisy, often being heard chirping at night, particularly around lighted houses. They feed on small insects, including mosquitoes and ants. The females, as is usual with geckos, lay two eggs. These eggs are quite adherent, both to each other and to structures on which they are laid. They have been found in holes in trees, under logs and rocks, in crevices at the bases of large palm fronds, and even in such places as unused keyholes in houses. The Mourning Gecko has been collected on about half a dozen of the Hawaiian Islands.

Tree Gecko, *Hemiphyllodactylus typus typus*

These geckos also have the basal part of the digits expanded. The terminal joints of the outer four digits on each foot are short, clawed, and set at an angle to the expanded part. The inner digits are vestigial and lack the terminal joints but may have tiny claws. They are short-legged little lizards, brown above, spotted or marbled with darker brown. There is usually a series of small, reddish dorsolateral spots. The tail has lighter and darker markings and a large, whitish, black-edged spot at the base. This gecko differs from most others in the United States in that it appears to avoid manmade structures and is instead a somewhat solitary, arboreal species living on trees and vines. The female lays two eggs and these are adherent, sticking to each other but not always to the surface on which they are deposited. They are laid in holes in trees, around the bases of palm fronds, on the trunks of coconut trees, and under the bark of woody trees. Tree Geckos are rather small, the head and body being generally less than 2½ inches in length and the tail, if complete, about the same. In the Hawaiian Islands this species occurs on Hawaii, Kauai, and Oahu.

IGUANIDS, FAMILY IGUANIDAE

This large family, with many hundreds of species, is almost confined to the New World and includes the majority of the lizards of the United States. As one would expect with such a large group, there is a great deal of variation, and it is not easy to define the family by listing a few characters that are found in all Iguanids and only in Iguanids. It is easier to say what is not an Iguanid. All members of the family have two pairs of legs, which separates them from the Worm Lizards and the Shovel-snouted Legless Lizards. There are no longitudinal grooves along the sides, which are covered with granular scales much smaller than the scales on the back and belly, as there are in the Lateral Fold Lizards. The combination of movable eyelids and round pupils separates the Iguanids from the Geckos and Night Lizards. The scales on the body are not smooth, flat, rounded, overlapping, and about equal in size, as they are in the Skinks. The belly scales are not quadrangular nor arranged either in transverse rows, as they are in the Beaded Lizards, or in eight longitudinal rows as they are in the Teiids. If your lizard hasn't been eliminated by any of these characters, it should be an Iguanid.

Anoles, Genus *Anolis*

These rather small, slender-bodied, long-tailed lizards differ from all others in the United States in that the male has a longitudinal loose fold of skin under the throat and neck which can be extended to form a large, fanlike structure. This fan is usually very brightly colored. The scales on the undersides of the fingers and toes are expanded to form padlike structures, but these scales are not divided. Anoles have movable eyelids and round pupils. All of our species are arboreal, though they may forage for insects on the ground. All of them reproduce by laying eggs. There are between 300 and 350 known species of this genus in tropical America, but only 3 occur in the United States.

Green Anole, *Anolis carolinensis* (Plate 8c)

In this species the tail lacks a distinct dorsal ridge, and the scales on the back are keeled. Green Anoles are attractive little animals, generally bright-green above when among green leaves, brown on a brown background. Their ability to change color rapidly gives them the common name of "Chameleon," but they are not so versatile as the true Chameleons of Africa. Males in the breeding season put on a spectacular display—bobbing up and down, turning bright-green, and extending the brilliant red throat fan. Large males may reach a head-and-body length of 2¾ inches. The tail is about twice as long and is seldom shed. Females are somewhat smaller. These are the common "Chameleons" that are so often sold as pets in circuses and sideshows. They do indeed make good pets but need to be supplied with live insects for food and to have water sprinkled on green leaves in the cage because they do not drink from a dish but will lap drops of water from foliage. Two races are found in the United States.

Carolina Anole, *Anolis c. carolinensis*

This race occurs from North Carolina, southward throughout Florida and westward to central Texas and Oklahoma. In the Mississippi Valley it ranges northward into Arkansas and Tennessee. The northern limits of the range vary from year to year, because in severe winters the northern populations are killed back, while when several rather warm winters follow one another, the Anoles extend northward again.

Cuban Anole, *Anolis c. porcatus*

This race, which is native to the island of Cuba, has been introduced and is now established in the Kaimuki district of Honolulu in the Hawaiian Islands.

Bark Anole, *Anolis distichus*

This species differs from the Carolina Anole in having the scales on the back smooth, rather than keeled, and from the Brown Anole in lacking a distinct ridge along the dorsal surface of the tail. Two races have been introduced into South Florida.

Bahaman Bark Anole, *Anolis d. distichus*

Individuals are pale-gray to dark-brown in color, and males have a pale-yellow throat fan. Large males reach a head-and-body length of nearly 2 inches. This race is now established in the Miami area of Florida.

Green Bark Anole, *Anolis d. dominicensis*

This race is pea-green or gray-green in life, with a pale-orange rather than a yellow throat fan. It is established and breeding along the Tamiami Trail in Miami, Florida.

Brown Anole, *Anolis sagrei* (Figure 56)

This Anole differs from the Green Anole and Bahaman Bark Anole in having the tail distinctly keeled above. Anoles of this species are ash-gray to brown. Large males may reach $2\frac{2}{3}$ inches in head-and-body length. Two races are found in Florida.

Cuban Brown Anole, *Anolis s. sagrei*

The throat fan is orange-red, sometimes flecked with brown, the light border practically unspotted. (When the fan is closed, the border appears as a white streak on the throat.) The tail crest is not so well developed as in the other race. This form of the Brown Anole has been introduced into Florida from Cuba and is now found in the Tampa–St. Petersburg region and on the East Coast from Palm Beach County southward.

Bahaman Brown Anole, *Anolis s. ordinatus*

The throat fan is orange, flecked with dark-gray and with a light border heavily spotted with dark. The tail crest is well developed. The Bahaman Brown Anole has been introduced into the region of Lake Worth in southeastern Florida and is also reported from South Miami.

Knight Anole, *Anolis equestris equestris*

A giant, generally pea-green Anole, with the top of the head studded with pronounced tubercles and with a yellow throat fan. Its large size (adults may exceed 15 inches in total length) and the rows of tubercles on each side of the top of the head will serve to distinguish this from all other Anoles in the United States. It is common in several localities in Dade County, Florida.

Desert Iguana, *Dipsosaurus dorsalis dorsalis* (Plate 8d)

These are rather large, desert-dwelling lizards in which the adult head-and-body length ranges from 4 to 5½ inches, and the tail is nearly twice as long. They differ from all other lizards in having a single row of enlarged, keeled scales down the middle of the back, while the rest of the dorsal scales are very small. They are grayish-brown in color, with an irregular pattern of reddish-brown and gray markings. Sometimes the reddish marks tend to form lines along the sides. These diurnal, terrestrial lizards, unlike most other reptiles, are largely vegetarians. Breeding occurs in April and early May, and the females go underground to lay their eggs in late June and July. There are three to eight creamy-white, soft-shelled eggs in a clutch. The only form of the genus found in the United States lives in the deserts of southeastern California, southern Nevada, extreme southwestern Utah, and western Arizona and also in Mexico.

Chuckwalla, *Sauromalus obesus*

These are large, vegetarian lizards big enough and tasty enough to serve as food for man. They differ from all other lizards of the western United States in lacking a median, unpaired scale at the tip of the upper lip. They are able to inflate themselves by taking air into the lungs; when not inflated, they show loose folds of skin on the neck and sides of the body. The scales on the back and sides are small and granular, and those on the belly are the same size or only slightly larger. Chuckwallas vary in color with age, sex, locality, conditions of heat and light, and state of activity. The young are crossbanded, especially on the tail. Adults usually have the head and fore part of the body darker, the tail lighter. They may retain traces of the juvenile banding and have yellow or orange scales scattered on the darker brown or gray ground color. Males frequently show a reddish wash. In the morning when the sun comes out they emerge from their hiding places in rocky crevices and bask until warm enough to begin foraging on the fruits, flowers, buds, and leaves of desert plants. They may be quite abundant in places but are difficult to collect. Their ability to swell up enables them to wedge themselves tightly into crevices from which it is difficult to dislodge them. Females lay six to ten white, soft-shelled eggs during the summer months. There are seven species of Chuckwallas in Mexico, but only one, with three races, occurs in the United States.

Western Chuckwalla, *Sauromalus o. obesus* (Plate 8e)

There are 3 to 5 dark bands and 2 to 4 light bands on the tail, and the tip is usually light. This form occurs in southeastern California, western Arizona, southern Nevada, and extreme southwestern Utah.

Arizona Chuckwalla, *Sauromalus o. tumidus*

The scales are larger and more spiny in this race, which is found in Arizona, south of the range of the Western Chuckwalla and south into Mexico.

Upper Colorado River Chuckwalla, *Sauromalus o. multiforaminatus*

There are 5 to 6 dark bands and 4 to 5 light bands on the tail, and the end of the tail is usually dark. This race is found in the Colorado River area and in south central Utah and extreme north central Arizona.

Collared and Leopard Lizards, Genus *Crotaphytus*

These are brightly marked, rather large, long-tailed, pugnacious lizards with a definite gular sac, a pouch formed by a fold of skin on the ventral surface immediately in front of the forelegs. The head is large and distinct from the neck. The dorsal scales are small and granular, the belly scales larger and overlapping. All the known species lay eggs. There are five species in the genus, three of them in the United States.

Collared Lizard, *Crotaphytus collaris*

These lizards can be recognized by the presence of 2 bright-black bands (sometimes broken at the midline) across the back of the neck. The ground color is very variable but often some shade of green. Females are duller and less strongly marked than males, and the young have crossbars. After mating, females carrying eggs often develop bright-red marks along the sides. The head is much wider than the neck, and the hind legs are long and powerful. These lizards often run on their hind legs, with the tail held out. The head-and-body length of adults may reach nearly 5 inches, and the tail is often twice as long. Collared Lizards live in rocky, hilly, arid regions and are primarily insectivorous. There are three forms of this species in the United States.

Eastern Collared Lizard, *Crotaphytus c. collaris* (Plate 8f)

The throat pouch of the adult male is deep-orange, the colors and markings of the rest of the body less intense than in the western race. This form ranges from southern Missouri and northern Arkansas, westward to northern and central Texas.

Western Collared Lizard, *Crotaphytus c. baileyi*

The throat pouch of the male is deep-green or bluish-green, the body bright-green and sharply defined, dark markings are present on the head and neck. This race ranges from southern and western Texas, westward through southwestern California and northward through the Great Basin as far as Idaho and Oregon.

Yellow-headed Collared Lizard, *Crotaphytus c. auriceps*

In the adult male, the head and forefeet are bright-yellow, the body bright-green with profuse white spots. This race is restricted to the upper Colorado and Green River basins in western Colorado and eastern Utah.

Reticulate Collared Lizard, *Crotaphytus reticulatus*

This species is like the Collared Lizard but has a reticulate dorsal pattern of narrow light lines separating grayish or reddish-brown areas. Some of these darker areas are much blacker than the adjacent ones, giving the impression of eight to twelve ocellilike black spots on the back. The black collar is indicated in males by black bars on the sides of the neck. The head width is at least equal to and often greater than the distance between the nostril and the ear. In habitat and habits these lizards are similar to the other Collared Lizards. This species occurs in southwestern Texas and adjacent Mexico.

Leopard Lizard, *Crotaphytus wislizeni*

This species lacks the collar, is more slenderly built, and has a narrower head; the head is always much less wide than the distance between the nostril and the ear. The dorsal pattern is one of dusky spots and usually whitish crossbars on a grayish ground color. Adults reach 5 inches in head-and-body length. Leopard Lizards are found in sandy, semidesert regions. Unlike the Collared Lizards, they seldom run on their hind legs, and they are apparently more apt to prey on other, smaller lizards. There are three races.

Long-nosed Leopard Lizard, *Crotaphytus w. wislizeni*

There are several rows of dark-brown spots on the back and sides, those toward the midline being much larger than those on the sides. Each has a circle of white dots at or near its border. The narrow white crossbars of the young are faint or absent in large adults. This race ranges from central Idaho and eastern Oregon, southward in the Great Basin into eastern and southern California, through Nevada, western Utah, most of Arizona and New Mexico, and into western Texas.

Blunt-nosed Leopard Lizard, *Crotaphytus w. silus*

This is the darkest of the races. The crossbars are wide and remain distinct even in the adults. This form is restricted to the San Joaquin Valley in California.

Pale Leopard Lizard, *Crotaphytus w. punctatus*

This is the lightest of the races. The dorsal color pattern consists of numerous small, round brown spots on a light background. The narrow light crossbands are faint in adults. This race is found in the Upper Colorado River Basin in eastern and southern Utah, western Colorado, northwestern New Mexico, and northern Arizona.

Horned Lizards, Genus *Phrynosoma*

There is nothing else like these animals in the United States. They are wide, flat-bodied lizards with very short tails and with the head bordered behind with a crown of sharp spines (horns) or with a projecting ridge. The short, squat body gives them a superficial resemblance to certain toads, and so they are sometimes called Horned Toads, rather than Horned Lizards. These animals are insect eaters found mostly in the deserts of the southwestern United States and northern Mexico. They are terrestrial, diurnal, and like many other lizards, are able to change in color from lighter to darker. They also have the startling ability to spurt blood from the eyes, which seems to disturb approaching predators. There are about fifteen species in the genus, seven of which occur in the United States.

Texas Horned Lizard, *Phrynosoma cornutum* (Plate 9a)

This lizard has the ventral scales keeled. The horns are relatively short and, as in most Horned Lizards, the crown of spines is not quite complete, but is interrupted in the midsection of the posterior border of the head. The two horns on either side of the gap are longer than the others. There are two rows of elongated, pointed scales forming a fringe along the side of the body between the front and hind legs. The general color is yellowish or reddish-tan, sometimes gray. There is a row of dark, oval spots on either side of a light middorsal line, and the belly is spotted. The maximum head-and-body length reported is 4¼ inches, and the tail is about half as long as the body. Mating occurs in April and May, and the eggs are laid in May and June in a burrow dug by the female. Clutches average twenty-two to twenty-three in number, and the young hatch in about 1½ months. The Texas Horned Lizard is found throughout most of Texas, Oklahoma, the westernmost part of Arkansas, northwestern Louisiana, southwestern Missouri, most of Kansas, the southeastern corner of Colorado, much of New Mexico, and extreme southeastern Arizona. An introduced population is now well established in central Florida.

Coast Horned Lizard, *Phrynosoma coronatum*

This species has smooth ventral scales. The crown and rows of fringing scales are like those of the Texas Horned Lizard. There is a large dark spot on either side of the neck, other smaller dark spots on the back and sides, and flecks and mottlings of dusky on the cream-yellow belly. Adults are 3 to 4 inches in head-and-body length. There are two races of this species in the United States.

San Diego Horned Lizard, *Phrynosoma c. blainvillei*

The scales on the top of the head are larger toward the center and are smooth and convex. This form occurs in the coastal part of southern California from about San Diego southward.

California Horned Lizard, *Phrynosoma c. frontale*

The scales on top of the head are all about the same size and are rough or ridged. This form occurs in the coastal region of California from San Diego northward to north of the San Francisco Bay area and a little farther north inland in the Sacramento Valley.

Short-horned Lizard, *Phrynosoma douglassi*

The horns are very small and inconspicuous in this species. As in the Texas and Coast Horned Lizards, the row of horns is incomplete, the horns on the right and left sides not touching on the midline. The ventral scales are smooth, the fringe scales between the front and hind legs in a single row. There is a row of dark blotches along each side of the middorsal line, and the tail is banded above. This species is found in a wide variety of situations, from open plains to mountain forests. The eggs are not buried in a hole in the ground, but are retained in the oviduct and the young are "born alive." Four races of this species are now recognized in the United States, but the differences between them are not well defined.

Pygmy Horned Lizard, *Phrynosoma d. douglassi*

This is the smallest of the races, adults not exceeding $2\frac{1}{2}$ inches in head-and-body length. The head spines are very short. The ground color is usually dark-brown or bluish, the blotches rather indistinct. The race is found in western Oregon and Washington, southern Idaho, extreme northern Nevada, and northeastern California.

Eastern Short-horned Lizard, *Phrynosoma d. brevirostre*

This race is somewhat larger, adult head-and-body lengths reaching 3 inches. It is the most wide ranging of the races, occurring in central and northwestern Kansas, central and western Nebraska, South and North Dakota, westward through most of Montana and southward through Wyoming into northeastern Utah and central Colorado.

Mountain Short-horned Lizard, *Phrynosoma d. hernandesi*

This is the largest of the races, adults reaching $3\frac{3}{4}$ inches in head-and-body length, and the spines of the crown are somewhat larger than in the other races. It is found from central Utah and western and southern Colorado, throughout much of Arizona and New Mexico, and into Trans–Pecos Texas and Mexico.

Salt Lake Horned Lizard, *Phrynosoma d. ornatum*

The color of the back is often nearly uniform gray, with the dorsal spots indistinct. This race occupies northern Utah in the vicinity of Salt Lake and adjacent parts of northeastern Nevada and southeastern Idaho.

Flat-tailed Horned Lizard, *Phrynosoma m'calli*

In this species the spines on either side of the gap in the crown at the midline are twice as long as any of the other spines. The tail is long and flat, and there are two rows of fringe scales. The dorsal color is gray or buffy with a dark middorsal stripe. This Mexican species enters the United States only in extreme southwestern Arizona and southeastern California.

Round-tailed Horned Lizard, *Phrynosoma modestum*

The four spines on the posterior margin of the head are about equal in length. This is the only one of the Horned Lizards in which the side of the belly is not trimmed with a fringe of spiny scales. There is a large black blotch on each side of the neck and above each groin. The tail is slender and rounded. This is a small species, adults reaching 2¾ inches in head-and-body length. In the United States it is found in western Texas, south and central New Mexico, and extreme southeastern Arizona.

Desert Horned Lizard, *Phrynosoma platyrhinos*

This species has a median gap in the crown of spines, and the four spines along the posterior margin of the head are about equal in length. There are dark blotches on each side of the neck and four or more dark blotches on each side of the back. The tail is banded with dark-brown. There is only one row of fringe scales along the side. Two of the three races occur in the United States.

Northern Desert Horned Lizard, *Phrynosoma p. platyrhinos*

The tail is rounded in this race, which ranges throughout most of central and northern Nevada, western Utah, and northward into southeastern Oregon and southern Idaho.

Southern Desert Horned Lizard, *Phrynosoma p. calidiarum*

The tail is usually somewhat flattened. This form ranges in southernmost Utah, southern Nevada, western Arizona, and southeastern California.

Regal Horned Lizard, *Phrynosoma solare*

This horned lizard can be told from all of the others by the absence of a gap in the crown of spines along the back of the head. They are large as Horned Lizards go, adults reaching about 4½ inches in head-and-body length. This species occurs in south central Arizona and northern Mexico.

Tree Lizards, Genus *Urosaurus*

The Tree Lizards, Side-blotched Lizards, and Rock Lizards are very similar and are often included in the same genus. In all of them at least some of the scales, particularly those on the tail, are keeled rather than smooth, but they do not have a single row of enlarged, keeled scales down the center of the back. The ventral scales are not much larger than most of the dorsal scales. They have an ear opening, and the eyelids are movable and without a transparent window. There are no fringes of scales along the edges of the toes, no enlarged toe pads, and no large spines festooning the back of the head. There is a fold of skin covered with small granular scales across the throat. This combination of characters should separate these three genera from all others in our area. Separating them from one another is a more difficult problem, since most of the differences are in skeletal characters that cannot be studied on intact specimens. Rock Lizards are larger and more flat-bodied with a distinctly banded tail. Side-blotched lizards usually have a dark spot behind the armpit and do not have any enlarged dorsal scales. Tree lizards usually have some of the dorsal scales enlarged. Habits may help identify them—Tree Lizards are most often found on trees, Rock Lizards on rocks, and Side-blotched Lizards on the ground—but some Tree Lizards are typically found on rocks, and Side-blotched Lizards can be found climbing on boulders and bushes. All of the Tree Lizards are diurnal insect eaters. Three species are found in the United States.

Small-scaled Tree Lizard, *Urosaurus microscutatus*

These are small Tree Lizards with very small scales on the back and sides, slightly larger scales down the center of the back, and large, keeled scales on the tail. They are dark-gray with blackish transverse bars or bands. The throat region in the male is blue with a yellowish center, and there are blue patches on the sides of the belly. Females lack the blue markings. The head-and-body length of these lizards is only about 2 inches, and the tail is a little less than twice as long. These "Tree" Lizards are found most often among rocks. Females lay four to eight soft-shelled eggs. In the United States the species is found in California from San Diego County southward.

Long-tailed Brush Lizard, *Urosaurus graciosus*

Members of this species are a little larger than the Small-scaled Tree Lizards, adults ranging from 2 to 2¼ inches in head-and-body length, with a tail often more than twice as long. There is a broad band of large, keeled scales down the middle of the back, and these scales are not separated by a central series of smaller scales, as in the Common Tree Lizard. These lizards are light- to dark-gray, usually with darker crossbands, and often a yellow or reddish patch on the throat. Males have blue-green patches on the belly. This lizard is found most often in the scrubby bushes of sandy desert areas. We have two races within our limits.

Western Brush Lizard, *Urosaurus g. graciosus*

The dorsal pattern is inconspicuous in adults of this race, which is found in southeastern California, southern Nevada, and western Arizona.

Arizona Brush Lizard, *Urosaurus g. shannoni*

The dorsal pattern consists of highly contrasting black marks on a gray ground color in adult males, brown on gray in females. This race is found in south central Arizona.

Common Tree Lizard, *Urosaurus ornatus*

These lizards are about the same as the Long-tailed Tree Lizards in head-and-body length, but they have somewhat shorter tails. The stripe of enlarged scales along the back is divided by a central stripe of much smaller scales. They are usually dark-colored lizards—either grayish, bluish, or brownish, and they tend to have rather vaguely defined crossbands of a darker hue on the back. Males have blue patches on the belly. The throat patch is orange or yellow in the females, variable in the males. These lizards are usually found climbing on bushes, rocks, or buildings. A number of races have been described in the United States, but the differences between them are not very clear, and the group is in much need of study. We will not attempt to define the races but simply give the ranges assigned to them.

Eastern Tree Lizard, *Urosaurus o. ornatus*

This form occurs in south central Texas east of the Big Bend region.

Smooth Tree Lizard, *Urosaurus o. levis*

This race is restricted to north central New Mexico.

Lined Tree Lizard, *Urosaurus o. linearis*

This form occupies central, southern, and southwestern New Mexico and central and southeastern Arizona.

Big Bend Tree Lizard, *Urosaurus o. schmidti*

As the name indicates, this is an inhabitant of the Big Bend region of Texas west of the Pecos River, extending northward into extreme southeastern New Mexico.

Colorado River Tree Lizard, *Urosaurus o. symmetrica*

This is the most western of the races, extending from southern and western Arizona into extreme southeastern Nevada and extreme southeastern California.

Northern Tree Lizard, *Urosaurus o. wrighti*

This is the most northern form, ranging from northern Arizona and northwestern New Mexico through western Colorado and eastern and central Utah to southwestern Wyoming.

Banded Rock Lizard, *Petrosaurus mearnsi* (Figure 57)

These lizards look rather like Collared Lizards but are flatter and do not have such broad heads. Some of the scales on top of the head are enlarged, and there are large, keeled, pointed scales on the tail, but the dorsal scales are small and granular. The dorsal pattern consists of a dark collar, often edged behind by white, several dusky crossbands on an olive-gray ground color, and a sprinkling of small white or bluish spots. The tail is banded. There is more or less blue on the underside, especially in the males. Adults reach nearly 4 inches in head-and-body length, and the tail is about twice as long. These insectivorous, diurnal lizards are found climbing among rocks in arid regions. Females apparently lay two or three eggs; otherwise the breeding habits are unknown. This species enters the United States only in southern California, ranging northward as far as Riverside County.

Side-blotched Lizard, *Uta stansburiana*

These small lizards are brownish in color, with longitudinal stripes, blotches, or many small spots. A large inky-blue spot behind the armpit on each side gives the species its common name. The spot is especially evident in males and may be absent in females. Males are able to change color and sometimes appear covered with pale-blue specks. Some of the head scales are enlarged; the dorsal scales are granular. There is a fold of skin covered with small granular scales across the throat region, and distinct external ear openings are present. Adults are 1¾ to 2½ inches in head-and-body length, and the tail is somewhat longer. These are ground-dwelling, insect-eating inhabitants of arid and semiarid regions. The eggs are laid in early summer, and the young hatch after about two months. Egg clutches ranging from one to four in number have been recorded. There are three races of this species in the United States, all very similar.

Northern Side-blotched Lizard, *Uta s. stansburiana* (Plate 9b)

The dorsal scales are small and weakly keeled in this race, and the dorsal blotches are not prominent. It ranges from northwestern New Mexico westward into northern Arizona, south central Nevada and extreme eastern California, northward through western Colorado, all of Utah except the southwestern part, southeastern Wyoming, southern Idaho, eastern Oregon, and south central Washington.

California Side-blotched Lizard, *Uta s. hesperis*

This is the largest of the races. The dorsal scales are small and strongly keeled, the back marked with prominent dark blotches. This is a form of the southern California coastal regions extending in the western half of California from the vicinity of San Francisco Bay southward.

Fig. 57. Banded Rock Lizard, *Petrosaurus mearnsi*

Fig. 58. Desert Side-blotched Lizard, *Uta s. stejnegeri*

Desert Side-blotched Lizard, *Uta s. stejnegeri* (Figure 58)

The dorsal scales are larger and usually strongly keeled in this race. The dark blotches are not so pronounced and females are usually striped. It occurs in southeastern California, southern Nevada, southwestern Utah, all of Arizona and New Mexico except the northern parts, and western Texas and southwestern Oklahoma.

Spiny Lizards, Genus *Sceloporus*

These small to moderate-sized lizards have the dorsal scales keeled, overlapping, and often sharply pointed, giving a bristly appearance. The scales of the middorsal row are not particularly enlarged. There is no complete fold of skin across the throat, though folds may be present on either side of the neck. The body is usually short and broad. Males usually have bright-blue patches on either side of the belly and often also blue on the throat. Females may also show these patches, but they are usually smaller and less intense in color than those of the males. Many of the species lay eggs, but in a few the young are born alive. These lizards are diurnal and primarily insectivorous, and most are agile climbers. There are over fifty species in the genus which ranges from western Canada, southward to Panama; fifteen of these species occur in the United States. Some of them are divided into a number of races, frequently based on the pattern of the breeding males. Females and young may be difficult to identify—use a combination of geography and the appearance of the males in the same area.

Clark's Spiny Lizard, *Sceloporus clarki*

These are gray, greenish, or bluish lizards, with narrow dark crossbands (indistinct in adults of one race) across the back and with more distinct dark crossbands on the front legs. The dorsal scales are large, keeled, and pointed. Males have blue throats and blue belly patches; females have dark lines on the throat. This is one of the larger Spiny Lizards—adults reach more than 5 inches in head-and-body length. They are found both on trees and on the ground in rocky, wooded, semiarid regions. The females lay eggs. There are two races.

Sonora Spiny Lizard, *Sceloporus c. clarki* (Plate 9c)

The pattern, except for the crossbars on the front legs, is indistinct in the adults. This race is found in southwestern New Mexico and southeastern Arizona except on the Colorado Plateau.

Plateau Spiny Lizard, *Sceloporus c. villaris*

The pattern remains distinct, even in large adults, and the animals appear bluer in color. This form is restricted to the edge of the Colorado Plateau in Arizona.

Blue Spiny Lizard, *Sceloporus cyanogenys*

This is one of the largest of our Spiny Lizards. Large adults reach 5½ inches in head-and-body length. The males are bright greenish-blue, the females and young duller, with indistinct crossbands. There is a distinct, light-bordered, black collar around the neck. Males also have bright-blue patches on the throat and sides of the belly. The dorsal scales are rather large and weakly keeled and are strongly pointed only on the sides. These lizards are found on rocky outcrops and dry earth banks. The young are born alive. This species is found in southern Texas.

Sagebrush Lizard, *Sceloporus graciosus*

This is a rather somber-colored *Sceloporus*, the dorsal color grayish-brown or olive, with orange or reddish markings in the armpits and on the sides. The dorsal scales are rather small, keeled, and pointed. The scales on the back of the thigh are small, granular, and mostly smooth. The throat is mottled light-blue in the males, the body patches darker. This is a small *Sceloporus*, the head-and-body length ranging from 2 to 2½ inches. The females lay eggs. Sagebrush Lizards are more terrestrial than most other Spiny Lizards. They are found on desert floors and arid mountain slopes. There are three races.

Great Basin Sagebrush Lizard, *Sceloporus g. graciosus*

This form usually has distinct dorsolateral dark and light stripes. It is characteristic of the Great Basin and ranges from northwestern New Mexico to eastern California and north to central Washington, Idaho, and Montana.

Northwestern Sagebrush Lizard, *Sceloporus g. gracilis*

The dorsal scales are smaller and the stripes less distinct in this California form of the Sagebrush Lizard, which occurs in the Sierra Nevadas and the coast range both north and south of San Francisco Bay.

Southern Sagebrush Lizard, *Sceloporus g. vandenburghianus*

This race is larger, and the blue ventral areas are more extensive. It occurs in isolated populations in southern California in the San Gabriel, San Bernardino, San Jacinto, and Santa Rosa mountains.

Mesquite Lizard, *Sceloporus grammicus disparilis*

This is a moderate-sized *Sceloporus*, gray or greenish in ground color, with from 4 to 6 narrow, dark, transverse lines across the back. Larger individuals may lose this pattern and be almost uniform in color. The dorsal scales are rather small, and the scales on the side of the neck are much smaller than those on the back of the neck. Adults reach nearly 3 inches in head-and-body length. They are shy, unobtrusive lizards, found on scrubby trees in arid regions. The young are born alive. In the United States this form is restricted to extreme southern Texas.

Yarrow's Spiny Lizard, *Sceloporus jarrovi jarrovi* (Figure 59)

This is a distinctive lizard in which the ground color is black with a light spot on each scale on the back and in which there is a distinct black collar around the neck, with a narrow, light border behind. Males have blue patches on the throat and sides of the belly. Females are duller in color but show the dark collar. The females bring forth their young alive. Adults range between $2\frac{1}{2}$ and $3\frac{1}{2}$ inches in head-and-body length. This is a mountainous species, found in rocky woodlands. It occurs in southeastern Arizona and southwestern New Mexico.

Desert Spiny Lizard, *Sceloporus magister*

This is a large Spiny Lizard, large individuals having a head-and-body length of $5\frac{1}{2}$ inches. The dorsal scales are large, keeled, and pointed. These lizards are yellow to light-brown, with a black patch on each shoulder edged with light behind. Males have the typical blue throat and belly marks. They are frequently found on the ground around rocks and bushes in arid and semiarid regions. Five races, based largely on the color patterns of the adult males, have been described for the United States.

Desert Spiny Lizard, *Sceloporus m. magister*

In this race the male has a broad black or purple stripe down the back, with a light stripe on either side. It is found in southcentral and southwestern Arizona, northward to Phoenix.

Twin-spotted Spiny Lizard, *Sceloporus m. bimaculosus*

Males have a double row of distinct black spots down the middle of the back. This race ranges from southwestern Texas to southeastern Arizona.

Orange-headed Spiny Lizard, *Sceloperus m. cephaloflavus*

Both males and females have yellowish-orange on the head, and males usually have 5 or 6 chevron-shaped bars on the back. This race is found in southeastern Utah, northeastern Arizona, northwestern New Mexico, and extreme southwestern Colorado.

Barred Spiny Lizard, *Sceloporus m. transversus*

This race has rather distinct black bars across the back. It is found from Inyo and Kern counties, California, to Mineral and Esmeralda counties, Nevada.

Fig. 59. Yarrow's Spiny Lizard, *Sceloporus jarrovi jarrovi*

Fig. 60. Southern Fence Lizard, *Sceloporus u. undulatus*

Yellow-backed Spiny Lizard, *Sceloporus m. uniformis*

In this race the middle part of the back is either plain-colored or has a row of faint, squarish blotches. It ranges from the region of Pyramid Lake, Nevada, southward and eastward into southwestern Utah and northern and central Arizona and westward in the Mohave and Colorado deserts of California and in San Benito and Fresno counties on the west side of the San Joaquin Valley.

Canyon Lizard, *Sceloporus merriami*

This is a rather distinctive Spiny Lizard, gray in color, with about a dozen dark spots on each side of the middorsal line, with small dorsal scales and with the scales along the sides granular. There is a fold of skin on either side of the throat region. These are small lizards, adults not reaching much more than 2 inches in head-and-body length. There are two races.

Merriam's Canyon Lizard, *Sceloporus m. merriami*

The underside of the tail is pale-blue, occasionally with faint traces of darker crossbands. This form is found in lowland desert canyons from Val Verde to Brewster County, Texas.

Big Bend Canyon Lizard, *Sceloporus m. annulatus*

The bands under the tail are distinct in this race, which is known only from the mountains of Brewster County, Texas.

Western Fence Lizard, *Sceloporus occidentalis*

This is a grayish, brownish, or greenish Spiny Lizard, with rather distinct dark spots or wavy crossbars on the back and sometimes longitudinal light stripes. The hind surfaces of the legs are yellow or orange in adults. The dorsal scales are keeled and pointed and not much larger than the scales on the sides and belly. This species is very similar to the Eastern Fence Lizard, but the two overlap only in a small area, in southwestern Utah and southeastern Nevada. Where they do overlap, mature males of *occidentalis* have a single throat patch, while in males of *undulatus* the throat patch is always divided. Females and young are more difficult to tell apart; female *occidentalis* sometimes have the throat patch divided, but the two parts are closer to the center of the throat, while in *undulatus* the patches are at the sides of the throat. Adults of the Western Fence Lizard reach $3\frac{1}{2}$ inches in head-and-body length. The females lay eggs. These lizards are found in many different habitats but seem to prefer rocky wooded regions. They are often found climbing on rocks, trees, or buildings. There are six races.

Northwestern Fence Lizard, *Sceloporus o. occidentalis*

Males usually have two very blue patches on the sides of the throat which may be connected by a lighter blue band. Females almost always have blue throat patches, too. The chest and area between the belly patches are usually pale. This race is found in the less humid parts of the coastal forest of Washington and Oregon, southward in the coast ranges as far as San Francisco Bay in California. In northern California it occupies the northern Sierra Nevadas and the Sacramento Valley, southward into the upper part of the San Joaquin Valley.

Island Fence Lizard, *Sceloporus o. becki*

The throat patch is black, with black lines radiating forward into the blue color of the chin. These lizards are restricted in distribution to the Channel Islands off the coast of southern California.

San Joaquin Fence Lizard, *Sceloporus o. biseriatus*

Males usually have a single blue throat patch (sometimes divided) marked with small, light flecks. The blue belly patches are usually black-bordered and separated by a light area. This race is restricted to the lower San Joaquin Valley, California.

Coast Range Fence Lizard, *Sceloporus o. bocourti*

The throat patches in the males are small, and they are usually absent entirely in the females. This form ranges south of San Francisco Bay as far as Santa Barbara County, California.

Great Basin Fence Lizard, *Sceloporus o. longipes*

Adult males almost always have a single, large blue throat patch. The chest and area between the belly patches are usually dark. This is a form of the Great Basin, ranging from Inyo and Mono counties in California, eastward through Nevada to the Wasatch Mountains of Utah, northward through southwestern Idaho, eastern Oregon, and southeastern Washington. There seems to be an isolated population in southern coastal California from the region of Los Angeles County southward.

Sierra Fence Lizard, *Sceloporus o. taylori*

In large males the entire belly is blue. This form is restricted to the Sierra Nevadas in California, above about 7,000 feet.

Texas Spiny Lizard, *Sceloporus olivaceus*

This is a grayish or reddish-brown Spiny Lizard, with rather indistinct longitudinal light stripes along each side and with several dark bars across the back. The dorsal scales are very large, strongly keeled, and strongly pointed. The males have narrow, light-blue patches without black borders on either side of the belly. Adults reach a maximum of $4\frac{3}{4}$ inches in head-and-body length. These are arboreal lizards, quick and agile but rather noisy climbers. They are found from southern Oklahoma through the Texas prairie region to the lower Rio Grande

Granite Spiny Lizard, *Sceloporus orcutti orcutti*

The males are strongly colored. The back is coppery to black, with a blue spot in the center of each scale, giving an iridescent appearance; the entire underside is blue. Sometimes the males have a rather broad purple stripe down the middle of the back. The females are apt to be banded like the young. The dorsal scales are large but not so strongly pointed and keeled as in the Desert Spiny Lizard. The maximum head-and-body length is 4¼ inches. Granite Spiny Lizards are found in rocky and scrubby semidesert regions in the mountains. They are often found on the ground but are also excellent climbers. This species occurs in southern California.

Crevice Spiny Lizard, *Sceloporus poinsetti*

This is a large lizard, reaching nearly 5 inches in head-and-body length, grayish to reddish in color and with a distinct, large black collar across the back of the neck. The collar is bordered by light areas. The tail is banded, especially toward the tip. Males have light-blue throat and belly patches. The blue patches are faint or absent in the females, and they, like the young, appear crossbanded. The dorsal scales are large, keeled, pointed, and projecting. In this species, females bring forth their young alive. Crevice Spiny Lizards are found among rocks in semiarid and arid regions in central and western Texas and southern New Mexico.

Bunch Grass Lizard, *Sceloporus scalaris slevini*

This species may be plain light-brown on the back or show a pattern of crescent-shaped blotches. There is usually a pair of light stripes on each side and a black patch in front of the shoulder. The scales along the side are arranged in rows parallel to those on the back, rather than at an angle to them, as in the other species of *Sceloporus*. This is a small lizard with a maximum head-and-body length of 2½ inches. It is found in the mountains of southeastern Arizona.

Eastern Fence Lizard, *Sceloporus undulatus*

These are usually rather dull-colored lizards, grayish in ground color, with indistinct, dark transverse bars or spots on the back and sometimes with dark or light longitudinal stripes. The dorsal scales are keeled and pointed and not much larger than those on the belly. The males almost always have blue on the throat and sides of the belly. This is the common Fence Lizard of the eastern and central United States. It is a widespread and variable species; to pick characters that will separate it from all other Spiny Lizards is not easy. Over much of its range, though, it is the only member of the genus and should be easy to identify. It is most similar to the Western Fence Lizard. See the discussion under that species for differences between the two. In central Florida, compare with the Florida Scrub Lizard and in southeastern Arizona and southwestern New Mexico with the Striped

Plateau Lizard. Fence Lizards are seen most often climbing on trees, bushes, rock piles, and as the name suggests, rail fences. There are nine races in the United States.

Southern Fence Lizard, *Sceloporus u. undulatus* (Figure 60)

The males may be almost entirely black underneath, except for the blue on the sides of the belly and throat. Adults may reach slightly more than 3 inches in head-and-body length. This form ranges from the coastal region of central South Carolina, westward through the southern half of Louisiana and southward in peninsular Florida to south of the Tampa Bay area.

Northern Fence Lizard, *Sceloporus u. hyacinthinus*

This race is slightly smaller and less strongly marked than the Southern Fence Lizard. The dorsal scales are smaller. It ranges from central New Jersey and southern Pennsylvania, southward to central South Carolina, Georgia, Alabama, and Mississippi, westward in the north through southern Ohio, Indiana, Illinois, and Missouri into eastern Kansas, and southward through eastern Texas nearly to the Mexican border.

Southern Prairie Lizard, *Sceloporus u. consobrinus*

This race has 2 light stripes on each side, the lower poorly defined, and the dark bars across the back are broken into spots. Males have a blue patch on either side of the throat, as well as on either side of the belly. The maximum head-and-body length is about 2¾ inches. This is a form of the southern prairies, ranging from southwestern Oklahoma, southern New Mexico, and extreme southeastern Arizona southward through Texas into northern Mexico.

Northern Prairie Lizard, *Sceloporus u. garmani*

The light stripes are well defined, the dorsal bars represented by spots; blue throat patches are lacking. This is a small race, the maximum head-and-body length being about 2½ inches. It ranges from central Oklahoma, northward into southern South Dakota and westward into southeastern Wyoming, northeastern Colorado, and the northeastern tip of the Texas panhandle.

Eastern Plateau Fence Lizard, *Sceloporus u. erythrocheilus*

In this race the lips of the breeding males are bright-red. The light stripes are poorly developed or lacking. In both males and females the blue throat patches meet on the midline. Adults may reach slightly over 3 inches in head-and-body length. This Plateau Lizard is found in northeastern New Mexico, Colorado east of the mountains, extreme southeastern Wyoming, and the western tip of the Oklahoma panhandle.

Northern Plateau Lizard, *Sceloporus u. elongatus*

The dark transverse bars on the back are well defined; the blue throat patches fail to meet in the middle; and the breeding males lack red on the lips. The maximum head-and-body length is 3¼ inches. This form occurs in northwestern New Mexico, northeastern Arizona, eastern Utah, western Colorado, and southwestern Wyoming.

Southern Plateau Lizard, *Sceloporus u. tristichus*

The light stripes are usually well developed in this race. The throat patches fail to meet in the middle. Maximum size is slightly less than in the Northern Plateau Lizard. This race is found in northeastern Arizona and southeastern Utah.

White Sands Fence Lizard, *Sceloporus u. cowlesi*

This distinctive lizard, extremely light in color with a broad light blue middorsal stripe, is found only in the White Sands National Monument, New Mexico.

Texas Rose-bellied Lizard, *Sceloporus variabilis marmoratus*

This is one of the most distinctive of the Fence Lizards. Males have pink belly patches edged with dark-blue. There is a pocket in the skin at the base of the tail just behind the hind leg. These characters are found in none of our other *Sceloporus*. Dorsally they are buffy to olive-brown lizards, with light longitudinal stripes and a double row of dark spots down the back. They are small lizards, adults reaching a head-and-body length of 2⅛ inches. They are often found on the ground in arid regions but can climb well on rocks, bushes, and fence posts. This is essentially a Mexican species, entering the United States only in southeastern Texas.

Striped Plateau Lizard, *Sceloporus virgatus*

This species resembles the Fence Lizards. There is on each side a dorsolateral light stripe, below this a brown stripe, then another light stripe and another dark stripe. There are usually pairs of dark-brown spots on the back and sometimes white spots as well. Both males and females lack blue patches on the sides of the belly and have small blue patches on the sides of the throat. After mating, the blue is more or less replaced by orange in females. Adults reach 2¾ inches in head-and-body length. This species is found in the mountains of southwestern New Mexico and southeastern Arizona at elevations above 5,000 feet. The Fence Lizard (*S. undulatus*) is found in the same general region but at lower elevations.

Florida Scrub Lizard, *Sceloporus woodi*

This moderate-sized Fence Lizard is restricted to the scrub region of central Florida. It differs from the Southern Fence Lizard, the only other *Sceloporus* found within its range, in having the middle part of the back tan and without distinct crossbars, while the Southern Fence Lizard has a grayish back with more or less distinct crossbars.

Fringe-toed Lizards, Genus *Uma*

These lizards are related to the Earless Lizards and Zebra-tailed Lizards. They differ from all our other lizards in having a fringe of long, pointed scales on the margins of the toes, an adaptation for moving through the fine sand of the deserts in which they live. The lower jaw is countersunk, the head wedge-shaped in profile, the body flattened, the eyelids thick and heavy, the body scales fine and granular, all further adaptations for moving through sand. The dorsal ground color is usually light, matching the color of the sand. The pattern consists of spots and reticulations. The undersurfaces are white, with dark lines on the throat and black bars toward the tip of the tail. Adults range from about 3 to 4½ inches in head-and-body length. These active, diurnal, insectivorous lizards are found around sand dunes. They are able to hide themselves by "swimming" into the sand. Females lay from one to four eggs. There are three species, two of which occur in the United States.

Fringe-toed Lizard, *Uma notata*

The black lines on the throat usually do not meet in the center, or if they do, they are not broadened to form crescent-shaped marks. The dorsal spots and reticulations form eyelike marks that are arranged in more or less regular rows. There are three races.

Colorado Desert Fringe-toed Lizard, *Uma n. notata* (Plate 9d)

A black blotch is present on the side. Adults have a bright-orange or red band along each side of the belly, brightest during the breeding season but always present to some degree. This race is found in the Colorado Desert of California.

Coachella Valley Fringe-toed Lizard, *Uma n. inornata*

There is no conspicuous black blotch on the side, although there may be a small cluster of black dots. During the breeding season, adults have a pinkish wash along the sides of the belly. This race is found in Coachella Valley and San Gorgonio Pass, Riverside County, California.

Cowles' Fringe-toed Lizard, *Uma n. rufopunctata*

A black lateral blotch is present. The belly is white except during the breeding season, when there is a pink wash along the sides. This race is found in the Sonoran Desert of southwestern Arizona.

Mohave Fringe-toed Lizard, *Uma scoparia*

The black lines on the throat form one or more crescents broadened in the central throat region. A black blotch is present on the side. The dorsal spots and reticulations form eyelike marks, but these do not appear to be arranged in rows. During the breeding season the males show a greenish-yellow color on the belly, and the females are pinkish along the sides. This form inhabits the Mohave Desert in southern California.

Earless Lizards, Genus *Holbrookia*

These are lizards of the western United States and northern Mexico. They differ from other lizards in our area in having the top of the head covered with numerous small, symmetrical scales and in lacking external ear openings. They are small, slender, rather flat-bodied, and long-legged lizards, with most of the scales nearly uniform in size and, with the single exception of the Keeled Earless Lizard, with the dorsal scales smooth. There is a fold of skin across the throat. The males have distinct, slanting black marks along the sides, except in the Spot-tailed Earless Lizard. These marks are faint or absent in the females. Females carrying eggs may be washed with pink or orange. Earless Lizards are inhabitants of sandy places and are primarily insectivorous. The females lay eggs. The four species all are found in the United States.

Spot-tailed Earless Lizard, *Holbrookia lacerata*

The markings under the tail are in the form of spots, rather than crossbands. These spots tend to fade out toward the tip. The back is marked with light-bordered dark blotches on a grayish brown ground color, and these marks continue onto the tail as paired blotches. The maximum head-and-body length is about 2¾ inches. There are two races in the United States.

Plateau Spot-tailed Earless Lizard, *Holbrookia l. lacerata*

The dark blotches on each side of the back usually form a single row on each side, and the hind legs are marked with dark bands. This form occurs in the Edwards Plateau region of central Texas.

Southern Spot-tailed Earless Lizard, *Holbrookia l. subcaudalis*

The dark blotches usually form two rows on either side of the back and the hind legs are spotted. This race occurs in southern Texas except for the lower Rio Grande Valley.

Lesser Earless Lizard, *Holbrookia maculata*

These are small lizards, about 2½ inches at most in head-and-body length and with the tail about the same length or shorter than the body

They are light-gray to brownish in color, more or less blotched, with a middorsal light line and with the underside of the tail unmarked. The ground color usually matches the color of the soil where the lizards live. The male has two black lines behind the armpit, often surrounded by a small blue area. During the breeding season, females have orange or yellow on the throat. A number of races have been described for the United States, but the differences between them are vague, and the ranges are not well known.

Northern Earless Lizard, *Holbrookia m. maculata*

This form ranges from extreme southern South Dakota through most of Nebraska except the eastern part, western and central Kansas, northeastern New Mexico, eastern Colorado, and extreme southeastern Wyoming.

Eastern Earless Lizard, *Holbrookia m. perspicua*

This race is found from south central Kansas to north central Texas.

Speckled Earless Lizard, *Holbrookia m. approximans*

This form occurs in extreme western Texas and southern and north central New Mexico.

Huachuca Earless Lizard, *Holbrookia m. pulchra*

This form is restricted to the high grassland region of southeastern Arizona above about 5,000 feet.

Colorado Plateau Earless Lizard, *Holbrookia m. campi*

This race is found on the Colorado Plateau in northwestern New Mexico, northeastern Arizona, southwestern Colorado, and southeastern Utah.

Western Earless Lizard, *Holbrookia m. elegans*

This form occurs in southeastern Arizona except for the area occupied by the Huachuca Earless Lizard.

Greater Earless Lizard, *Holbrookia texana*

This is the largest of the Earless Lizards, the adults sometimes exceeding 3 inches in head-and-body length. They are grayish or brown in color, usually with irregularly spaced dark spots and small, light flecks on the back. They have several broad black bands on the under surface of the tail. Males have two big black lines in a blue patch on the side near the hind leg. Females may have orange throats. There are two races in our area.

Texas Earless Lizard, *Holbrookia t. texana*

The dark spots on the back, if present, are not prominent, and the ground color is darker in this race. It occurs in central and western Texas and southeastern New Mexico.

Southwestern Earless Lizard, *Holbrookia t. scitula*

The ground color is light-gray; there are prominent black spots on the back and many orange, red, or yellow spots on the sides. This form ranges in Texas west of the Pecos, in south central and southwestern New Mexico and southeastern and central Arizona.

Keeled Earless Lizard, *Holbrookia propinqua propinqua*

This lizard differs from all the other Earless Lizards in having keels on the dorsal scales, but the scales are so small that the keels may be hard to see. There are no spots or bands under the tail. The only other Earless Lizard that lacks markings under the tail is the Lesser Earless Lizard, which is not found in the same region. The black lines on the side of the male are behind the armpit and are not surrounded with blue. The maximum head and body length is nearly $2\frac{1}{2}$ inches, and if the tail is complete, it is usually longer than the head and body. In the United States this lizard is restricted to Texas south of the vicinity of San Antonio.

Zebra-tailed Lizard, *Callisaurus draconoides* (Plate 9e)

These are moderate-sized, long-tailed, long-legged lizards that dwell in sandy places. They are similar to the Earless Lizards and Fringe-toed Lizards and, like them, have small scales on top of the head, small, granular scales on the back, and a fold of skin across the throat. They differ from the Earless Lizards in having external ear openings and from the Fringe-toed Lizards in lacking fringing scales on the toes. The undersurface of the tail is marked with distinct black and white bands. Like many other lizards they are able to change from light to dark, depending largely on the temperature. There are rows of more or less well-marked dark spots on the back and a dusky patch under the throat. Males have wedge-shaped black bars in bright-blue patches on the sides of the belly. Adults reach $3\frac{1}{2}$ inches in head-and-body length. They are very rapid, insectivorous, diurnal lizards, with the habit of holding the tail up and waving it to and fro when disturbed. Females lay two to six eggs. This species is restricted to the southwestern United States and northern Mexico, with three races, all very similar, in the United States. These races can hardly be identified except by a specialist who has a good series at hand.

Colorado Desert Zebra-tailed Lizard, *Callisaurus d. rhodosticus*

This form ranges in southern Nevada, extreme southwestern Utah, southeastern California, and western Arizona.

Nevada Zebra-tailed Lizard, *Callisaurus d. myurus*

This race occurs in central Nevada north of the range of the Colorado Desert Zebra-tailed Lizard.

Arizona Zebra-tailed Lizard, *Callisaurus d. ventralis*

This race is found in south central Arizona.

Curl-tailed Lizard, *Leiocephalus carinatus armouri*
(Figure 61)

Superficially these lizards look something like Spiny Lizards but they have a rather striking habit of curling the long, thin tail like a watch spring above the body, and this distinguishes them from any other lizard in our region. The color is gray to brownish, with the sides generally somewhat darker than the back. The tail is usually more or less banded, and the head irregularly marked with black. The scales on the back are rather large, keeled, and pointed. Those in the central row are somewhat enlarged and form a crest on the tail. The adult is about 3½ inches in head-and-body length. This is a tropical lizard that has been introduced into Palm Beach and Dade counties, Florida, from the Bahamas.

LATERAL FOLD LIZARDS, FAMILY ANGUINIDAE

All members of this family in the United States have a deep groove running along each side. The skin in the groove is usually covered with granular scales much smaller than the platelike scales on the back and belly. (The groove is lacking in members of the family in other parts of the world.) The family is widespread in both the Old and New Worlds but contains only a few genera, and of these, only two are found in the United States. Separating them is easy—Alligator Lizards have legs, and Glass Lizards lack them.

Glass Lizards, Genus *Ophisaurus*

With their long, slim bodies and lack of legs, these lizards are more apt to be mistaken for snakes than for other lizards and indeed they are sometimes called Glass Snakes. Their movable eyelids and external ear openings will distinguish them from any snake. Like the Alligator Lizards, they have a long groove down each side of the body. The tail is very long and very fragile. There are ten species in the genus, three of which occur in the United States. All American species lack legs, although some of the Old World forms do have very short limbs. Glass Lizards are apt to be found where the grass is tall and thick and are particularly apt to be active in the morning or late in the evening. Insects form the main part of their diet but they also eat other smaller lizards and snakes. Females lay from eight to seventeen eggs.

Fig. 61. Curl-tailed Lizard, *Leiocephalus carinatus armouri*

Fig. 62. Texas Alligator Lizard, *Gerrhonotus liocephalus infernalis*

Slender Glass Lizard, *Ophisaurus attenuatus*

This Glass Lizard differs from both of the other species in having narrow, dark stripes on the side below as well as above the lateral groove. There is a dark middorsal stripe, which may be broken into blotches in large adults. The maximum head-and-body length is $11\frac{3}{8}$ inches. This most widespread of all of our Glass Lizards is divided into two races.

Western Slender Glass Lizard, *Ophisaurus a. attenuatus*

The tail is somewhat shorter in this race, which ranges west of the Mississippi except in the north, where it extends into Illinois, extreme western Indiana, and southern Wisconsin. Westward it reaches southeastern Nebraska, central Kansas and Oklahoma, and eastern Texas as far south as the Rio Grande.

Eastern Slender Glass Lizard, *Ophisaurus a. longicaudus*

The tail is longer in this race, which is found in the southeastern states from southeastern Virginia to southern Florida and west to the Mississippi, except in the high mountains.

Island Glass Lizard, *Ophisaurus compressus*

This form has no dark stripe below the lateral groove. It does have a dark stripe above the groove and generally a rather distinct middorsal dark stripe which may be broken into a series of dashes. It is the smallest of the species, with a maximum head-and-body length of $6\frac{5}{8}$ inches. It is found in the coastal region of South Carolina and Georgia and through most of Florida east and south of the Suwannee River.

Eastern Glass Lizard, *Ophisaurus ventralis* (Plate 9f)

This species has no longitudinal dark stripe on the side below the groove and no distinct middorsal stripe. The young are tan, but old adults may be green in color. Large adults may reach $11\frac{1}{2}$ inches in head-and-body length. The Eastern Glass Lizard is found on the coastal plain from North Carolina to central Louisiana and throughout all of Florida.

Alligator Lizards, Genus *Gerrhonotus*

These rather large lizards of the western continental United States can be separated from all of our other lizards by the presence of front and hind legs and of a deep groove where the skin is folded in along the side of the body. This groove permits expansion of the body when the belly is gorged with food or when the female is packed with eggs. Our only other lizards with such a groove are the Glass Lizards, which lack legs. Alligator Lizards have more or less quadrangular scales arranged in parallel rows. The legs are short, the tail long. The dorsal pattern usually consists of crossbands, often irregular or broken into spots or blotches. These are terrestrial lizards, primarily solitary, secretive, slow moving and quiet. Some species lay eggs, others give birth to living young. There are five species with ten races found in the United States. They are rather difficult to distinguish, but when geography is taken into account, it should be possible to identify most of the forms, since only two of the species, the Northern and Southern overlap in range.

Northern Alligator Lizard, *Gerrhonotus coeruleus*

These are moderate-sized ($3\frac{1}{2}$ to $5\frac{1}{4}$ inches in head-and-body length) Alligator Lizards, greenish, olive, or bluish on the back, usually with brownish spots or blotches, which may unite to form irregular crossbands. The belly is light, sometimes marked with faint dark stripes that run between the scale rows. The eye is dark. The tail is less than twice the head-and-body length. The young are born alive. They lack crossbands but have a broad, light stripe down the back. The ranges of the Northern and Southern Alligator Lizard overlap, but the two are usually found in different situations. The northern species prefers cool, moist woodlands and is found not only farther north, but also at higher elevations; the southern is more apt to be found in drier, warmer woods or open grassy areas. There are four races of the Northern Alligator Lizard.

San Francisco Alligator Lizard, *Gerrhonotus c. coeruleus*

There are usually dark blotches or crossbands on the back, and the scales are heavily keeled. This form occurs in western California, both north and south of the San Francisco Bay area.

Sierra Alligator Lizard, *Gerrhonotus c. palmeri*

The adults usually lack a broad, light-colored area on the back, and there are distinct dark spots on the head and a dark line below the eye. This is a form of the Sierra Nevada in California.

Northern Alligator Lizard, *Gerrhonotus c. principis*

Adults usually have a broad tan or golden-brown band on the back, which is lighter than the color of the sides. The dark markings on the back are reduced or absent. This form occurs from extreme north-western California to southern British Columbia and Victoria Island and eastward along the Washington–Canadian border, turning southward into northern Idaho and western Montana.

Shasta Alligator Lizard, *Gerrhonotus c. shastensis*

Many of the scales on the body are light-tipped. The race occurs in northern California north of the Sierra Nevada and extends into southwestern Oregon, where it meets the range of the Northern Alligator Lizard. It ranges southward to meet the ranges of the Sierra and San Francisco Alligator Lizards north of the region of San Francisco Bay.

Arizona Alligator Lizard, *Gerrhonotus kingi nobilis*

This rather small Alligator Lizard is only about 3 to 5 inches in head-and-body length. The ground color is gray to brown, and there are 9 to 12 irregular crossbands on the back. The iris of the eye is usually orange to pink. The young hatch from eggs and are strongly crossbanded. This is a mountainous form, terrestrial and diurnal, found in open woodlands and grassy places. A single race enters the United States in southeastern Arizona and southwestern New Mexico.

Texas Alligator Lizard, *Gerrhonotus liocephalus infernalis* (Figure 62)

This, the largest Alligator Lizard in our country, has a maximum head-and-body length of about 8 inches and looks something like a small alligator. It is yellowish to reddish-brown on the back, with irregular crossbands. Many of the scales in the crossbands are very pale, so that the impression is one of light crossbands on a dark background. The tail, like the body, is banded, but the legs and head are plain-colored. The young hatch from eggs and are strikingly cross-banded. These terrestrial, diurnal lizards are found among bushes on rocky slopes. They eat both invertebrates and small vertebrates. Only one race of this Mexican species enters the United States in the Edwards Plateau and Big Bend regions of Texas.

Southern Alligator Lizard, *Gerrhonotus multicarinatus*

This is a gray to reddish-brown or yellowish lizard, darker on the sides than on the back. Adults are about 4 to 6½ inches in head-and-body length, with the tail more than twice as long as the head and body if it hasn't been broken. The crossbands on the back are more regular than in the Northern Alligator Lizard and are usually darker on the sides than in the middle of the back. If there are dark markings on the belly, they tend to form dim longitudinal stripes down the centers of the scale rows. The iris of the eye is yellow. The young hatch from eggs and have a broad, light band down the back but no crossbands. There are three races in our region.

California Alligator Lizard, *Gerrhonotus m. multicarinatus* (Plate 10a)

There is a row of red blotches down the center of the back. This form ranges along the California coast from about Los Angeles to the region of Fort Bragg. In the southern half of its range it is restricted to the area east of the San Joaquin Valley, but in the north it ranges across the Sacramento Valley to the Sierra Nevadas.

Oregon Alligator Lizard, *Gerrhonotus m. scincicauda*

There are no red blotches on the back. This form ranges from northwestern California to the Columbia River Basin in northern Oregon and southern Washington.

San Diego Alligator Lizard, *Gerrhonotus m. webbi*

There are red blotches on the back, and the dorsal scales are more strongly keeled than in the other races. This form occurs on the slopes of the Sierras east of the San Joaquin Valley, reaching the coast in the vicinity of Los Angeles and extending southward through southwestern California into Lower California.

Panamint Alligator Lizard, *Gerrhonotus panamintinus*

This is a pale-colored Alligator Lizard with broad, regular dark crossbands. The young are also strikingly crossbanded. The iris of the eye is pale-yellow. This species is known from only a few specimens from the Panamint and Inyo Mountains of Inyo County, California.

BEADED LIZARDS, FAMILY HELODERMATIDAE

These are the only poisonous lizards. They are large, stout-bodied, short-legged, and short-tailed, with scales and pattern very reminiscent of Indian beadwork—hence the name Beaded Lizard. The family includes only a single genus with two species, one in the United States and one in Mexico.

Gila Monster, *Heloderma suspectum*

Adults are from 12 to 16 inches in head-and-body length, with a tail from one-third to one-half as long. The tail is blunt and heavy and often somewhat constricted at the base. The color pattern of the young consists of irregular dark and light bands across the back, with spots of the light color, yellowish, orange, or reddish, included in the dark bands. The tail is also marked with light and dark bands. Adults of one race retain the juvenile pattern. In the other race the bands break up to form a blotched or reticulate pattern. These lizards are most often active at night or at dusk. Despite their slow, awkward appearance, they are able to climb shrubs and bushes, probably to search for eggs and nestling birds. They are quite omnivorous—eating birds, eggs of birds and reptiles, small rodents and rabbits, and occasionally other lizards. While there is no doubt that their bite is poisonous, they are not aggressive; most bites are the result of careless handling. The lizard does not strike like a rattlesnake, but rather takes a fast grip with its jaw and chews its victim while the poison works in. The severity of the symptoms varies greatly, but usually the bite is not fatal to man. There are two races.

Reticulate Gila Monster, *Heloderma s. suspectum* (Plate 10b)

Adults lose the banded appearance of the young. This race is found in central and southern Arizona and southwestern New Mexico and south into Mexico.

Banded Gila Monster, *Heloderma s. cinctus*

Adults retain the banded juvenile pattern. This race is found in the drainage of the Colorado River in western Arizona, southern Nevada, southwestern California, and southwestern Utah.

CALIFORNIA LEGLESS LIZARDS, FAMILY ANNIELLIDAE

These small legless lizards differ from snakes in having eyes with movable lids. They can be told from the Glass Lizards by the lack of external ear openings and from Worm Lizards by the presence of small eyes with movable lids. The family includes a single genus with two species, one found in California and Lower California, the other restricted to Lower California.

California Legless Lizard, *Anniella pulchra* (Plate 10c)

These are small, slender, shiny lizards about 8 of 9 inches in total length and about $\frac{1}{4}$ inch in diameter. The scales are smooth and shiny, and the tail is blunt. Legless lizards are commonly found living in loose, sandy soil, in which they readily burrow, and are also abundant in the leaf mold in forested regions in some localities. The one to four young are born alive. There are two races.

Silvery Legless Lizard, *Anniella p. pulchra*

This race is silvery-gray or yellowish, with a thin, dark, middorsal stripe. It ranges in western California from San Francisco Bay southward into Lower California.

Black Legless Lizard, *Anniella p. nigra*

Adults are dark-brown to black above, the young lighter in color. This race has a restricted distribution along the coast of California from Monterey Bay to Morro Bay.

NIGHT LIZARDS, FAMILY XANTUSIIDAE

These small, spotted, or blotched lizards have vertical pupils and immovable eyelids with a transparent window through which they see. In this they resemble many Geckos, but unlike Geckos, they have the top of the head covered with large, symmetrical scales. The scales on the back are small and granular; those on the belly larger, squarish, nonoverlapping, and arranged in regular rows. This is a small family with few members, which are found only from the southwestern United States to Panama and in Cuba. There are two genera in the United States.

Night Lizards, Genus *Xantusia*

These small, soft-skinned, secretive lizards of the western United States are terrestrial and quite nocturnal; you seldom see one during the day unless you find it hiding under the branches of a yucca or in the crevice of a rock. The permanently closed and transparent eyelids, the vertical pupils, the enlarged, symmetrical scales on the head, and the regular rows of squarish scales on the belly will separate them from all other lizards except the Island Night Lizards, which are larger, have 2 rows of small scales above the eyes, and 16 rows of scales across the belly. Night Lizards of the genus *Xantusia* have a single row of small scales above the eyes, and the belly scales are in 12 or 14 rows (count them about midway between the front and hind legs). These little lizards feed primarily on insects, and the females give birth to one to three young at a time. There are three species in the western United States.

Arizona Night Lizard, *Xantusia arizonae*

These rather flat-bodied lizards have the olive, gray, or brown back marked with small black dots which are generally arranged in 7 or 8 irregular, longitudinal rows. There are 12 longitudinal rows of scales across the belly. Adults reach 2⅜ inches in head-and-body length, and the tail is somewhat longer. This species is found on rocky slopes along the southern edge of the Colorado Plateau in central Arizona.

Granite Night Lizard, *Xantusia henshawi* (Figure 63)

This is another rather flat-bodied little lizard, less than 3 inches in head-and-body length. The back is marked with large, ovoid dark spots on a yellowish background, which may appear simply as a reticulation of thin lines between the spots. There are 14 longitudinal rows of scales across the belly. Like the Arizona Night Lizards, these lizards are found among large rocks in arid and semiarid regions. The species occurs in southern California west of the San Bernardino Mountains and southward into northern Lower California.

Desert Night Lizard, *Xantusia vigilis*

This form is patterned something like the Arizona Night Lizard, but the spots on the back are smaller and usually run together to form streaks. Sometimes spots are practically lacking. The Desert Night Lizard is not so flat-bodied as the other two and is smaller—adults are less than 2 inches in head-and-body length. The belly scales are in 12 longitudinal rows. These Night Lizards can be found under fallen dead branches and among the leaves of yuccas and in pack rat nests in desert and semidesert places. There are four races, two of which occur in the United States.

Fig. 63. Granite Night Lizard, *Xantusia henshawi*

Fig. 64. Six-lined Race Runner, *Cnemidophorus s. sexlineatus*

Common Desert Night Lizard, *Xantusia v. vigilis* (Plate 10d)

The ground color is olive to dark-brown in this race. It occurs from southern California, southward into northern Lower California and eastward into northwestern Arizona, southern Nevada, and extreme southwestern Utah.

Utah Desert Night Lizard, *Xantusia v. utahensis*

The ground color is yellowish, with orange or reddish-buff in the head-and-shoulder region. This form is restricted to the Henry Mountains in Garfield County, southeastern Utah.

Island Night Lizard, *Klauberina riversiana*

Like the other Night Lizards, these have immovable eyelids with clear windows, vertical pupils, large scales on top of the head, small granular scales on the back, and squarish scales on the belly. They are larger than the Night Lizards of the genus *Xantusia*, adults reaching a maximum head-and-body length of 3¾ inches. There are 16 longitudinal rows of belly scales. Island Night Lizards are grayish-brown in color, with dark spots or reticulations which sometimes form stripes. These lizards eat plants, as well as animal food. Females give birth to three to nine young. They are found only on three islands off the coast of southern California: San Clemente, Santa Barbara, and San Nicolas.

TEIIDS, FAMILY TEIIDAE

This is a large family of New World lizards, especially common in South America. Only one genus is abundant in the United States, but it is divided into a bewildering variety of forms. They are all rather slim-bodied animals with well-developed legs and with exceptionally long tails (two or more times as long as the head and body). They have movable eyelids, enlarged scales on top of the head, small granular scales on the back and sides, and large, quadrangular belly scales arranged in 8 longitudinal rows.

Whiptails and Race Runners, Genus *Cnemidophorus*

Superficially, these lizards look a good bit like Striped Skinks, not only in general body shape, but also in the typically striped pattern and in the frequent presence of a blue or sometimes reddish tail in the young. The small, granular scales on the back make them look dull, rather than shiny. The granular dorsal scales and 8 regular rows of enlarged, quadrangular belly scales will serve to identify a specimen in hand, but catching one of these alert, wary, agile, and very speedy creatures is another story. They are diurnal, most often seen foraging for insects on the ground in open country. When alarmed, they take refuge under bushes or in burrows, sometimes those of other animals, sometimes ones that they have dug themselves. All are oviparous.

The basic dorsal pattern is one of light, longitudinal stripes on a dark background. There may be a paravertebral stripe on either side of the middorsal line, a dorsolateral stripe, and a lateral stripe on each side, giving a 6-striped pattern. The 2 paravertebral stripes may fuse to form a single middorsal stripe, resulting in a 5-striped pattern. Or a separate median vertebral stripe may be present between the 2 paravertebral stripes to make a 7-striped pattern. Sometimes this vertebral stripe is split, giving an 8-striped pattern. A striped pattern (sometimes with spots as well) is usually present in the young; it may be retained by the adults or may be more or less modified. Sometimes light spots develop in the dark fields between the stripes. The light stripes are sometimes also broken into spots so that the animal appears spotted rather than striped. Sometimes the light spots of the dark areas fuse with the broken light stripes to give an appearance of alternating dark and light bars. Sometimes the dark part of the pattern is reduced so that it appears simply as a dark reticulation on a light background. Occasionally an unpatterned phase is found. The final adult pattern is usually characteristic for each form, but it may be late in developing. Beside pattern and coloration, the number of dorsal scales around the body midway between the front and hind legs and the number of scales between the paravertebral light lines are useful characters when the lizard is in hand.

Whiptails are perhaps the most difficult to identify of all our lizards. Locality and habitat may help, but many of the species overlap in both. There are twelve species in the United States, most of them in the Southwest.

Giant Spotted Whiptail, *Cnemidophorus burti*

This is a large, spotted species. The young have 6 or occasionally 7 light stripes on a dark background, spots in the dark fields, and an orange or reddish tail. The adults are spotted, with the stripes reduced or absent. There is red on the head and neck and sometimes on the back as well. These lizards are frequently found in brushy places near streams in arid and semiarid country below 5,000 feet. The two races in our area are quite different.

Giant Spotted Whiptail, *Cnemidophorus b. stictogrammus*

This is our largest Whiptail—adults may exceed 5 inches in head-and-body length. There are 98 to 115 dorsal scales around the middle of the body and 5 to 11 scales separating the paravertebral stripes. Large adults show little or no trace of stripes. The reddish wash is apt to be confined to the head and neck, and the undersurfaces are pale and unspotted. Other Spotted Whiptails occurring in the same area are smaller. The Chihuahua develops spots in the dark areas, but the stripes are usually distinct even in large adults. The Southern Whiptail (a race of the Western Whiptail) usually retains the stripes, and the throat, chest, and undersides of the forelegs are usually dark. The Giant Spotted Whiptail is found in southeastern Arizona, the extreme southwestern corner of New Mexico, and south into Mexico.

Red-backed Whiptail, *Cnemidophorus b. xanthonotus*

This is a smaller race, the adults not exceeding 4 inches in head-and-body length. The reddish suffusion on the back stops abruptly on the upper sides, which are a dark greenish-gray. The light spots are small but well defined on the back and sides, and traces of the light stripes remain. This race is known only from the Organ Pipe National Monument in Pima County, Arizona.

Chihuahua Whiptail, *Cnemidophorus exsanguis*

Adults of this variable species have both stripes and spots in the dark areas between the stripes. The fewest spots are in the area between the two paravertebral stripes, which are separated by 2 to 8 small granular scales. The tail may be tan, pinkish, or greenish, and the ventral surfaces are pale and unspotted. Young lack spots and have 6 or 7 light lines (the vertebral may be faint, broken, or absent). Adults may reach $3\frac{3}{4}$ inches in head-and-body length. Other spotted Whiptails whose ranges overlap that of the Chihuahua Whiptail include the Giant Spotted, which is much larger and loses the stripes; the Texas Spotted, which has paired vertebral stripes in the young and 10 to 21 scales between the paravertebral stripes; the Big Bend, in which the stripes fade on the posterior third of the body; the New Mexican, which has a wavy vertebral stripe and 9 to 13 scales between the paravertebrals; and the Checkered, which has more of a banded or blotched appearance in the region where the two overlap. Chihuahua Whiptails are found most often in the uplands from Trans–Pecos Texas through much of New Mexico to central Arizona.

Texas Spotted Whiptail, *Cnemidophorus gularis*

This is another Whiptail that as an adult has both light stripes and light spots in the dark fields between the stripes. The vertebral stripe is less well defined than the others and may be divided in the young. There are 10 to 21 scales between the paravertebral stripes. Adult males have a pink or orange throat and a dark-blue belly. Females are paler on the belly. The spots are poorly developed or absent in the young, and the tail is reddish. Adults reach $3\frac{1}{2}$ inches in head-and-body length. Adult Race Runners lack spots, and the young have a blue tail. Chihuahua Whiptails have only 2 to 8 scales between the paravertebral stripes. Little Striped Whiptails lack spots and have a bluish tip to the tail. Young of the Checkered and Marbled Whiptails have spots and the adults a more checkered, barred, or mottled appearance. The Big Bend Whiptail has the stripes faded on the posterior third of the body. The Texas Spotted Whiptail is found in open, arid, and semiarid prairie country from southern Oklahoma throughout most of Texas, except for the more humid east and the northern part of the northern panhandle.

Orange-throated Whiptail,
Cnemidophorus hyperythrus beldingi

This Whiptail is a dark-brown to black lizard, with 6 light stripes (sometimes the paravertebrals are more or less fused) without spots and with an orange throat. Adults range from 2 to 2½ inches in head-and-body length. The only other Whiptail in the same area is the Coastal Whiptail, a race of the Western Whiptail. The Coastal Whiptail has spots, as well as stripes, in the dorsal pattern and black spots on the throat and chin. The Orange-throated Whiptail is found in brushy, arid regions of extreme southwestern California from southwestern San Bernardino County, south into Lower California.

Little Striped Whiptail, *Cnemidophorus inornatus*

This small Whiptail fails to develop spots. There are usually 6 or 7 light lines on a reddish-brown to black ground color (light in White Sands region of New Mexico). Sometimes the stripes are absent. The tail is bluish toward the tip, and the undersides are also bluish, especially in males. Young have bright-blue tails. There are 52 to 72 small scales around the body. Adults are from 2 to 2¾ inches in head-and-body length. Most of the other Whiptails that overlap the range of this species develop spots and have orange or reddish tails as juveniles. The Desert-grassland Whiptail has a greenish tail. The Plateau Whiptail is larger and usually has more scales at midbody (65 to 85). This species is found in open short grass areas from western Texas through much of New Mexico to Cochise County, Arizona.

New Mexican Whiptail, *Cnemidophorus neomexicanus*

This Whiptail has both stripes and spots, and the spots are present even in the young. There are 7 light stripes, the vertebral one appearing wavy. The undersurfaces are pale-blue, the tail bright-blue in the young, blue-gray in adults. There are 11 to 13 scales between the paravertebral stripes. Adults range from 2½ to 3 inches. The other spotted and striped Whiptail within the range of this species is the Chihuahua Whiptail, which has 2 to 8 scales separating the paravertebral stripes. The larger Checkered and Western Whiptails lack the pale-blue underparts. The New Mexican Whiptail is found in arid and semiarid lowlands of the Rio Grande Valley of extreme western Texas and New Mexico. There are isolated populations west to Lordsburg, New Mexico.

Big Bend Whiptail,
Cnemidophorus scalaris septemvittatus

This rather large Whiptail has both stripes and spots as an adult, but the stripes tend to spread and fade on the posterior third of the body. The undersides are white or pale-blue, sometimes with black spots. There are 77 to 98 small scales around the body. The Chihuahua Whiptail in the eastern part of its range has 74 or fewer scales at midbody. The Texas Spotted is bluer beneath and does not have the stripes fading posteriorly. This is primarily a Mexican form that enters the United States only in the Big Bend region of Texas.

Six-lined Race Runner, *Cnemidophorus sexlineatus*

In spite of its name, individuals of this widespread species may have 7 or 8 light stripes instead of 6. There are no spots in the dark fields. The stripes may be somewhat faded in old males and the belly washed with blue. Young have light-blue tails. Adults may reach 3½ inches in head-and-body length. Over most of its range, this is the only species of *Cnemidophorus* present.

Six-lined Race Runner, *Cnemidophorus s. sexlineatus* (Figure 64)

This race has 6 light stripes. It is found in open woodlands and fields from Maryland south through Florida, west to eastern Texas, and north in the Mississippi Valley to southern Minnesota.

Prairie Lined Race Runner, *Cnemidophorus s. viridis*

In addition to the 6 primary stripes, this race has a light vertebral stripe which may be narrowly divided. The foreparts are bright-green in adults. This race is found mostly in open grasslands from southern South Dakota to the Gulf Coast of Texas and from central Missouri west to southeastern Wyoming, eastern Colorado, and eastern New Mexico.

Checkered Whiptail, *Cnemidophorus tesselatus*

Hatchlings of these lizards have 6 to 8 light stripes and sometimes an additional light stripe below the lateral one on each side. Light spots are present in the dark fields. As the lizard grows, the light spots become more numerous and usually spread to fuse with the light stripes. These stripes tend to be broken so that the lizard has a checkered or barred appearance. At the extreme north of the range, the stripes and spots remain separate. The undersurfaces are plain or with a few scattered black spots. Adults may reach 4⅕ inches. Checkered Whiptails resemble Western Whiptails, but the dorsal pattern of the former is usually coarser in appearance, and adults have fewer, if any, black spots on the chest. These lizards are found most often in open, rocky places in arid regions. They range from western Texas to extreme southeastern Arizona and north into southeastern Colorado.

Western Whiptail, *Cnemidophorus tigris*

This is another species in which spotting is well developed and the adult pattern may appear more mottled or barred than striped. The young are marked with black and yellow and have blue tails. Adults usually have more or less black on the undersides, and the color difference between the light and dark parts of the dorsal pattern is usually less marked than in the young. They may reach 3¾ inches in head-and-body length. They are lizards of more or less open, arid, and semiarid regions. Six races are now recognized in our area.

Great Basin Whiptail, *Cnemidophorus t. tigris* (Plate 10e)

Adults have 4 light lines on the back. The front legs are marbled with black, and the thighs are black with white vertical bars. The belly and chest are usually checkered with black. This race is found from eastern Oregon and west central Idaho, south through northeastern and southeastern California, Nevada, western and central Utah, and western Arizona.

Southern Whiptail, *Cnemidophorus t. gracilis*

The young have 4 to 6 light stripes and light spots in the dark fields. Adults often retain traces of the tan stripes. The dark areas may be broken into series of rectangular spots or appear as wavy lines. The chin, chest, and belly are usually darkened and may be black in large adults. This race is found in southeastern and central Arizona.

Marbled Whiptail, *Cnemidophorus t. marmoratus*

Young of this race have many light spots that tend to be arranged in longitudinal rows on a dark-brown or black ground color. Adults are variously crossbanded or marbled and usually have scattered black spots on the chin, throat, and chest. The chest, and often the chin, is pink or orange in adults. This race occurs in western Texas and southern New Mexico.

Coastal Whiptail, *Cnemidophorus t. multiscutatus*

Adults retain the light stripes, though they may tend to fade on the posterior part of the body. The dark areas are variously spotted or broken. The chin is whitish, often with distinct, large black spots. This race is found along the southwestern coastal area of California.

California Whiptail, *Cnemidophorus t. mundus*

This race usually has 8 light stripes, though the lateral ones may be indistinct. The dark areas are broken into spots. The chin is white or marked with small black spots. This race occurs in western and central California from the region of Point Conception to the region of Lassen Peak.

Northern Whiptail, *Cnemidophorus t. septentrionalis*

Adults usually have 4 to 6 yellow stripes and light spots in the dark fields. These dark fields end in front of the level of the hind legs. There are small black spots on the throat. This race is found from western Colorado and northwestern New Mexico through eastern and southern Utah and northern Arizona.

Desert-grassland Whiptail, *Cnemidophorus uniparens*

This is a small, unspotted Whiptail. There are 6 well-developed, yellowish to white light stripes and usually a trace of a seventh (vertebral). The areas between the stripes are reddish-brown to black. The tail is bluish-green to olive-green. The chin has a bluish suffusion, and the undersides are unspotted. Adults reach $2\frac{3}{4}$ inches in head-and-body length. Most of the other species within its range have spots, and the young, if unspotted, have reddish tails. The larger unspotted Plateau Whiptail and the Little Striped Whiptail have a bluish rather than greenish tip to the tail. This is chiefly a lowland species, often found in dense, shrubby country but also in open grasslands. It occurs from central and southeastern Arizona, eastward to the Rio Grande Valley of New Mexico and to El Paso, Texas.

Plateau Whiptail, *Cnemidophorus velox*

This Whiptail has 6 or 7 light stripes on a dark-brown or black ground color and lacks conspicuous spots. (Some scales in lateral dark areas may develop light edges in large individuals.) There are 63 to 85 small scales around the body and 5 to 10 between the paravertebral stripes. The belly is plain white or faintly bluish, and the tip of the tail is pale-blue in adults, bright-blue in the young. Adults reach $3\frac{1}{2}$ inches in head-and-body length. Other unspotted Whiptails in the same region are the Desert Grassland, which has a greenish tail, and the smaller Little Striped, which usually has more blue on the belly. Both these species are also more often found in lowlands, in grassy or shrubby areas, while the Plateau Whiptail is more common in mountain woodlands. It is known from the Colorado Plateau region of Colorado, Utah, New Mexico, and Arizona.

Ground Lizard, *Ameiva ameiva petersi*

A well-established colony of these is located in Miami, Florida. They are similar to the Whiptails and Race Runners but can be told on close inspection from them by distinctly enlarged scales on the undersides of the chin between the lower lip scales. They are believed to have come from Colombia, South America.

WALL LIZARDS, FAMILY LACERTIDAE

This is a large family of Old World lizards that are the counterparts of the foregoing New World Teiids. The two groups are very similar in superficial characteristics, but the Wall Lizards differ in having only 6 rows of wide scales down the belly. Only one species occurs in the United States.

Italian Wall Lizard, *Lacerta sicula campestris*

This species, which can be differentiated from the preceding Teiids by the 6, rather than 8, longitudinal rows of scales down the belly, has existed in this country as a breeding colony in certain areas in Philadelphia for over forty years.

SKINKS, FAMILY SCINCIDAE

This is a large family of lizards, but most of the species live in the Old World. Only five genera are found in our area—three in the continental United States (one with species also in Hawaii) and two introduced into Hawaii. All of our skins have smooth, shiny scales, those on the head enlarged, those on the body flat, rounded, overlapping and more or less the same size. The legs are short, the pupil of the eye round, the tail long and very easily shed. Some skinks develop a transparent window in the lower eyelid but only in the Snake-eyed Skink, found in Hawaii, are the eyelids immovably fused. Skinks are active, agile lizards. Many of them are terrestrial, a few are arboreal, others are burrowing forms with reduced limbs.

Striped Skinks, Genus *Eumeces*

The Striped Skinks are bright, shiny lizards with flat, smooth, overlapping scales. It is the absence of keels or ridges on the scales that gives the lizards the shiny appearance. Striped skinks differ from all our other skinks in having the lower eyelid scaly and without a transparent disk in its center. The legs are well developed and have five toes. In most of the species the young and adults tend to be striped, although the striping may disappear in older individuals. The young frequently have a bright-blue tail (sometimes pink) and adults, particularly breeding males, often develop orange or red coloring on the head. These skinks are diurnal and primarily insectivorous. Females lay eggs and often guard them until they hatch. There are about sixty species of *Eumeces* throughout the world—thirteen occur in our country.

Coal Skink, *Eumeces anthracinus*

These are moderate-sized skinks, gray or brown in ground color with two narrow light lines running along each side, separated by a broad, dark band $2\frac{1}{2}$ to 4 scales wide. The upper light line is on the edges of the third and fourth scale rows counting down from the middle of the back. The stripes extend onto the tail but not onto the head in front of the eyes. These skinks are often found on wooded hillsides and near springs. The maximum head-and-body length is $2\frac{3}{4}$ inches. There are two races.

Northern Coal Skink, *Eumeces a. anthracinus*

The young have blue tails but otherwise resemble the adults. This form ranges from western New York through the mountains to eastern and central Kentucky. Scattered colonies that occur in the southern Appalachians to North Georgia and Alabama are apparently intergrades between this and the southern race.

Southern Coal Skink, *Eumeces a. pluvialis*

The young are black, with reddish lips and bluish tail, and the adults usually have faint, dark stripes or rows of dots down the center of the back. This race is found from southern Missouri and eastern Kansas south into northeastern Texas and northwestern Louisiana. East of the Mississippi it ranges from southern Louisiana to the Apalachicola region of Florida.

Short-lined Skink, *Eumeces brevilineatus*

This is a greenish gray to brownish lizard without any distinct markings on the body but with a light line from the jaw to the shoulder and another passing over the eardrum. Males have orange along the jaw and young have a blue tail. The maximum head-and-body length is 2⅝ inches. This species is usually found near water in central and southern Texas.

Mountain Skink, *Eumeces callicephalus*

In this skink the central part of the back is light-brown with a lighter dorsolateral stripe on each side from the head to the base of the tail. There is a dark-brown band below the light stripe and usually a second light line below the dark band. There are poorly defined light lines on the head, and the tail is bluish. The scales on the side are in rows parallel to the rows on the back. Adults are 2 to 2½ inches in head-and-body length. This Mexican species enters our country only in the mountains of southeastern Arizona and extreme southwestern New Mexico.

Mole Skink, *Eumeces egregius*

These are small, slender skinks, less than 2½ inches in head-and-body length, with the tail in most populations orange to red in color (blue in young and some adults of one race). The dorsal ground color is brownish, and there are light longitudinal stripes along the side. Mature males usually have orange on the lips, neck, and sides. Mole Skinks are among the most fossorial of the skinks and generally are found either burrowing in loose sand or resting below logs or piles of debris in sandy places. There are five races.

Florida Keys Mole Skink, *Eumeces e. egregius*

The dorsolateral light stripes are the same width throughout and are on the second scale row. They may fade out on the body. There are also well-defined lateral light stripes, and the tail is red or brownish-red even in adults. Mature males often have orange on the belly. This race is confined to the Keys of southern Florida.

Cedar Key Mole Skink, *Eumeces e. insularis*

The dorsolateral light stripes are rather indistinct and are confined to the second scale row; the lateral light stripes are sometimes lacking. The tail color varies from dull-orange to maroon. Hatchlings are almost black in color. This race is found only on Cedar Key and Seahorse Key off the west coast of peninsular Florida.

Blue-tailed Mole Skink, *Eumeces e. lividus*

The tail is bright-blue in the young and some adults. The dorsolateral light stripe widens just behind the head to include the second and third scale rows and behind the shoulder is confined to the third scale row. This race is limited to the Lake Wales Ridge in Polk and Highland counties, Florida.

Peninsula Mole Skink, *Eumeces e. onocrepis*

The tail may be brown, red, orange, yellow, pink, or lavender. The dorsolateral light stripe is at least partly on the third scale row. This race is found in peninsular Florida south of Alachua and Putnam counties except for the area occupied by the Blue-tailed race.

Northern Mole Skink, *Eumeces e. similis*

The tail is reddish-brown to orange. The dorsolateral light stripe is confined to the second scale row and is the same width throughout. This race is found on the coastal plain of Georgia, northern Florida, and Alabama.

Five-lined Skink, *Eumeces fasciatus* (Plate 10f)

This is the common blue-tailed Skink of the eastern United States. Young animals have 5 longitudinal light lines on a black background along the back and a bright blue tail. In older individuals the stripes tend to fade, though usually some trace remains, and the dorsal ground color becomes brownish. The tail loses its bright-blue color. Adult males may have orange on the head. The scales in the middle row under the base of the tail are about twice as wide as the scales in the other rows. There are usually fewer than 30 rows of scales around the middle of the body. Two other skinks found in the same part of the country are very similar. Southeastern Five-lined Skinks have narrow light stripes, and all the scales under the base of the tail are about the same size. Broad-headed Skinks are larger, and the adult males have a spectacular, swollen orange head. Adult Five-lined Skinks reach a maximum head-and-body length of $3\frac{1}{8}$ inches. Five-lined Skinks are found in or near moist woodlands. In the eastern part of the range they are usually seen on the ground, but in Texas they are quite arboreal. They are found from southern New England to extreme northern Florida, westward to Wisconsin and eastern Texas. Scattered colonies have been reported as far west as Nebraska and South Dakota.

Gilbert's Skink, *Eumeces gilberti*

These are brownish, rather large skinks that reach a head-and-body length of 4½ inches. Young have a broad dorsolateral light line from the snout to the tail, below this a dark band, and then a broad lateral light line from the edge of the lip to the tail. In adults the stripes are usually reduced or lost entirely. The tail of the young is blue in some races, pink in others, and adults may have a reddish tail. The scale rows on the side of the body are parallel to the rows on the back. These skinks resemble the Western Skinks, but in that species the adults are smaller and retain the stripes. Where the ranges of the two species overlap, young Gilbert's Skinks have pink tails, and young Western Skinks have blue tails. There are five races.

Greater Brown Skink, *Eumeces g. gilberti*

The young have blue tails, and the adults lose the stripes and develop bright-red heads. This form occurs in the northern Sierra Nevadas of California.

Variegated Skink, *Eumeces g. cancellosus*

The young have pink tails, washed with blue above, and the adults have red heads. This form is restricted to eastern Contra Costa and Alameda counties, southwestern San Joaquin County, and northwestern Merced County, California.

Northern Brown Skink, *Eumeces g. placerensis*

Young have blue tails. The juvenile stripes are retained longer than in the Greater Brown Skink, and adults may show traces of them on the neck. This is a form of the foothills of the Sierra Nevadas below 2,500 feet and the San Joaquin Valley in Yuba, Nevada, Placer, Sacramento, Eldorado, Amador, and San Joaquin counties in California.

Western Red-tailed Skink, *Eumeces g. rubricaudatus*

The tails of the young are pink, without a blue wash. Adults lose the stripes and develop red heads. This race is found in the southern Sierra Nevadas and Coast Range of southern California and eastward in isolated localities to southern Nevada.

Arizona Skink, *Eumeces g. arizonensis*

The tail is yellow above, pink below in the young, probably completely pink in the newly hatched. Adults retain the juvenile coloring, though they are somewhat duller and have orange on the head. This form is restricted to Yavapai and Maricopa counties, Arizona.

Southeastern Five-lined Skink, *Eumeces inexpectatus* (Figure 65)

This is another skink with 5 light lines along the back on a brown or blackish ground color. Adults tend to retain the stripes. The central row of scales under the tail is not widened as it is in the Five-lined Skink and Broad-headed Skink. The light stripes, particularly the middorsal one, are narrow. The young have blue tails and adults become reddish around the head, particularly the males during the breeding season. These lizards are usually seen on the ground but are able to climb well. Adults reach a maximum of 3½ inches in head-and-body length. This species ranges through the southeastern states from Virginia southward through Florida and westward to Louisiana and southeastern Arkansas.

Broad-headed Skink, *Eumeces laticeps* (Figure 66)

This is our largest skink, adults reaching 5½ inches in head-and-body length. Young and adult females are like the Five-lined Skink and Southeastern Five-lined Skink in coloration; but large breeding males, with their tan bodies and swollen, bright orange-red heads, are unmistakable. Very young individuals may have 7 instead of 5 light lines. The scales of the middle row under the tail are enlarged. There are usually 30 to 32 rows of scales around the middle of the body. This species is more arboreal than the other Five-lined Skinks, but it may also be found foraging for insects on the ground. It is a lizard of the southeastern states, ranging from extreme southern Pennsylvania and Maryland, westward into Kansas and Oklahoma, southward as far as northern Florida and eastern Texas.

Many-lined Skink, *Eumeces multivirgatus*

The pattern of this species is variable but is composed primarily of numerous alternating light and dark longitudinal stripes except in some adults of the Two-lined Skink. One of the light stripes is restricted to the third row of scales counting down from the middle of the back. There may be only 4 or 5 light stripes in the young, but young adults may have more. Juveniles have blue tails. This is a moderate-sized skink with a head-and-body length of nearly 3 inches. There are two races.

Many-lined Skink, *Eumeces m. multivirgatus*

Adults have a prominent, light middorsal stripe bordered by well-marked dark lines. This is a skink of the plains, found in southwestern South Dakota, southeastern Wyoming, central and western Nebraska, and northeastern Colorado.

Fig. 65. Adult male Southeastern Five-lined Skink, *Eumeces inexpecta*

Fig. 66. Adult male Broad-headed Skink, *Eumeces laticeps*

Two-lined Skink, *Eumeces m. epipleurotus*

The middorsal light stripe is faint or absent in adults, though prominent in the young. This more mountainous race is found in southwestern Colorado, southeastern Utah, Arizona, New Mexico and Trans–Pecos Texas.

Great Plains Skink, *Eumeces obsoletus*

This is a large skink, with a maximum head-and-body length of about 5 inches, gray, tan, or brown in color. In the adults most of the dorsal scales tend to have dark borders, which give these skinks a salt-and-pepper appearance. The young are shiny black with a bright-blue tail and white and orange spots on the head. The scales along the sides are in rows which run at an angle to the dorsal scale rows, rather than parallel to them. As you would imagine from the name, this is a skink of the Great Plains, ranging from extreme southeastern Wyoming, southern Nebraska, and extreme southwestern Iowa through all but eastern Texas and into Arizona.

Prairie Skink, *Eumeces septentrionalis*

This is a moderate-sized brown or brownish-gray skink with a head-and-body length of about 3 inches. Like the Many-lined Skinks, Prairie Skinks are marked with a number of light and dark longitudinal stripes. The dorsolateral light stripes are on the fourth or fourth and fifth scale rows counting down from the midline of the back. None of the dark stripes is more than 2 scale rows wide. The light lines extend onto the tail. The lower sides of the body and the belly are often tinged with blue. This is a terrestrial lizard, often found hiding under stones. Young have blue tails, and breeding males have orange on the sides of the head. There are two races.

Northern Prairie Skink, *Eumeces s. septentrionalis*

There are longitudinal stripes in the middorsal region, as well as on the sides. This race ranges from southern Manitoba, south through eastern North Dakota to extreme northeastern Oklahoma and east to the Chicago region of Illinois.

Southern Prairie Skink, *Eumeces s. obtusirostris*

The stripes in the middorsal region are faint or absent. This form occurs from south central Kansas southward through central Texas and into extreme northwestern Louisiana.

Western Skink, *Eumeces skiltonianus*

This moderate-sized, brownish skink has 2 broad, light lines on the back from the snout onto the tail and another broad lateral light line on each side from the edge of the lip to the tail. The area between the dorsal and lateral light lines is much darker than the area between the 2 dorsal light lines. As in so many skinks, the tail is blue in the young but darker in older individuals, and the breeding adults usually have red on the lips and chin. The pattern is very similar to that of Gilbert's Skink. Western Skinks are smaller (adults $2\frac{1}{2}$ to $3\frac{1}{4}$ inches in head-and-body length); they retain the striped pattern as adults; and the tail is always blue in the young. These skinks are found in open bushy places and grassy slopes of rocky ridges, where they forage for insects during the day. There are three races.

Western Skink, *Eumeces s. skiltonianus*

The dorsal light stripes are narrow, and the lateral light stripes are bordered below by a narrow dark line. This race is found from British Columbia south through Washington east of the Cascade Mountains, northern Idaho, and western Montana; through Oregon except the northwestern corner; into northwestern Nevada, northeastern California south to Placer and Yuba counties, and western California south along the coast into northern San Diego County.

Great Basin Skink, *Eumeces s. utahensis*

The dorsal stripes are wider, and there is no dark border below the lateral light stripe. This race is found from southern Idaho into Nevada except the western edge, Utah in the Great Basin, and south into northern Arizona.

Coronado Island Skink, *Eumeces s. interparietalis*

The dark stripes on the body extend more than half the length of the tail in this race. It ranges from southern San Diego County, California, southward into Lower California.

Four-lined Skink, *Eumeces tetragrammus*

These skinks are generally grayish above, with a blue tinge along the sides and with 2 light lines on each side that end in about the region of the hind legs. These light lines do not have dark borders. The tail is bright-blue in the young, the jaws reddish in adult males. The maximum head-and-body length is 3 inches. These secretive skinks are found in the Lower Rio Grande Valley.

Sand Skink, *Neoseps reynoldsi* (Figure 67)

This small, slender, shiny, delicate little lizard literally swims in sand. It is easily identified by its shiny scales and very weak legs, with only one toe on each of the front legs and two on the hind. Sand Skinks are pale-gray to light-brown in color and reach a maximum

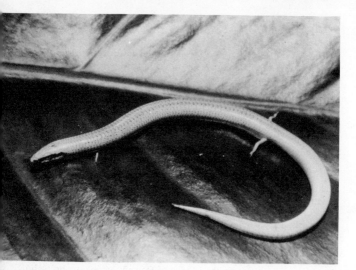

Fig. 67. Sand Skink, *Neoseps reynoldsi*

Fig. 68. Queen Snake, *Regina s. septemvittata*

head-and-body length of $2\frac{3}{4}$ inches. They are burrowers but occasionally come to the surface of the ground under logs or boards lying on the ground. They are seldom seen, but you can sometimes catch one by rolling logs in sandy places. This is the only member of the genus, and it is restricted in its natural distribution to the sand ridge of central Florida. It is, perhaps, introduced into Dade County, Florida.

Azure-tailed Skink, *Emoia cyanura*

These lizards have the typical, rounded, smooth, overlapping skink scales. The eyelids are movable, and the lower lid contains a transparent brille, or window, through which the skink can see when the eyes are closed. This is one of the most brightly marked lizards of Hawaii, with a broad, light middorsal stripe and bluish-tinted tail. Some, though, are melanistic and appear very dark. Azure-tailed Skinks are very like the Ground Skinks in general appearance. They differ from the Ground Skinks of the United States in having blue tails. The head-and-body length is about 2 inches and the tail nearly 3 inches. Azure-tailed Skinks occur both in dry lowlands and more moist woods at higher elevations on the islands of Hawaii, Molokai, and Oahu.

Snake-eyed Skink, *Ablepharus boutoni poecilopleurus*

These little lizards are called Snake-eyed Skinks because the eyelids are fused together but are transparent, so that the lizard sees through the lids of the closed eye. They differ from all our other skinks in having immovable eyelids. These agile little lizards are generally greenish or brownish above, spotted and marbled with black and with light lateral stripes bordered by narrow, darker stripes. They are generally found around the rocks, cliffs, and sand hills along the coast. It is practically impossible to catch these extremely wary and active lizards by hand. Most specimens are collected by shooting them with .22 shells. The females generally lay two sticky-shelled eggs, but many females may lay in one spot, so that as many as seventy eggs have been found in a single clump. Adults have a head-and-body length of about 2 inches, and the tail, which is extremely fragile, may be $2\frac{1}{2}$ inches. Newly hatched young are less than 2 inches in total length but are able to run around and fend for themselves within just a few seconds after escaping from the egg. These lizards are widespread throughout the Pacific Islands and are found on most of the larger islands of the Hawaiian archipelago.

Ground Skinks, Genus *Lygosoma*

The Ground Skinks of the United States differ from Sand Skinks in normally having the full complement of five toes on each foot and from Striped Skinks in having a transparent window in the lower eyelid. They can be told from Snake-eyed Skinks by their movable eyelids and from Azure-tailed Skinks by the lack of a blue tail. Like our other skinks, they have enlarged scales on the head and smooth, shiny, rounded, overlapping scales on the body. They are small and agile, with long, fragile tails. The head and body are 2 inches or less in length, the tail somewhat longer. They feed primarily on insects and such related forms as small spiders and seem to be essentially ground lovers. There are three species within the United States.

Ground Skink, *Lygosoma laterale* (Plate 11a)

This is the only Ground Skink of the continental United States. It is a small, shiny brown skink, easily recognized by its small size, the absence of light stripes down the back, the presence of dark stripes on the sides, and the presence of a "window" in the lower eyelid. Ground Skinks are typically found under the leaf mold in wooded areas, but they are inclined to come out and range over the surface of the leaf mold late in the afternoon, particularly on sunny days. Females lay one to five eggs. This species ranges from New Jersey, westward to Kansas, southward to the Gulf of Mexico, and throughout Florida.

Metallic Skink, *Lygosoma metallicum*

This skink has a definite, bronzy, metallic sheen on the back and sides. Small brown spots on the back sometimes form a dark middorsal line. It can be told from the Moth Skink by the absence of a light middorsal stripe. Females lay one to four eggs. This skink, an inhabitant of Australia, was first taken in Hawaii around 1917 and is now very common on the island of Oahu.

Moth Skink, *Lygosoma noctua noctua*

This brightly marked little skink is golden-brown above, with a light middorsal stripe edged with dark-brown spots. It is slightly smaller than the Metallic Skink. It seems to be more apt to climb than the other Ground Skinks and also perhaps is more active at night. Females have been reported to bear living young. The fate of this skink in Hawaii is a mystery, for while it was once very abundant, there have been no definite records of its having been taken there since 1920.

RINGED LIZARDS, FAMILY AMPHISBAENIDAE

Members of this rather widespread family of burrowing, snakelike lizards are characterized by having rings of flat scales encircling the body and tail. They all lack external ear openings, and only a few possess visible legs. They are represented in the United States by a single species, which is restricted to Florida.

Worm Lizard, *Rhineura floridana* (Plate 11b)

This burrowing lizard looks so much like a large pinkish-gray worm that it is often confused with the true worms. Adults range from 7 to slightly over 12 inches in total length, about the size of a big earthworm, and the fact that the scales are arranged in rings around the body and tail adds to the wormlike appearance. The tail is very short. There are no external limbs, no ear openings, nor in adults is there any external evidence of eyes. These lizards spend practically their entire lives in burrows in loose sand, where they feed on earthworms, termites, and spiders. They are sometimes plowed up or may be forced to the surface by exceptionally heavy rains. They are restricted to northern and central peninsular Florida.

Snakes

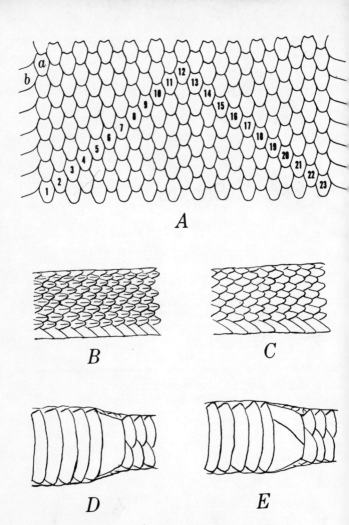

SCALE ARRANGEMENTS OF SNAKES

A. Dorsal view of snake skin showing how scale rows are counted and (a) dorsal scales and ends of (b) ventral scales.
B. Lateral view of snake with keeled scales.
C. Lateral view of snake with smooth scales.
D. View of single anal plate.
E. View of divided anal plate.

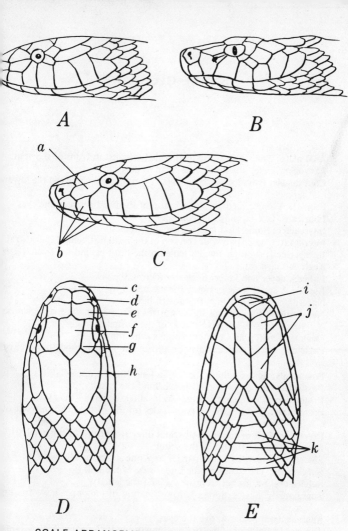

SCALE ARRANGEMENTS OF HEADS OF SNAKES

A. Lateral view of head of harmless snake.

B. Lateral view of head of Cottonmouth, a poisonous snake.

C. Lateral view of head of snake indicating (a) the loreal scale and (b) the labials.

D. Dorsal view of head of snake indicating the (c) rostral scale, (d) internasal scales, (e) prefrontal scales, (f) frontal scales, (g) supraocular scales, and (h) parietal scales.

E. Ventral view of head of snake indicating (i) mental scale, (j) chin shields, and (k) ventral scales.

SNAKE GLOSSARY

Anal plate: The single or divided scale lying just in front of the vent.

Azygous: Single, not divided, median in position.

Chin shields: Paired scales on a snake's throat region between the lower labials.

Frontal: A single median plate on top of the head between the eyes.

Imbricate: Overlapping, like shingles.

Intercalary: Something inserted or interpolated.

Internasal: One or two scales on top of the head just behind the rostral.

Interparietal: A single medial scale on the head behind the frontal.

Keel: A sharp ridge.

Labials, upper and lower: Scales bordering the jaw.

Loreal: A small scale between the nasal and the preocular.

Nasal: The scale in which the nostril lies.

Nasal valves: Fleshy flaps in the nostrils of some aquatic snakes whose function is to keep water out of the nostrils.

Oculars: Small scales lying in contact with the eye.

Parietals: Large paired scales on top of the head behind the level of the eyes.

Postlabials: Scales behind the jaw in line with the upper labials.

Postnasal: One or two scales just behind the nasal.

Postoculars: One or more small scales directly behind the eye.

Prefrontals: One or two pairs of scales on top of the head in front of the frontal.

Preocular: One or more small scales directly in front of the eye.

Rostral: Plate at the tip of the snout.

Shield: An enlarged scale, particularly one in the head region.

Subcaudals: The scales on the under side of the tail.

Suboculars: Scales between the eye and the labials.

Supralabials: Scales along the lower margin of the upper jaw—the lip scales.

Supraoculars: Scales above the eyes.

Temporals, anterior: One or two longitudinal, elongated scales, lying one above the other, behind the postoculars and between the parietals and upper labials.

Ventrals: The laterally enlarged scales on the lower surface of a snake

Snakes

PROBABLY more people are interested in snakes than in any of the other kinds of animals in this book. This may be partly because snakes seem so different. We think of a normal animal as having a body divided into head, trunk, and tail, with front and hind limbs. The absence of limbs makes it hard to see at a glance that the snake really does have the normal divisions of the body and also imposes on the snake modes of locomotion that seem unnatural to many people. Also unnatural to us is the "unwinking stare" that results simply from the fact that the eyelids of the snake are immovably fused and transparent. This characteristic will separate the snakes from two of our three kinds of legless lizards which might be confused with them. Glass Lizards and California Legless Lizards can close their eyes. The Florida Worm Lizard has vestigial eyes and looks more like a big earthworm than a snake. The same might be said of the Blind Snakes, but they are not found in Florida. Snakes also lack external ear openings.

Snakes are covered with scales, those on the body overlapping and arranged in regular rows. The scales on the head are usually enlarged and regular in arrangement. They vary from species to species (and sometimes within a species) in number, size, and shape and have been given individual names. Usually the ventral scales are enlarged and form a single row down the belly. The scales under the tail are known as caudals, or subcaudals, and are usually in two rows, occasionally in one. The smaller scales on the back and sides are all considered dorsal scales. The number of dorsal scale rows is an important character. Make your count at midbody, that is, about halfway between the place where the enlarged head scales give way to the smaller dorsal scales and the region of the vent. This region is indicated by a single or double scale which separates the belly scales from the caudal scales and is the only scale that can be lifted up. Whether this anal scale is single or divided is also an important characteristic. The dorsal scales may be smooth, or some or all of them may be keeled.

Males usually have longer tails (and more subcaudal scales) than females. It is not easy to tell the sex of a snake, but the base of the tail is usually swollen in adult males, more tapering in females.

Color and markings are often very variable in snakes, and in many species the young look entirely unlike the adults. But pattern is very important in the identification of snakes, because (along with size and general build) it is all that you can see of a snake without having it in hand. Many snakes are distinctively patterned. Certain conventions are used in referring to elements of the pattern. Lines that run lengthwise along the animal's body are called stripes. If they run crosswise, they are called crossbands if they do not cross the belly scales, rings if they do. Spots refer to rounded markings, blotches to large and more irregular ones, specks to small, irregular ones.

In spite of the loss of legs, external ears, and movable eyelids, snakes seem to be a very successful group. There are many different kinds, and they live successfully in a wide variety of places—from ocean to desert, from the tropics to Alaska, in trees, on the ground, and under the ground. Some lay eggs; others bear living young. All are carnivorous. Few kinds in our region are poisonous. The best advice that can be given about poisonous snakes: Learn to recognize the snakes in your region that are poisonous and let them alone.

BLIND SNAKES, FAMILY TYPHLOPIDAE

These highly aberrant little worm-shaped creatures have been classified both as lizards and as snakes but are now generally placed with the snakes. Certainly anyone trying to identify one would turn first to the snakes. They are small, with cylindrical bodies and very short tails. The belly scales are not enlarged, and the eyes appear as black spots beneath the head shields. There are rows of teeth on the upper jaws but never more than one enlarged tooth on either side of the lower jaw.

Brahminy Blind Snake, *Typhlops braminus*

These tiny snakes are brown or blackish above, lighter below, with the snout, anal region, and end of tail often whitish. They are less than 7 inches long. These secretive little burrowers have been introduced into the Hawaiian Islands, probably from the Philippines. All the present Hawaiian records are from Honolulu. The female lays from two to seven elongate eggs, each ½ inch or less in length.

SLENDER BLIND SNAKES, FAMILY LEPTOTYPHLOPIDAE

This is another family of small blind snakes, which superficially resemble earthworms. They differ from the Typhlopidae in lacking teeth on the upper jaw but having rows of them on the lower jaw.

Slender Blind Snakes, Genus *Leptotyphlops*

This genus is found in Asia, Africa, and tropical America, as well as in the United States. Its members are slender little snakes, usually less than 15 inches long. In life they look semitransparent and often have a silvery-pink or purplish cast to the skin. The eyes are merely small black spots beneath the head scales. They can be told from all of our other snakes except the Sea Snakes and the Blind Snakes of the genus *Typhlops* by the ventral scales, which are not enlarged but are about the same size as the scales on the other parts of the body. Since the Sea Snakes are large and brightly colored, have flattened tails, and live in the sea, there can be no confusion between them and the Slender Blind Snakes. They can be separated from the other Blind Snakes by the arrangement of the teeth.

Slender Blind Snakes feed largely on termites. They spend most of their time buried in the ground or in a termite nest and wander on the surface only early in the evening. Snakes of this genus lay eggs, usually about four. There are two species in the United States.

Texas Blind Snake, *Leptotyphlops dulcis*

This species can be told from the Western Blind Snake by the presence of supraocular scales above the ocular scales which enclose the eyes; in the Western Blind Snake there are no supraocular scales. There are two races of this form in the United States.

Plains Blind Snake, *Leptotyphlops d. dulcis*

This race has a single supralabial scale on each side between the enlarged ocular scale and the nasal. It ranges from central Oklahoma, westward through the panhandle and southward through central Texas into northern Mexico.

New Mexico Blind Snake, *Leptotyphlops d. dissecta*

In this race there are 2 supralabial scales between the ocular and the nasal. It is more northern in distribution, ranging from southern Kansas into Oklahoma and southwestward through western Texas, southern New Mexico, southeastern Arizona, and adjacent parts of Mexico.

Western Blind Snake, *Leptotyphlops humilis*

Western Blind Snakes are like the Texas Blind Snakes but lack supraocular scales above the oculars which cover the eyes. There are some half a dozen or more subspecies of this species, but only four of them occur in the United States. They are quite similar in coloration and structure, and range should be considered in identifying the various races.

Southwestern Blind Snake, *Leptotyphlops h. humilis* (Plate 11c)

This race has 12 scale rows around the tail. It is darker in color than the Desert Blind Snake. It occurs in extreme southern Nevada and southern California, except in the desert region east of the San Fernando Mountains, and extends into central and southern Arizona east of the range of the Desert Blind Snake.

Desert Blind Snake, *Leptotyphlops h. cahuilae*

This is a light-colored desert race with 12 scale rows around the tail. It is restricted to the desert regions of southwestern Arizona and southeastern California.

Trans-Pecos Blind Snake, *Leptotyphlops h. segregus*

This race, which can be separated from the other three by the fact that it has only 10 rows of scales around the tail instead of 12, occurs in southeastern Arizona, southern New Mexico, and westernmost Texas.

Utah Blind Snake, *Leptotyphlops h. utahensis*

This race is very like the Southwestern Blind Snake but has more scales on the back. It is restricted to southeastern Nevada and the extreme southwestern corner of Utah.

BOAS, FAMILY BOIDAE

Boas are rather primitive snakes, as is shown by the presence of vestigial hind limbs, which usually appear externally as minute spurs on either side of the vent. The eyes are not reduced, and teeth are present on both upper and lower jaw. The scales on the underside of the chin between the lower labials are not conspicuously enlarged, but the ventral scales are considerably larger than the dorsals. Boas are mainly snakes of the tropics. There are none in Hawaii, and only two genera reach the continental United States.

Rosy Boa, *Lichanura trivirgata*

Rosy Boas are built like typical Boas, heavy bodied with short, blunt tails, but they are somewhat smaller than one generally expects a Boa to be. The average length of adults is only about 2 feet, although an occasional individual may reach $3\frac{1}{2}$ feet. The scales are small and smooth, and those on top of the head are not enlarged. The eye is rather small, the pupil vertical. The dorsal pattern usually consists of 3 longitudinal, broad reddish-brown stripes on a bluish, tan, or gray ground color.

These are rather slow-moving, deliberate snakes, generally most active in the early evening or during the night, although they sometimes are seen abroad during the day. They make excellent pets, as they are extremely gentle and never attempt to bite. When disturbed in the wild, they are apt to roll themselves up in a ball with the head tucked into the center. Unlike many snakes, they bring forth the young alive, rather than lay eggs.

There are three races in the United States.

Mexican Rosy Boa, *Lichanura t. trivirgata*

This race has clearly defined chocolate-brown stripes on a light, drab background. The belly is cream with occasional black flecks. This western Mexico form has been reported from the United States only from the Organ Pipe National Monument in extreme southern Arizona.

Coastal Rosy Boa, *Lichanura t. roseofusca* (Plate 11d)

The longitudinal stripes are poorly defined and poorly contrasted, sometimes obscured, and the ground color is darker in this race. The belly is heavily flecked or may be completely dark. It occurs in southwestern California and adjacent Lower California.

Desert Rosy Boa, *Lichanura t. gracia*

In this light-colored desert race the three longitudinal stripes are more sharply and clearly defined, though they may have saw-toothed edges. The belly is mottled with brown. It is found in southeastern California and southwestern Arizona.

Rubber Boa, *Charina bottae* (Plate 11e)

Like Rosy Boas, Rubber Boas have small, smooth scales and small eyes with vertical pupils. They differ from Rosy Boas in having larger, somewhat irregular scales on top of the small, blunt head, and in lacking longitudinal stripes down the back. They are usually unpatterned snakes with a "rubbery" look, brown, greenish-brown or yellowish above, yellow below. Maximum length is 29 inches.

Rubber Boas are predominantly snakes of mountainous regions. They are distinctly partial to humid situations and are often found in coniferous woodlands, where they tend to burrow in the loose soil. They are very inoffensive, never attempting to defend themselves by biting. If disturbed, they also tend to ball up. They also bear living young. The three races of this snake differ chiefly in size and in number of scales.

Pacific Rubber Boa, *Charina b. bottae*

This race occurs in mountainous parts of California from south of the San Francisco Bay area, west and east of the central valley to the Lake Tahoe region of Nevada and northward through western Oregon and western Washington to southern British Columbia. Not counting the ventrals there are 45 or more scale rows at midbody.

Southern Rubber Boa, *Charina b. umbratica*

This is the smallest race, apparently not reaching 1 foot in length. It is known only from a couple of small, isolated populations in southern California. Scale rows at midbody number 44 or fewer; less than 192 ventral scales.

Rocky Mountain Rubber Boa, *Charina b. utahensis*

This race is somewhat larger than the Pacific Rubber Boa but has fewer scale rows. It is the most widespread of the three races, extending from northwestern California eastward through northern and central Nevada into Utah, northward into western Wyoming and western

Montana, throughout Idaho, most of Oregon and Washington and into southern British Columbia. Scale rows at midbody number 44 or fewer; 192 or more ventral scales.

COLUBRIDS, FAMILY COLUBRIDAE

This enormous family includes the great majority of the snakes of the world. Experts have been trying for years to divide this huge and heterogeneous assemblage into more manageable subgroups, but so far there is little agreement as to what these subgroups should be. Colubrid snakes lack vestiges of hind limbs. They have rows of teeth on the upper and lower jaws but do not have enlarged, grooved, poison-injecting fangs in the front of the upper jaw (a few have grooved teeth connected to poison glands in the rear part of the jaw). The belly scales are broadened so that a single row covers the underside of the body. The head scales are usually large and regularly arranged. There are thirty-eight genera belonging to this family in the United States alone.

Water Snakes, Genus *Natrix*

These are the familiar snakes so often seen around the ponds and streams of eastern North America. The genus occurs in both the New and the Old World. The species in the United States are all more or less aquatic and many of them can be seen basking on limbs and logs around water on bright, sunny days. The dorsal scales are strongly keeled and occur in 21 or more rows at midbody. The anal plate is divided (except in some specimens of Plain-bellied Water Snakes). The tail is short; the head is broad and distinctly set off from the neck; the caudal scales are in a double row. Most are rather large, heavy-bodied snakes, though some are small and slender. The dorsal pattern usually consists of blotches, spots, or crossbands (stripes in two races of the Banded Water Snake) and is often obscure in large adults. Although often killed by fishermen as "moccasins," they all are harmless although some of the large ones can give a painful bite and may draw blood. There are seven species in the United States, some with a number of races. Individual specimens are sometimes hard to identify, since there is a good bit of color variation in some species, and the markings of large adults are frequently obscure.

Green Water Snake, *Natrix cyclopion*

These snakes of the southeastern states are heavy bodied, dark-greenish to brown, with an indistinct pattern of middorsal dark bars alternating with a lateral series. The Green Water Snakes can be told from all other American species of *Natrix* by the presence of a row of small scales between the eye and the scales along the upper lip. There are 27 to 31 rows of scales at midbody.

Like all American *Natrix*, this species is viviparous; the females give birth to young in July and August. The number of young born at a time may be nearly two dozen, and they are about 9 to 10 inches long at birth.

This is a species of the lower Atlantic and Gulf coastal plain and upper Mississippi Valley. It is divided into two subspecies.

Green Water Snake, *Natrix c. cyclopion*

The belly is yellowish anteriorly, brown on the posterior two-thirds, with whitish spots. Adults range from 2½ to slightly over 4 feet long. This race ranges along the Gulf Coast from the Apalachicola River, Florida, west to Arkansas and Texas, and then northward in the Mississippi Valley to the southern tip of Illinois and Indiana.

Florida Green Water Snake, *Natrix c. floridana*

This eastern subspecies is similar to the Green Water Snake of the Mississippi Valley but differs in having the belly whitish or yellowish, not darkened behind. It reaches a greater maximum length—the record is over 6 feet. It is found along the coastal plain from South Carolina to the Apalachicola River of Florida and throughout peninsular Florida.

Plain-bellied Water Snake, *Natrix erythrogaster*

This species, in which the unspotted belly is uniform in coloration—red, orange, or yellow—is sometimes known as the Copperbelly. Like the other *Natrix*, it has keeled scales and usually a divided anal plate. It lacks the small scales below the eye of the Green Water Snake. The young are brightly blotched, but adults tend to lose the markings on the back and sides, and most old individuals are plain-colored above. This is one of the larger species of Water Snakes, adults sometimes exceeding 5½ feet in total length.

The Copperbelly has a pronounced tendency to wander away from water, particularly in hot, humid weather.

This species, which occupies much of the eastern and central United States east of New Mexico, is divided into four races.

Red-bellied Water Snake, *Natrix e. erythrogaster*

In this race the back of the adult is a uniform brown or reddish-brown in color (blotched in young) and the belly is orange-red. It ranges from Delaware to northern Florida and westward into southeastern Alabama.

Yellow-bellied Water Snake, *Natrix e. flavigaster*

This race is very similar to the Red-bellied Water Snake, but the general tone of the body is paler; the belly is yellowish, rather than orange-red, and the back gray, rather than reddish-brown. It is found from northern Georgia, westward to eastern Texas and northward through the Mississippi Valley into southern Iowa.

Northern Copperbelly, *Natrix e. neglecta*

Similar to the Red-bellied Water Snake but generally darker in coloration. This race occurs in western Kentucky, Indiana, Illinois, Ohio, and southern Michigan, mostly as disjunct populations in swampy areas.

Blotched Water Snake, *Natrix e. transversa*

This race differs from the other three in having the blotching of the young persist in the adult; otherwise it is rather similar. The belly is essentially plain yellow and may be faintly spotted. This is the most western of the races, occurring from Missouri and Kansas, south and westward through Texas to extreme southeastern New Mexico and into northern Mexico.

Brazos Water Snake, *Natrix harteri*

This central Texan form is a rather small Water Snake, not reaching 3 feet in length, with 21 to 25 rows of scales, 4 rows of dark spots down the back and sides, and a pink belly.

Very little is known of the life history of this species. The female, as in all other North American *Natrix*, gives birth to living young which are about 8 or 9 inches long. Two races have been described.

Brazos Water Snake, *Natrix h. harteri*

There is a row of dark dots down each side of the belly. This race is found along the Brazos River in central Texas.

Concho River Water Snake, *Natrix h. paucimaculata*

The spots on the belly are reduced or absent. This race is found along the Concho and Colorado rivers in central Texas.

Diamond-backed Water Snake, *Natrix rhombifera rhombifera*

The Diamond-backed Water Snake, one of our largest Water Snakes, can be recognized by the series of light rhomboidal or diamond-shaped spots down the back, alternating with light blotches along the sides. The scales are in 27 to 33 rows. Adults average from 3 to 4 feet in total length, but some specimens over 5 feet long have been recorded.

These big Water Snakes are found in all sorts of aquatic situations—sloughs, ponds, river bottoms, small creeks, big lakes, cypress swamps, even ditches and water tanks. They are rather vicious and will bite fiercely if roughly handled. The number of young, which are born from August to early November, ranges from eighteen to sixty-two. They may be 12 inches long at birth.

The Diamond-backed Water Snake ranges from Indiana and Illinois, southward through western Kentucky, Tennessee and Alabama and westward into Kansas, throughout most of Oklahoma and eastern Texas into Mexico.

Brown Water Snake, *Natrix taxispilota* (Plate 11f)

The Brown Water Snake is large and heavy bodied, with a series of large, squarish, dark blotches down the back alternating with similar markings on the side. The whole snake may be dark, with the blotches hardly showing. There are no small scales under the eyes, as there are in the Green Water Snake, and the belly has conspicuous dark markings. There are 27 to 33 scale rows.

This large Water Snake of the southeastern states is commonly seen hanging on limbs near or over water, particularly along streams and large stream-fed lakes. Like its relative to the west, the Diamond-backed Water Snake, the Brown Water Snake tends to be ill-natured and will bite viciously if annoyed. It has disturbed more than one fisherman by dropping unannounced from an overhanging limb into the boat. Broods of up to forty young are born in August and September. The young are generally 10 inches or less in length at birth, despite the fact that this is one of the largest Water Snakes.

This is a southeastern snake, ranging from extreme southeastern Virginia, southward throughout Florida and westward to extreme eastern Louisiana.

Common Water Snake, *Natrix sipedon*

This is the Common Water Snake of the northern and eastern United States. The adults are generally marked with rather distinctive dark crossbands on the neck and forepart of the body. Farther back the crossbands break up into alternating dorsal and lateral blotches. Coloration is very variable, tan, gray, or reddish, and some individuals are practically uniform black above. They have from 21 to 25 rows of keeled scales. These snakes are very closely related to the Banded Water Snakes and very easy to confuse with them. In general, the two can be told apart by the fact that the Common Water Snake lacks conspicuous markings around the head and lip scales, while the Banded Water Snake usually has a distinct dark stripe running from behind the eye back toward the angle of the jaw. Also, the belly markings of the Common Water Snake are not clear-cut and generally tend to be semi-circular or half-moon-shaped, while the belly markings of the Banded Water Snake are more distinctly outlined, more prominent, and more apt to be squarish or triangular in shape. Adults of the Common Water Snake range from 2 to 3½ feet in length, although occasional specimens may reach 4½ feet.

This is the common "moccasin" Water Snake so well known to fishermen and so often killed in the mistaken belief that it is poisonous. The number of young in a brood may range from less than a dozen to over seventy. They are born from early August through early October and range from 6 to nearly 10 inches in length at birth.

Three races of this species are known.

Northern Water Snake, *Natrix s. sipedon*

The dark crossbands on the neck and back are generally larger than the spaces between them in this race. It is found from central Maine, westward to South Dakota and Colorado and southward into North Carolina and Tennessee, extreme northern Georgia and Alabama, and northern Oklahoma.

Midland Water Snake, *Natrix s. pleuralis*

This race is similar to the Northern Water Snake, but the dark markings on the back are generally narrower than the spaces between them. It ranges from South Carolina, southwestward to extreme western Florida, Alabama and eastern Louisiana, northwestward into Oklahoma, and northward into southern Illinois and Indiana.

Lake Erie Water Snake, *Natrix s. insularum*

This Water Snake is nearly uniform brown above. It occurs on the islands of the Put-in-Bay Archipelago in Lake Erie.

Banded Water Snake, *Natrix fasciata*

This is the southern counterpart of the Common Water Snake of the northeastern United States. Where the ranges overlap, it can be told from the Northern Water Snake by the rather distinct dark stripe running downward and backward from behind the eye and by the distinct, discrete, often squarish or triangular belly markings. Not all races are banded. Those that are commonly have the bands extending the whole length of the body. Coloration is variable—often there is a good bit of red. The inland races are very similar to the Northern Water Snakes both in general build and in habits.

There are six races of this species.

Banded Water Snake, *Natrix f. fasciata* (Plate 12a)

This race is found from eastern North Carolina, southward into southern Georgia and northern Florida and westward into extreme southern Mississippi.

Florida Water Snake, *Natrix f. pictiventris*

There are wormlike red or black markings on the belly and frequently dark spots on the sides between the crossbands. This is the Banded Water Snake of peninsular Florida, except for the coastal marsh regions.

Broad Banded Water Snake, *Natrix f. confluens*

In this race the dorsal crossbands are quite broad, and there are fewer than 18 of them on the body. No other Banded Water Snake has so few crossbands. It ranges in the Mississippi River Valley from extreme southern Illinois, southward through western Tennessee, western Alabama, and all of Louisiana and westward into southeastern Oklahoma and eastern Texas.

Atlantic Salt Marsh Snake, *Natrix f. taeniata*

This is a small, slender, laterally compressed Water Snake, more striped than blotched in appearance (at least on the forepart of the body). It is found in the salt marshes of the Atlantic coast of Florida from the vicinity of Daytona Beach southward to the vicinity of Vero Beach.

Mangrove Water Snake, *Natrix f. compressicauda*

The coastal marsh snake of southern Florida also has a laterally compressed body but is larger than the Atlantic Salt Marsh Snake and lacks stripes. It is found along the southern coast of Florida from the vicinity of Vero Beach on the east coast to Tampa Bay on the Gulf coast.

Gulf Salt Marsh Snake, *Natrix f. clarki*

This is the Gulf Coast counterpart of the Atlantic Salt Marsh Snake and, like it, is a striped rather than a banded snake. It ranges from the vicinity of Tampa Bay westward to southern Texas.

Striped Water Snakes, Genus *Regina*

These snakes all have a dorsal pattern of dark-brown or black stripes on a lighter ground color (the stripes are sometimes hard to see in old, dark individuals) and light stripes on the lower sides. If there are dark markings on the belly, they form regular rows or stripes. The lip scales are light-colored and unmarked, the rest of the head dark. They are more slenderly built than most members of the genus *Natrix*, with narrower heads. The dorsal scales are in 19 rows and are keeled except in the Striped Swamp Snake. The anal plate is divided. The genus contains four species, all from the United States.

Glossy Water Snake, *Regina rigida*

This is a small, shiny snake, olive to brown in color, with two more or less evident dark-brown stripes along the back and two rows of distinct black spots down the yellow belly. The largest specimen recorded was about 32 inches long. This very secretive little snake is quite aquatic. Most specimens are found foraging among water hyacinths or other aquatic plants, but they are also found around the edges of shallow ponds in pine flatwoods. They feed on small aquatic vertebrates and crayfish. The life history is not well known. They are viviparous and the newborn young have essentially the same pattern as the adults. Three races of this species are recognized.

Glossy Water Snake, *Regina r. rigida*

Dark shadings on the edges of the scales of the first few dorsal rows in the neck region give the appearance of lines on the sides of the throat in this race. They are found along the Atlantic coastal plain from New Kent County, Virginia, to northern Florida.

Delta Water Snake, *Regina r. deltae*

There are no dusky lines on the sides of the throat. This race and the next differ only in average scale counts and there is considerable overlap. It is found on the Mississippi Delta.

Gulf Coast Water Snake, *Regina r. sinicola*

This race ranges from central Georgia and the panhandle of Florida to eastern Texas, exclusive of the region of the Mississippi Delta.

Graham's Water Snake, *Regina grahami* (Plate 12b)

This Striped Water Snake is olive-brown in color, with yellowish stripes which are black-bordered below and lie just above the ventral scales on each side. There is sometimes a light stripe down the middle of the back. The belly is generally plain but may tend to have a median row of dark spots or grayish areas down the center. Maximum size is a little less than 4 feet. These snakes are more apt to be found hiding under logs or stones than they are in the open. From six to twenty-five young are born at a time; they are from 8 to 10 inches long at birth. This species ranges from Louisiana and eastern Texas, northward into Iowa and Illinois.

Queen Snake, *Regina septemvittata*

This is one of the larger of the Striped Water Snakes. It differs from most of the others in having 4 dark stripes down the belly, 2 near the midline, 2 at the sides. The stripes are most evident in the neck region in adults. In other Striped Water Snakes the belly is either plain or has 1 or 2 rows of dots. Adults average less than 2 feet in length, but specimens slightly greater than 3 feet have been recorded.

The Queen Snake seems particularly fond of rocky streams but is also found in other aquatic habitats. It has a rather specialized diet, feeding mostly on soft-bodied crayfish. The young are born from July through early September and are over 9 inches long. Two subspecies of this form are known.

Queen Snake, *Regina s. septemvittata* (Figure 68)

This is a snake with black stripes on the brown back and sides. It ranges from the Great Lakes region, southward nearly to the Gulf Coast and westward into Arkansas and Missouri.

Mobile Queen Snake, *Regina s. mabila*

The Gulf Coast race differs from the northern race in being darker on the back and sides, with no dorsal dark stripes apparent. It is restricted to the Gulf Coast in southern Alabama and extreme western Florida.

Striped Swamp Snake, *Regina alleni*

These are small, shiny, brownish, aquatic snakes. Most of the dorsal scales are smooth, but those on the tail are keeled. As with other Striped Water Snakes, the anal plate is divided. These characters, plus the brownish color and broad, yellowish stripe along the side of the body, will separate this snake from all others in the southeastern states. This is probably the most aquatic snake in this region; individuals are commonly found among the roots of the water hyacinths in shallow water. The young are born in the spring and summer and look much like the adults except for size. They range from 6 to 7 inches in length, compared to 12 to 20 inches for the adults. There are two races.

Striped Swamp Snake, *Regina a. alleni* (plate 12c)

The belly is plain buff or salmon. This race is found from the Okefenokee Swamp region of Georgia, south through peninsular Florida to the region of Lake Okeechobee.

Everglades Swamp Snake, *Regina a. lineapiatus*

The belly is marked with a median row of distinct black spots or an indistinct dark line. This race is found in southern Florida.

Kirtland's Water Snake, *Clonophis kirtlandi*

This small, slender snake of the Ohio Valley has 19 rows of keeled scales, a divided anal plate, a loreal scale, 4 more or less evident rows of dark spots on a brown or grayish ground color on the back and sides, and a row of round black spots down each side of the red belly. The head is short and hardly distinct from the neck. Adults are less than 2 feet long. Although it is frequently grouped with the Water Snakes, this species is more terrestrial. While it may enter water, it is more often found in wet meadows, where it feeds on earthworms and other soft-bodied invertebrates. It has developed to a fine degree the common Water Snake habit of flattening the head and body when disturbed. Kirtland's Water Snake is found from western Pennsylvania, westward to central Illinois, northward into southernmost Michigan, and southward to the northern border of Kentucky.

Black Swamp Snake, *Seminatrix pygaea* (Figure 69)

These small black snakes with bright-red bellies and smooth dorsal scales characteristically live among the water hyacinths in the southeastern states. The color pattern and the smooth dorsal scales in 17 rows will distinguish them from all other snakes in the region. The young are born alive in late summer and early autumn and at birth range from about 5 to 5½ inches in length. Litters of from three to thirteen young have been recorded. Adults range from about 10 to over 18 inches in length.

The three recognized subspecies can be told apart by the number of ventral scales.

North Florida Swamp Snake, *Seminatrix p. pygaea*

This race has 118 to 124 ventral scales. It is found on the coastal plain of Georgia and northern Florida.

South Florida Swamp Snake, *Seminatrix p. cyclas*

There are fewer than 118 ventrals in this race. It occupies the southern half of peninsular Florida.

Carolina Swamp Snake, *Seminatrix p. paludis*

This race has 127 or more ventrals. It is found on the coastal plain of North and South Carolina.

Brown Snakes, Genus *Storeria*

These gentle little snakes have keeled dorsal scales, divided anal plates, and lack a loreal scale. Most of them are brown on the back, although they may be gray, reddish, or black. They are easily confused with several other small brownish snakes. They can be told from Ground Snakes, Worm Snakes, Ringneck Snakes, Yellow-lipped Snakes, Kirtland's Water Snakes, and Black-headed Snakes by the keeled scales and from Earth Snakes by the lack of a loreal scale. They differ from Garter Snakes in having a divided, rather than a single anal plate and in the absence of the loreal. The genus is North American in distribution; there are three species in the United States.

Brown Snake, *Storeria dekayi*

These are slender, short-headed little snakes, with 2 rows of small dark spots (sometimes inconspicuous) down the back and with small black dots along the sides of the yellow, brown, or pinkish belly. There are dark markings on the labial scales and a dark spot at the angle of the jaws (except in the Florida race). Young have a yellow collar. They differ from the closely related Red-bellied Snakes in having 17 rather than 15 rows of scales (except in the Florida race, which also has 15). Red-bellied Snakes also usually have a more brightly colored belly.

ig. 69. Black Swamp Snake, *Seminatrix pygaea*

g. 70. Eastern Garter Snake, *Thamnophis s. sirtalis*

Mexican Brown Snakes have few or no dark markings on the labials and lack the dark spot at the angle of the jaws. Adult Brown Snakes are 10 to 18 inches long.

This is probably the most urban of all our snakes; it is not uncommon to find quite large populations in city parks and vacant lots. They are viviparous, giving birth to living young. From three to twenty-four young may be born at one time to a single female. The young are generally born during August and are about 3½ to 4½ inches long.

This species is divided into four subspecies. The races are not well marked—there are wide areas of intergradation and much overlap of characteristics.

Northern Brown Snake, *Storeria d. dekayi*

The dorsal scales are in 17 rows; the anterior temporal shields are marked with a dark band; and the spots down the back are usually not connected from side to side. This race ranges from southern Maine to Virginia and westward through Pennsylvania.

Midland Brown Snake, *Storeria d. wrightorum*

This race is similar to the Northern Brown Snake, but the dorsal spots are connected by narrow crossbands. It ranges from Wisconsin, east to the Carolinas and south to the Gulf Coast from Louisiana to western Florida.

Texas Brown Snake, *Storeria d. texana*

The anterior temporal shields are not marked with black bars. This is a snake of the western plains, ranging from Minnesota southward to Texas and northern Mexico.

Florida Brown Snake, *Storeria d. victa*

This Brown Snake differs from the other Brown Snakes in having only 15 rows of dorsal scales, instead of 17, and in lacking the dark spot at the angle of the jaws. There is a light band across the head in the Florida Brown Snake, across the neck in the Florida Red-bellied Snake; the Florida Brown Snake has 130 to 148 ventral scales, while the Florida Red-bellied Snake has 114 to 126. This race is restricted to southeastern Georgia and peninsular Florida.

Red-bellied Snake, *Storeria occipitomaculata*

The Red-bellied Snakes differ from all the Brown Snakes except the Florida Brown Snake in having only 15 rows of dorsal scales. The coloration is very variable and some may be completely black. Usually, though, the plain brown back, faintly striped, the red belly, and the distinct light spots or bands at the back of the head will separate them from Brown Snakes. Adults range from 8 to 12 inches in length, with specimens of 16 inches having been recorded.

Red-bellied Snakes are quite similar to Brown Snakes in habits, but are more often found in wooded areas near bogs and swamps. The female gives birth to free-living young. As many as twenty-one have been born to a single female at one time; most clutches though range from five to ten in number. The young are born from June to September and are about 3 to 4 inches long.

This species of the eastern and central United States has three races.

Northern Red-bellied Snake, *Storeria o. occipitomaculata*

This subspecies is generally dark above, rather bright-red below, with three light spots on the neck. It is found from Maine to southern Georgia, westward through Louisiana and northward into eastern Dakotas.

Florida Red-bellied Snake, *Storeria o. obscura*

The Florida race is apt to be paler above than the northern form, and the belly may not be nearly so bright-red. The three white spots, so characteristic of the northern race, tend to fuse to form a light band across the neck. Check the account of the Florida Brown Snake for differences between these two Florida forms. This race is found in southeastern Georgia and in Florida to about the middle of the peninsula.

Black Hills Red-bellied Snake, *Storeria o. pahasapae*

This race is similar to the Northern Red-bellied Snake but has the light spots on the neck reduced or absent. It is known only from the Black Hills of western South Dakota and eastern Wyoming.

Mexican Brown Snake, *Storeria tropica limnetes*

This race of a Mexican and Central American species occurs in the United States only in the Gulf coastal marshes of Texas and Louisiana. It resembles the Brown Snake, but the dark spots on the labials are reduced or absent, and there is no dark spot at the angle of the jaws.

Garter Snakes, Genus *Thamnophis*

This is a group of moderate-sized to small snakes, usually striped in appearance, which are active in the daytime and range in habitat from quite terrestrial to extremely aquatic. Although restless when picked up, they are usually not pugnacious, though most of them do have the unpleasant habit of releasing foul-smelling mucus from the anal scent glands when first handled. They have keeled dorsal scales in from 17 to 23 rows, a loreal scale, and from 6 to 9 upper labials. Many of them are very like Water Snakes in appearance and habits; the best way to tell them apart is by the anal plate, which is divided in Water Snakes, normally single in Garter Snakes (divided in a few individuals of some species).

The snakes of this genus range from the Atlantic to the Pacific and from Alaska to lower Central America. Twelve species occur in the United States and many of them have a number of races, so that there are no less than thirty-nine named forms now recognized for the United States. With such a welter of forms and with many of them being very similar in appearance, it is extremely difficult to identify many of the Garter Snakes. However, we can divide them into groups, which makes identification somewhat easier.

One group includes species, generally either rather small or slender, which have lateral stripes that reach onto the fourth row of scales from the bottom up on the front part of the body. This includes the Eastern Ribbon Snake, the Western Ribbon Snake, the Short-headed Garter Snake, Butler's Garter Snake, the Mexican Garter Snake, and the Plains Garter Snake. The two species of Ribbon Snakes differ from the others in the group in having the tail make up more than one-fourth of the total length. These two can generally be separated by range alone. Where they do overlap, specimens of the Eastern Ribbon Snake have a broad, brown stripe on either side of the belly, while in the Western Ribbon Snake the stripe is narrow or lacking. The other four species have the tail less than one-fourth the total length. The Short-headed Garter Snake has only 17 rows of dorsal scales, while the Plains Garter Snake has 21 rows. Butler's and Mexican Garter Snakes both have 19 rows, but their ranges are entirely different.

In the other group of Garter Snakes, if a lateral stripe is present, it does not reach onto the fourth row of scales on the front part of the body (except in the Texas race of the Common Garter Snake). This group includes most of the Garter Snakes of the United States. The Common Garter Snake and Northwestern Garter Snake both have 7 rather than 8 upper labials, and the Common Garter Snake normally has 19 rows of dorsal scales, while the Northwestern usually has 17. The other four species have 8 upper labials. The Black-necked Garter Snake has only 19 rows of dorsal scales; the other three generally have 21 (some races of the Western Garter Snakes usually have 19 but can be separated from the Black-necked by pattern). The four species which usually have 21 scale rows are the Western Terrestrial, Western Aquatic, Narrow-headed, and Checkered. The Narrow-headed Garter Snake is unstriped; in the Western Garter Snakes the lateral stripes may be obscure but, if present, are on the second as well as third row of scales anteriorly, while in the Checkered Garter Snake the anterior part of the lateral stripe is on only the third row of scales. The Western Terrestrial Garter Snake has rather broad, squarish, internasal scales, and the sixth upper labial is considerably higher than wide. The Western Aquatic has elongate, pointed internasals and the sixth upper labial not noticeably higher than wide. In regions where the two overlap, they are usually represented by races that differ in color pattern.

Eastern Ribbon Snake, *Thamnophis sauritus* (Plate 12d)

The Ribbon Snake is a very slender Garter Snake, with lateral stripes that involve the fourth row of scales on the anterior part of the body and with a tail more than one-fourth the total length. There is a broad, brown stripe down either side of the belly. Adults average about 2 feet in length, though occasional specimens may exceed 3 feet.

These snakes are partial to low, wet places, a habitat preference that helps distinguish them from other Garter Snakes of the eastern and central states. They are often found climbing in bushes. The young are born alive in July and August. The broods are rather small for Garter Snakes, ranging from about five to twenty. The young are 8 to 10 inches long at birth.

There are four races of the Eastern Ribbon Snake.

Eastern Ribbon Snake, *Thamnophis s. sauritus*

This Ribbon Snake is reddish-brown on the back, with a yellow dorsal stripe. It occurs from southern New England, eastern New York, New Jersey, and eastern Pennsylvania, west-southwestward through southern Ohio and southern Indiana to the Mississippi River, south to the northern edge of Lake Pontchartrain on the west and to northwestern Florida and Georgia on the east.

Northern Ribbon Snake, *Thamnophis s. septentrionalis*

The Northern Ribbon Snake is dark-brown or black above. It is found from Maine, westward through southern Ontario and western New York to Michigan and Indiana.

Southern Ribbon Snake, *Thamnophis s. sackeni*

This race is tan or brown above, with a tan dorsal stripe and yellow lateral stripes. It ranges from southern South Carolina southward throughout peninsular Florida except for a narrow strip along the central Gulf Coast.

Coastal Ribbon Snake, *Thamnophis s. nitae*

This Ribbon Snake is very dark on the back, at least anteriorly, with the dorsal stripe obscure or absent and the lateral stripes light blue in color. It is found only along the Gulf Coast of north central Florida.

Western Ribbon Snake, *Thamnophis proximus*

The Western Ribbon Snake is like the eastern species but is somewhat stouter and longer, and the brown stripes on the belly are usually narrow or absent. There are two pairs of light spots on the parietal scales, which fuse where the scales meet. Similar spots may be present in Eastern Ribbon Snakes, but they are smaller, duller, and generally separate. Adults may reach 4 feet in length.

Western Ribbon Snakes are usually found near water and may occasionally climb in bushes. They feed mostly on amphibians and fish. The number of young in a brood ranges from four to twenty-seven. The young are usually born in July and August and range from 6 to 9 inches in length.

This species occurs in the central United States from southern Wisconsin through Texas and south into Central America. Six races have been described, four from the United States. These races intergrade very extensively, and many specimens probably should not be identified to race.

Black-backed Ribbon Snake, *Thamnophis p. proximus*

This race has a black back, with a narrow orange dorsal stripe. It lacks dark stripes on the sides of the belly. It is found from Indiana and southern Wisconsin, west through southern Iowa and eastern Nebraska and south into Louisiana and eastern Texas.

Gulf Coast Ribbon Snake, *Thamnophis p. orarius*

This Ribbon Snake has an olive-brown back, a broad gold dorsal stripe, and no dark stripes on the belly. It occurs along the Gulf Coast from Mississippi through Texas and into Mexico.

Red-lined Ribbon Snake, *Thamnophis p. rubrilineatus*

As the name indicates, the dorsal stripe is bright-red. The rest of the back is olive-brown or olive-gray, and the ventral stripes are narrow or absent. This race is found in the Edwards Plateau region of central Texas.

Orange-lined Ribbon Snake, *Thamnophis p. diabolicus*

The dorsal stripe is orange in this race, and there are narrow, dark stripes along the sides of the belly. This is the westernmost Ribbon Snake, found from western Texas and New Mexico to extreme southern Colorado.

Short-headed Garter Snake, *Thamnophis brachystoma*

This little Garter Snake is the only one which has the anterior lateral stripe involving the fourth row of scales and a maximum of 17 rows of dorsal scales. The adults are generally from 12 to 18 inches long, though occasional specimens may approach 2 feet. It is commonly found under stones, boards, and planks in low, wet meadows bordering creeks and seldom wanders more than $\frac{1}{4}$ mile from water of some sort. The young are born in late summer and range from 5 to 6 inches in length. This species has a restricted range in southwestern New York and northwestern Pennsylvania.

Butler's Garter Snake, *Thamnophis butleri*

This species differs from the Short-headed Garter Snake in having 19 rather than 17 rows of scales on the body. Range alone should separate it from the Mexican Garter Snake, which also has 19 scale rows. These two differ in number of upper labials, 7 in Butler's, 8 or 9 in the Mexican Garter Snake. The coloration is variable; the lateral stripes may be orange and the ground color olive-brown to black. Adults average around 18 inches in length; occasional specimens may exceed 2 feet. Butler's Garter Snake resembles the Short-headed Garter Snake in habits. The young are born in late summer and may be 7 inches long at birth. This species ranges from southern Ontario and Ohio westward through Indiana, with a disjunct population in southeastern Wisconsin.

Mexican Garter Snake, *Thamnophis eques megalops*

This is a rather stout-bodied Garter Snake in which the lateral stripe on the front part of the body involves the fourth row of scales. It usually has 19 scale rows at midbody and 8, occasionally 9, upper labials. There are paired black blotches at the back of the head. Adults are generally larger than the other Garter Snakes in which the anterior lateral stripe involves the fourth row of scales. They average 2 or more feet in length and large individuals may reach 3⅓ feet. Very little is known of the life history of this snake. It apparently feeds on fish and frogs. One female gave birth to twenty-five young on June 15, and the young averaged about 9½ inches in length. This snake is found in western Texas, New Mexico, and southern Arizona and ranges southward on the Mexican Plateau.

Plains Garter Snake, *Thamnophis radix*

The Plains Garter Snake differs from the others in which the anterior part of the lateral stripe includes the fourth scale row by having usually 21 rows of dorsal scales, rather than 19 or fewer. Between the dorsal and lateral stripe are 2 rows of alternating black blotches, and there is another row of dark spots below the lateral stripe. It is a moderate-sized Garter Snake, ranging from 1½ to 3½ feet in length. Like so many Garter Snakes, it prefers marshes, wet meadows, and bogs. The young are born in late summer; the broods may range from thirteen to forty in number, with the young averaging about 7 inches in length. This species feeds on all sorts of food—fish, frogs, earthworms, and insects. There are two subspecies.

Eastern Plains Garter Snake, *Thamnophis r. radix*

The dark blotches are large, and there are fewer than 155 ventral scales in this race, which ranges from central Ohio westward to central Iowa and from central Wisconsin south to northern Missouri.

Western Plains Garter Snake, *Thamnophis r. haydeni*

The black blotches are smaller and more numerous than in the eastern race, and there are usually 155 or more ventral scales. This race ranges from Canada, south to northwestern Texas and northeastern New Mexico and from the western half of Minnesota and Iowa, west to the Rockies.

Common Garter Snake, *Thamnophis sirtalis*

This is the familiar Garter Snake of the United States, our most widely distributed and probably our best-known snake. It is the only snake to reach Alaska. The lateral stripe on the front part of the body does not extend onto the fourth row of scales (except in the Texas Garter Snake); there are 19 rows of scales at midbody and usually only 7 upper labials. (Sometimes the Northwestern Garter Snake has this combination of 7 upper labials and 19 scale rows, although typically it has only 17 rows.) The Common Garter Snake is rather large for a Garter Snake, averaging about 2 feet in adult length, with occasional specimens exceeding 4 feet.

The Common Garter Snake is a familiar sight throughout its range. It is more terrestrial than many of the other Garter Snakes and may be found on land in brush piles, bushes, and thickets quite some distance from water. The female gives birth to young which range from 5 to 9 inches in length. This snake will eat practically anything that wiggles and is small enough for it to swallow.

There are nine recognized races of this Garter Snake in the United States. There is one wide-ranging race occupying the eastern and central United States, another in the Great Plains, a Great Basin form that extends into Alaska, and a series of forms more limited in distribution, one in Texas, one in New Mexico, and four along the Pacific Coast. We will discuss them in this order. All the western races, including *parietalis* of the Great Plains but not *annectens* of central Texas, have more or less well-developed red markings between the dorsal and lateral stripes. Because of the extreme variability of this species, range may be the best means of identification.

Eastern Garter Snake, *Thamnophis s. sirtalis* (Figure 70)

Usually there are three yellowish stripes with a double row of black spots between the dorsal and lateral stripe on each side. The color is very variable and sometimes the spots are more conspicuous, sometimes the stripes. This form ranges in eastern North America from southern Canada throughout Florida and westward to central Minnesota and eastern Texas.

Red-sided Garter Snake, *Thamnophis s. parietalis*

This is another widespread, variable race. The light markings between the dorsal and lateral stripes are mostly on the skin between the scales and are usually red. The stripes are broad and rather dull. This is a snake of the Great Plains, from Canada southward through Minnesota, Missouri, Arkansas, most of Oklahoma, and eastern Texas and westward into northern Colorado, eastern and northern Wyoming, and most of Montana.

Valley Garter Snake, *Thamnophis s. fitchi*

The ground color of the back is darker than in the Red-sided Garter Snake, and the red markings do not reach so close to the dorsal stripe. It occurs in California, west of the Colorado and Mohave deserts (except for a narrow strip along the coast), northwestern Nevada, northern Utah, Idaho, extreme western Montana, Oregon except the northwestern part, Washington east of the Cascade Range, and extends through British Columbia to extreme southeastern Alaska.

Texas Garter Snake, *Thamnophis s. annectens*

The orange dorsal stripe is very broad and the lateral stripe is on rows two, three and four. Markings between the stripes are pale-yellow, rather than red. This form is restricted to an area in northern and central Texas south of the Oklahoma border, with an isolated population in the Texas panhandle.

Rio Grande Garter Snake, *Thamnophis s. ornata*

The ground color is paler than in the Red-sided Garter Snake, and the dorsal stripe has a continuous black border. This race occurs along the Rio Grande Valley from southern Colorado through New Mexico to the Mexican border.

California Red-sided Garter Snake, *Thamnophis s. infernalis*

This race resembles the Red-sided Garter Snake, but the stripes are narrower and bright-yellow. It is found along the coastal region of California, west and south of the area occupied by the Valley Garter Snake, from Humboldt County to San Diego County.

San Francisco Garter Snake, *Thamnophis s. tetrataenia*

This race is like the Red-sided Garter Snake but is darker, and the top of the head is red. It has the most restricted range of any of the races, being confined to San Mateo County on the San Francisco Peninsula.

Red-spotted Garter Snake, *Thamnophis s. concinnus*

The dorsal ground color is black, with the dark color extending onto the belly. The red markings on the sides are reduced. The head is red, the stripes narrow and sharply defined. This is a snake of the Northwest, occurring in the coastal region of northern Oregon and southern Washington.

Puget Sound Red-sided Garter Snake, *Thamnophis s. pickeringi*

This race resembles the Red-spotted Garter Snake but has a dark head. It is found along the coastal region of southern British Columbia throughout Vancouver Island and in the western part of the state of Washington.

Northwestern Garter Snake, *Thamnophis ordinoides*

This is a rather small Garter Snake of the northwestern United States. Adults usually range from 1 to 2 feet in length; the maximum recorded is 26 inches. The fact that the lateral stripe does not reach onto the fourth row of scales on the anterior part of the body and that it has 7 upper labials will separate it from all other Garter Snakes except the Common Garter Snake, *Thamnophis sirtalis*. From this it can generally be told by having only 17 rather than 19 rows of body scales. The posterior chin shields are about the same size as the anterior ones in the Northwestern Garter Snake, considerably longer than the anterior ones in the races of *sirtalis* found in the same region. Coloration and pattern are very variable—individuals may be striped, spotted, or plain. There is often a red dorsal stripe.

The Northwestern Garter Snake inhabits meadows, clearings, and rights-of-way for railroads and highways near, but generally not in the heavy, humid forests of the Puget Sound lowlands. It is generally fairly close to some dense undercover, into which it can glide when alarmed.

There is only a single form of this species. It ranges from southern Vancouver Island and the mainland of adjacent British Columbia southward through Washington and Oregon, mostly west of the Cascade Mountains as far as Del Norte County, California.

Black-necked Garter Snake, *Thamnophis dorsalis*

This moderate-sized Garter Snake (1½ to 3 feet in length) bears a large black blotch on either side of the neck, and there are dark spots between the stripes. There is no red along the sides. It differs from the other Garter Snakes in which the anterior part of the lateral stripe does not involve the fourth row of scales in having 8 upper labials and usually 19 rows of dorsal scales. It is characteristically found in the vicinity of mountain streams. It is definitely a snake of mountainous and hilly regions and usually is found not far from water, although during wet weather it may range away from the streams. There are two subspecies of this form known from the United States.

Western Black-necked Garter Snake, *Thamnophis d. dorsalis*

The Western Black-necked Garter Snake ranges from southern Utah and Colorado southward through the eastern half of Arizona and most of New Mexico and western Texas into Mexico.

Eastern Black-necked Garter Snake, *Thamnophis d. ocellata*

The black spots above and below the light lateral stripe impinge on it to give it a wavy appearance. This race is found in the Edwards Plateau region of Texas, west to the Big Bend.

Western Terrestrial Garter Snake, *Thamnophis elegans*

This variable species usually has a well-defined dorsal stripe and a lateral stripe that includes the second and third scale rows, but not the fourth. There are usually 19 or 21 rows of dorsal scales and 8 upper labials. The internasal scales are broad and squarish, and the sixth and seventh upper labials are higher than wide. Western Aquatic Garter Snakes have the internasals elongate and rather pointed and the sixth and seventh upper labials hardly higher than wide. These two species are very similar structurally, but in regions where they overlap they are represented by races that usually can be separated by color and pattern. Check the accounts of the races in your area. Habits may also help—Western Terrestrial Garter Snakes, although often found near streams or ponds, are more apt to hunt their food on land and to take refuge on land when chased. They are found in a wide variety of habitats, from open grassland to forests and from sea level to high mountains. They eat soft-bodied invertebrates, such as slugs and earthworms, and any vertebrates small enough to be swallowed. The young are born alive. Adults are from $1\frac{1}{2}$ to $3\frac{1}{2}$ feet in length. There are four races in the United States and one in Lower California.

Wandering Garter Snake, *Thamnophis e. vagrans*

In this widely distributed race the dorsal stripe is dull-yellow to brown, and narrow. The areas between the dorsal and lateral stripes are usually light with small dark spots. But the spots may be absent or so enlarged that the snake appears more spotted than striped. In the Puget Sound region these areas are black with small, light flecks. This race occurs from western Canada, southward nearly to the Mexican border in New Mexico and from extreme western South Dakota and the panhandle of Oklahoma and adjacent Texas to east central California.

Mountain Garter Snake, *Thamnophis e. elegans*

The yellow or orange dorsal stripe is quite conspicuous, occupying most of 3 rows of scales. The ground color lateral to this stripe is dark, with faint light specks scattered through it. The race is found in the Sierra Nevada range of California, north in the mountains through Oregon, and in extreme western Nevada.

Klamath Garter Snake, *Thamnophis e. biscutatus*

This race has a quite distinct broad dorsal stripe, and the dorsal ground color on each side is quite dark with light flecks. The belly is light-gray. The Klamath Garter Snake is more aquatic than other members of the species, acting more like the Western Aquatic Garter Snakes. It has a restricted range in the central part of extreme northern California and south central Oregon.

Coast Garter Snake, *Thamnophis e. terrestris*

This Garter Snake has a distinct, usually bright-yellow dorsal stripe about 3 scale rows wide. There are usually bright-red or orange flecks on the sides and belly. It occurs along the coast of California from the vicinity of Santa Barbara north into extreme southwestern Oregon.

Western Aquatic Garter Snake, *Thamnophis couchi*

This is another very variable species. Usually the dorsal stripe is not clearly marked (except in the Aquatic and Santa Cruz races) and the snake appears more blotched or spotted. There are 19 or 21 rows of scales. The internasals are elongated and pointed, and the posterior upper labial scales are about as high as they are wide. These snakes are seldom found more than a few feet from water, to which they retreat when disturbed and in which they catch most of their food. The races vary in size—the Santa Cruz Garter Snake reaches only about 2 feet in length, while the Giant Garter Snake may reach 4¾ feet. There are six races, all found in California, with one extending into Oregon and another into Nevada.

Sierra Garter Snake, *Thamnophis c. couchi*

In this race the dorsal stripe is faint, dull, narrow, and usually confined to the front part of the body. The lateral stripe is usually more distinct; the area between the stripes is checkered with dark blotches. This mountain-dwelling snake occurs in eastern California and western Nevada.

Oregon Garter Snake, *Thamnophis c. hydrophila*

The dorsal stripe is dull and narrow, the lateral stripe indistinct or lacking, the dark markings conspicuous in this race. It occurs in the coastal region of northern California and southern Oregon, and in the interior north and east of the range of the Aquatic Garter Snake.

Aquatic Garter Snake, *Thamnophis c. aquaticus*

This race has a distinct yellow or orange dorsal stripe occupying 2 or 3 rows of scales and distinct lateral stripes. The throat is yellow and the belly blotched with orange or yellow. It is found in the region north of San Francisco Bay in California, extending in the mountains between the two arms of the range of the Oregon Garter Snake.

Giant Garter Snake, *Thamnophis c. gigas*

The dorsal stripe is inconspicuous, and the lateral stripes are usually indistinct in this large race. The dorsal spots are well marked, and the head and belly are brown. The race occupies the Great Valley of California between the Coast Ranges and the Sierra Nevadas south of the San Francisco Bay area.

Santa Cruz Garter Snake, *Thamnophis c. atratus*

This race has the most distinct and clear-cut dorsal stripe of any of the aquatic group, and the lateral stripes are usually conspicuous. The areas between the stripes are dark. The chin is yellow, the belly blue or greenish. This race is found along the coast south of the San Francisco Bay area to the vicinity of Salinas.

Two-striped Garter Snake, *Thamnophis c. hammondi*

In this race there is no dorsal stripe; instead the back is plain olive, gray, or brownish. Lateral stripes are present and are bordered with dark spots. This race is restricted to the coastal region of California from the vicinity of Salinas south to the vicinity of Santa Marta.

Narrow-headed Garter Snake, *Thamnophis rufipunctatus*

This is another Garter Snake found in the vicinity of mountain streams. It differs from all the other Garter Snakes in having 8 upper labials, 21 rows of dorsal scales, and no dorsal or lateral stripes. The brown back is marked with reddish-brown, black-bordered spots. Adults are less than 3 feet long. A snake of the Southwest, it is restricted in the United States to the highlands of central and southeastern Arizona and southwestern New Mexico, extending south into Mexico.

Checkered Garter Snake, *Thamnophis marcianus*

This is a rather small Garter Snake, the adults about 2 feet long, although one is reported at 3½ feet. Unlike most Garter Snakes, it seems to be largely active at night. It is a light-brown snake with 8 upper labials and 21 rows of dorsal scales. The anterior part of the lateral stripe is usually confined to the third row of scales. Between the dorsal and lateral stripes the sides are checkered with squarish black blotches. The young are born in June and July, the broods ranging from six to eighteen. The babies are sometimes nearly 8 inches long at birth.

Two subspecies have been described in the United States, but the differences are very slight, and range had best be considered primarily in making identification.

Eastern Checkered Garter Snake, *Thamnophis m. marcianus*

This subspecies ranges from central Oklahoma southward through central Texas and into northern Mexico.

Western Checkered Garter Snake, *Thamnophis m. nigrolateris*

This has a more westerly range, from southwestern Kansas, and eastern Colorado, through western Texas, southern Arizona and New Mexico into extreme southern California and southward into Mexico.

Lined Snake, *Tropidoclonion lineatum*

These rather small, moderately stout, grayish-brown snakes are marked with 3 light stripes, one down the middle of the back and one along each side, and with a double row of conspicuous, half-moon-shaped dark spots on the belly. The scales are keeled, the anal plate is single. The combination of single anal plate and double row of strongly marked half-moons down the belly should separate this snake from others. Lined Snakes average only about 12 inches long; the record is 21 inches.

This snake is quite common within its range and occurs in all sorts of places—woods, open prairies, and vacant lots in cities. It prowls at night, when it can be found on open ground. During the day it is usually hidden under rocks or logs. The young are born alive during August, and the broods may range from two to twelve in number, although they average around seven or eight. The young are about 4 to 5 inches long. Apparently this snake feeds primarily on earthworms. The only species has been divided into four races, which differ chiefly in the average number of ventral and subcaudal scales. Since the numbers overlap, however, range is more useful in identifying the four races.

Northern Lined Snake, *Tropidoclonion l. lineatum* (Plate 12e)

This form ranges from Iowa westward into southeastern South Dakota and south through eastern Nebraska into Kansas. It intergrades with the next race in an area extending from south central Nebraska across central Kansas. There is a disjunct population in eastern Colorado.

Central Lined Snake, *Tropidoclonion l. annectens*

This race extends from central Kansas southward through central Oklahoma into northern Texas, where it intergrades with the Texas form. There are isolated populations in Illinois and Missouri.

Texas Lined Snake, *Tropidoclonion l. texanum*

This form is restricted to east central Texas.

New Mexican Lined Snake, *Tropidoclonion l. mertensi*

This race is limited to northeastern New Mexico.

Earth Snakes, Genus *Virginia*

These little snakes, which are restricted to the eastern and central United States, are easy to confuse with several other kinds of small, plain-colored snakes. They can be told from Brown Snakes and Black-headed Snakes by the presence of a loreal scale and from Ground Snakes by the fact that the loreal scale touches the eye and there are 5 or 6 upper labials (7 in Ground Snakes). Worm snakes have 13 rows of smooth scales, Earth Snakes 15 or 17 rows of scales that are usually more or less keeled. The Yellow-lipped Snake has smooth scales and a dark line through the eye.

Rough Earth Snake, *Virginia striatula* (Figure 71)

This is a small, light reddish-brown snake with a pointed snout. It has 5 upper labials, and the scales are rather distinctly keeled. Adults range from 7 to 10 inches in length, with the record being nearly 13 inches. These are secretive snakes, usually found in or near wooded regions, where they can sometimes be collected under the bark of rotten logs, particularly in low country near creeks and river bottoms. From three to thirteen young are born alive in the summer time. They are about 4 to 5 inches long at birth. The Rough Earth Snake is distributed from Virginia to northern Florida and westward to south-eastern Kansas and eastern Texas.

Smooth Earth Snake, *Virginia valeriae*

The Smooth Earth Snakes differ from the Rough Earth Snakes in having 6 rather than 5 upper labials. The dorsal scales are weakly keeled or at times practically smooth. The adults are about the same size as the Rough Earth Snakes. Like them also, they are usually found hiding under logs, stones, or trash on the ground in or near wooded regions. The young are born in August and run from about $3\frac{1}{2}$ to $4\frac{1}{2}$ inches long. The Smooth Earth Snake is divided into three subspecies.

Eastern Earth Snake, *Virginia v. valeriae*

The scales are in 15 rows throughout the length of the body. They are mostly smooth, but faint keels are sometimes present. This race ranges from New Jersey to northern Florida, westward to southern Ohio and all but extreme western Alabama.

Mountain Earth Snake, *Virginia v. pulchra*

The weakly keeled scales are in 15 rows on the front part of the body, 7 rows from about midbody backward. This race occurs in the mountains and high plateaus of western Pennsylvania and adjacent parts of Maryland and West Virginia.

Fig. 71. Rough Earth Snake, *Virginia striatula*

Fig. 72. Southern Hognose Snake, *Heterodon simus*

Western Earth Snake, *Virginia v. elegans*

The scales are in 17 rows throughout the length of the body. The race ranges from southern Indiana, south to the Gulf and west to eastern Kansas and central Texas. There are disjunct colonies in Iowa.

Hognose Snakes, Genus *Heterodon*

In spite of their moderate size, these pug-nose snakes are among our most spectacular. They are commonly known as Spreading Adders or Puff Adders, because if one is disturbed, it flattens and spreads its head and neck like a cobra spreading its hood, hisses loudly, and presents a threatening mien that has surely many times frightened an enemy away. If this bluff fails to work, the snake may roll over on its back, open its mouth, loll out its tongue, and "play dead." If you turn it over on its belly, it gives the show away by promptly flopping over on its back again. Usually these snakes quickly become tame in captivity and then no longer put on this display. As the name indicates, Hognose Snakes have an upturned snout with a keel on top. The dorsal scales are keeled, the anal plate divided. The genus occurs only in North America; there are three species.

Eastern Hognose Snake, *Heterodon platyrhinos* (Plate 12f)

The Eastern Hognose Snake is stout-bodied, generally blotched in appearance, but may be plain black. It can be told from the others by the underside of the tail, which is usually distinctly lighter in color than the underside of the belly, and by the prefrontal scales on top of the head, which are in contact, not separated by small scales. The snout is not so sharply upturned as in the other two species. In keeping with their habit of feeding primarily on toads, these snakes are generally found in rather dry, sandy country. The females lay eggs in early or midsummer, sometimes laying as many as forty or more at a time. The young hatch from late July to early September and may be nearly inches long at hatching. The adults range from $1\frac{1}{2}$ to $2\frac{1}{2}$ feet, the record is $45\frac{1}{4}$ inches. This species is found in the eastern and central United States from southern New Hampshire, south throughout Florida and westward into western Texas, Oklahoma, Kansas, Nebraska and southeastern South Dakota.

Southern Hognose Snake, *Heterodon simus* (Figure 72)

The smallest of the Hognose Snakes, this species is generally found the vicinity of live oak hammocks of the lower southeastern states. differs from the Eastern Hognose Snake in having the prefrontal scales on top of the head separated from one another by a series of small scales. The snout is more sharply upturned, the underside of the tail about the same color as the belly. It differs from the Western Hognose Snake in lacking large masses of black pigment on the underside of the belly and tail. In general habits it is like the other

Hognose Snakes, although it is seldom seen except in the very hottest summer weather. The other Hognose Snakes feed primarily on toads of the genus *Bufo*, but this one seems to restrict its diet very largely to Spadefoot Toads (genus *Scaphiopus*). Practically nothing is known of its breeding habits. The largest known specimen is only slightly more than 2 feet in length, and most adults are much less. This species ranges from southeastern North Carolina, southward to central Florida and westward to southern Mississippi.

Western Hognose Snake, *Heterodon nasicus*

This is the Hognose Snake of the dry western prairies, found especially in sandy regions. Like the other two it is stout-bodied and blotched, with keeled scales, a divided anal plate, and an upturned snout which is keeled above. It can be told from both the other species by the belly, which is marked with large jet-black areas interspersed or checkered with white or yellow markings. Like the other two, this species is a toad eater. The female lays from five to twenty-four eggs in July and August; they hatch in late August and early September. The hatchlings are about 7 inches long. The adults are intermediate in size between the Eastern and Southern Hognose Snakes, ranging from 16 to 32 inches in length. The species is divided into three subspecies.

Plains Hognose Snake, *Heterodon n. nasicus*

This race differs from the Mexican Hognose Snake in having 9 or more small scales between the prefrontals. The blotches on the back are more sharply defined and more numerous (more than 35 in males, more than 40 in females) than in the Dusty Hognose Snake. The Plains Hognose Snake ranges from southern Canada, southeastward into Minnesota and northwestern Nebraska, south to western Oklahoma and northwestern Texas, and to the west in central and eastern Montana and eastern Wyoming, Colorado, and New Mexico. There are isolated populations in Illinois.

Mexican Hognose Snake, *Heterodon n. kennerlyi*

The Mexican Hognose Snake has only 2 to 6 small scales between the prefrontals. It is found from extreme southern Texas to southeastern Arizona and south into Mexico.

Dusty Hognose Snake, *Heterodon n. gloydi*

Like the Plains Hognose Snake, this race has 9 or more small scales between the prefrontals, but there are fewer dark blotches on the back (fewer than 33 in males, fewer than 38 in females) and the blotches are usually less sharply defined. It is distributed from southeastern Kansas southward throughout most of Texas and into extreme southeastern New Mexico. There is an isolated population in southeastern Missouri

Yellow-lipped Snake, *Rhadinaea flavilata* (Figure 73)

This small, slender snake of the pine flatwoods of the southeastern states is easy to recognize. It is light reddish-brown to golden-brown above, plain yellow below, with a dark line passing through the eye and the upper lip below this dark line distinctly yellow. It has smooth dorsal scales and a divided anal scale. There is sometimes a faint suggestion of narrow dorsal and lateral stripes, but these are never prominent. It is most easily collected by tearing up rotten pine stumps in flatwoods. The eggs are laid in late summer and hatch in early fall. Adults range from 10 to about 16 inches in length, and the newly hatched young are 6 to 7 inches long. This species is found in the coastal region from mid-North Carolina southward through about two-thirds of the Florida peninsula and westward into eastern Louisiana.

Ringneck Snake, *Diadophis punctatus*

These are pretty, gentle little snakes, plain-colored above, bright-yellow, orange, or red below, with (usually) a bright collar on the back of the neck. The back may be plain gray, olive, brown, tan, or almost black. The brightly colored belly is frequently marked with black spots. The neck ring is sometimes interrupted and occasionally obscure or absent (especially in the Regal Ringneck). The scales are smooth, the anal divided, the loreal scale present. Some Brown Snakes and Black-headed Snakes also have a light collar, but they lack the loreal scale. Ringneck Snakes are slender little snakes; only one race (*regalis*) exceeds 2 feet in length, and most are much smaller.

These are secretive snakes, most often found under rocks, logs, and boards lying on the ground in wooded areas. They feed on just about any small, soft-bodied animals they can catch—salamanders, worms, insects. When threatened, they may coil the tail in a tight spiral, exposing the bright color of the underside, and wave it at the intruder. This behavior is most common in those in which the underside of the tail is bright-red. Ringneck Snakes are oviparous. The number in a clutch is small, from one to seven, and the hatchlings are only about 4 or 5 inches long.

This variable species extends from the Atlantic to the Pacific and is divided into eleven races. The western races usually have the ventral color extending up onto one or more of the dorsal scale rows on the anterior part of the body, while in the eastern races the bright color is confined to the belly scales.

Southern Ringneck Snake, *Diadophis p. punctatus* (Plate 13a)

The black spots on the belly are clearly defined semicircles arranged in a single median row. The neck ring is usually interrupted. There are 15 scale rows. This race ranges along the coastal plain and piedmont from southern New Jersey to Mobile Bay and south throughout peninsular Florida.

Fig. 73. Yellow-lipped Snake, *Rhadinaea flavilata*

Fig. 74. Worm Snake, *Carphophis amoenus*

Northern Ringneck Snake, *Diadophis p. edwardsi*

The belly is typically unspotted, although sometimes there is an incomplete line of rather ill-defined black spots. The neck ring is uninterrupted. There are 15 scale rows. This race is found from southern Canada throughout the northeastern states, south in the Appalachians to northern Georgia and northeastern Alabama and west to southeastern Illinois and in the Great Lakes region through Wisconsin.

Mississippi Ringneck Snake, *Diadophis p. stictogenys*

The small belly spots tend to form a median row, but the spots are not usually so regular in shape as in the Southern Ringneck and are usually paired. Dorsal scales are in 15 rows. The neck ring is narrow and often interrupted. This is a form of the lower Mississippi Valley from southern Illinois to Mobile Bay and west to eastern Texas.

Prairie Ringneck Snake, *Diadophis p. arnyi*

There are usually 17 scale rows; the neck ring may or may not be interrupted; the belly spots are usually scattered. This race ranges from southwestern Wisconsin and northwestern Illinois, west to eastern Colorado and south through much of Texas.

Regal Ringneck Snake, *Diadophis p. regalis*

This is the largest of the Ringneck Snakes and has the highest number of ventrals—more than 206 in males and more than 220 in females. There are 17 scale rows. The belly is spotted with black; the neck ring is sometimes obscured or absent. The extent to which the yellow color of the belly invades the dorsal scales varies from a single spot on a few of the anterior scales of the first row to nearly covering the first and second rows. Adults average about 2 feet in length, the maximum reported is $2\frac{1}{2}$ feet. This race extends in the mountains from southeastern Idaho south through western Utah, southeastern Nevada, and eastern Arizona into Mexico, east through New Mexico to Trans–Pecos Texas, where it intergrades with the Prairie Ringneck Snake.

San Diego Ringneck Snake, *Diadophis p. similis*

In this race there are usually 15 rows of dorsal scales, and the ventral color extends one-half to two-thirds of the width of the lowest row of dorsal scales. There is a moderate amount of black spotting on the belly. The race occurs from southwestern San Bernardino County south into Lower California.

San Bernardino Ringneck Snake, *Diadophis p. modestus*

This race has 17 dorsal scale rows on the anterior part of the body, a belly usually conspicuously spotted with black, and the ventral color not extending above the first row of dorsal scales. It is found in northern San Diego County and southern Los Angeles County, east to the San Bernardino Mountains.

Monterey Ringneck Snake, *Diadophis p. vandenburghi*

This race has 17 scale rows anteriorly, and the ventral color extends over at least 1½ of the lower rows of dorsal scales. The belly is very sparsely spotted. The neck ring is rather wide and uninterrupted. It ranges from Ventura County to Santa Cruz County, California.

Pacific Ringneck Snake, *Diadophis p. amabilis*

There are usually 15 dorsal scale rows; the neck ring is quite narrow, from 1 to 1½ scale lengths wide, and is sometimes interrupted; the ventral color covers ½ to 1½ of the lower rows of dorsal scales; the belly may be spotted with small black dots. This race occurs in the foothills of the central valley of California and the San Francisco Bay region.

Coral-bellied Ringneck Snake, *Diadophis p. pulchellus*

This race has 15 rows of dorsal scales, a broad, prominent, uninterrupted neck ring, and a belly almost or quite unspotted with black. The 2 lower rows of dorsal scales show the ventral color but lack black flecks. It ranges on the western slopes of the Sierra Nevadas.

Northwestern Ringneck Snake, *Diadophis p. occidentalis*

This is a race with 15 rows of dorsal scales, with a prominent, uninterrupted neck ring 1½ to 2 scale lengths wide and with the ventral color extending onto 1½ or more of the lower rows of dorsal scales, which are flecked with black. It occurs in western Idaho, the Columbian basin of southern Washington and western Oregon, and on the Pacific Coast as far south as Sonoma County, California.

Worm Snake, *Carphophis amoenus* (Figure 74)

These small, pink-bellied snakes have the general appearance of large earthworms. The back is brown, gray, or black, and the bright color of the belly extends up onto the dorsal scales. The small size and wormlike appearance, together with the smooth, shiny scales in 13 rows and the divided anal plate will separate Worm Snakes from other small, unpatterned snakes. Adults are usually less than a foot long; the record is 14¾ inches.

Worm Snakes are secretive and are generally found beneath bark, rotting logs, or stones lying on the ground. The females lay from two to eight eggs in June and July. The young hatch out in August and early September and are 3 to 4 inches long. As might be expected for such small snakes, their food is mostly small invertebrates, such as earthworms, slugs, and insects.

The three subspecies of this snake are quite closely related, and in identifying them, range should certainly be taken into consideration.

Eastern Worm Snake, *Carphophis a. amoenus*

This race is usually brown above; the pink color of the belly does not extend on to the third row of dorsal scales; and the prefrontals and internasals are usually separate. It ranges from southern New England, southward to central Alabama.

Midwest Worm Snake, *Carphophis a. helenae*

The Midwest Worm Snake usually has the prefrontal and internasal shield on either side fused. It is found from southern Ohio to southern Illinois and southward to the Gulf in Mississippi and eastern Louisiana.

Western Worm Snake, *Carphophis a. vermis*

The Western Worm Snake has the prefrontals and internasals separate, and the ventral color reaches at least onto the third row of dorsal scales. It ranges from southern Iowa and Nebraska to northern Louisiana.

Rainbow Snake, *Abastor erythrogrammus* (Plate 13b)

This large, brightly colored, shiny snake can be told at a glance from all other snakes within its range by the bright-red and black stripes running along the back and the red, yellow, and black belly. The scales are smooth, the anal plate divided. The tail ends in a sharp spine. Adults may reach 5 feet in length, but most are between 3 and 4 feet.

This snake is both fossorial and aquatic. It is frequently plowed up or dug up from loose, sandy soil in the vicinity of marshes and is also often found in springs and spring runs. It eats large aquatic salamanders, fish, frogs, and earthworms. The eggs are laid in burrows in sandy soil. Clutches of from twenty-two to fifty have been reported. The young hatch in early fall and are about 8 to 10 inches long.

This species ranges in the coastal plain from southern Maryland to central Florida and west as far as the Mississippi River.

Mud Snake, *Farancia abacura*

This is another large, brightly colored, very aquatic snake of the southeastern states. The dorsal scales are smooth and glossy, the anal divided; a tail spine is present. The pink or red of the belly extends up on the sides in about 50 bands separated by bands of the black dorsal color which extend onto the belly, so that the sides have a checkered look. Adults may reach 6½ feet, but most are about 4 feet long.

Mud Snakes seem to feed largely on the big aquatic salamanders, *Siren* and *Amphiuma*. Females lay from 15 to over 100 eggs in damp soil and under piles of moist debris in early summer. In one case at least, the female was reported to stay with the eggs. The young are less than 10 inches long at hatching.

There are two subspecies of this snake.

Eastern Mud Snake, *Farancia a. abacura* (Figure 75)

There are 53 or more red bars on the side (not counting those on the tail). This race ranges from southeastern Virginia to southern Florida and west to southern Alabama.

Western Mud Snake, *Farancia a. reinwardti*

There are 52 or fewer red bars on the side, and they generally do not extend so far dorsally as those of the Eastern Mud Snake. This race extends from Alabama to eastern Texas and north in the Mississippi Valley to southern Illinois.

Black-striped Snake, *Coniophanes imperialis*

This is a small (about 16 inches) brown burrowing snake with a distinct dark dorsal stripe and another dark stripe down each side of the body and with a sharply defined light line running from the nostril through the upper part of the eye to the temporal scale. The upper labials are white, with tiny, scattered black dots. The belly is reddish. The scales are smooth, the anal divided. Not much is known of the life history of these little burrowers. They feed on other small vertebrates, toads, lizards, snakes, baby mice. This member of a Central American genus reaches the United States only in extreme southeastern Texas.

Racer, *Coluber constrictor*

The Racer is a rather large, slender, very agile, and fast snake; often all you have is a glimpse of one as it darts away through the grass or bushes. Adults are generally uniformly colored, but the young are conspicuously blotched or spotted. Racers have smooth dorsal scales and a divided anal plate. Their smooth scales, their lack of contrasting markings on the back, and their build and behavior will separate them from most similar species. They can be told from the Coachwhips and Whip Snakes by the fact that they have 15 rows of scales immediately in front of the vent, while the others have no more than 13. Adult Racers usually range from 3 to 5 feet in length, though occasional specimens may exceed 6 feet.

Racers are found in open woodlands and grassy areas. They are egg-laying snakes, the number of eggs recorded for a single clutch ranging from three to forty. Most records for hatching have been in the latter part of July and the first two weeks of August, but one has been recorded in October. Hatchlings range from 11 to nearly 14 inches in length and are brightly blotched or spotted.

Eight races of this wide-ranging species are recognized in the continental United States.

Northern Black Racer, *Coluber c. constrictor* (Plate 13c)

These are the largest of the Racers. The back is uniformly dark bluish-black in adults, and the belly is dark-gray. The chin and throat

Fig. 75. Eastern Mud Snake, *Farancia a. abacura*

Fig. 76. Western Coachwhip, *Masticophis f. testaceus*

are blotched gray and white, and the eye is brown. This race occurs in the eastern United States, west into Ohio and extreme southeastern Illinois, south in the mountains and piedmont to extreme northwestern Mississippi and central Alabama and Georgia. It is absent from the northern parts of Maine, New Hampshire, Vermont, and New York.

Buttermilk Snake, *Coluber c. anthicus*

This is the only Racer that is not uniformly colored above. The back has a more or less speckled look; the ground color is olive, tan, or blackish, with tinges of green and gray, and is irregularly sprinkled with light scales of olive-buff, pearl-gray, or white. This race is restricted to central and western Louisiana and adjacent Texas.

Eastern Yellow-bellied Racer, *Coluber c. flaviventris*

The back is rather dark—brown, gray, olive, or blue; the belly is yellow, greenish, or bluish. There are usually 7 upper labials. This is a snake of the plains, from northern Ohio and Michigan to the Rockies and from the Canadian border to southeastern Texas.

Brown-chinned Racer, *Coluber c. helvigularis*

This race is like the Southern Black Racer, but the chin is light-tan or brown or mottled with tan and brown; it is never all white or blotched with black. The labial scales always have a tan suffusion. The eye is brown as in the Northern Black Racer, not orange or red as in the Southern Black Racer. This form is restricted to the area along the Apalachicola and Chipola rivers in western Florida.

Western Yellow-bellied Racer, *Coluber c. mormon*

The back is plain brown, olive, bluish, or gray in this race, and the belly is yellowish or greenish. It is the Racer of the Far West, found throughout much of California, Oregon, Idaho, and Washington into British Columbia, east to western Montana, and Colorado. In the arid Southwest it is found in scattered localities in the mountains.

Southern Black Racer, *Coluber c. priapus*

This race of the southeastern states is similar to the Northern Black Racer but smaller, and the iris of the eye is usually bright-red or orange, not brown as in the northern race. There is usually more white on the chin in the southern race. It ranges in the coastal plain from southeastern North Carolina to eastern Texas and southeastern Oklahoma, north in the Mississippi Valley to southern Indiana and Illinois and south through the Florida peninsula to the Keys. Its range in Florida is interrupted by that of *helvigularis* in the panhandle and of *paludicola* in South Florida.

Everglades Racer, *Coluber c. paludicola*

This is a light-colored Racer, bluish or greenish-gray above and whitish or light-blue below. It is primarily confined to the Everglades of southern Florida, but there is an outlying population on Cape Kennedy.

Rio Grande Racer, *Coluber c. oaxaca*

This small Racer does not exceed 40 inches in length. The back is some shade of green, the belly yellowish. The young are marked with spots and narrow, dark crossbands, rather than blotches. This race is found along the lower east coast of Texas and south into Mexico.

Whip Snakes, Genus *Masticophis*

Like the closely related Racers, these are long, slim, agile snakes with smooth scales and a divided anal plate. There are 11 to 13 scale rows just in front of the vent. There are four species of Whip Snakes in the continental United States, each with two or more subspecies.

Sonora Whip Snake, *Masticophis bilineatus*

This species has 17 rows of scales at midbody and 2 or 3 light lateral stripes, which do not reach the tail. They are fairly large snakes, adults in general ranging between 3 and 5 feet, with a maximum of 6 feet. These Whip Snakes are found in mountainous regions, in open woodlands and brushy areas. They are often found climbing in bushes and trees but are sometimes found on fairly open ground. Apparently they feed primarily on birds. Like the Racers they are egg-layers, though few clutches have been recorded. The young of this species, like the adults, are striped. Two subspecies of this snake are known.

Sonora Whip Snake, *Masticophis b. bilineatus*

The ground color of the back is bluish-gray, greenish-gray, or grayish-brown, becoming lighter on the posterior third of the body. The belly is pale-yellow. If there are spots on the chin, they are inconspicuous. This race occurs in southeastern Arizona and southwestern New Mexico and extends southward into Mexico.

Ajo Mountain Whip Snake, *Masticophis b. lineolatus*

This race is restricted to the Organ Pipe Cactus National Monument in Pima County, Arizona. It differs from the Sonora Whip Snake in having narrower light stripes and the chin conspicuously marked with well-defined spots. The ground color of the back is darker, and the dorsolateral stripe is narrow, only about half as wide as it is in *b. bilineatus*.

Coachwhip Snake, *Masticophis flagellum*

The Coachwhip has the dorsal scales in 17 rows at midbody and lacks any well-defined longitudinal stripes. The back may be uniformly colored; it may be darker anteriorly and lighter posteriorly, or there may be dark crossbands on the anterior part of the body. This is the largest of the Whip Snakes, and specimens are known to exceed 100 inches in length. While able to climb, Coachwhips do not seem to be as arboreal as Sonora Whip Snakes and are often found in open grasslands and semideserts, as well as in brushy and wooded areas. These snakes apparently have a tendency to roam at night. They are often found dead on highways, run over by cars. They eat small rodents, lizards, and snakes, as well as birds. The females deposit from eight to twenty-four eggs in June and July. The young are 12 to 16 inches long and are marked with narrow, dark crossbands. Coachwhips are found throughout the southern half of the United States from North Carolina to California. Six races are now recognized in the United States. The color within the races is very variable, and sometimes two distinct color phases are found.

Eastern Coachwhip, *Masticophis f. flagellum*

Anteriorly the dorsal color is black or dark-brown, fading to brown and finally light-brown and tan posteriorly. The extent of the dark color is very variable. There are no dark crossbands on the neck or body in the adults, nor is there a light stripe crossing the loreal scale. In the northwestern part of the range, specimens may be black, with more or less red on the hind part of the body and tail. This race ranges from North Carolina, southward throughout peninsular Florida and west to eastern Texas, Oklahoma, and Kansas.

Banded Red Racer, *Masticophis f. cingulum*

This form is a dark red-brown, broken by pale-pink crossbands, which are frequently doubled or paired on the posterior part of the body. It occurs from Santa Cruz County, Arizona, southward into Sonora, Mexico.

Lined Whip Snake, *Mastocophis f. lineatulus*

In this subspecies the back is light-brown anteriorly, becoming reddish posteriorly. The anterior dorsal scales each have a dark stripe down the center. There are no crossbands on the neck and no white line crossing the loreal scale. The posterior part of the belly and underside of the tail are red. This mountainous race is found in the United States only in southern New Mexico, though it ranges widely in Mexico.

Red Racer, or Western Black Racer, *Masticophis f. piceus*

This race has two common names because it comes in two quite distinct colors: red and black. The red phase has dark crossbands on the neck and anterior part of the body and a horizontal white stripe through the loreal scale. In the black phase the back is completely black. Sometimes intermediates are found which are black anteriorly, pink or red posteriorly. This race ranges from central and southern Nevada, southward through California and New Mexico into Lower California and northwestern Mexico. The black phase is restricted to southern California and Arizona in the United States but is widely distributed in Mexico.

San Joaquin Whip Snake, *Masticophis f. ruddocki*

This name is used for the light-yellow Whip Snake of the San Joaquin Valley and west central California. It lacks the dark head and dark neck bands of the Red Racer.

Western Coachwhip, *Masticophis f. testaceus* (Figure 76)

This is similar to the Eastern Coachwhip but differs in color, for the anterior part is not distinctly darker than the posterior part of the body. The back is brown, olive, tan, yellowish, pink, or red, and the belly is pale, often coral-pink or coral-red. Adults sometimes show traces of the juvenile crosslines or of wide crossbands. This race ranges from southern Nebraska through western and central Kansas and Oklahoma, eastern Colorado, and New Mexico, all of Texas except the eastern third, and south into Mexico.

Striped Racer, *Masticophis lateralis*

This species has the dorsal scales in 17 rows at midbody and a single light lateral stripe on each side, which continues to or onto the tail. Adults reach 5 feet in length. This is an agile, striped Racer often found in the neighborhood of water near the banks of ponds, lakes, and rivers, and it may escape by moving into the water. Two subspecies are known.

California Striped Racer, *Masticophis l. lateralis*

This race has the underside of the head and neck spotted with buff. The stripes are yellow and the ground color of the back is dark, the tail lighter. It ranges from northern California, south through California west of the Sierra crest into Lower California. It is missing from most of the interior valley and is replaced in the San Francisco Bay area by the next race.

Alameda Striped Racer, *Masticophis l. euryxanthus*

This race, which occurs east of San Francisco Bay, differs from the California Striped Racer in having the underside of the head and neck unspotted and the lateral stripes broader and orange in color.

Striped Whip Snake, *Mastocophis taeniatus*

The Striped Whip Snake differs from all other Whip Snakes in having the dorsal scales in 15 rows, rather than 17, at midbody. This species is quite distinctly marked on the sides with narrow, dark longitudinal stripes on a cream or grayish or even reddish background (except in Ruthven's Whip Snake). The back between the lighter sides is dark. The belly is generally pale-yellowish or tan, and the underside of the tail is pink or red. Within its range this species is apparently quite ubiquitous, having been recorded from all sorts of habitats. It has a strong tendency to climb and is often found in trees and bushes. It is a long Whip Snake, ranging up to 6 feet in length. Four subspecies are known in the United States.

Desert Striped Whip Snake, *Masticophis t. taeniatus*

This subspecies has five narrow, dark stripes on a cream background on the side. The back is brown. The shields on top of the head have light edges. It ranges from southeastern Washington through eastern and central Oregon and southern Idaho and through Utah and Nevada southward to Arizona and New Mexico, just entering Texas and California.

Central Texas Whip Snake, *Masticophis t. ornatus*

This form differs from the other Striped Whip Snakes in having one or more longitudinal white patches or streaks on the sides on the anterior part of the body. The head shields are edged with light. It occurs in central and western Texas, southward into Mexico.

Ruthven's Whip Snake, *Masticophis t. ruthveni*

The lateral stripes are quite reduced and sometimes entirely absent except for traces in the neck region. The anterior margins of the dorsal scales are cream-colored. In the United States it is restricted to extreme southeastern Texas and ranges south into Mexico.

Schott's Whip Snake, *Masticophis t. schotti* (Figure 77)

This race is similar to the Desert Striped Whip Snake, from which it differs in having a greenish-gray or bluish-gray dorsal ground color and in lacking the light edges to the head shields. It is restricted to southern Texas and northeastern Mexico, between the ranges of the two preceding races.

Green Snakes, Genus *Opheodrys*

These are charming little snakes, slender and graceful, bright-green above, plain-yellow, greenish, or white below. As gentle as they are lovely, they make excellent pets. Two American species of this genus are known.

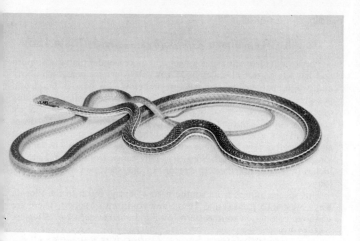

Fig. 77. Schott's Whip Snake, *Masticophis t. schotti*

Fig. 78. Mountain Patch-nosed Snake, *Salvadora g. grahamiae*

Rough Green Snake, *Opheodrys aestivus* (Plate 13d)

The Rough Green Snake is longer and more slender than the Smooth and has keeled dorsal scales in 17 rows. It is a light pea-green above and white, pale-yellow, or pale-green below. Its slender build and pea-green color make it very unlikely that it can be confused with any other snake of the United States. These snakes are arboreal and are generally found climbing in vines and bushes. The females lay from four to eleven eggs in midsummer, and the young hatch in late August and September. The hatchlings are grayish-green and about 7 to 8 inches long. Adult Rough Green Snakes usually range from about 22 to 32 inches in length, but there is a record of one specimen over 40 inches long.

This species ranges from southern New Jersey, south to the Florida Keys, west into Kansas and Texas, and south into Mexico. There are scattered colonies in southeastern Iowa and northeastern New Mexico.

Smooth Green Snake, *Opheodrys vernalis*

The Rough Green Snake is essentially a climber, but the Smooth Green Snake is a "grass snake." The bright pea-green color and slender build will separate it from other snakes in the United States, except the Rough Green Snake, from which it can be told by its smooth dorsal scales in 15 rows. The females lay from three to twelve or more eggs in June, July, and August and sometimes even into September; the young hatch in late August, September, and October. They are dark olive-gray in color and less than 6 inches long. Both the Green Snakes are insectivorous. The Smooth Green Snake is not so long as the Rough; most adults are between 1 and 2 feet in length, and the largest on record is only about 26 inches long. There are two races of the Smooth Green Snake.

Eastern Smooth Green Snake, *Opheodrys v. vernalis*

This race ranges across the northern part of the eastern United States and southern Canada from Nova Scotia west to Minnesota and extreme northern North Dakota and south in the Appalachians as far as North Carolina in isolated populations.

Western Smooth Green Snake, *Opheodrys v. blanchardi*

This race is very similar to the eastern race, but the average number of ventral scales is higher. It occurs south and west of the range of the Eastern form, from northern Indiana westward through the Dakotas and northeastern Missouri, with isolated populations in southern Ohio, south into Texas and in the mountains as far west as Utah.

Speckled Racer, *Drymobius margaritiferus margaritiferus* (Plate 13e)

This moderate-sized snake is very similar to the Racers in form but has some of the dorsal scales weakly keeled. The scales are in 17 rows at midbody, and the anal plate is divided. The distinctive pattern should make it easy to tell from all other Racers. It is uniformly dark-green, dark-brown, or black above, but each scale has a little light spot in the center, which gives the whole snake a decidedly speckled appearance. There is a black spot behind the eye. The belly is plain yellowish, but the posterior edges of the belly plates are sometimes dark. Adults are from 30 to 40 inches long; the record is 50. The species ranges from the Gulf Coast of Mexico northward into the southern tip of Texas, but only a few specimens have ever been reported from north of the Rio Grande.

Indigo Snake, *Drymarchon corais*

These are large, heavy-bodied, dark-colored snakes with smooth scales in 17 rows and a single anal plate. Two races are found in the United States.

Eastern Indigo Snake, *Drymarchon c. couperi* (Plate 13f)

This is a large, heavy, inky blue-snake of the southeastern states. The chin and sides of the head may be reddish. Its shiny dark-blue color, together with the smooth scales and undivided anal plate, will distinguish it from any other snakes in the region. In spite of their large size, they are very gentle and generally rather easy to feed in captivity; they make excellent pets and are often seen in snake charmer shows. They eat small mammals, birds, frogs, and other snakes. Eggs are laid in early summer and hatch in the fall. The young may be up to 2 feet long at hatching, and the adults may reach $8\frac{1}{2}$ feet in length. The Eastern Indigo Snake ranges from southern South Carolina, south throughout peninsular Florida and west into southern Alabama. It is apparently separated by a wide gap from the next race.

Texas Indigo Snake, *Drymarchon c. erebennus*

This race is very like the Eastern Indigo Snake, but there is a tendency for the anterior part of the body to be brownish rather than blue-black; there is sometimes a trace of a pattern; there are dark lines below the eye; and the third from last upper labial is generally quadrangular, rather than triangular, in shape. In behavior and life history the two races are apparently very similar. The range of the Texas Indigo Snake in the United States is limited to southern Texas.

Patch-nosed Snakes, Genus *Salvadora*

These are known as Patch-nosed Snakes because the rostral scale is enlarged, projecting, and curved back over the top of the snout. The scales are smooth and the anal plate divided. The structure of the rostral scale will distinguish Patch-nosed Snakes from all others in the United States except the Leaf-nosed Snakes, from which they differ strikingly in pattern. Patch-nosed Snakes are usually striped; Leaf-nosed Snakes are blotched or spotted. The average adult is only about 30 inches long, but some reach nearly 4 feet. These strikingly striped snakes are terrestrial and able to crawl with considerable speed. The females apparently lay eggs, and lizards seem to be the main staple of diet. Two species of this genus are found in the southwestern United States.

Western Patch-nosed Snake, *Salvadora hexalepis*

Identifying individual Patch-nosed Snakes is precarious if one does not have the benefit of a library containing complete descriptions of the various forms. In general, Western Patch-nosed Snakes differ from Mountain Patch-nosed Snakes in having 9 upper labials on each side, rather than 8. The posterior chin scales are separated by 2 or 3 smaller scales. Habitat will also help identify the species. Western Patch-nosed Snakes are found mostly in arid or semiarid country. Mountain Patch-nosed Snakes are found in wooded mountains in the western part of the range, in prairies to the east. There are four races of Western Patch-nosed Snakes.

Desert Patch-nosed Snake, *Salvadora h. hexalepis*

There is a broad, light stripe down the center of the back, and there are dark stripes on the sides. The top of the head is gray. There are usually 2 or 3 loreal scales, and 1 upper labial reaches the eye. This form occurs in southwestern Arizona and southeastern California east of the San Bernardino Mountains.

Big Bend Patch-nosed Snake, *Salvadora h. deserticola*

The loreal shield is single, and 2 upper labials reach the eye. This race is found west of the Pecos in Texas and in southern New Mexico and southeastern Arizona.

Mohave Patch-nosed Snake, *Salvadora h. mojavensis*

The pattern is sometimes obscure, or the light dorsal stripe may be marked with crossbars. No upper labials reach the eye. This form is found in southern and central Nevada, northwestern Arizona, and southeastern California north of the range of the Desert Patch-nosed Snake.

Coast Patch-nosed Snake, *Salvadora h. virgultea*

The top of the head is brown, and the light stripe down the center of the back is narrower than in the Desert Patch-nosed Snake. This race occupies the coastal region of southern California south of Point Conception.

Mountain Patch-nosed Snake, *Salvadora grahamiae*

Mountain Patch-nosed Snakes can generally, but not always, be told from Western Patch-nosed Snakes by the presence of 8 rather than 9 upper labials on each side. Also the posterior chin shields are in contact or separated only by 1 small scale. We have two races in our country.

Mountain Patch-nosed Snake, *Salvadora g. grahamiae* (Figure 78)

This race usually has a single dark stripe on either side of the light dorsal stripe. It has a limited and discontinuous distribution in extreme southern Arizona, New Mexico, and the Trans–Pecos region of Texas; possibly there are other isolated populations of this snake.

Texas Patch-nosed Snake, *Salvadora g. lineata*

There are two dark stripes on each side in this race. It is found in central Texas east of the Pecos, ranging south into Mexico and north into south central Oklahoma.

Leaf-nosed Snakes, Genus *Phyllorhynchus*

These are small snakes about 12 to 15 inches long, rather heavy-bodied, with the scales heavily to very weakly keeled, a single anal plate, and the rostral shield enlarged into an augerlike structure, as though it were used for boring into the sand. There is a maximum of 21 scale rows. All Leaf-nosed Snakes have a pattern of dark dorsal spots or blotches on a light background. Snakes of this genus live in the southwestern deserts and, like most desert animals, are nocturnal. They feed on eggs, lizards, and insects. The females lay from two to four rather large eggs at a time. The genus is divided into two species.

Saddle Leaf-nosed Snake, *Phyllorhynchus browni*

This species differs from the Spotted Leaf-nosed Snake in having the dorsal blotches large, conspicuous, and fewer than 17 in number on the body not including the tail. There are three races, two of which occur in the United States.

Pima Leaf-nosed Snake, *Phyllorhynchus b. browni* (Figure 79)

The dark blotches are noticeably wider than the spaces between them along the center of the back. This race occurs in southern Arizona.

Maricopa Leaf-nosed Snake, *Phyllorhynchus b. lucidus* (Figure 80)

The dark blotches are about as wide as the spaces between them along the center of the back. This rare snake is found in northeastern Maricopa County, Arizona, along the bases of the mountains from near Cave Creek to Indian Wells.

Fig. 79. Pima Leaf-nosed Snake, *Phyllorhynchus b. browni*

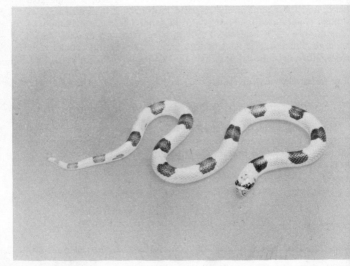

Fig. 80. Maricopa Leaf-nosed Snake, *Phyllorhynchus b. lucidus*

Spotted Leaf-nosed Snake, *Phyllorhynchus decurtatus*

There are more than 17 dorsal blotches (not including the tail spots), and the blotches are smaller and not so distinct and sharply set off as are those of the Saddle Leaf-nosed Snake. Two races of this species are found in the United States.

Clouded Leaf-nosed Snake, *Phyllorhynchus d. nubilis*

The body blotches are usually as wide as or wider than the interspaces. This Mexican form extends into southern Arizona, where it is restricted to the vicinity of Tucson in Pima County.

Western Leaf-nosed Snake, *Phyllorhynchus d. perkinsi*

The body blotches are narrower than the interspaces. This is the most widespread of the Leaf-nosed Snakes, occurring in southern Nevada, along the western border of Arizona, and in southwestern Arizona and southeastern California southward into Mexico.

Rat Snakes, Genus *Elaphe*

Rat Snakes, or Chicken Snakes, as they are sometimes called, are large, often richly colored snakes that are characteristic of the eastern United States and extend westward as far as Utah and Arizona. The pattern is usually quite bright and is generally characteristic for each species. The young are blotched, adults may or may not be. These snakes tend to be flat-bottomed, with the sides sloping up steeply, not bowed out as they are in most snakes. The scales are in 25 or more rows and are weakly keeled along the top part of the back, but along the sides the keels fade out, and the scales are smooth (young may have all scales smooth). The anal plate is divided. The Rat Snakes include some of our largest snakes; the Black Rat Snake may exceed 100 inches in total length. Rat Snakes (and some other snakes also) often vibrate the tip of the tail rapidly when disturbed. In dry leaves the resulting noise may cause them to be mistaken for Rattlesnakes. They are primarily terrestrial snakes, but some of the species are quite arboreal. There are five species of this widespread genus in the United States.

Corn Snake, *Elaphe guttata*

In this species the back is marked with a distinctive pattern of blotches, and the bands on the neck cross the parietal scales to join on the top of the head, forming a spear-shaped mark. A dark stripe behind the eye continues onto the neck. There are no subocular scales. This brightly marked, often reddish, quite arboreal snake perhaps got the name "Corn Snake" from its habit of frequenting corn cribs, for it feeds on rodents, and where rodents are to be found Corn Snakes are often present. Females lay from twelve to twenty-four eggs in midsummer. Corn Snakes usually average from 3 to 4 feet in length, although specimens of 6 feet have been recorded. There are three rather well-marked subspecies.

Corn Snake, *Elaphe g. guttata* (Plate 14a)

This gaudy snake has the red markings on the back strongly bordered with black, distinctive black checkerboard markings on the belly, and the underside of the tail marked with distinctive bold dark stripes. It ranges from southern New Jersey, southward through peninsular Florida and westward to eastern Louisiana.

Rosy Rat Snake, *Elaphe g. rosacea*

This paler version of the Corn Snake is found on the Florida Keys. It is less strongly marked, and the black checkerboard pattern of the belly is not so conspicuous.

Great Plains Rat Snake, *Elaphe g. emoryi*

This western race is smaller and duller in color than the Corn Snake, the blotches more gray or brown than red and the ground color light-gray. It ranges from southwestern Illinois and southwestern Iowa across Missouri and Kansas to eastern Colorado, south through most of Oklahoma and Texas and eastern New Mexico. There is an isolated population west of the Continental Divide in western Colorado, eastern Utah, and northwestern New Mexico.

Rat Snake, *Elaphe obsoleta*

Rat Snakes are large snakes with the characteristics of the genus. The species is divided into eight races. Some of these races are quite spectacularly marked and are so unlike in overall appearance and pattern that it may seem strange they are considered to be closely related. But the young are very similar, and many of the races are known to intergrade. The young are blotched and lack a spear-shaped mark on top of the head. The dark line behind the eye does not continue past the corner of the mouth. We will discuss the pattern variations of the adults for the different races, rather than for the species as a whole.

Black Rat Snake, *Elaphe o. obsoleta* (Figure 81)

This is a familiar Black Snake of the northeastern states. Adults are usually shiny-black above, sometimes brownish, and occasionally retain traces of the juvenile blotches. The chin and throat are white. This race ranges from southern Vermont, southward to northern and central Georgia and westward to eastern Minnesota, Nebraska, Kansas, and Oklahoma.

81. Juvenile Black Rat Snake, *Elaphe o. obsoleta*

82. Glossy Snake, *Arizona elegans*

Baird's Rat Snake, *Elaphe o. bairdi*

Adults have 4 rather dull stripes and frequently traces of the juvenile blotches as well. They are grayish-brown snakes with an orange wash. They are found from central Texas to the Big Bend region and south into Mexico.

Key Rat Snake, *Elaphe o. deckerti*

This is a yellowish-brown snake with dark stripes. Sometimes the juvenile blotches can be seen on the adult. The chin and throat are yellow, the eye pink or red, the tongue black. It is restricted to extreme southern Florida and the Keys.

Texas Rat Snake, *Elaphe o. lindheimeri*

This is a variable race, blotched like the Gray Rat Snake, but usually the blotches are less sharply set off from the ground color. The top of the head may be black. This race is found in central and eastern Texas. It intergrades with the Gray Rat Snake in a broad area in western Louisiana and eastern Texas.

Yellow Rat Snake, *Elaphe o. quadrivittata*

This snake has four distinctly marked, dark longitudinal stripes on a yellow or tan background. The chin and throat are white and the belly whitish mottled with gray. The iris of the eye is gray or yellow. It ranges along the southeastern coast from the Carolinas into northern and central Florida and west to the region of the Apalachicola River.

Yellow Rat Snake, *Elaphe o. rossalleni*

Like the Yellow Rat Snake, this race is striped, but it tends to be orange or pink rather than yellow and brown, and the stripes are usually not so distinct. The tongue is red. It is found in southern Florida from the region just north of Lake Okeechobee to the southern part of the Everglades.

Gray Rat Snake, *Elaphe o. spiloides*

This is another variable, blotched Rat Snake. The blotches are sharply set off from the ground color, and the overall tone is usually gray. It is a snake of the lower Mississippi Valley, ranging from about the Apalachicola region of Florida and southern Georgia, westward through Louisiana into eastern Texas and northward into southern Illinois and southern Missouri.

Gulf Hammock Rat Snake, *Elaphe o. williamsi*

This snake has both blotches and stripes, dark on a whitish ground color. It is restricted to the Gulf Hammock region of Florida.

Trans-Pecos Rat Snake, *Elaphe subocularis*

This species differs from all the other Rat Snakes in having scales between the eye and the upper labials; these subocular scales give the species its name. It is a yellowish, dark-blotched snake, but the ends of the H-shaped blotches tend to run together to form stripes. It is a Mexican form ranging into the United States only in the Trans-Pecos region of Texas and extreme southern New Mexico.

Green Rat Snake, *Elaphe triaspis intermedia*

This Rat Snake, a Mexican species, can be told from all our other Rat Snakes by the fact that the adult is uniformly greenish-gray above. There is no distinctive belly pattern. Only this one race enters the United States in southern Arizona.

Fox Snake, *Elaphe vulpina*

This is a large (more than 5 feet), handsome snake with dark brown blotches on a yellowish background. The head is often reddish and lacks a spear-shaped mark. Its large size and bright color make it conspicuous, and it is often killed by mistake for some poisonous species. It is essentially a snake of the open country, rarely found in thickly wooded areas and rarely a climber. It is not uncommonly found around yards or farm buildings and briar patches. The females lay from six to slightly more than two dozen eggs in the latter part of June and through July. There are two races.

Western Fox Snake, *Elaphe v. vulpina*

This race ranges from Nebraska, eastward to the Upper Peninsula of Michigan and south and east to central Indiana and northern Missouri.

Eastern Fox Snake, *Elaphe v. gloydi*

The dorsal blotches are larger and fewer in number than in the Western Fox Snake. This race occurs in southern Ontario, eastern Michigan, and north central Ohio.

Glossy Snake, *Arizona elegans* (Figure 82)

These snakes look like small editions of the Bull Snakes but have smooth rather than keeled scales. They are moderate in size, with the snout rather sharp and the lower jaw countersunk. These snakes have darker blotches on a pale background and a plain yellow, buffy, or white belly. The dorsal scales are in 27 to 31 rows; the anal plate is single; there are two prefrontal scales. Glossy Snakes are rather gentle, not at all pugnacious. They prefer sandy, even desert areas and are mostly nocturnal. They can usually be collected in the early part of the night when the air is warm. Females lay from three to twenty-four eggs, which hatch in August, so far as is known. These snakes feed primarily on lizards. Adults range from about $1\frac{1}{2}$ to $4\frac{1}{2}$ feet in total length. This is the only species in the genus, and it is divided into seven races. They differ in the form and number of blotches, but there is overlap in characteristics between the races, and, as is so often true, it is best to take geography into consideration when trying to identify one.

Texas Glossy Snake, *Arizona e. elegans*

This and the next race differ from the others in having 29 or 31 scale rows rather than (usually) 27. This is the darkest of the races. The dorsal blotches are large, 2 to 4 scale rows wide and extending from side to side over 13 to 15 scale rows. It occurs in central and western Texas and southeastern New Mexico.

Kansas Glossy Snake, *Arizona e. blanchardi*

This race is like the Texas one but the blotches tend to be slightly smaller and more numerous. They are 2 to 3 scale rows wide and extend over 12 to 13 scale rows. It occurs north of the Texas race, ranging in the northern panhandle of Texas, western Oklahoma, western Kansas, south central Nebraska, and the eastern part of Colorado and northeastern New Mexico.

Mohave Glossy Snake, *Arizona e. candida*

This and all the following races usually have no more than 27 rows of scales at midbody. The Mohave Glossy Snake is a light-colored snake; the dorsal blotches are narrower than the interspaces between them and extend from side to side over about 9 scale rows. This race is restricted to the Antelope Valley and extreme western Mohave Desert in Inyo, Kern, Los Angeles, and San Bernardino counties, California.

Desert Glossy Snake, *Arizona e. eburnata*

This is another light-colored race with narrow dorsal blotches that only extend about 7 scale rows. It is found in southeastern California, southern Nevada, extreme southwestern Utah, and northwestern and southwestern Arizona southward into Mexico.

Arizona Glossy Snake, *Arizona e. noctivaga*

The blotches are slightly wider than the spaces between. The lower labials are practically unspotted, and there are no dark marks on the edges of the belly scales. This form occurs in southern and western Arizona, between the ranges of *eburnata* and *philipi*.

California Glossy Snake, *Arizona e. occidentalis*

This resembles the Arizona Glossy Snake but has marks on the edges of the belly plates and usually spots on the lower labials. The two are separated geographically by the lighter colored desert races. This race occupies the San Joaquin Valley in California from central San Joaquin County to the Tehachapi Mountains and the coastal region of southern California from Los Angeles County southward into Lower California.

Painted Glossy Snake, *Arizona e. philipi*

The body blotches extend over 11 scale rows. This form occurs in south central New Mexico, extending into central and southeastern Arizona, the extreme western tip of Texas, and northern Mexico.

Pine Snakes, Gopher Snakes and Bull Snakes, *Pituophis melanoleucus*

These large, powerfully built snakes are well known throughout most of the United States. They have keeled scales in 27 to 37 rows and a single anal plate. They differ from other snakes in the United States in usually having 4 rather than 2 prefrontal scales. Most have dark blotches on a lighter ground color. (One race may be dark-brown or black above and below.) The largest adults may exceed 8 feet in length. They are perhaps best known for their habits. When one is approached, instead of attempting to slip away quietly, it is apt to hiss loudly and threateningly, vibrate its tail rapidly, and lunge at the intruder. Although they do well in captivity, they are seldom as gentle and docile as the Indigo Snakes. They feed mostly on small mammals and thus help control rodents. In the East they are found most often in dry, sandy areas in or near pine woods. In the West they are found in a variety of habitats, from woods to deserts. They are able both to climb and to burrow. Females lay from three to twenty-four eggs in the summer. The eggs hatch in the fall, and the hatchlings are about 1 to 1½ feet long. Ten races of this species are found in the United States.

Northern Pine Snake, *Pituophis m. melanoleucus*

In this race the blotches are distinctly black, particularly on the front part of the body, although they may be brown toward the tail. They stand out clearly against the light ground color, so that this looks like a black-and-white snake. It ranges from southern New Jersey, southward to north Georgia and westward into Kentucky and Tennessee. It is rather spotty in distribution, being apparently absent from a large area of the coastal plain in Virginia and North Carolina. Isolated populations have been reported in central Alabama and southern Indiana.

Florida Pine Snake, *Pituophis m. mugitus* (Figure 83)

This is a rusty-brown snake with the brown dorsal blotches rather indistinct. It ranges on the coastal plain from southern South Carolina south throughout most of Florida and west to Alabama.

Fig. 83. Florida Pine Snake, *Pituophis m. mugitus*

Fig. 84. Short-tailed Snake, *Stilosoma extenuatum*

Black Pine Snake, *Pituophis m. lodingi*

This is a very dark snake with the dorsal blotches quite indistinct. Some individuals are uniform black or very dark brown above and below. The race occurs in a restricted region from southern Alabama to extreme eastern Louisiana.

Louisiana Pine Snake, *Pituophis m. ruthveni*

The anterior blotches are dark-brown and not sharply defined, those toward the tail are lighter in color and more distinct. This subspecies ranges from central Louisiana to eastern Texas.

Bull Snake, *Pituophis m. sayi* (Plate 14b)

This race is yellowish with dark blotches, 41 or more along the middle of the back. The rostral scale is distinctly higher than wide. It is a snake of the western plains, ranging from Illinois and Wisconsin westward throughout most of Montana, southward through northern and eastern Wyoming, eastern Colorado and New Mexico and most of Texas.

Sonora Gopher Snake, *Pituophis m. affinis*

The dorsal blotches are usually brown and separate, rather than tending to run together. The ground color on the sides is cream or buffy. The rostral scale is little if at all higher than wide. This race occurs throughout most of Arizona and New Mexico, northward into southern Colorado, westward into southern California, and southward through extreme western Texas.

Great Basin Gopher Snake, *Pituophis m. deserticola*

The rostral scale is little if any higher than wide. The blackish anterior dorsal blotches are expanded so that they come together with the lateral blotches, leaving light spots on the back, particularly anteriorly. This subspecies ranges from southern British Columbia, south through eastern Washington, Oregon, and California, throughout Nevada and Utah to extreme western Colorado and Wyoming and throughout most of Idaho.

Pacific Gopher Snake, *Pituophis m. catenifer*

In this race the dorsal blotches may be dark-brown or black, but they are distinctly separated from one another. The ground color of the sides is washed with gray. This race ranges from coastal Oregon southward through western and central California as far south as Santa Barbara County.

San Diego Gopher Snake, *Pituophis m. annectans*

The black dorsal blotches tend to run together, but they are much smaller and more numerous (averaging about 75) than in the Great Basin Gopher Snake. This race is found on the coastal region of southern California from about Santa Barbara County southward into northern Lower California.

Santa Cruz Island Gopher Snake, *Pituophis m. pumilus*

This is a dwarf race. Adults do not reach 3 feet in length, and there are 29 or fewer rows of dorsal scales, while the other races usually have more than 29 rows. It is found only on Santa Cruz Island, California.

Short-tailed Snake, *Stilosoma extenuatum* (Figure 84)

These are secretive, burrowing snakes of the dry pine woods of central Florida. They are exceptionally slender, and their tail is less than one-tenth the total length. Their build, smooth dorsal scales, single anal plate, and pattern of 60 to 70 dark-brown spots separated by yellow, orange, or red interspaces on a silvery-gray dorsal ground color will separate them from any other Florida snake. They feed on small snakes and lizards, which they kill by constriction. The breeding habits are unknown. Adults range from 14 to 26 inches in total length, but most are less than 20 inches.

In spite of the fact that this species is restricted to the dry pine lands of central Florida, two subspecies are recognized.

Eastern Short-tailed Snake, *Stilosoma e. extenuatum*

There are 6 lower labials on one or both sides and/or the internasals are fused with the prefrontals. This race is found in Central Florida from Putnam County to Polk County.

Western Short-tailed Snake, *Stilosoma e. arenicolor*

There are 7 lower labials, and the internasals and prefrontals are separate. This form is found from Alachua County to Pinellas County.

King Snakes, Genus *Lampropeltis*

This widespread genus with many species ranges from Canada to South America. These snakes have smooth scales in 17 to 27 rows and a single anal plate. One loreal scale is present; the scales on the underside of the tail are divided. King Snakes are moderate in size and have rather short tails. They vary greatly in pattern. They may be crossbanded, blotched, speckled, ringed, striped, or nearly plain-colored. Almost always, there are at least some dark markings on the belly. Many of the species are very brightly colored. They are terrestrial snakes that feed mainly (though not entirely) on other snakes, which they subdue by constriction. There are six species of this genus within our limits.

Gray-banded King Snake, *Lampropeltis mexicana*

Gray-banded King Snakes differ from other members of the genus in having an alternating sequence of black, red, black, white, gray, white markings on the back. They are rather small snakes, between 2 and 3 feet long. The longest reported specimen is less than 4 feet. They inhabit desert and semidesert areas and, like so many desert snakes, are apparently most active at night. They feed mainly on lizards. They are very rare snakes in our region, known only from Trans–Pecos Texas. There are two races in the United States, others in Mexico.

Davis Mountain King Snake, *Lampropeltis m. alterna*

The gray dorsal bands are broad in this race and are crossed by narrow, interrupted black bands. These alternate with somewhat broader, white-edged, black bands, some of which enclose red scales. The red scales may be scattered or form discrete patches. There are from 15 to 34 of these red markings on the back. This race is found in the Big Bend and Davis and Guadaloupe mountain areas of Trans–Pecos Texas.

Trans-Pecos King Snake, *Lampropeltis m. blairi*

The dorsal pattern consists of black-bordered red saddles alternating with white-bordered gray saddles. The red markings are much broader than in the Davis Mountain King Snake. There are 13 or 14 of them along the back. This race is known only from Terrell and Valverde counties in Trans–Pecos Texas.

Prairie King Snake, *Lampropeltis calligaster*

This rather small, slender King Snake has a dorsal pattern of brown, reddish, or greenish blotches narrowly bordered in black and alternating with a series of smaller lateral blotches. The ground color is lighter brown. The dorsal blotches may barely reach, but do not extend broadly onto, the fifth row of scales. Older specimens may darken so that the blotches are obscured and may develop dusky stripes. This is a form of open lands, found usually in prairies, pastures, plowed and uncultivated fields, along roads, and occasionally in mixed woodlands and bottomlands. It feeds primarily on small snakes, rodents, lizards, and frogs. From four to thirteen eggs are laid, generally in July; they hatch in late August and September. Adults range from $2\frac{1}{2}$ to nearly 4 feet in length. The largest may slightly exceed 4 feet. Hatchlings range from 7 to 9 inches. There are two races of the Prairie King Snake.

Prairie King Snake, *Lampropeltis c. calligaster*

In this race there are usually about 60 concave, dark-edged markings on the back. There are 25 to 27 dorsal scale rows. Large adults may be almost uniformly black or marked with dusky stripes. This race ranges from Indiana westward to Nebraska, southward through northern Mississippi to the Gulf Coast in western Louisiana and Texas. In Texas it extends south to Matagorda Bay and west into the panhandle.

Mole Snake, *Lampropeltis c. rhombomaculata*

This slightly smaller version of the Prairie King Snake seldom has more than about 55 dorsal dark blotches, and these are generally well separated. There are 19 to 23 scale rows. Adults may be plain brown or marked with dusky stripes. This race extends from Maryland south to north central Florida and west to eastern Tennessee and southeastern Louisiana.

Milk Snake, *Lampropeltis triangulum*

In this species the basic pattern is a series of red or brown rings or blotches bordered by black and separated by yellow or white or light-gray. The red areas are always surrounded by black and never come in contact with the light areas. If the pattern is blotched, the blotches extend well onto the fifth row of scales or lower. These snakes are known as Milk Snakes because of the old wives' tale that they are able to suck milk from a cow—something that no snake can do. There are ten different subspecies in the United States. The first three races are blotched snakes; the rest have a ringed appearance though the rings may not go all the way around the body, and the red rings are sometimes broken at the middorsal line. There is a good deal of variation in adult size. The maximum recorded is 4½ feet, but most are probably between 2 and 3 feet long.

Eastern Milk Snake, *Lampropeltis t. triangulum*

In this race the dorsal blotches are chocolate-brown or reddish-brown on a gray or tan background. The usual appearance is of a gray snake with dark-reddish or brown blotches along the back. The dorsal blotches do not reach the belly. There are smaller blotches along the sides and the belly is checkered black and white. There is frequently a Y- or V-shaped mark on the back of the head. This snake ranges from Maine to Minnesota in the north and in the mountains south to northern Alabama and Georgia.

Coastal Plain Milk Snake, *Lampropeltis t. temporalis*

This is a more brightly colored race. The reddish dorsal blotches are large and reach the belly scales, at least on the front part of the body. There is usually a broad, light collar. The lateral blotches are reduced or absent. It is the snake of the central Atlantic coastal plain, ranging from New Jersey southward to North Carolina.

Red Milk Snake, *Lampropeltis t. syspila*

The dorsal blotches are larger and fewer in number than in the Eastern Milk Snake. They are usually red, set in a light ground color of white, gray, or buff. They do not extend onto the belly scales. The lateral blotches are small or lacking. This snake is found in the north central United States, ranging from Indiana and Kentucky westward into Oklahoma and South Dakota.

Scarlet King Snake, *Lampropeltis t. doliata* (Plate 14c)

This is a ringed snake. The black bordered red rings are quite wide and separated by rather narrow yellowish rings. The rings usually continue across the belly. There are 19 rows of dorsal scales (other Milk Snakes with a ringed pattern have 21 or more). Adults seldom exceed 24 inches in length. The harmless Scarlet King Snake looks very like the common venomous Coral Snake but has a red nose, and the red and yellow colors are separated by black. The Coral Snake has a black nose, and the red and yellow are in contact. This is a southeastern race, ranging from North Carolina south throughout Florida and westward to the Mississippi River in the coastal plain. It has also been reported from some higher elevations both in the Mississippi Valley and along the Atlantic Piedmont.

Louisiana Milk Snake, *Lampropeltis t. amaura*

This race has 21 rows of dorsal scales and broad red bands which extend onto the belly scales and may cross them completely. The black rings are narrow and interrupted on the belly. The top of the head is black, the snout usually reddish but may be speckled with black or white. Occasionally it is black like a Coral Snake's, but, as in all Milk Snakes, the red and yellow are separated by black, not in contact as they are in the Coral Snake. This race is found on the western Gulf coastal plain, from southern Arkansas and southeastern Oklahoma to the Gulf Coast.

Mexican Milk Snake, *Lampropeltis t. annulata*

In this race the red areas are broad but are restricted to the back and sides and do not reach the belly. The black rings are rather broad, especially on the belly, which they cross completely. The snout is black. This is the King Snake of central and southern Texas and northeastern Mexico.

Pallid Milk Snake, *Lampropeltis t. multistrata*

This is a pale-colored Milk Snake in which the black areas are reduced and the red is replaced with orange. The belly is without black markings or has only a very few scattered ones. The snout is light. This race occurs from central Nebraska, northward and westward into southeastern Montana.

Western Milk Snake, *Lampropeltis t. gentilis*

The black bands are rather wide and tend to encroach on the red bands dorsally, sometimes cutting them in two. The red bands extend onto the belly and may cross it or be interrupted by a black bar at the midline. The head is mostly black. This race is found on the lower plains, ranging from southern Missouri through most of Kansas and Oklahoma into the panhandle of Texas and northeastern and eastern New Mexico.

New Mexican Milk Snake, *Lampropeltis t. celaenops*

Both the black and the light bands are expanded both middorsally and ventrally, and the red extends only to the lateral edges of the belly scales. This race is known from extreme southern Utah and the Rio Grande drainage of New Mexico.

Utah Milk Snake, *Lampropeltis t. taylori*

The black rings are expanded middorsally and frequently interrupt the red rings. The red rings extend onto and usually cross the belly scales. This race is found in central and northeastern Utah, western Colorado, and northern Arizona.

Common King Snake, *Lampropeltis getulus*

This is the familiar black and white King Snake of most of the United States. The basic pattern is one of black or dark-brown scales with oval, white, or yellow centers. Variations in pattern within the species result from the presence of regions where the scales are entirely yellow or white and other regions where the scales are entirely black or from variations in different parts of the body of the extent of the light areas in the individual scales. Most of the races have either a speckled or a banded appearance, but some appear plain-colored. One color phase of the California race is striped. As would be expected of a species that occupies such a wide range, these snakes are found in many different habitats, from moist woodlands to semideserts. They also eat many different animals, both vertebrates and invertebrates. Eggs are laid in the early summer and hatch in the late summer and fall. The hatchlings are usually about 10 to 12 inches long. Most adults are between 2½ and 4 feet, but one individual of the Eastern King Snake is reported to have reached 82 inches. This species ranges from New Jersey south throughout Florida and west to California. It is absent from the northern part of the country and from the Rocky Mountain region. Ten races of this snake are recognized at present.

Eastern King Snake, *Lampropeltis g. getulus* (Figure 85)

Most of the scales on the back are shiny black with the yellow, creamy, or white scales restricted to narrow crossbands which fork and

g. 85. Eastern King Snake, *Lampropeltis g. getulus*

. 86. Great Plains Ground Snake, *Sonora e. episcopa*

join along the sides. The snake appears to be black with a light chain of narrow links extending up and down the back. This race extends from New Jersey south to central Florida and west into southeastern Alabama, except for an area in the Florida panhandle where it is replaced by the Blotched King Snake.

Florida King Snake, *Lampropeltis g. floridana*

This race is very similar to the Eastern King Snake, but the ground color is not quite so dark, and the bands of light-yellowish across the back are wider and less sharply marked. The dark blotches are more numerous, usually 50 or more, while there are typically less than 50 in the Eastern race. Sometimes the light areas invade the dark to such an extent that the dark blotches can hardly be made out. This race occurs from central Florida to south of Lake Okeechobee.

South Florida King Snake, *Lampropeltis g. brooksi*

The scales all over the back tend to be so uniformly light, with dark-brown or black margins, that it is hard to distinguish any crossbands at all, though keen observation and a little imagination can demonstrate that they are really there. The general appearance is of a speckled yellowish snake. The form is restricted to southern Florida in the Everglades region.

Blotched King Snake, *Lampropeltis g. goini*

In this form the light bands across the back are so wide that the dark areas appear as isolated oval blotches. There are fewer than 25 of these blotches. This race is restricted to the region of the Chipola and Apalachicola River valleys in western Florida.

Eastern Black King Snake, *Lampropeltis g. niger*

The chainlike pattern is so faint or incompletely indicated that the snake appears shiny-black. There are usually some traces of yellow spots in the scales, particularly along the sides. The belly is checkered with black and yellow. This is the King Snake of the upper Mississippi and Ohio valleys, ranging from southern Ohio, Indiana, and Illinois and southwestern West Virginia, south into northern Mississippi and Alabama.

Speckled King Snake, *Lampropeltis g. holbrooki*

This is called Speckled King Snake because the light dots on the back are so uniformly distributed that they give the snake a salt-and-pepper appearance. It is a snake of the plains region, extending from eastern Texas and southern Alabama, northward and westward into Iowa and Nebraska.

Sonora King Snake, *Lampropeltis g. splendida*

In this form, most of the scales have yellow centers, except for some along the back which form a series of oval, dark blotches. The sides appear speckled. It is found in the southwestern United States, ranging from central Texas into southern and central New Mexico and southeastern Arizona and southward into northern Mexico.

Western Black King Snake, *Lampropeltis g. nigritus*

This is a plain-colored race, dark-brown or black above, with little sign of bands or stripes. It is primarily Mexican, entering the United States only in extreme southern Arizona.

Yuma King Snake, *Lampropeltis g. yumensis*

The ground color is deep-brown or black with narrow white or yellowish cross bars. The scales in the light areas are dark at the base. Some of the crossbars may end at the middorsal region, with those of the opposite side alternately spaced, especially on the posterior part of the body. The face and underparts of the head are white, heavily marked with black. In the United States this subspecies ranges from extreme southeastern California almost to Phoenix, Arizona.

California King Snake, *Lampropeltis g. californiae* (Plate 14d, e)

This race comes in two patterns. In one, the ground color is black or dark-brown with a prominent middorsal line of yellow, which breaks up into spots on the tail; the lower 3 or 4 rows of scales usually have light centers which form several rows of broken lines of little yellow spots. In the other pattern the ground color is dark-brown or black and there are from about 30 to 50 clear whitish or yellowish rings across the back which widen as they descend onto the sides. The light scales usually do not have dark bases. The dark markings on the face and underside of the head are not so heavy as in the Yuma King Snake. This race extends from Oregon, south through California and east into southern Utah and northwestern Arizona.

Sonora Mountain King Snake, *Lampropeltis pyromelana*

In this species the pattern is made up of black rings separated by narrow yellow or buffy rings. The black rings are often interrupted with scarlet-red areas. The pattern is thus similar to that of the Milk Snakes, but the Mountain King Snakes have proportionately longer tails, with a higher number of subcaudal scales (59 to 79). There are usually more than 40 light rings. The top of the head is black; the snout is light-colored. These are rather small King Snakes. Most adults range from 1½ to 2 feet long. The maximum reported length is 41 inches. Little is known of the habits of these snakes of the southwestern mountains. There are three races in the United States and others in Mexico.

Arizona Mountain King Snake, *Lampropeltis p. pyromelana*

In this form there are 10 lower labials on each side and generally more than 43 light rings across the back. It is found in southwestern New Mexico and central and eastern Arizona north of the Huachuca Mountains.

Utah Mountain King Snake, *Lampropeltis p. infralabialis*

There are only 9 lower labials on each side. This race occurs from the Grand Canyon region of Arizona, northward through central Utah and into eastern Nevada.

Huachuca Mountain King Snake, *Lampropeltis p. woodini*

There are 10 lower labials on each side and generally less than 43 white bands across the back. This race is restricted to the Huachuca Mountains of southern Arizona and adjacent parts of Mexico.

California Mountain King Snake, *Lampropeltis zonata*

This species is very like the Sonora Mountain King Snake but differs in having a dark snout, sometimes marked with red, and in usually having fewer than 40 light bands on the body. The amount of red within the dark bands is very variable. It approaches even more closely some of the Milk Snakes and perhaps should be included in that species. These are common snakes in the large canyons throughout the mountains of the California region, where their bright colors attract attention. As with the Eastern King Snakes, many tales are told of these snakes seeking out Rattlesnakes to kill them. They are probably no fonder of Rattlesnakes than of any other snakes, but where Rattlesnakes are common they are an important item in the diet of the King Snake. King Snakes are immune to Rattlesnake venom, and the Rattlesnakes defend themselves not by striking, but by attempting to fend the attacker off with a loop of the body. Because of their bright colors, these King Snakes are often supposed to be venomous, like the Coral Snakes. Other than the facts that they are snakes of the mountains and are oviparous, very little is known of the habits and life history. They are moderate-sized snakes; adults may be slightly more than 3 feet long. They feed on lizards and mice, as well as other snakes. There are five subspecies now recognized in the United States.

St. Helena Mountain King Snake, *Lampropeltis z. zonata*

In this race the posterior margin of the first white ring around the head is behind the posterior margin of the mouth. The snout is dark, and more than sixty percent of the red bands are confluent across the top of the back. This form occurs in California north of the San Francisco Bay area in Lake, Mendocino, Napa, and Sonoma counties.

Coast Mountain King Snake, *Lampropeltis z. multifasciata*

In this race also the posterior margin of the first white ring is behind the mouth, and more than sixty percent of the red bands are confluent across the back. It can be told from the St. Helena Mountain King Snake by the presence of red markings on the snout. The black markings are usually narrower, especially on the sides. This race is found south of the San Francisco Bay area from Santa Clara County to Ventura County or perhaps to the extreme western edge of Los Angeles County.

Sierra Mountain King Snake, *Lampropeltis z. multicincta*

This race can be recognized by the fact that less than sixty percent of the red bands are confluent across the back. The snout is black, as in the St. Helena Mountain King Snake, and the posterior margin of the first white ring is behind the mouth. This is a snake of the Sierra Nevada Mountains, ranging from Kern County, California, northward into Washington.

San Bernardino Mountain King Snake, *Lampropeltis z. parvirubra*

In this form the posterior margin of the first white ring around the head is at least on or anterior to the last upper labial. The snout is dark. There are 37 or more triads (combinations of red, black, and light rings) around the body. This race ranges from Los Angeles County into San Bernardino County and north-central Riverside County, California.

San Diego Mountain King Snake, *Lampropeltis z. pulchra*

Like the San Bernardino race, this one has the first white ring on or anterior to the last upper labial; however, there are 36 or fewer triads of rings around the body. It occurs in southern California in Los Angeles, Orange, Riverside, and San Diego counties.

Scarlet Snake, *Cemophora coccinea*

These small snakes are patterned with bright-red, yellow, and black rings on the body. They can be told from both the Coral Snakes and the Scarlet King Snakes by their glistening white or yellow belly; in the other two, some or all of the rings go completely around the body, so the belly is patterned. The top of the head and tip of the snout are typically red in Scarlet Snakes, and there is a black band across the top of the head. These secretive snakes are most often found on the ground under lumber piles, pieces of bark, or stones. They feed on small lizards, snakes, frogs, and reptile eggs. Females lay from three to eight eggs in early summer. Adults usually range from 14 to 20 inches in length, but an occasional one may exceed 30 inches. Three races have been described.

Florida Scarlet Snake, *Cemophora c. coccinea*

The black bands extend to the first or second dorsal scale row and enclose the red bands laterally. The first black band on the body does not reach the parietal scales and is usually separated from them by 2 or more scales. This is the race of peninsular Florida.

Southeastern Scarlet Snake, *Cemophora c. copei* (Plate 14f)

The black bands on the body are like those of the Florida race but the first usually either touches the parietals or is joined to the black head band. This race ranges from New Jersey, southern Indiana, southwestern Illinois, and southeastern Missouri, southward to the Gulf coast, including northern Florida, westward to eastern Texas.

Texas Scarlet Snake, *Cemophora c. lineri*

The black bands do not extend below the third scale row and do not enclose the red bands laterally. This race is known only from two specimens from Kenedy County, Texas.

Long-nosed Snake, *Rhinocheilus lecontei*

These are moderate-sized snakes with rather pointed heads, smooth scales, and a single anal plate. They can be told at once from all other harmless snakes by the fact that most of the scales on the underside of the tail are in a single row. The only other snakes in the United States that show this condition are the poisonous Rattlesnakes, Copperheads, and Moccasins. These snakes have a speckled appearance. The dorsal pattern consists of a series of large black or dark-brown, light-bordered blotches alternating with narrow bands of red, yellow, or white. The dorsal blotches narrow as they extend down the sides and become spotted with light. The light areas on the sides are usually spotted with black, sometimes so heavily as to form dark lateral blotches. Adults of this species average about 2 feet in length, although specimens slightly over 3 feet have been recorded. These snakes are found in desert and semidesert areas. They are nocturnal burrowers and feed largely on lizards and small rodents. The few reports on life history indicate that between five and eight eggs are laid in July. There are three subspecies, two of which occur in the United States.

Western Long-nosed Snake, *Rhinocheilus l. lecontei*

This race is very variable in color pattern. At one extreme are individuals with red between the dorsal blotches and with heavy dark spotting and dark blotches on the sides. At the other extreme are individuals with fewer and longer dorsal blotches, without red coloring, and with few if any dark spots or blotches on the sides. Intermediates between these two color phases are frequently found. This race ranges from southern Idaho through Nevada, western Utah, California, and western and southern Arizona.

Texas Long-nosed Snake, *Rhinocheilus l. tessellatus* (Plate 15a)

The snout is more sharply pointed in this race and usually has an upward tilt. This race occupies Texas, except the eastern part, western Oklahoma, southwestern Kansas, and all except northwestern New Mexico.

Sharp-tailed Snake, *Contia tenuis* (Plate 15b)

These are small, secretive snakes, generally found under logs and boards where there is enough moisture to support the slugs on which they feed. They have smooth scales, a divided anal plate, a loreal scale, and a single preocular. The tail is short and conical, ending in a sharply pointed scale. The color above may be light-brown, reddish-brown, yellowish-brown or grayish and there may be a weakly developed pattern. The character that gives the species away is the ventral coloration. Each ventral scale is white or cream-colored, with a very sharply defined black anterior border which results in a black-and-white barred effect on the belly. The maximum reported size is $1\frac{1}{2}$ feet, but most adults are about a foot long. Very little is known of the life history of these snakes. They lay eggs, apparently in the summer, and these eggs presumably hatch in the fall. This species occurs from the vicinity of Puget Sound to south central California in the coast region and also in the Sierra Nevadas.

Ground Snakes, Genus *Sonora*

These are small snakes (adults average 10 to 12 inches in length, with a maximum of 19 inches) with smooth scales and a divided anal plate. The dorsal scales are in 13 to 15 rows; a loreal scale is present; and there are 7 upper labials. These snakes are nearly impossible to identify from pattern for striped, banded, collared, streaked, and uniform individuals of the same species can be found under the same rock at the same time. A frequent pattern is one of dark crossbands, separated dorsally by red or orange interspaces. Banded ones may look like Shovel-nosed Snakes, but in that genus the snout is flattened and the upper jaw extends noticeably beyond the lower. The dorsal scales of *Sonora* are frequently marked with dark blotches. These are secretive, burrowing snakes, found in open country under rocks and debris or around vacant lots in urban areas. They feed primarily on insects, spiders, and other small invertebrates. They are egg layers, with up to six eggs reported in a clutch. At the present time they are generally placed in three species, two of which occur in the United States. Range may help identify them.

Ground Snake, *Sonora episcopa*

The belly is plain white or yellowish, the back very variable in color and pattern. Dark blotches on the dorsal scales may form rows of dots or streaks. This form occurs in the eastern part of the range of the genus and is divided into two subspecies.

Great Plains Ground Snake, *Sonora e. episcopa* (Figure 86)

Members of this race typically have 15 scale rows. It ranges from southwestern Missouri and northwestern Arkansas to southeastern Colorado and south through central and western Texas and eastern New Mexico.

South Texas Ground Snake, *Sonora e. taylori*

This race has 13 scale rows, and apparently lacks the pattern variations that are so marked in the other race. The back is brown, frequently with indications of light lateral stripes. The top of the head is often darker than the back. It is found in southeastern Texas.

Western Ground Snake, *Sonora semiannulata*

As the name indicates, this species is more western in distribution. It is very like the preceding species, but range will separate most of them. (See the Trans–Pecos Ground Snake.) There are five subspecies.

Santa Rita Ground Snake, *Sonora s. semiannulata*

The pattern consists of dark crossbands separated by red areas on the back. The belly is unmarked. This form is restricted in distribution to the Santa Rita Mountains of extreme southern Arizona.

Trans-Pecos Ground Snake, *Sonora s. blanchardi*

This race may be nearly uniform in dorsal coloration or marked with dark crossbands, with or without red in the interspaces, or there may be a red middorsal stripe. It is the only race of this species which overlaps in range the similarly varied *episcopa*. The two can usually be separated by the number of subcaudal scales. Males have 53 or more and females 45 or more in the Trans–Pecos Ground Snake; males have 52 or fewer and females usually fewer than 46 in the Great Plains Ground Snake. The barred form of the Great Plains Ground Snake has fewer (less than 30) more widely spaced bars. The Trans–Pecos Ground Snake is found in Texas west of the Pecos, extreme southern New Mexico, and adjacent parts of Mexico.

Grand Canyon Ground Snake, *Sonora s. gloydi*

This is a banded race; the dark crossbands are wide and extend down onto and frequently cross the belly. It is found in the Grand Canyon region of northwestern Arizona and southwestern Utah.

Great Basin Ground Snake, *Sonora s. isozona*

If crossbands are present, few if any cross the belly. If crossbands are lacking, the color of the back may be the same as that of the sides, or it may be brighter but fade gradually into the brown, gray, or reddish of the sides, or there may be a red middorsal stripe. This is a snake of the Great Basin, ranging from southern Arizona north and westward through eastern California and Nevada into extreme southern Idaho and Oregon.

Vermilion-lined Ground Snake, *Sonora s. linearis*

This race lacks crossbands but has a bright-scarlet, sharply defined line down the middle of the back. The stripe is narrower and more sharply edged than in the striped form of the Great Basin Ground Snake. This form occurs in southeastern California east of the San Bernardino Mountains.

Shovel-nosed Snakes, Genus *Chionactis*

These are small burrowing snakes with 15 rows of smooth scales and a divided anal plate. The head is small, with little or no neck constriction. There is a sharp angle between the belly and the side. The lower jaw is countersunk within the longer upper jaw; the snout is shovel-shaped; and there are well-developed valves on the nostrils—all adaptations for burrowing in sand. This is another group of small, crossbanded snakes of the Southwest. The dark bands may or may not cross the belly. The white or yellow interspaces may be suffused with red, have well-marked red saddles, or have dark spots on the scales which form more or less distinct secondary crossbands. These snakes might be confused with the Sand Snakes, which have 13 rather than 15 rows of scales and are more stoutly built, or with the banded Ground Snakes, which lack well-developed nasal valves. They differ from Coral Snakes in that the red markings, if present, do not form complete rings around the body. These nocturnal, desert-dwelling snakes feed on insects and other small invertebrates. Adults are 10 to 17 inches long. There are two species.

Western Shovel-nosed Snake, *Chionactis occipitalis*

This species differs from the Ground Snakes, genus *Sonora*, in having a flat-topped snout and usually more than 21 dark bands across the body. There are four races in the United States.

Mohave Shovel-nosed Snake, *Chionactis o. occipitalis* (Plate 15c)

There are no red saddles in the interspaces between the dark bands. There are 25 to 41 usually brown bands on the body; typically most of them do not cross the belly. This race occurs in southeastern California (north of the range of the next race) and extends into extreme southern Nevada and the western edge of central Arizona.

Colorado Desert Shovel-nosed Snake,
Chionactis o. annulata (Plate 15c)

There are 18 to 25 dark bands on the body, and usually most of them cross the belly. There are frequently narrow red saddles in the interspaces. This race ranges from the southeastern tip of California and southwestern Arizona south into Mexico.

Nevada Shovel-nosed Snake, *Chionactis o. talpina*

The primary dark bands are brown, and there are dark marks in the interspaces that give the effect of secondary brown crossbands. This is the northernmost of the races, occurring in south central Nevada and extreme western California.

Tuscon Shovel-nosed Snake, *Chionactis o. klauberi*

This is like the Nevada race, but the primary dark bands are black or very dark-brown, and the narrow secondary bands are more distinct. This race occurs in south central Arizona.

Organ Pipe Shovel-nosed Snake, *Chionactis palarostris organica* (Figure 87)

There are generally fewer than 21 dark bands on the body, and the snout is convex rather than flat-topped above. There are broad red saddles in the interspaces, and the yellow ground color is reduced to narrow rings between the red and black. This race is known only from western Pima County, Arizona.

Banded Sand Snake, *Chilomeniscus cinctus* (Plate 15d)

These small, rather stout-bodied snakes, some 7 to 10 inches long, have a yellowish or reddish ground color with from 19 to 49 distinct dark-brown or black bands on the body and tail. The bands on the body may extend across the belly and those on the tail usually form complete rings. The belly otherwise is whitish. The scales are smooth and shiny and in 13 rows. The anal plate is divided. The rostral plate at the tip of the snout is very large; the head is flattened and chisel-shaped, and nasal valves are present—characteristics that reflect the burrowing habits of this species. It burrows in the loose sand of the true deserts and, like many desert animals, is strictly nocturnal. Banded Sand Snakes feed on insects. Other than this, little is known of their habits or life history. They are found in central and southwestern Arizona and south into Mexico.

Hook-nosed Snakes, Genus *Ficimia*

This is a genus of small blotched or banded snakes in which the broad rostral scale is turned up in front. The snout looks like that of

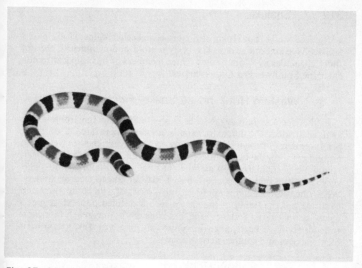

Fig. 87. Organ Pipe Shovel-nosed Snake, *Chionactis palarostris organica*

Fig. 88. San Diego Night Snake, *Hypsiglena t. klauberi*

a Hognose Snake, but Hognose Snakes have keeled scales; Hook-nosed Snakes have smooth scales. The body is stout and cylindrical, the tail short, the scales in 17 or 19 rows. Three members of this Mexican genus enter the Southwestern United States.

Western Hook-nosed Snake, *Ficimia cana*

In this species the rostral scale is separated from the frontals, the anal is divided, the loreal is usually absent. There are 30 or more black-bordered, brownish crossbands on a gray, pinkish, or yellowish ground color on the back and 8 to 14 on the tail. The bands in the head region are particularly well marked. The belly is glistening white. This very rare little snake appears to be a burrower and to feed on spiders. When one is touched, it is apt to go into a series of wild contortions and to thrust out the lining of the cloaca with a decided pop. Most specimens are only about 8 inches long, but large adults may reach 14 inches. Individuals have been taken in central and western Texas, southern New Mexico, and southeastern Arizona.

Sonora Hook-nosed Snake, *Ficimia quadrangularis desertorum*

The rostral is separated from the frontal; the anal is single, the loreal present. The black dorsal blotches are squarish and the ground color between the blotches is creamy white in the center of the back, reddish on the sides. The belly is nearly plain-white. Adults are 6 to 12 inches long. This rare Mexican snake has been found in the United States only in Santa Cruz County, Arizona.

Mexican Hook-nosed Snake, *Ficimia olivacea streckeri*

This form differs from the other two representatives of the genus in having the rostral and frontal broadly in contact. The anal is divided, the loreal absent. The black crossbands are narrow and indistinct or broken into a series of dots; the head is practically without pattern. The ground color is gray, the belly purplish. Adults range from 10 to 19 inches. In the United States this form is restricted to extreme southern Texas.

Night Snake, *Hypsiglena torquata*

These are small, rather slender, cylindrical snakes with smooth scales in 19 or 21 rows (in the forms in our area) and a divided anal plate. The pupil is a vertical elipse; the pattern above is of many dark-brown or gray spots on a background of gray or yellowish; the ventral surfaces are white or creamy yellow. The maximum reported length is 26 inches, but most adults are about 12 to 18 inches. Very little is known of the habits of these snakes. As the name indicates, they are active at night and are generally found under stones or logs in arid or semiarid regions.

They feed mostly on lizards although small frogs, insects, and other little animals are also taken. They lay eggs, but other than this little is known about their breeding habits. Six races of one species are found in the United States. Range will be the biggest help in identifying some of them.

Desert Night Snake, *Hypsiglena t. deserticola*

There are 3 blotches across the back of the neck, the middle one broadened posteriorly to cover most of the nape. This race ranges through southeastern California, extreme northwestern Arizona, western Utah, most of Nevada, and northward through western Idaho and eastern Oregon into southeastern Washington.

San Diego Night Snake, *Hypsiglena t. klauberi* (Figure 88)

This race also has 3 neck blotches, but the middle one is not enlarged posteriorly. This is a snake of the lower West Coast, ranging from about the region of San Luis Obispo Bay in California southward into northern Lower California.

Mesa Verde Night Snake, *Hypsiglena t. loreala*

This race differs from all others in having two rather than one loreal on each side. It is found in eastern Utah, southwestern Colorado, northwestern New Mexico, and extreme northeastern Arizona.

California Night Snake, *Hypsiglena t. nuchalata* (Plate 15e)

The dorsal scales are in 19 rows at midbody. All our other races have 21 rows. This form occurs on the slopes bordering the Great Valley of California, west of the Sierra Nevadas and east of the Coast Ranges.

Spotted Night Snake, *Hypsiglena t. ochrorhyncha*

This race can usually be told from the other Night Snakes by the fact that instead of having 3 blotches across the nape of the neck, it has only 2 or a single narrow band. It occurs throughout most of Arizona and western New Mexico and ranges southward into northern Mexico and eastward into the southern edge of Texas west of the Pecos.

Texas Night Snake, *Hypsiglena t. texana*

The dorsal spots are larger in this race than in the Spotted Night Snake. It occupies all of Texas except the extreme eastern edge and the extreme southwestern edge west of the Pecos, most of New Mexico, western Oklahoma, a southern strip along the border of Kansas, and southeastern Colorado.

Texas Cat-eyed Snake,
Leptodeira septentrionalis septentrionalis (Plate 15f)

These snakes have the head conspicuously wider than the neck and are marked along the back with large dark blotches that extend down on each side to the first row of scales. The ventral scales usually have dark posterior edges. Cat-eyed Snakes have vertical pupils, smooth scales, a single loreal, and a divided anal plate. Adults average about 2 feet in length, but occasional ones may exceed 3 feet. They feed largely on frogs. Other than the fact that they lay eggs, little is known of their breeding habits. This representative of a widespread tropical genus reaches the United States only in the extreme southern tip of Texas.

Lyre Snakes, Genus *Trimorphodon*

These are slender, blotched snakes with a narrow neck and enlarged head, vertical pupils, and a lyre-shaped mark on the head. Two or 3 loreal scales are present. The scales are smooth, and the anal plate may be either divided or entire. These snakes are nocturnal and can be found abroad at night, particularly in rocky places. The adults average about 3 feet in length; the longest known individual exceeded 3½ feet. The one species of which we know the feeding habits is a lizard eater; probably the others are also. The female lays eggs. Three species of this largely Mexican and Central American genus enter the Southwestern United States.

Sonora Lyre Snake, *Trimorphodon lambda*

This species has 23 to 34 light-centered, dark dorsal blotches, not counting those on the tail, and the spaces between the blotches are generally narrower than the blotches themselves. The anal plate is usually divided. This species is found in southwestern Utah, southern Nevada, extreme southeastern California, and western and southern Arizona.

California Lyre Snake, *Trimorphodon vandenburghi*
(Plate 16a)

The blotches are usually more numerous in this species than in the Sonora Lyre Snake, and the anal plate is almost always entire. It occurs in southern California.

Texas Lyre Snake, *Trimorphodon vilkinsoni*

This species has fewer dorsal blotches, generally less than 23, and the spaces between the blotches are distinctly wider than the blotches themselves. In the United States it is restricted to the border of Texas along the Rio Grande, west of the Pecos River, and to extreme southern New Mexico.

Mexican Vine Snake, *Oxybelis aeneus auratus*

This is an extremely slender snake, quite arboreal, with an elongated pointed head that immediately sets it off from any other snake in the United States. The snout in front of the eye is four times as long as the eye. Adults are 3 to 5 feet in total length. These snakes are gray above, grading into yellowish-brown or tan in the head region. They probably live primarily on lizards. They are egg layers, but other than this we know next to nothing of the life history. This snake is found in the United States only in the mountain regions of extreme south central Arizona.

Black-headed Snakes, Genus *Tantilla*

These small snakes are uniform in body color, usually brown above and often with pink or red on the belly. Most of them have a black cap and some of them a black collar, as well. They have smooth scales in 15 rows and a divided anal plate and lack a loreal scale in front of the eye. Most adults are less than 1 foot long; the largest recorded specimen is about 20 inches. They are secretive snakes, usually found buried under rocks and piles of debris. Apparently they feed solely on insects and other soft-bodied invertebrates small enough for them to capture. They lay from one to four eggs in midsummer, and these eggs hatch in early fall. Seven species occur in the United States. They are very variable and, as in so many cases, identification is often difficult without access to the extensive original literature. Fortunately, the species are to a large extent separated geographically. There is some overlap, but in most parts of the country only one species will be found. The following synopsis should help in identifying them.

Crowned Snakes are the only ones found east of the Mississippi River. Usually they have a light collar that includes the tips of the parietal scales on the head and is followed by a broad black band. Flat-headed Snakes are found in the midwestern states west of the Mississippi River. The cap on the head is usually not much darker than the color of the back. It extends beyond the parietals, and its posterior border is concave. These snakes have only 6 upper labials on each side (other species normally have 7). Plains Black-headed Snakes have a black cap that extends 2 to 5 scale lengths beyond the parietals and has a concave or pointed posterior border. There is no light collar. This species overlaps the ranges of both the Flat-headed Snakes and the Western Black-headed Snakes, and in these areas, especially in central Texas, identification may be troublesome. In Western Black-headed Snakes the dark cap extends for 0 to 3 scale lengths behind the parietals; its posterior border is usually rather straight; a white collar is more or less developed. When it is well marked, it is usually followed by a row of dark spots. And finally there are three species that are found only in the Mexican border region of Texas and Arizona. The Hooded Snake has the black of the cap extending down to cover the scales of the lips and between the lower jaws and lacks a white collar. The Val Verde Black-headed Snake has the black cap reaching to the tips of the parietals, from which a trident-shaped black mark extends into the white collar. The black band behind the collar is broad and well marked. The Huachuca Black-headed Snake has a well-marked white collar that crosses the tips of the parietals. Behind this the posterior black border is very narrow or may be reduced to a row of dark spots.

Crowned Snake, *Tantilla coronata*

These small snakes are tan or brown above, white or grayish below, often washed with pink or yellow on the belly. There are three races.

Southeastern Crowned Snake, *Tantilla c. coronata* (Figure 89)

The dark cap reaches to or almost to the mouth under the eye and near the angle of the jaw. This race is found in the southeastern states from central Virginia to northern Florida, west to the Mississippi River and north to southern Indiana. It is replaced in the southern Appalachians by the next race.

Appalachian Crowned Snake, *Tantilla c. mitrifer*

This is a darker race in which the black cap usually does not reach the labial scales near the angle of the jaws. It is restricted to the southern Appalachians in western North Carolina, eastern Tennessee, northwestern South Carolina and northern Georgia.

Florida Crowned Snake, *Tantilla c. wagneri*

The white collar is reduced or absent and the anal is occasionally single in this peninsular Florida race.

Flat-headed Snake, *Tantilla gracilis*

This is a brownish snake with a salmon pink belly. It has only 6 upper labials and the head usually is only a little darker than the rest of the body. There are two races, hard to separate except by counting scales.

Slender Flat-headed Snake, *Tantilla g. gracilis*

The Slender Black-headed Snake usually has 127 or fewer ventrals and 41 or fewer subcaudals in the female, 119 or fewer ventrals and 50 or fewer subcaudals in the male. This race extends from southern Texas northward into south central Oklahoma, northwestern Louisiana and southwestern Arkansas.

Northern Flat-headed Snake, *Tantilla g. hallowelli*

This race usually has 128 or more ventrals and 42 or more subcaudals in the female, 120 or more ventrals and 51 or more subcaudals in the male. It occurs north of the former in northern Arkansas and Oklahoma, southern Missouri, western Kansas, and extreme southwestern Illinois.

Fig. 89. Southeastern Crowned Snake, *Tantilla c. coronata*

Fig. 90. Arizona Coral Snake, *Micruroides euryxanthus euryxanthus*

Plains Black-headed Snake, *Tantilla nigriceps*

These snakes are yellowish-brown to brownish-gray above, whitish below, with a pink or orange midventral line. The black head cap is not bordered posteriorly by a light collar, and there are 7 upper labials. This species has two races, and again it is necessary to count scales to separate them.

Plains Black-headed Snake, *Tantilla n. nigriceps*

The female has 150 or more ventrals, the male 136 or more. This form ranges from southern Nebraska through western Kansas, eastern Colorado, southward through western Oklahoma, western Texas, and through most of New Mexico into southeastern Arizona.

Texas Black-headed Snake, *Tantilla n. fumiceps*

The female has 150 or fewer ventrals, the male 138 or fewer. This form is restricted to a north–south oriented area ranging from extreme southern Texas, northward into south central Oklahoma.

Western Black-headed Snake, *Tantilla planiceps*

In this species there is frequently an indication of a narrow, dark middorsal stripe, and there may be traces of lateral stripes. The belly is usually red. There are five races in the United States.

Mexican Black-headed Snake, *Tantilla p. atriceps*

The black cap usually extends less than 1 scale length beyond the parietals and does not extend down below the angle of the mouth. If a light collar is present, it is narrow and not bordered behind by dark spots. Females have 159 or fewer ventrals, males 151 or fewer. This race is found from western Texas through southern New Mexico into southern Arizona and south into Mexico.

Chihuahua Black-headed Snake, *Tantilla p. yaquia*

The light collar is usually present and bordered by dark spots. The head cap extends onto the throat scales below the angle of the jaws. There is a conspicuous light spot behind the eye. This is a Mexican race that has been found in the United States only in the vicinity of Bisbee, Arizona.

Utah Black-headed Snake, *Tantilla p. utahensis*

The cap usually extends about 1½ scale lengths behind the parietals but does not extend down below the angles of the jaws. The light collar is usually inconspicuous, narrow, and not marked behind by dark spots. There are 162 to 174 ventrals in females, 153 to 165 in males. This race is found from western Colorado through southern Utah, north-western Arizona, and southern Nevada into the Sierra Nevada Mountains of California.

Desert Black-headed Snake, *Tantilla p. transmontana*

This is a light-colored race. The head cap extends $1\frac{1}{2}$ to $2\frac{1}{2}$ scale lengths beyond the parietals and reaches down behind the angle of the jaws onto the throat scales. The light collar is present but may be inconspicuous and may or may not be marked behind with a row of dark dots. There are 187 or more ventrals in the females, 175 or more in the males. This race is known from San Diego and Riverside counties, California.

California Black-headed Snake, *Tantilla p. eiseni*

This race is like *transmontana* but is usually darker in color. There are 185 or fewer ventrals in the females, 175 or fewer in the males. It ranges from Fresno County, California, into Lower California.

Hooded Snake, *Tantilla cucullata*

Only two specimens of this species are known. The black cap extends $3\frac{1}{2}$ or 4 scale lengths behind the parietals and reaches down onto the labials and throat scales. One of the specimens is about 13 inches long, the other over 20 inches. Both were taken in Brewster County, Texas.

Val Verde Black-headed Snake, *Tantilla diabola*

This species is based on a single specimen from Val Verde County, Texas. There is a conspicuous light spot behind the eye. The light collar is nearly divided by a posterior extension of the black cap, and the black band behind the collar is broad. The single specimen is less than 9 inches long.

Huachuca Black-headed Snake, *Tantilla wilcoxi wilcoxi*

The broad light collar crosses the tips of the parietals, and the dark band behind is narrow or reduced to a row of spots. This is a Mexican form that enters the United States only in the Huachuca Mountains of extreme southern Arizona.

CORAL SNAKES, FAMILY ELAPIDAE

These snakes are poisonous. The enlarged fangs in the front part of the upper jaw are grooved and fixed in position; that is, they cannot be folded back along the jaw, as can the fangs of Rattlesnakes. The family is widespread in Africa, Asia, Australia, and tropical America, but only two genera are found in the United States. Both of them are strikingly marked with red, yellow or whitish, and black rings that go entirely around the body. The order of the rings is yellow, red, yellow, black, yellow, red, yellow, black. Many harmless snakes have rather similar patterns of red, yellow, and black rings, but none combines the characteristics of having the red and yellow rings in contact and the red rings continuing across the belly.

Arizona Coral Snake, *Micruroides euryxanthus euryxanthus* (Figure 90)

Arizona Coral Snakes differ from the Eastern Coral Snakes by the arrangement of the bands on and just behind the head. The snout and top of the head are black to the angles of the jaws. Then comes a yellow or white ring that barely touches the parietals and is immediately followed by a broad red ring. The next ring is yellow or white, the next one black. The light rings are quite wide, not narrow as they are in the Eastern Coral Snake. This species seems to be subterranean in habits and secretive in nature. It is largely nocturnal and feeds on other small snakes and lizards. The breeding habits are unknown. The maximum length is 1¾ feet. This snake is found in southern and central Arizona, southwestern New Mexico, and also occurs in adjacent Mexico.

Eastern Coral Snake, *Micrurus fulvius* (Figure 91)

The snout and head are black to behind the level of the eyes. Then comes a broad yellow band across the back of the head, followed by a broad black ring, a narrow yellow ring, and a broad red ring. The yellow rings are narrower than in the Arizona Coral Snake. The order of the rings on the body—yellow, red, yellow, black, yellow, red, yellow —the black snout, and the fact that all rings cross the belly will separate this Coral Snake from all the harmless ringed snakes in its range. These snakes are by nature rather gentle and somewhat secretive. Although they have the reputation of being nocturnal, I think most herpetologists would admit that they have encountered as many of them in the daytime as at night, if not more so. Their burrowing habits permit them to live in quite highly developed residential neighborhoods, but their inoffensive nature generally prevents their causing trouble to man. They eat other snakes, lizards, and frogs. They lay three to twelve eggs in late June. The eggs hatch in late September, and the young are about 7 inches long. Most adults are between 2 and 3 feet in length; the record is nearly 4 feet. There are two races.

Eastern Coral Snake, *Micrurus f. fulvius*

Black spots are usually present in the red rings on the back and are often concentrated to form 2 rather large black spots. This race of the southeastern lowlands ranges from North Carolina to southern Florida and westward to the Mississippi River.

Fig. 91. Eastern Coral Snake, *Micrurus fulvius*

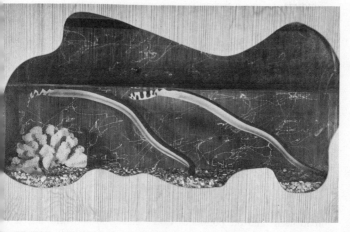

Fig. 92. Yellow-bellied Sea Snake, *Pelamis platurus*

Texas Coral Snake, *Micrurus f. tenere* (Plate 16b)

The black spots in the red zones are more numerous and are irregularly distributed in this race, which ranges from southern Arkansas and western Louisiana to southern Texas and northern Mexico.

SEA SNAKES, FAMILY HYDROPHIDAE

These marine relatives of the Coral Snakes swim in the open seas and feed on fish. The body is flattened from side to side, and the tail is strongly compressed laterally and paddle-shaped. Like the Coral Snakes, they are poisonous and have fixed fangs in the front of the upper jaw.

Yellow-bellied Sea Snake, *Pelamis platurus* (Figure 92)

These are rather small snakes with a maximum length of about 3 feet. The anterior part of the body is dark-brown or black above and yellow or orange below, and the tail is yellow with dark vertical bars. The ventral scales are little if any wider than the dorsal scales. The females give birth to living young, usually in tidepools in remote rocky reefs and islands. This species ranges from Madagascar across the Indian and Pacific oceans to the Pacific Coast of the Americas. It does not reach the continental United States but is present in the Gulf of California. A few specimens have been recorded from the waters of the island of Oahu in Hawaii.

PIT VIPERS, FAMILY VIPERIDAE

Most of our poisonous snakes belong to this family. The very large fangs in the front part of the jaws are hollow, and the bones in which they are set can be rotated. At rest the fangs are folded back along the jaws. When the snake strikes, the fangs are swung forward. All the members of this family in our area belong to a group known as Pit Vipers because they have a deep pit on either side of the face between the eye and the nostril. (Do not try to use this characteristic to identify live snakes in the field!) Most of the scales under the tail are in a single row and the pupil is vertical. Pit Vipers normally have a pattern of blotches or crossbands, but these may be obscure in large adults, which then appear practically unicolor. They are heavy-bodied snakes, with the head noticeably wider than the neck. This is not an infallible means of recognizing poisonous snakes because some harmless snakes have broad heads and the poisonous Coral Snakes do not. Still, any unknown blotched or plain-colored snake with a stout body, narrower neck, and broad head should be approached with caution. When in doubt let it alone. The wisest plan is to learn in advance what poisonous snakes are in your area and how to recognize them.

Our Pit Vipers fall into two groups: the Copperheads and Cottonmouths, which lack a rattle at the end of the tail, and the Rattlesnakes.

Copperheads and Cottonmouths, Genus *Agkistrodon*

Copperheads and Cottonmouths have a facial pit, weakly keeled scales, a single anal plate, and a single row of scales under most of the tail, which is pointed at the tip and lacks a rattle. They may, however, vibrate the tail when disturbed. They give birth to living young, and the young have a bright-yellow tip to the tail. In the United States there are two species: the Copperheads are the "upland moccasins" and the Cottonmouths are the "water moccasins."

Copperhead, *Agkistrodon contortrix*

These are usually rather brightly colored snakes with a crossbanded pattern in tones of orange, copper, chestnut, or reddish-brown. They are somewhat smaller than Cottonmouths and usually have 23 scale rows. There is a loreal scale, and the labials do not reach the eye. Although normally inoffensive, if disturbed, they can be quite pugnacious and are, of course, dangerous. They are rather gregarious, usually living on wooded hillsides and in rocky, mountainous regions and also tending to congregate in abandoned and undisturbed ruderal areas. As might be expected with snakes that attract so much attention, the life history is fairly well known. Females give birth to from two to eleven young in the fall of the year, late August and early September. The young are about 8 or 9 inches long at birth. Adults range between 2 and 3 feet in length but sometimes exceed 4 feet. There are five subspecies in the eastern and southern states.

Southern Copperhead, *Agkistrodon c. contortrix*

This race has the narrowest dark crossbands of any. The bands are constricted in the middorsal region and are sometimes broken to form lateral, sometimes alternating, triangles. The ground color and centers of the crossbands are lighter than in the northern race. There are dark blotches along the sides of the belly, which is otherwise rather pale. This form occurs from Virginia southward to the Florida panhandle, west to eastern Texas, and northward in the Mississippi Valley to Arkansas, southern Illinois, and southeastern Missouri.

Broad-banded Copperhead, *Agkistrodon c. laticinctus*

This richly colored Copperhead can be told from all except the Trans–Pecos race by the fact that the dorsal dark bands are broader in the middle of the back than are the light areas they separate. The dark markings extend onto the belly scales, but the ventral ground color is lighter than in the Trans–Pecos Copperhead. This race is found from southern Kansas, southward through Oklahoma and central Texas to the Gulf.

Northern Copperhead, *Agkistrodon c. mokasen* (Plate 16c)

In this race the dark bands are only about half as wide on the middle of the back as they are on the sides of the body. They are hour-glass-shaped but not so narrow middorsally as in the southern race. This form ranges from Massachusetts to eastern Kansas, except in the Marias des Cygnes-Osage River drainage south in the highlands to Alabama east of the Mississippi and through the Ozarks and adjacent parts of Texas west of the Mississippi.

Osage Copperhead, *Agkistrodon c. phaeogaster*

This race can be recognized by having the crossbands narrow in the middle back (3 to 5 scales) and by having the very dark crossbands narrowly edged with white so that they stand out sharply against the light background. It is confined to the major portion of the Marias des Cygnes-Osage River drainage in eastern Kansas and central Missouri.

Trans-Pecos Copperhead, *Agkistrodon c. pictigaster*

This race is similar to the Broad-banded Copperhead in dorsal pattern but differs from it in the very dark belly which is marked with light areas that extend down from the sides. It is limited to the Big Bend region of Texas west of the Pecos River.

Cottonmouth, *Agkistrodon piscivorous*

These are the "moccasins" of the eastern and southern United States. (Harmless Water Snakes of the genus *Natrix* are also often called "moccasins.") Young Cottonmouths resemble Copperheads in pattern, but they darken as they grow older, so that large adults are dark-brownish, or blackish, and the crossbands are indistinct. The Cottonmouth usually has 25 scale rows and lacks a loreal scale in front of the eye. The labials reach the eye. It is a snake of the southeastern states, where it lives around swamps, lakes, and marshy places. As the scientific name indicates, it feeds extensively on fish. Like the Copperhead, this species is a live bearer; young number from one to fifteen and are born in August and September. Most of the young are from 8 to 12 inches long. Adults are usually between 3 and 4 feet, but the largest recorded was over 6 feet. This species is often pugnacious and has a dangerous bite; it should be avoided. When one is threatened, it usually rears up and opens its mouth widely to show the conspicuous white lining from which it gets its common name. There are three subspecies.

Eastern Cottonmouth, *Agkistrodon p. piscivorous*

The snout is light, and there is generally a rather distinct, broad, dark band that passes posteriorly through the eye, leaving the margin of the upper lip pale. The belly is lighter than the back. This race occurs in the southeastern states from Virginia southward to southern Georgia and westward through most of Alabama.

Florida Cottonmouth, *Agkistrodon p. conanti*

This race can be recognized by the fact that two dark vertical stripes border the edge of the rostral scale at the tip of the snout. It occurs from southern Georgia southward throughout Florida and westward to southeastern Alabama.

Western Cottonmouth, *Agkistrodon p. leucostoma*

This race is smaller and darker, with the head markings obscure or absent. It is a snake of the Mississippi Valley, ranging from southern Alabama northward to southern Illinois and central Missouri and through extreme southeastern Kansas, eastern Oklahoma and central and southern Texas.

Pigmy Rattlers and Massasaugas, Genus *Sistrurus*

These are small, usually blotched or spotted Rattlesnakes with various shades of gray, tan, brown, or black, with a small rattle and the characteristic facial pit and vertical pupil of the other Rattlesnakes. They can be told from members of the genus *Crotalus* by the presence on top of the head of 9 enlarged, regularly arranged scales. *Crotalus* has many small, irregular scales on top of the head. Like other Rattlesnakes, members of this genus give birth to living young. There are three species, two of which occur in the United States.

Massasauga, *Sistrurus catenatus*

The Massasauga differs from the Pigmy Rattlesnake in having a short and stocky tail and a better-developed rattle. The pattern is of rounded, dark spots or crossbars on the back and sides. The light spaces between the spots on the back are narrower than the spots. Massasaugas are rather small snakes, adults averaging about 2 feet or less in length with a maximum of $3\frac{1}{2}$ feet. They feed on mice and frogs and have broods of up to twelve young which are $5\frac{1}{2}$ to $9\frac{1}{2}$ inches long at birth. This is a snake which changes its habitat in different parts of its range. In the northeastern states it is primarily a snake of bogs and swamps; in the southwestern states it is primarily a snake of the desert grasslands. There are three races. They apparently intergrade extensively, and the limits of the ranges are not very clear.

Eastern Massasauga, *Sistrurus c. catenatus* (Plate 16d)

This is a dark race, usually with black or dark-brown blotches on a brownish or grayish ground color. The belly is black with irregular light markings. Some individuals are almost completely black. This is the Massasauga of the northeast, found from northwestern New York and northwestern Pennsylvania through the lower peninsula of Michigan, northern and central Ohio and Indiana, westward throughout most of Illinois and into southern Wisconsin, extreme southeastern Minnesota, eastern and southern Iowa and northern Missouri. It apparently intergrades with the Western Massasauga in southeastern Nebraska and northeastern Kansas.

Western Massasauga, *Sistrurus c. tergeminus*

This race is lighter in color than the Eastern Massasauga, and the belly is light with some dark markings. It occurs from southeastern Nebraska, southward through Kansas, Oklahoma, and central Texas to the Gulf Coast.

Desert Massasauga, *Sistrurus c. edwardsi*

This is a small, pale-colored desert race, with a pale belly, plain or lightly flecked with gray or brown. It is the snake of the southwestern arid grasslands, occurring in extreme southeastern Arizona, south central New Mexico and western Texas. A separate population in southeastern Colorado is apparently intermediate between this and the Western Massasauga.

Pigmy Rattlesnake, *Sistrurus miliarius*

Pigmy Rattlesnakes have slender, pointed tails and very small rattles. The spots on the back are more widely separated than in the Massasauga and there is often a red middorsal stripe. Pigmy Rattlesnakes seem to feed more on lizards and snakes than do Massasaugas, or indeed most Rattlesnakes. They also seem to have more irritable and cantankerous dispositions than the Massasaugas. The female gives birth to broods of five or six young which average about 8 or 9 inches in length. Adults are usually less than 2 feet long, with a maximum of 31 inches. There are three races.

Carolina Pigmy Rattlesnake, *Sistrurus m. miliarius*

The ground color is lighter in this race than in the next and the belly is pale, lightly flecked, or mottled rather than heavily blotched. This form ranges from southern North Carolina through most of South Carolina except the southernmost tip and through north central Georgia westward through mid-Alabama.

Dusky Pigmy Rattlesnake, *Sistrurus m. barbouri* (Figure 93)

This is a dark race with dark stippling on the gray ground color. The belly is heavily marked with large, dark spots. It is found from southernmost South Carolina through southern Georgia, southern Alabama, southeastern Mississippi, and throughout Florida.

Fig. 93. Dusky Pigmy Rattlesnake, *Sistrurus m. barbouri*

Fig. 94. Western Diamondback Rattlesnake, *Crotalus atrox*

Western Pigmy Rattlesnake, *Sistrurus m. streckeri*

This is the lightest of the races, and the middorsal markings are often in the shape of narrow crossbars rather than rounded spots. This is the Pigmy Rattlesnake of the lower Mississippi Valley, ranging throughout most of Mississippi except the extreme southern part, north to southern Tennessee and southern Missouri and west into Oklahoma and eastern Texas.

Rattlesnakes, Genus *Crotalus*

These snakes can be easily recognized by the conspicuous and spectacular rattle at the end of the tail. In newborn young the rattle consists of a single "button," and a new joint is added each time the snake sheds. In addition, these Rattlesnakes have a vertical pupil, a pit on the side of the face between the eye and the nostril, a head conspicuously broader than the neck, and the top of the head, at least back of the eyes, is covered with many small scales rather than a regular number of large, symmetrical plates. Rattlesnakes feed primarily on rodents, although many of the smaller species also take smaller items of food, such as lizards. All of them give birth to living young. The genus ranges from southern Canada, southward throughout most of the United States, Mexico, Central America, and South America east of the Andes into northern Argentina. There are 59 named forms. Of this number, 26 occur in the United States, and these are grouped into 13 species. Many of the species are extremely difficult to identify without detailed descriptions; however, it is possible with the aid of certain characters and geographic distribution to place many of the individuals one encounters in the proper species. The following synopsis should help.

There are only two species in the United States that normally have 21 scale rows; one of these is easily recognized by the triangular projections of the supraocular scales to form "horns" above the eyes—this is the Sidewinder (one race usually has 23 scale rows). The other form with 21 scale rows is the Twin-spotted Rattlesnake. This is a small species with a distinctive pattern of 2 rows of spots down the back and smaller spots on the sides. Species that usually have 23 rows of scales are the Timber Rattlesnake, the Rock Rattlesnake, the Tiger Rattlesnake, and one race (Panamint) of the Speckled Rattlesnake. The Timber Rattlesnake is the only member of this genus in the eastern United States except for the large Eastern Diamondback Rattlesnake, from which it differs not only in the smaller number of dorsal scale rows, but also in having a pattern of bands rather than diamond-shaped blotches on the back. The Rock Rattlesnake, Tiger Rattlesnake, and Panamint Rattlesnake had best be separated from one another by range. Of the Rattlesnakes that usually have 25 scale rows, the Arizona Ridge-nosed Rattlesnake can be recognized by the ridge across the top of the nose, the light vertical stripe on the snout, and the fact that the end of the tail is striped rather than banded, as it is on other Rattlesnakes. In the Southwestern Speckled Rattlesnake, the dorsal blotches are formed by clumps of small dots. The Western Diamond-back Rattlesnake has a light line behind the eye which reaches the mouth in front of the angle of the jaw. The Mohave Rattlesnake and Western Rattlesnake usually have a similar light line that passes above the angle of the jaw. These two can be separated by pattern. The Mohave Rattlesnake has the tail marked with conspicuous black rings that are narrower than the light spaces between them, and both colors are in strong contrast to the color of the back. In the Western Rattlesnakes the colors of the tail are not sharply set off from the colors of the back and the dark rings are not narrower than the light. There is one species that characteristically has 27 scale rows; this is the Black-tailed Rattlesnake, in which the tip of the snout and tail of the adult are usually coal-black. Finally there are two species with 29 scale rows; the Eastern Diamondback Rattlesnake of the Eastern United States and the Red Diamond Rattlesnake of southern California. Range alone is enough to separate them.

Eastern Diamondback Rattlesnake, *Crotalus adamanteus* (Plate 16e)

This is not only the largest of the Rattlesnakes, but in mass is one of the largest poisonous snakes of the world. Specimens 96 inches long have been recorded, and such specimens reach a weight of around 15 pounds. No Diamondbacks of this size have been found in recent years, however. Most adults today range from about 3 to 6 feet in length. There are 29 scale rows. The name comes from the dorsal pattern of light-bordered, dark, diamond-shaped blotches. There are 2 light lines on the side of the face. Females give birth to from eight to fourteen young about 14 inches long. This snake ranges from the coastal region of North Carolina southward throughout the peninsula of Florida and westward into southern Mississippi and extreme southeastern Louisiana.

Western Diamondback Rattlesnake, *Crotalus atrox* (Figure 94)

Somewhat smaller than its eastern counterpart, but still an impressively large snake, this species has from 25 to 27 scale rows. It also has light-edged dark diamonds on the back, but they are not so sharply marked and may be indistinct, so that the snake appears speckled. The tail has black and light rings of about equal width and sharply set off from the colors of the back. Adults average about $4\frac{1}{2}$ feet in length, and large specimens may reach nearly $7\frac{1}{2}$ feet. The young are also smaller than those of the Eastern Diamondback, averaging only about 1 foot long at birth. The Western Diamondback ranges from the southern border of eastern and western Kansas and west central Arkansas south through most of Oklahoma and most of Texas except the eastern border, westward through southern and central New Mexico, Arizona and southeastern California and south into Mexico.

Sidewinder, *Crotalus cerastes* (Figure 95)

This small, stout Rattlesnake can be easily recognized by the triangular, horny projections of the supraocular scales above the eyes. The dorsal scales are in 21 or 23 rows and the pattern is of faint to distinct spots and blotches. The ground color is very variable and usually matches the color of the sand where the snake lives. Adults average only about 18 inches in length, although large specimens may exceed 30 inches. These are desert dwelling snakes found most often in sandy regions. There are three subspecies.

Mohave Desert Sidewinder, *Crotalus c. cerastes*

The first segment of the rattle is brown in adults, and there are usually 21 rows of scales. This race is found in southern Nevada, extreme southwestern Utah, western Arizona just south of the Nevada state boundary and southeastern California.

Sonora Sidewinder, *Crotalus c. cercobombus*

The first segment of the rattle is black in adults, and there are usually 23 scale rows. This race is restricted to south central Arizona and adjacent Mexico.

Colorado Desert Sidewinder, *Crotalus c. laterorepens*

The first segment of the rattle is black in adults, and there are normally 21 scale rows. This race occupies the area between the ranges of the other two in southwestern Arizona and extreme southeastern California.

Timber Rattlesnake, *Crotalus horridus*

This snake of the eastern United States usually has 23 or 25 scale rows and a dorsal pattern of frequently V-shaped dark crossbands on a background that may range from yellow through brown to black. Some specimens are nearly uniform black above. Adults average about 3½ feet in length, although one that reached 6 feet 2 inches has been recorded. There are two races.

Timber Rattlesnake, *Crotalus h. horridus* (Plate 16f and Figure 96)

The head is usually unpatterned in this race. It ranges from southern Vermont and New Hampshire southward into Maryland, western Virginia, western North and South Carolina, northern Georgia and northern Alabama, northward through Kentucky into Illinois, Indiana, southern Michigan, and southern Wisconsin. West of the Mississippi River it is found from southeastern Minnesota to southeastern Nebraska, eastern Kansas and Oklahoma and northeastern Texas.

Fig. 95. Sidewinder, *Crotalus cerastes*

g. 96. Immature Timber Rattlesnake, *Crotalus h. horridus*

Canebrake Rattlesnake, *Crotalus h. atricaudatus*

This race has a broad stripe running back from the eye, a red middorsal stripe, and frequently 25 scale rows. It ranges from the coastal region of southeastern Virginia southward into northern Florida as far south as Alachua County and westward into eastern Texas. In the Mississippi Valley it ranges northward into southern Illinois.

Rock Rattlesnake, *Crotalus lepidus*

This is a small Rattlesnake with 23 rows of scales and a pattern of narrow, dark, sometimes indistinct, widely spaced bands across the back. The ground color is usually greenish or bluish-gray, sometimes pinkish-tan, with a mottling of flecks or blotches between the dorsal bands. This is a mountain dwelling species that extends into the southwestern states from Mexico. There are two races.

Mottled Rock Rattlesnake, *Crotalus l. lepidus*

The dark crossbands are often rather indistinct, and the mottling on the ground color sometimes forms secondary bands. In the United States this form is found only in southwestern Texas and extreme southeastern New Mexico.

Banded Rock Rattlesnake, *Crotalus l. klauberi* (Figure 97)

The dark crossbands are more distinct and there are few or no dark marks between them. This form is found in extreme western Texas, south central and southwestern New Mexico, and southeastern Arizona.

Speckled Rattlesnake, *Crotalus mitchelli*

This species usually has from 23 to 25 rows of scales and a dorsal pattern of blotches or bands formed of clusters of small dots. These snakes are very variable, both in color and in shape of the dorsal blotches. Most adults are from 2 to 4 feet long. These are rock-dwelling snakes of the arid southwest. The typical race occurs only in Lower California, but two other races are found in the United States.

Southwestern Speckled Rattlesnake, *Crotalus m. pyrrhus*

This form has rather indistinct blotches and bands. There is usually a small row of scales between the rostral and the prenasals. It occurs in western Arizona, southern California, the extreme southern tip of Nevada, and southwestern Utah.

Panamint Rattlesnake, *Crotalus m. stephensi*

This race has a more distinct dorsal pattern and is more noticeably banded. The rostral and prenasals are in contact. It ranges in southern Nevada and adjacent parts of California.

Fig. 97. Banded Rock Rattlesnake, *Crotalus l. klauberi*

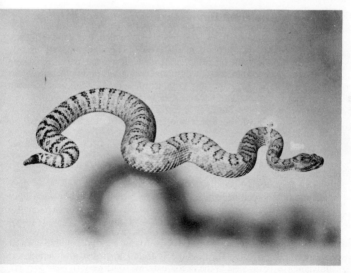

Fig. 98. Great Basin Rattlesnake, *Crotalus v. lutosus*

Northern Black-tailed Rattlesnake,
Crotalus molossus molossus

This Rattlesnake usually has 27 scale rows, a black tail and frequently a black snout, and distinctive light areas or spots within the dark dorsal bands. The individual scales are a single color—that is, the lines separating light and dark areas of the pattern run between the scales, not across them. Adults average about 3 feet in length, but specimens over 4 feet have been recorded. Broods are rather small, those that are known averaging about five young. This is another mountain-dwelling snake found most often in rocky places. In the United States it occurs in central and western Texas and southern and central New Mexico and Arizona.

Twin-spotted Rattlesnake, *Crotalus pricei pricei*

These small Rattlesnakes have the dorsal scales in 21 rows and a dorsal pattern of two rows of dark spots. Adults range from about $1\frac{1}{2}$ to slightly over 2 feet in length. This is another inhabitant of rocky places in the arid mountains of the Southwest. It has a rather extensive range in western and northern Mexico but in the United States is restricted to the southeastern corner of Arizona.

Red Diamond Rattlesnake, *Crotalus ruber ruber*

This is a Diamondback Rattlesnake in which there are typically 29 scale rows and a general reddish color. The diamonds are usually light-edged and may be rather indistinct. The head pattern is quite faded in adult specimens. The light and dark rings on the tail are about equal in width. This is a rather large Rattlesnake—adults average from about $2\frac{1}{2}$ to 5 feet. The females give birth to about eight young at a time. In the United States it is restricted to southwestern California, from the coast to the desert foothills west of the San Bernardino Mountains.

Mohave Rattlesnake, *Crotalus scutulatus scutulatus*

This Rattlesnake usually has 25 scale rows, a dorsal pattern of dark diamonds bounded in light on a green or brown ground color, a light stripe behind the eye which passes above the angle of the jaws, and a tail pattern of narrow black and broader gray rings that contrast sharply with the color of the back. Adults average about 3 to $3\frac{1}{2}$ feet in total length but may exceed 4 feet. About eight young are born at a time. The Mohave Rattlesnake is found in desert and semidesert lowlands in Texas west of the Pecos, extreme southwestern New Mexico, a large part of Arizona, southern Nevada, the southwestern tip of Utah, and in southeastern California west of the southern Nevada boundary.

Tiger Rattlesnake, *Crotalus tigris*

This species has typically 23 scale rows, a rather small head for a Rattlesnake, and a pattern of numerous, somewhat poorly defined dark dorsal crossbands composed of dots. The rostral and prenasals are in contact, and there are only 2 internasals. Adults are about $1\frac{1}{2}$ to 3 feet in total length. This is another snake of the canyons and rocky foothills of desert mountains. It occurs in south central Arizona and adjacent parts of Mexico.

Western Rattlesnake, *Crotalus viridis*

These snakes have a dorsal pattern of squarish or round blotches or diamonds, usually 25 scale rows, and a white line running from behind the eye to pass above the angle of the jaw. The rostral scale is in contact with the prenasals and also with three or more internasal scales. There are dark and light rings on the tail, but the change from the color and pattern of the back to that of the tail is gradual. These snakes are primarily diurnal in habits and are found most often in grassy areas in the central and western United States. There are eight races. They range in size from $2\frac{1}{2}$ feet maximum size in the small Midget Faded Rattlesnake and Hopi Rattlesnake to about 5 feet in the Prairie Rattlesnake. The number of young ranges from four to twenty-one, the larger races having the larger broods. Although some of the races are rather strikingly marked, geography had better be considered seriously in identifying the subspecies.

Prairie Rattlesnake, *Crotalus v. viridis*

The ground color is usually green or greenish-brown, sometimes brown. The blotches are dark-brown, narrowly bordered with white. This form ranges from southern Canada throughout most of Montana and into eastern Idaho, western North Dakota, most of Wyoming, South Dakota, Nebraska and Kansas, the eastern half of Colorado, western Oklahoma and Texas, and throughout most of New Mexico.

Midget Faded Rattlesnake, *Crotalus v. concolor*

This is one of the most distinctive of the Western Rattlesnakes. It is a small, pale-colored race, the pattern often obscure in the adults. It is found in eastern Utah, western Colorado, and extreme southwestern Wyoming.

Hopi Rattlesnake, *Crotalus v. nuntius*

This is the Rattlesnake usually used by the Hopi Indians in the snake dance. It is a small race, generally pink or reddish in color, the blotches well defined. Adults range from 20 to 30 inches long. It is found in northeastern Arizona, extreme northwestern New Mexico, south central Utah, and extreme southwestern Colorado.

Grand Canyon Rattlesnake, *Crotalus v. abyssus*

In adults of this race the general color is bright-reddish and the blotches tend to be obscure. The young are more like the Prairie Rattlesnake in pattern. This race is found only in the Grand Canyon.

Great Basin Rattlesnake, *Crotalus v. lutosus* (Figure 98)

This race is lighter in color than the Prairie Rattlesnake, the ground color usually light-brown or gray. The blotches are narrower, the light line behind the eye broader. As the name implies, it is a snake of the Great Basin, ranging in southern Idaho, southeastern Oregon, northwestern California, most of Nevada, western Utah and southward into extreme northwestern Arizona.

Arizona Black Rattlesnake, *Crotalus v. cerberus* (Figure 99)

This is a very dark race; some specimens are nearly black. The dorsal blotches are often diamond-shaped and lack light lateral borders. This race occupies most of central Arizona, just reaching extreme western New Mexico.

Southern Pacific Rattlesnake, *Crotalus v. helleri*

This is another dark race with diamond-shaped blotches, which, in this form, are completely bordered with light. It is found in the coastal region of southern California and northern Lower California.

Northern Pacific Rattlesnake, *Crotalus v. oreganus*

The color is somewhat lighter in this race than in the Southern Pacific Rattlesnake, and the blotches tend to be hexagonal or rounded rather than diamond-shaped. They are wider than the interspaces between them. This race ranges from the region of San Luis Obispo Bay northward through most of California into southern and central Oregon, eastward away from the coast in the Puget Sound region through eastern Washington, western Idaho and southern British Columbia.

Ridge-nosed Rattlesnake, *Crotalus willardi*

This distinctive Rattlesnake has the scales of the tip of the snout turned up to form a ridge on the top of the nose and the end of the tail striped rather than ringed. The blotches on the back are separated by light interspaces but merge with the ground color on the sides. There

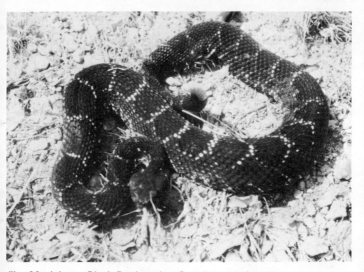

Fig. 99. Arizona Black Rattlesnake, *Crotalus v. cerberus*

Fig. 100. Chihuahua Ridge-nosed Rattlesnake, *Crotalus w. silus*

are 25 to 27 scale rows. It is a small snake, adults not exceeding 2 feet in length. About three to six young are born at a time. Of the three races of this species, two are found in the United States.

Arizona Ridge-nosed Rattlesnake, *Crotalus w. willardi*

This race has a conspicuous white vertical stripe on the face. It is found in wooded regions of the Santa Rita and Huachuca mountains of southeastern Arizona.

Chihuahua Ridge-nosed Rattlesnake, *Crotalus w. silus* (Figure 100)

This race lacks the white stripe on the face. In the United States it is known only from the Animas Mountains of extreme southwestern New Mexico.

SELECTED REFERENCES

SINCE no single volume can be expected to cover adequately every aspect of the amphibian and reptile fauna of an area the size of the United States, the user of this book may find it advantageous to refer to other sources in connection with this one. The following eight volumes are particularly recommended. The first of these is a list and diagnosis of every species of vertebrate known to occur in the continental United States. The next two are superbly illustrated, carefully prepared handbooks written for restricted areas—the first for the Eastern United States and the second for the Western United States. The remaining five are concerned with particular groups and contain detailed descriptions of the species in those groups, together with rather extensive discussions of their variations and life history.

BLAIR, W. FRANK, BLAIR, ALBERT P., BRODKORB, PIERCE, CAGLE, FRED R., AND MOORE, GEORGE A., *Vertebrates of the United States.* 2nd ed. New York, McGraw-Hill, 1968.

CONANT, ROGER, *A Field Guide to Reptiles and Amphibians.* Boston, Houghton Mifflin, 1958.

STEBBINS, ROBERT C., *A Field Guide to Western Reptiles and Amphibians.* Boston, Houghton Mifflin, 1966.

BISHOP, SHERMAN C., *Handbook of Salamanders.* Ithaca, Comstock Publishing Associates, 1943.

CARR, ARCHIE, *Handbook of Turtles.* Ithaca, Comstock Publishing Associates, 1952.

SMITH, HOBART M., *Handbook of Lizards.* Ithaca, Comstock Publishing Associates, 1946.

WRIGHT, ALBERT HAZEN, AND WRIGHT, ANNA ALLEN, *Handbook of Frogs and Toads.* Ithaca, Comstock Publishing Associates, 1949.

———, *Handbook of Snakes.* Vols. I and II. Ithaca, Comstock Publishing Associates, 1957.

Index

BOLDFACE figures refer to the page numbers of the black and white photographs. Color photographs are referred to by plate number.